Politics, Punishment, and Populism

STUDIES IN CRIME AND PUBLIC POLICY
Michael Tonry and Norval Morris, *General Editors*

Police for the Future
David Bayley

Incapacitation: Penal Confinement and the Restraint of Crime
Franklin E. Zimring and Gordon Hawkins

The American Street Gang: Its Nature, Prevalence, and Control
Malcolm W. Klein

Sentencing Matters
Michael Tonry

The Habits of Legality: Criminal Justice and the Rule of Law
Francis A. Allen

Chinatown Gangs: Extortion, Enterprise, and Ethnicity
Ko-lin Chin

Responding to Troubled Youth
Cheryl L. Maxson and Malcolm W. Klein

Community Policing, Chicago Style
Wesley G. Skogan and Susan M. Hartnett

Making Crime Pay: Law and Order in Contemporary American Politics
Katherine Beckett

Crime Is Not the Problem: Lethal Violence in America
Franklin E. Zimring and Gordon Hawkins

Hate Crimes: Criminal Law and Identity Politics
James B. Jacobs and Kimberly Potter

Politics, Punishment, and Populism
Lord Windlesham

Politics, Punishment, and Populism

LORD WINDLESHAM

New York   Oxford
Oxford University Press
1998

Oxford University Press

Oxford   New York
Athens   Auckland   Bangkok   Bogota   Bombay
Buenos Aires   Calcutta   Cape Town   Dar es Salaam
Delhi   Florence   Hong Kong   Istanbul   Karachi
Kuala Lampur   Madras   Madrid   Melbourne
Mexico City   Nairobi   Paris   Singapore
Taipei   Tokyo   Toronto   Warsaw

and associated companies in
Berlin   Ibadan

Copyright © 1998 Oxford University Press, Inc.

Published by Oxford University Press, Inc.
198 Madison Avenue, New York, New York 10016

Oxford is a registered trademark of Oxford University Press

Library of Congress Cataloging-in-Publication Data
Windlesham, David James George Hennessy, Lord, 1932–
Politics, punishment, and populism / Lord Windlesham.
p. cm. – (Studies in crime and public policy)
Includes bibliographical references and index.
ISBN 0-19-511530-9
1. Criminal justice, Administration of—United States.
2. Crime prevention—United States.
3. Gun control—United States.
4. Pressure groups—United States.
I. Title. II. Series.
HV9950.W56 1998
364.973—dc21   97-51415

1   3   5   7   9   8   6   4   2
Printed in the United States of America
on acid-free paper

Preface

Like others before me, I came from outside to study the penal system and ended with some wider impressions of the workings of government in America as it approaches the close of the twentieth century. Crime in the United States has some uniquely destructive characteristics, but the prevalence of criminal offending, the fear it creates, and the political reactions it provokes are shared by many other industrialized countries. As democratic forms of government have spread throughout Eastern Europe and the states of the former Soviet Union, they too have experienced some of the malign consequences of greater individual freedom and prosperity.

After ten years writing about developments in penal policy and the administration of justice in Britain, my interest was caught by the populist surge of opinion in California that spread so rapidly with the enactment of "three strikes and you're out" sentencing laws nationwide. This phenomenon led me to make a parallel study of the policies contemporaneously before Congress in the passage of the Violent Crime Control and Law Enforcement legislation in 1993–94 and the British Parliament in the Criminal Justice and Public Order and Police and Magistrates' Courts Acts of the same year. The results were published in volume 3 of my work on *Responses to Crime* (Oxford: Clarendon Press, 1996). With the encouragement of the Oxford University Press in New York and the general editors of its Studies in Crime and Public Policy series, the American part of that volume has been revised and expanded. It now forms the first five chapters of this book.

In any exploration of legislative history the most interesting question is "What happened next?" The later chapters of this book aim to provide an answer by analyzing the course of events in a setting where the Republican Party had won control of both houses of Congress in the midterm elections held in November 1994, but with President Clinton still at the head of the administration. Behind these institutional changes was the constant pressure of public opinion, by far the most significant factor in the framing and execution of federal criminal policy.

Although the book is primarily a narrative account of the policies on crime enacted by the 103rd and 104th Congresses, and a discussion of the influences that determined them, the observant reader will notice that in places I have presumed to add some opinions of my own about their thrust and motivation. Several of these are critical, but they are put forward in the belief that those who stand further away from a mountain sometimes can see its contours more clearly than those who live on it.

Many debts have been accumulated that call for acknowledgment. A short stay in the summer of 1994 as a visiting fellow at the Earl Warren Legal Institute at the University of California, Berkeley, was the starting point. The Law Library of Congress has been a superb resource and a welcoming base for my research in Washington, D.C. The Reference Center of the United States Information Service in London, the Bodleian Law Library and the Rhodes House Library in Oxford, each combined a store of valuable material and helpful staff. Above all else is my gratitude to Princeton University for appointing me to the John L. Weinberg/Goldman Sachs and Co. Visiting Professorship during six months' sabbatical leave from Brasenose College, Oxford, in 1997. The support and friendship of colleagues at the Woodrow Wilson School of Public and International Affairs were an experience I shall not forget. Acting as faculty director of a policy task force on gun control in the undergraduate program gave me an opportunity to get to know, and admire, some of the next generation of policy makers. At all of these places and elsewhere the names listed below are only a selection of the many people, whether consulted formally or in informal discussions, who helped to deepen my understanding, correct my errors, and inform my conclusions. It goes without saying that none has any responsibility for the opinions expressed in this book.

At Princeton: Michael Danielson, Jameson Doig, Brian Howe, Stanley Katz, Patricia Schroeder, and Nathan Scovronick; two outstanding librarians: Rosemary Allen Little, Public Administration, Politics and Law Librarian at the University Library, and Laird Klinger, the Librarian of the Woodrow Wilson School; and Shirley Canty for her secretarial assistance. At the Library of Congress, Prosser Gifford, Director of Scholarly Programs, once again was my sponsor. Robert Gee, Chief of Public Services for the Law Library of Congress, and two of the staff in the Reading Room, David Rabasca and Nancy Wynn, were expert guides over much unfamiliar terrain. Others whom I should like to thank include John Brademas, Lynn Curtis, Anthony Doob, Julian Epstein, Jenni Gainsborough, Jane Grall, Lawrence Greenfeld, Marvin Kalb, Robert Litt, Kent Markus, Marc Mauer, Pat Mayhew, E. Leo Milonas, Mark Moore, Mitchell Sklar, Frank Sullivan, William Suter, Robert Walker, Nicole Winger, and Marlene Young. The entire manuscript was word-processed by my secretary in Oxford, Patricia Spight, who for many years has so capably and willingly carried the additional burden of preparing my books for publication.

Contents

Politics, Punishment, and Populism

Chapter 1

———

The Politics of Crime

I

For the politician in a representative democracy, populism is a slippery concept. The aspirant to public office knows that electoral success is a prerequisite for the exercise of influence and power and that in order to gain more votes than rival candidates it is imperative to ascertain the opinions of the voters, and then to satisfy them. Elected politicians everywhere are keenly aware of the need to keep their ears close to the ground. The skill lies in interpreting the signals that are picked up, some loud but irregular, others fainter but more consistent, and the uses to which they are then put. Once elected to the representative assembly, the successful political candidate becomes a legislator, a more dignified status, with a voice and a vote in reaching decisions on policies and making laws. It takes some newly elected representatives longer than others to realize that the function of any legislative assembly worth the name is not simply to transmit undiluted the outpourings of raw public opinion but, in the felicitous language of James Madison, "to refine and enlarge the public views, by passing them through the medium of a chosen body of citizens, ..."[1]

In the closing years of the twentieth century, neopopulist forces have been in the ascendant in American politics, whether at national, state, or local level.

3

The panorama is vast, but the outlines are familiar. In the foreground is a large black cloud of discontent, shutting off the sun from the nourishing sense of well-being that it might be expected would be enjoyed by the citizenry of the most economically prosperous nation on earth, and one with a long, if not altogether untarnished, tradition of individual freedom. As it has developed in modern times, neopopulism has taken on many negative characteristics. There is a consciousness of remoteness and resentment at being powerless and detached from the decision-taking process. Frustration and resentment lead to suspicion of those closer to the seats of power, especially anonymous nonelected officials or experts, and an attraction toward simplistic solutions to complex problems. In the early stages attitudes may not have hardened into opinions on particular issues. But the soil is fertile, and slender shoots, cultivated by rhetoric, can grow rapidly and branch out into unexpected directions.

These features provide the general context for the inquiry that follows. The focus, however, is a narrower one: the constant play of public opinion, fortified by populist rhetoric and dissipated by the demands of legislative compromise, before, during, and after the enactment of a single federal law designed to counter crime. The long and detailed Violent Crime Control and Law Enforcement Act of 1994[2] was arguably the major legislative achievement of the 103rd Congress, coinciding with the first two years of the Clinton presidency. Its eventual shape and content synthesized the sometimes conflicting strands of opinion that dictated policies toward crime since the Nixon era. It is instructive to identify and explore the impulses that stimulated and fed the latent currents of populist sentiment. How was the interest of politicians engaged and retained? Should their actions be viewed as legitimate responses to the true interests of those whom they represented, or as calculated exploitation or manipulation in the pursuit of political advantage?[3] How did Congress handle a major presidential initiative, and what was the impact on national crime policy when the Republicans won control of both Houses after the congressional elections in November 1994?

Because rates of violent offending escalated so rapidly since the 1970s, a pervasive fear of crime was generated which was far-reaching and genuine. Numerous horrific incidents, extensively publicized, hardened the public reaction. The resulting climate of opinion, with its symptomatic punitive overtones, was not peculiar to the United States. A pattern of high crime rates, leading to widespread victimization and fear of crime was only too familiar in many other countries of the developed world, where the perception of a remorseless increase in the frequency and severity of crime had become a dominating issue of public concern.

The insecurity and anxiety caused by crime impose restrictions on people's lives. Public anger, fueled by the mass media, demands a political response. The clamor for action is orchestrated by elected representatives and candidates who are running for election. It is too early in the narrative to generalize about motives and stratagems. Yet there can be no doubt that in the formation of popular opinion it is perceptions that count. The reality may be different. In the last quarter of a century, the popular perceptions in America have been that criminal offending has reached intolerable levels, that violence is omnipresent, that no one is safe, and that lawmakers and law enforcement have not been effective in protecting the majority of the people from the harmful acts of a malevolent and predatory minority. Strongly held as they are, each is a partial misconception, although derived from truisms. But these were the assumptions that drove policies toward crime over a period that saw some profound changes in the justice system.

When considering the reality, we should note that public interest in crime can drive up media coverage even where published data show, as was the case in 1993, that there was no appreciable increase either in overall crime or violent crime rates. Taken over a longer period, cumulative trends, reinforced by fear-inducing criminal stereotypes,[4] are likely to condition public attitudes and beliefs. The electronic news media have disseminated a consistent message that crime, frequently portrayed as life-threatening, has become a perilous aspect of everyday life. Whether or not news values stand for anything more than a volatile indication of audience interest is debatable, but whatever the selection process for news items the fact is that at the time of the introduction of the Clinton crime bill in 1993, a count by a reputable research organization showed that a record number of crime stories were broadcast by the three major television networks to a national audience.[5]

With a total of 1,698 stories in the main evening newscasts, crime occupied the first place in the top ten television news topics of 1993. The economy (1,457 stories) was second, and health issues (1,096 stories), third. Taken together, these three topics accounted for nearly one-third of the 13,474 news stories broadcast on the ABC, CBS, and NBC evening newscasts. An average of nearly five stories per night meant that the coverage of crime was approximately double that for 1992, with murder stories tripling from 104 stories in 1992 to 329 in 1993. On policies, as against news reports, gun control measures such as the Brady bill led the way (138 stories). Other policy options, including more prisons, stiffer sentencing policies, and extra money for law enforcement and crime prevention, received less media attention. Relatively few stories, 66 out of the total of 1,698, focused on illegal drugs, representing a reduction of 83 percent since 1989 when the concentration on the war on drugs was at its height and 518 stories were broadcast. Declining concern about the economy correlated with indicators showing a recovery in economic activity, thus opening up space for crime or some other social issue to take its place as the leading topic in media coverage and also in the opinion polls.[6]

II

Crime statistics exist in profusion, but they are a morass through which it is hazardous to try and lay down any certain path. First of all there is a distinction to be made between crimes reported to and recorded by the law enforcement agencies, and victimization surveys taking account of a much wider range of offences, whether or not they are reported to the police. Both are regularly published, but the results are neither entirely consistent nor entirely comparable.[7] Over the years the findings have indicated that the rate of increase is considerably higher in the police figures than the trends shown in victimization surveys. There are several explanations for the discrepancies. Recorded crime figures are subject to such noncriminal factors as the greater availability of telephones or the necessity to report break-ins to domestic or business premises, or loss of property, to support insurance claims.

Then there is a great bulk of so-called victimless crimes, notably those associated with drug taking, which never come to light. Within the home or domestic setting it is commonplace even for incidents of serious assault or abuse between partners, members of the family, or acquaintances to go unreported. Victims may be unwilling to report violence or contact the police because they are incapacitated by their injuries, fearful of reprisals, habituated to violence, or have a continuing relationship with their assailant. Statistics for admission to hospital casualty departments of patients with serious nonaccidental injuries typically reveal a high proportion that have not been reported. On average it is estimated that less than two-thirds of aggravated assaults resulting in injury are reported to the police. Minor thefts, vandalized cars, and other less serious offenses may not be reported because the victim has no confidence that the police will be able to catch the offender. Recording practices vary, and changes in methods of enforcement will have an effect on the volume of crime recorded. In the presentation of the statistics, whether showing increases or decreases, there is a strong public relations element.

The Department of Justice administers two statistical programs to measure the magnitude, nature, and impact of crime in the United States. In public administration, as in legislation, the term ''program'' denotes an organized set of activities directed toward a common purpose or goal, undertaken or proposed by an agency to carry out its given responsibilities.[8] First is the Uniform Crime Reporting (UCR) program, dating back to 1929, supplemented by the newer National Crime Victimization Survey (NCVS), which began in 1973. The Uniform Crime Reports collect data each month on a list of offenses, known as index crimes, which have come to the attention of law enforcement agencies throughout the nation. Information compiled by UCR contributors is forwarded to the Federal Bureau of Investigation (FBI), either directly from local law enforcement agencies, or through state-level UCR programs in forty-four states and the District of Columbia.

The index is made up of the violent crimes of murder and nonnegligent manslaughter, forcible rape, robbery, and aggravated assault; the property crimes of burglary, larceny-theft, and motor vehicle theft; and arson, the last being added by congressional edict in 1979. Unless they fall under existing categories of offense, hate crimes are excluded from the index, although they are separately reported.[9] In addition to the primary collection of data on crime index offenses (part I), the UCR program also solicits monthly data on persons arrested for all crimes except traffic violations (part II offenses).[10] The resulting reports, published annually, are a method of estimating fluctuations in the overall volume and rate of increase or decrease of reported crime. The annual publication includes statistics for each state and certain metropolitan areas, and for the United States and its regions.

The second national measurement, the NCVS, publishes information obtained by way of sample surveys conducted by the Census Bureau[11] on crimes suffered by individuals or households, whether or not they have been reported to law enforcement. Much detailed information is assembled about victims and offenders, as well as the frequency and nature of the crimes of rape, personal robbery, aggravated and simple assault, household burglary, personal and household theft, and motor vehicle theft.[12] The NCVS excludes homicide, arson, commercial crimes, and crimes against children under the age of twelve, all of which are included in the UCR. While the UCR is a measure based on actual crime counts, the NCVS is an estimate derived from the results of nationwide sample surveys. Each set of statistics is hedged about with qualifications, but together they amount to the best approximation there is of the extent and nature of criminal offending in America. Until 1993, sampling methods of the NCVS were constant, with the resulting annual reports being tolerably reliable indicators of trends during the 1980s and early 1990s. It must be repeated that the UCR data is dependent on the extent to which offenses are reported to law enforcement and recorded by the police or other agencies. Both the patterns of reporting and recording practices can and do vary. If, whatever the reasons, victims, witnesses, and others become less disposed to report criminal incidents, it may be misleading to draw the conclusion that the overall volume of crime has decreased. Conversely, if there is an increase in the number of instances of violent behavior reported to law enforcement, for example domestic assaults, it does not follow that the actual volume of violent crime has gone up in proportion to the number of reported incidents.

With these reservations, it is safe to say that the overall picture portrayed by the statistics between 1982 and 1992 did not match the public perception. According to the UCR, per capita rates of recorded property crimes fell slightly over the decade, but with an increase of about one-third in violent crime, mainly in the category of aggravated assault. The NCVS statistics, however, showed a different picture. Although complicated by a change in methodological design in 1993, the survey indicated generally downward trends both in property and violent crime. The trends continued between 1992 and 1995 when the legislation analyzed in this book was being considered by Congress. A comparison between the two systems of measuring changes in per capita national crime rates is set out in table 1.

There is ample evidence that perceptions are influenced more by violent crime than by property crime or statistics on the overall rate of offending. Although it was not discernible at the time, the surge in violent offending, especially that part of it committed by adults,[13] had begun to recede by 1992. Over the next five years there was a steady decline in the UCR year-on-year figures, both for violent crime and homicide. At the time that the crime bill

Table 1. Crime Trends in the United States, 1982–1995

	1982–1992		1992–1995	
	Uniform Crime Reports	National Crime Victimization Survey (pre-redesign)	Uniform Crime Reports	National Crime Victimization Survey (post-redesign)
Property crime[a]	−3%	−27%	−5%	−11%
Violent crime[b]	+33%	−6%	−10%	−7%
Total[c]	+1%	n.a.	−6%	n.a.

Sources: Federal Bureau of Investigation, U.S. Department of Justice, *Crime in the United States,* Uniform Crime Reports, 1982–95 (Washington, D.C.: U.S. Government Printing Office 1982–95); Bureau of Justice Statistics, U.S. Department of Justice, *Criminal Victimization in the United States,* National Crime Survey Reports, 1982–95 (Washington, D.C.: 1982–95).

Notes: The table shows changes in per capita crime rates. The rates for the UCR figures are based on total population. For the NCVS, they are based on households for property crime, and on those aged twelve or more for violent crime.

[a] For the UCR, property crime comprises burglary, larceny, and vehicle theft. For the NCVS for the years 1982–92 it comprises all crimes against households (burglary, motor vehicle theft, and household larceny); for 1992–95 it comprises the same crimes against households, together with personal larcenies.

[b] For the UCR, violent crime comprises murder and nonnegligent manslaughter, forcible rape, robbery, and aggravated assault. For the NCVS for 1982–92 and 1992–95, it comprises all rape, robbery, and aggravated and simple assault.

[c] Because of different bases, no overall per capita rate can be calculated for the NCVS.

was introduced in the autumn of 1993, however, the fixed perceptions shared by lawmakers and the general public alike were of an ever-rising tide of violence that had started to engulf the United States in the late 1960s and early 1970s. In 1993, the scale of violent offending was demonstrated by a total in excess of 1.9 million incidents of violent crime reported. (See table 2.) The national rate was 746 per 100,000 inhabitants, rising to a rate of 975 offenses of violent crime per 100,000 in the cities.[14]

The total number of recorded murders during 1993 was 24,526 (see table 3, falling to 23,326 in 1994, and 21,597 in 1995. High as they are these figures are unlikely to represent the actual total. Each year a significant number of missing persons are recorded and no one can estimate how many of those who disappear might have been murdered. Taken over a longer period, the murder rate has been relatively constant. In 1980 it was 10.2 per 100,000 inhabitants, falling to 7.9 in 1984 and 1985 before moving up again to 9.4 in 1990, and steadying between 9.4 and 9.8 per 100,000 in the early 1990s. By the mid-1990s it had fallen to 8.2 in 1995, with provisional figures showing a drop below 8.0 for 1996. While it is to be hoped that a reduction in criminality is the main cause of the decline in the number of homicides, it may not be the whole explanation. The advent of trauma centers at hospitals in nearly all major urban areas has led to a marked improvement in the number of victims who survived after being treated for gunshot wounds. In reporting the findings of

Table 2. Violent Crime in the United States, 1990–1995

Year	Number of Offenses	Change from Previous Year	Rate per 100,000 Population	Change from Previous Year
1990	1,820,130	+10.6%	731.8	+10.4%
1991	1,911,770	+5.0%	758.1	+3.6%
1992	1,932,270	+1.1%	757.5	−0.1%
1993	1,926,020	−0.3%	746.8	−1.4%
1994	1,857,670	−3.5%	713.6	−4.5%
1995	1,798,790	−3.2%	684.6	−4.1%

Source: Federal Bureau of Investigation, U.S. Department of Justice. *Crime in the United States,* Uniform Crime Reports for 1990–95 (Washington, D.C.: U.S. Government Printing Office, 1990–95).

a research study that indicated that 92 percent of patients who required hospitalization due to firearms injuries survived, the UCR commented in 1995 that this factor might have influenced the decline in the homicide rate.[15]

In 1993 the chances of becoming a murder victim were more than twice as high in metropolitan areas (11 victims per 100,000 inhabitants) as in the rural counties and in cities outside metropolitan areas, where the rate was 5 victims per 100,000.[16] Within the metropolitan areas there were marked discrepancies. Violent crime is disproportionately concentrated in the low-income, predominantly black, districts, where the risks of being murdered, assaulted or robbed are far higher than in the middle- and upper-income, predominantly white, districts. As one well-informed commentator has written, "[N]ever before has violent crime been so concentrated among teenage and young adult male inner-city blacks."[17] The most ominous of the UCR statistics are that in 69.6 percent of the murders, 42.4 percent of the robberies, and 25.1 percent of aggravated assaults, a firearm was the weapon used. Between 1992 and 1993 assaults with firearms rose by 5.0 percent.[18] The statistics for each of these categories showed a rise on the previous year. Firearm injuries were far and away the leading cause of death in 1993 for young black males between the ages of fifteen and twenty-four.[19] At 162 deaths per 100,000 of the population, firearm deaths dwarfed the comparable rates for suicide (16.4 per 100,000), deaths resulting from motor vehicle crashes (35.0 per 100,000), HIV infection (6.9 per 100,000), and all other diseases (in aggregate amounting to 15.2 per 100,000).[20] For whites in the same age group, the death rate from firearm injuries was much lower, at 32.0 per 100,000.

III

This resumé does not aim to pursue the disagreements that exist over the gathering and interpretation of statistical data. What stands out from any analysis is the salience of violence, and the recourse to physical force and firearms that distinguishes crime in America from any other developed nation state. It

Table 3. Murder in the United States, 1990–1995

Year	Number of Offenses	Change from Previous Year	Rate per 100,000 Population	Change from Previous Year
1990	23,438	+9.0%	9.4	+8.8%
1991	24,703	+5.4%	9.8	+3.9%
1992	23,760	−3.8%	9.3	−4.9%
1993	24,526	+3.2%	9.5	+2.1%
1994	23,326	−4.9%	9.0	−5.8%
1995	21,597	−7.4%	8.2	−8.3%

Source: Federal Bureau of Investigation, U.S. Department of Justice, *Crime in the United States,* Uniform Crime Reports for 1990–95 (Washington, D.C.: U.S. Government Printing Office, 1990–95).

Note: ''Murder'' includes nonnegligent manslaughter. The index offense is defined in the UCR as the willful killing of one human being by another. The classification is based on police investigation as opposed to the determination of a court, medical examiner, coroner, jury, or other judicial body. It does not include deaths caused by negligence, suicide, or accident; justifiable homicides; attempts to murder or assaults to murder, which are classified as aggravated assaults.

is the consciousness of life-threatening personal violence that has led so many Americans, and not only in the big cities where the risk is greatest, to live in fear. Making an intercity comparison of crime patterns between Los Angeles and Sydney, and New York City and London, Franklin Zimring and Gordon Hawkins demonstrated the extent to which American criminals kill and wound their victims far more often than elsewhere in the developed world. Whereas the incidence of theft and burglary in Los Angeles and Sydney, two multicultural cities of comparable size,[21] was broadly similar, robbery[22] and homicide were notably dissimilar. In 1992 Los Angeles reported 39,508 robberies while Sydney reported 4,942, one-eighth of the Los Angeles rate.[23]

For homicide the differential was greater still. Fifty-three homicides were reported by the police in Sydney during 1992, a crime volume equal to 5 percent of the total of 1,094 homicides reported by the Los Angeles police in that year. The difference between the two cities in rates of criminal homicide exceeded an order of magnitude.[24] The pattern emerging from a comparison between London and New York City crime rates was even more surprising than the Sydney/Los Angeles comparison, and to the same effect. Whereas in 1990 London experienced considerably more theft than New York, and a rate of burglary that was 57 percent higher, the robbery rate was less than one-fifth of the robbery rate in New York. Here again, homicide stood out starkly with homicide rates in London being less than one-tenth of those in New York.[25] Thus the distinguishing factor between the four cities was not the overall amount of crime experienced, but rather the more harmful character of the crimes.

The findings of this illuminating survey have direct relevance to national policies toward crime in the United States. A country's crime rate, it is argued, is substantially independent of its rate of lethal violence. The death rate from crime in England and Wales, to take one example, was the lowest in a sample of twenty developed countries, although the overall crime rate was just above the average.[26] Failure to differentiate between the grave dangers to personal security posed by violent crime and the generality of non-violent offending, harmful and distressing as it is, can divert attention away from finding the most effective means of achieving greater public safety. Muggings in the streets and armed robberies by strangers are more an aspect of a propensity toward violence than part of a broader pattern of crimes against property. It is the violent strain in American social life that leads to the special destruction and disorganization caused by crime, and spreads such corrosive anxiety and fear. In framing crime control policies, violence and its favored instrument, the handgun, should have priority over all else.

In any society penal policy is misdirected if resources, including prosecutions, criminal trials, and prison places, are not deployed selectively. The contention that violence is the key to grasping the essentials of the overall crime problem in the United States is persuasive. In the well-chosen words of Zimring and Hawkins:

> Chronically high rates of lethal violence generate insecurities in the United States that are qualitatively different from those found in other advanced countries. Lethal violence is the most serious social control problem in every developed nation; it is by far a more serious problem in the United States than in any society with which we would care to compare ourselves.[27]

An example of a priority target is that whereas adult homicide rates remained relatively stable between 1985 and 1992, the rate at which young men aged fourteen to seventeen killed increased steeply. According to one estimate, the homicide rate for young white males went up by about 50 percent, and for young black males it tripled.[28] In 1992 the proportion of all killings by young men in the fourteen-to-seventeen age range reached 15 percent. Unlike the direct impact on opinion of adult homicides, where many killings (e.g., of family members or acquaintances) take place behind closed doors, the high profile of inner-city violent behavior by youths heightened the fear of the public at large of random killings, robberies, or assaults by strangers in the street or public places.

By the early 1990s crime, depicted by President Clinton as "the great crisis of the spirit that is gripping America today,"[29] was firmly established at or close to the top of the list of issues of greatest public concern. It was also the most politicized, dominating the electoral landscape. Politicians running for elective office, whether local, state, or federal, had no cause to consult opinion polls to be reminded of the strength of the feelings aroused by criminal offending, above all the violent crimes that colored attitudes toward all other forms of offending. The anger, fear, and resentment were only too evident. A wave of populism, already aroused and gathering strength, reached all parts of the nation, including those where the risks of victimization were least. Unlike other upsurges of populist sentiment, the tide did not stop at the doors of professional, business, or academic homes. The elites were frightened too. Their homes might be better protected, and located in safer neighborhoods, but in the streets of the cities they were as vulnerable. The pervading climate of violence, the extent of actual or reputed victimization, reflected and magnified by media exposure, and supplemented by the velocity of news about violent crime within personal networks, came together in the creation of a public mood characterized by retribution and punitive values.

Criminologists might warn against oversimplification and exaggeration, but elected representatives almost without exception recognized an imperative need to respond to such a ubiquitous mood, and in many cases sought to exact political advantage from a fearful, sometimes vindictive, public. To be tough on crime had become transformed from slogan to electoral necessity. Politicians of contrasting views could not afford to allow their opponents to occupy the high ground unchallenged, so they too joined in the chorus of rhetorical toughness. The transfer of such a powerful current of popular opinion into federal legislation that was workable and preserved the principles of justice was to be a severe test of America's political institutions.

IV

Before embarking on a detailed study of the politics and substance of the legislation on violent crime control and law enforcement enacted by the 103rd Congress, a brief rehearsal of the fundamentals of the American system of criminal justice may be called for. First are the separate, although overlapping, federal and state criminal jurisdictions. Historically the responsibility for detecting, prosecuting, and punishing crimes lay with each individual state, and not with the federal government. That responsibility remains today, with some 95 percent of all prosecutions for violent crime being tried in state courts. If offenders are convicted and sentenced to a term of imprisonment, they are confined in a local jail or state-run prison. Throughout the twentieth century, however, the criminal jurisdiction of the federal courts, and the substantive and procedural provisions imposed by Congress, have been greatly enlarged. Laws intended to curb the misuse of narcotic or other dangerous drugs, and to penalize those who trade in them or use them, have been the main cause in recent years, although the expansionist trend was clear enough before.

Federal offenses accumulated steadily from the early years of the century onward: breaches of immigration laws, customs violations, tax frauds, crimes committed on the high seas or subsequently in the air. Then came laws aimed at regulating the social evils, as they were seen at the time, of gambling, child labor, and prostitution, followed by prohibition of the sale of liquor in the 1920s and 1930s. The earlier enactments fell clearly enough under the heading of offenses against the regulations necessary for the conduct of a modern federated state. Later regulatory legislation relied upon the device of prohibiting interstate transportation, rather than interfering directly with local activities, so bringing into play the commerce clause of the Constitution. But the legislators in Washington had to tread with care, for the doctrine of states' rights emphatically included the right to make and enforce the laws to be observed in their own state on all matters not specifically reserved to the federal government. Federal courts were able to try only those classes of case designated to be within their jurisdiction by federal law. Everything else fell within the jurisdiction of the state systems.[30]

The expansion of the federal criminal jurisdiction and the emergence of a national system of criminal justice were made possible, if not inevitable, by advances in technology, particularly in rail and air transportation. Lawrence Friedman has pointed out that the shrinking of distance coincided with economic developments and the electronic news media to make a reality of the national ideal implicit in the concept of federalism. As the years passed, state boundaries were of less and less significance in determining the way of life of millions of Americans. Many crimes became interstate: criminals too had "wheels and wings."[31] Not only was offending by individuals mobile and not confined within state boundaries, but so was large-scale organized crime. Nor, it was contended, should be the law enforcement agencies of federal government, most notably the Federal Bureau of Investigation.

The Bureau of Investigation, later renamed the Federal Bureau of Investigation, was established by the Attorney General in 1908 as part of the Department of Justice. The status and influence of the FBI grew under the long period when J. Edgar Hoover was director, from 1924 until his death in 1972. Today it is the principal investigative arm of the Department of Justice and is charged with gathering and reporting facts, locating witnesses, and compiling evidence in cases involving the federal jurisdiction. Priority areas are organized crime, drugs, counterterrorism, white-collar crime, foreign counterintelligence, and violent crime.

Responding to these developments, the number of federal offenses multiplied rapidly. Drugs, stolen goods and merchandise of every sort, securities and money frequently crossed state lines, calling for combined action by enforcement authorities and the ability to prosecute offenders in federal district courts. Driving stolen motor vehicles across state lines and dealing in stolen vehicles that had moved from one state into another had been federal offenses since 1919. Following the outcry over the Lindbergh baby case in 1932, kidnappers who had taken victims held for ransom or reward over state boundaries became subject to federal investigation and prosecution.[32]

To non-Americans it seems strange that the interstate commerce clause of the Constitution should have been pressed into service to facilitate and validate the growth of the federal criminal jurisdiction. In enumerating the powers granted by the people to their government, the Constitution conferred on the Congress power "[t]o regulate Commerce with foreign Nations, and among the several States, and with the Indian Tribes."[33] In the formative years of the Republic, national control was needed to prevent unneighborly trade rivalries between the states, such as the imposition of tariffs on imports by one state from another and retaliatory action. The commerce power did much to create national markets but, as construed by the Supreme Court, it also became a prime source to justify the exercise of national authority and to restrain state action.

A historic development occurred in the 1960s when the commerce power was invoked for the purpose of banning racial discrimination in places of public accommodation under Title II of the Civil Rights Act of 1964.[34] For the purposes of section 201 of the Act, commerce meant travel, trade, traffic, commerce, transportation, or communication among the several states, or between the District of Columbia and any state. Inns, hotels, motels, or other establishments providing lodgings for transient guests were brought within the ambit of the statute, as were restaurants and other facilities principally engaged in selling food for consumption on the premises where a substantial portion of the food was supplied from outside the state. Places of public accommodation included gasoline stations, motion picture house, theaters, concert halls, sports arenas and stadiums, and other places of exhibition or entertainment. The constitutionality of these provisions was upheld by the Supreme Court in *Heart of Atlanta Motel v. United States*[35] and *Katzenbach* v. *McClung*.[36] During the Senate hearings on the bill the previous year, the Attorney General, Robert Kennedy, argued that racial discrimination in the South amounted to an injustice that needed to be remedied: "We have to find the tools with which to remedy that injustice." In the administration's judgment the commerce clause provided the most apt constitutional tool. To some commentators, however, as to the sceptical members of the Senate Committee on Commerce, it was straining the meaning and purpose of the "affecting commerce" rationale to make it the basis of civil rights legislation, which would have been better addressed by way of the Fourteenth Amendment.[37]

Although the connections between the original purposes of the commerce clause and its modern applications might often seem tenuous, the increasingly intense searches for constitutional justifications among the powers expressly granted by the Constitution, in the words of one scholarly critic, made the commerce clause "a frequently attractive and often hospitable base for the assertion of regulatory authority."[38]

By the mid-1990s with federal regulatory authority coming under more critical scrutiny, the constitutional wheel began to turn once again. In 1995, for the first time in nearly sixty years, the Supreme Court in *United States v. Lopez*[39] struck down a federal statute on the ground that it exceeded the authority of Congress. There was nothing novel in the setting aside of a federal enactment on constitutional grounds. In the 1994–95 term alone the Supreme Court had invalidated provisions of three other statutes, two because of their incompatibility with the First Amendment, and one as a contravention of the separation-of-powers doctrine.[40] Since *Marbury v. Madison* in 1803[41] a total of 129 federal statutes had been invalidated by the Supreme Court. The significance lay in the fact that no act had been overturned on commerce clause grounds since 1936.[42]

The Gun-Free School Zones Act of 1990[43] had been enacted at a time of public and congressional concern about a series of shooting incidents at schools. It made it a federal offense for any individual knowingly to possess a firearm at a place that the individual knows, or has reasonable cause to believe, is a school zone.[44] There was little evidence of prior thought having been given to the constitutional authority necessary to give effect to what was regarded by its sponsors in the Congress as an expression of their legislative concern to combat crime by reducing the risk of firearms misuse at or in the vicinity of schools, so backing up a prohibition that in various forms already existed in over forty states. It was only later, when the Court of Appeals for the Fifth Circuit reversed the decision of a U.S. District Court to deny a motion to dismiss the indictment of a high-school student in Texas who had carried a concealed handgun and ammunition to his school and had been prosecuted under federal rather than state law,[45] that the commerce clause was invoked as the source of authority enabling Congress to legislate.

By a fateful coincidence the oral argument in *Lopez* was heard by the Supreme Court on the same day, November 8, 1994, when the voters were sending to Washington in large numbers legislators committed to limiting the power and role of federal government. Six months later, on April 26, 1995, in affirming the Fifth Circuit's judgment that the law forbidding the possession of guns in or near schools was invalid as being beyond the powers of Congress under the commerce clause,[46] the Supreme Court, by a majority of five Justices to four,[47] held that the act exceeded the authority of Congress to regulate commerce since the possession of a gun in a local school zone was not an economic activity that substantially affected interstate commerce.

The Chief Justice, William Rehnquist, delivering the opinion of the Court, described the Act as a criminal statute that by its terms had nothing to do with commerce or any sort of economic enterprise, however broadly one might define those terms. Nor was the possession of a gun at a local school an economic activity that might, through repetition elsewhere, substantially affect any sort of interstate commerce. Lopez was a local student at a local school; there was no indication that he had recently moved in interstate commerce, and there was no requirement that his possession of a firearm had any concrete tie to interstate commerce.[48]

Justice Breyer, joined by three other Justices, led the dissent. In his opinion the statute fell well within the scope of the commerce power as the Court had understood it over the last half-century.[49] The courts must give Congress a degree of leeway in determining the existence of a significant factual connection between the regulated activity and interstate commerce, both because the Constitution delegated the commerce power directly to Congress and because the determination required an empirical judgment of a kind that a legislature was more likely than a court to make with accuracy. The traditional words "rational basis" captured that leeway. The specific question before the Court was not whether the regulated activity sufficiently affected interstate commerce, but rather whether Congress could have had a rational basis for so concluding. Viewing the commerce connection not as a technical legal conception but as a practical one, he concluded that the answer to the question must be yes.[50]

Oblique in approach, necessarily so in the light of the facts of the case, and recondite as Breyer's reasoning was, it is hard to fault a reported off-the-cuff reaction by his former colleague at the Harvard Law School, Laurence Tribe. In calling the decision a dramatic move by the Court, Tribe, an eminent constitutional authority, added, "[I]f ever there was an Act that exceeded Congress's commerce power, this was it."[51]

V

Whether the decision in *Lopez* will stand as an isolated move against the hitherto prevailing climate of judicial restraint in challenging the legitimacy of established laws, or whether it is a precursor of climatic change, still remains to be seen. The fundamental doctrine, that the Constitution establishes a federal government of delegated, enumerated, and so limited powers is unchanged. That the interpretative climate surrounding the doctrine does change, however, was seen in the conflict between the Supreme Court, the administration, and Congress in the 1930s over the legitimacy of the legislation giving effect to President Roosevelt's New Deal program. In 1936, the decision of the Supreme Court in *Carter v. Carter Coal Company*[52] marked the culmination of a series of decisions invalidating important components of the New Deal, to Roosevelt's great displeasure, on the grounds that the transactions which federal laws sought to regulate were not part of commerce, and that their effect on commerce was indirect rather than direct. Less than a year later, in a decision described by Rhenquist, C.J., in *Lopez* as a watershed,[53] the Court changed course. Writing for the majority in *NLRB v. Jones and Laughlin Steel Corporation*,[54] a case about the right to union membership by employees in the steel industry, Hughes, C.J., abandoned the distinction between direct and indirect effects on interstate commerce, holding that intrastate activities that had "such a close and substantial relation to interstate commerce that their control is essential or appropriate to protect that commerce from burdens or obstructions" fell within Congress's power to regulate.[55] Thus it was the reinterpretation of the commerce clause by the Supreme Court in 1937 that provided a way of preserving the sanctity of the Constitution by finding new and broader grounds for determining the scope of congressional power.

Intricately linked to the limitations on congressional and executive power is the division of authority between federal and state government. The relationship is one that fluctuates according to the needs of the time and the climate of national opinion. Not only the Congress and the courts, but the political leaders who attain the highest elective office determine the parameters. During the presidency of John F. Kennedy, federal power was directed toward obtaining for black Americans the basic legal and political rights enjoyed by white Americans. The "Great Society" measures promoted by Lyndon Johnson went further, recognizing that the life chances for African-Americans were diminished by the incidence of poverty, substandard living conditions, especially in the inner cities, and lack of educational and employment opportunities. The determined resistance mounted by the defenders of states' rights in the courts failed, but it was not long before the neoconservative attitudes of the next era once again adjusted the federal-state balance. When exposing his vision of a "new federalism," a term used by President Johnson to convey an opposite meaning,[56] President Reagan proclaimed his intention to restrict the activities of federal government by reducing or eliminating a large number of social welfare and other programs, the cuts falling mainly on federal aid to state and local governments. He did so not simply because he wanted to bring down the high level of public expenditure and its adverse effect on the American economy, but

> because he judged these activities to be inefficient, unnecessary, and sometimes positively harmful. He also claimed that they were improper under the Constitution—not so much in the strict sense that they violated specific provisions of our fundamental law as in the larger philosophical and historical sense that they offended against the true meaning of the document.... [A]ccordingly, President Reagan promised to "restore the balance between levels of government."[57]

An echo of Reagan's creed was sounded by his successor, George Bush, when he signed the Crime Control Act into law in 1990. The President said he was disturbed that certain provisions unnecessarily constrained the discretion of state and local governments. The examples he gave were rural drug enforcement and drug-free school zone programs, correctional options incentives, and "most egregiously" the ban on the possession of firearms at school zones (added as a Democrat initiative in the Senate), which he described as inappropriately overriding legitimate state firearms laws with a new and unnecessary federal law.[58] Three years later his premonitory remarks were to be cited in the decision of the U.S. Court of Appeals in the *Lopez* case.[59]

If President Clinton's policies fell short of the more sharply defined goals set by Johnson and Reagan, appearing at times to steer an erratic course between the polarities, on certain issues—health care and crime being his legislative priorities for the 103rd Congress—he showed that on occasion he was ready to deploy federal power and executive authority to act upon what he identified as the true interests of the majority of the people.

Apart from the federal/state duality, there are countless dissimilarities between American and British parliamentary institutions. As two well-informed British authors have aptly remarked, despite a shared heritage the two greatest legislatures of the free world are "separated by a width of incomprehension, an Atlantic of the mind, which prevents each from benefiting from the acquired wisdom of the other."[60] In recent years the gap, already so wide, seems if anything to have grown. The weaknesses of each system are accentuated, and the strengths taken for granted. Trust in government suffers as a result. The characteristics of congressional lawmaking are diffuse and nonstatic. They include the extraordinary ease with which legislation can be introduced, however improbable the chances of enactment; the barely visible party discipline; the decisions to hold, or withhold, public hearings by committees or subcommittees; the building of coalitions and their disintegration; the laxity in enforcing rules on relevance in the House; the blurring of the distinctions between the procedures for authorizing and appropriating expenditures; the readiness to add or discard large or small provisions in conference, sometimes resulting in statutory provisions being enacted without any consideration on the floor of either chamber; and the threatened or actual use of the presidential veto. All of these features will be encountered in the unfolding of the narrative.

The separation between the executive and the legislature, at state as well as federal level, is absolute, in practice as well as in constitutional design. There is no question of the executive dominating the lawmaking process in the way it does in Britain,[61] even when the President's party has a majority in the Senate and the House. For two years of Clinton's first term he had that advantage, but, as we shall see, it was no easier for him to get his policy aims enacted than it had been for his immediate Republican predecessor in office, George Bush.

Since power is fragmented, and party discipline ineffective, the progress of major items of legislation through Congress is unpredictable and prone to outside pressures. Local allegiances count for much, particularly in the House where representatives have to face their electorates every two years. No representative can afford to distance himself or herself from the views of constituents without risking the loss of electoral support. They must be seen and heard, regularly and articulately, advancing matters of concern to their districts in Washington. For these reasons, cross-party alliances come together on specific issues. An instance can be found in the conflicting reactions to the policy of enlarging federal controls on firearms exemplified in the voting record of congressmen from the run-down inner-city areas of the industrialized states, and the rural and farming regions of the South and West. The Republican supporters of gun control in the House of Representatives typically came from urban or suburban districts with high rates of violence and street crime, whereas most of the Democrats who were opposed to gun controls represented rural districts. On issues of this sort, where local attitudes are deeply entrenched, there is always the potential for the opinions of local voters to override party affiliation and the interests of the leadership in Congress.

No introduction to the scrutiny of the passage of a particular legislative enactment would be complete without remarking on the role and influence of organized groups. A multitude of groups dedicated to promoting the entire spectrum of current policy preferences are continuously at work at the grass roots. They are instrumental in bringing local opinion, or factions of local opinion, to bear on elected representatives. Moreover, as politicians need to raise financial support for their costly election campaigns, national interest groups and political action committees can and do play a crucial part in helping or impeding a candidate's return to Washington, and on voting decisions once there. The sums of money now involved in campaign finance are huge. In the congressional midterm elections held in November 1994, the Federal Election Commission estimated that in total over half a billion dollars was spent on campaigns. Candidates were left with an estimated debt of more than $70 million.[62] Although during the campaign it was a Republican theme to castigate the Washington elite, with lobbyists being described as a blight on the political process, it was not long before they and their clients were being solicited by some of the large number of newly elected congressmen to make donations to repay campaign debts.[63]

Those who provide the money are not philanthropists. They expect something in return from those who are elected. Both are keenly aware that the candidates who fail to raise the money to finance an effective campaign are those most likely to fail at the polls. The host of representatives and lobbyists who cluster around the Capitol, seeking access to legislators and working to advance the interests of major national associations, labor unions, special interest groups, U.S. and foreign companies, and many other corporate or individual interests, are an enduring part of the political system. Whether or not regarded as a blight, the rapidity with which lobbyists established links with members of the first Congress for forty years to be dominated by the Republican Party showed that the rules of the game had not changed, only some of the players.

At a more elevated level of constitutional discourse, Congress is, and has been for generations, a stronghold of particular interests of every sort. Presidents and party leaders may initiate proposals of general application that they regard as being in the national interest, but they are conscious of the truth of the dictum that "Congress is a center of resistance to actions in the general interest and an initiator of actions to benefit partial interests."[64] Hence a state of disharmony between the White House and the legislators on Capitol Hill is unavoidable and, on one view, is integral to the healthy functioning of American democratic institutions.[65]

The statutory restrictions on the manufacture, transfer, and possession of certain firearms contained in the Violent Crime Control and Law Enforcement Act of 1994 afford a vivid case history of the interplay between interest group pressures and lawmaking. Like the gun control proposals in the crime bills that failed to make headway in the 101st and 102nd Congresses, these provisions, central to the President's appeal to the national public, were subjected to intense and sustained opposition from one of the most formidable, feared, and well-financed of all interest groups, the National Rifle Association (NRA). The impact of the NRA will be noted, and the sources of its political strength analyzed, at the successive stages of the 1994 legislation and its aftermath in the 104th Congress.

In contrast, the influence of another organized group, drawing its support and legitimacy from a very different constituency, was apparent in the rooted

hostility of the Congressional Black Caucus (CBC) in the House of Representatives to the punitive orientation of the crime bill, and in particular to the
extension of the death penalty to a long list of federal offenses. Members of
the caucus were convinced that the death sentences that were passed in those
states where capital punishment was lawful discriminated against African-
Americans. Many of them shared with the voters who had sent them to Congress a deep distrust of the police, the prosecutors, and the courts, all of which
were believed to be biased against them. These were far from the only organized interests brought to bear during the passage of the 1993–94 legislation on
crime, but they were two of the most prominent.

VI

Twenty-five years earlier, in 1968, another Democratic-controlled Congress
had passed another omnibus crime bill,[66] although with little more than lukewarm support from the Johnson Administration. It contained some watered-
down restrictions on the sale and purchase of firearms, which were strengthened a few months later[67] in the aftermath of the assassinations by shooting
of Martin Luther King and Senator Robert Kennedy. Thereafter the Democratic
preference, apart from some of the more conservative southern Democrats, was
to address the causes of crime committed within state jurisdictions, rather than
to convert various crimes against state laws into federal offenses. Richard
Nixon, who became President in succession to Lyndon Johnson in 1969, campaigned against Hubert Humphrey on a law-and-order platform, amongst other
matters. At least for presidential politics, and to some extent for congressional
politics, crime was largely a Republican issue for the next two decades.

During the late 1960s and early 1970s some southern Democrats in the
Senate, led by Senator John McClellan of Arkansas, espoused the cause of
reforming and recodifying federal criminal law, gaining the support of some
Republican senators. A national commission, with McClellan and other members of Congress included in the membership, was established under the chairmanship of former Governor Edmund Brown of California, which produced a
final report in 1971.[68] A new and comprehensive code was proposed to replace
Title 18 of the United States Code, comprising a reclassification of virtually
all federal penal statutes, together with the rules for interpreting them and the
procedures for imposing sanctions for their violation. Important areas of judge-
developed law were incorporated into associated statutory provisions, thus providing for the first time a single, basic source of federal criminal law.[69]

Although the executive branch, in the shape of Nixon and his Attorney
General, John Mitchell, responded positively, institutional inertia had to be
guarded against within the Department of Justice during the long-drawn-out
consideration of the necessary legislation by the Senate and, to a lesser extent,
the House of Representatives. Like many other codification proposals, it was
when the general arguments for simplicity, rationality, consistency, and accessibility encountered the political controversies that legislators saw arising out

of the detailed proposals that the trouble began. A bill introduced in the Senate came under attack both from the Left and the Right, with the deletion being sought of its two most divisive sets of proposals: those involving defenses to criminal conduct and those involving a series of provisions on espionage and the disclosure of classified information. Shorn of these controversial features, but with the addition of a sentencing commission to set detailed guidelines for the imposition of sanctions on federal offenders, a revised bill was the subject of floor debate in the Senate over a period of eight days in January 1978. In the upshot it was passed by a vote of seventy-two votes to fifteen.

In the House some far-sighted and sophisticated Democrats, Don Edwards of California and Robert Kastenmeier of Wisconsin among them, did not share the senators' optimism about the advantages of a sentencing commission. Although no action was taken on the Senate bill in the 95th Congress, the House of Representatives set to work on preparing its own bill. In the 96th Congress, after the House Subcommittee on Criminal Justice had held numerous hearings and met in over one hundred sessions, a bill was reported that only partially recodified federal criminal statutes and made limited changes to sentencing procedures.[70] It too failed to make progress.

Later legislative initiatives were no more successful, while opposition outside Congress mounted. Criticism from civil liberties groups was vehement and prolonged. In support of recodification it was explained that many of the criticisms of provisions in the draft code were misguided as they were no more than counterparts of current law. But controversial accretions had formed around the original framework during the years of Republican administrations, and there was ineradicable suspicion that anything backed by Nixon and Mitchell was unlikely to further the cause of civil liberties. From another quarter, the voices of indignant moralists were heard. A number of conservative organizations, including religious organizations, expressed alarm at what they perceived as the code's unduly lenient approach toward pornography, sex offenses, prostitution, and drug trafficking. At the same time, it was censured for being excessively severe toward corporate crime. It was not altogether a caricature to comment that their complaints added up to an indictment that the code would permit vice to flourish while hounding innocent businessmen into bankruptcy or prison.[71]

Codification efforts were abandoned by Congress in 1982 after more than a decade of inconclusive legislative deliberation. Apart from the merits or demerits of its content, a draft criminal code was singularly ill-suited to the ways of congressional lawmaking. The essence of the code was its intended consistency, harmony, and structure.[72] The familiar tactic used to progress legislation through Congress of producing multiple proposals as a basis for compromise was simply not available. Nor could the code survive being broken up into separate pieces from which legislators could pick and choose. In the end the piecemeal approach prevailed. Although no further action was taken to renew the aim of inclusive codification, certain segments taken from the earlier bills were incorporated in an anti-crime package that was enacted in late 1984 as the Comprehensive Crime Control Act.[73] The whole of the code bill's sentencing provisions, originally regarded by McClellan as a sweetener to liberal opinion,[74] were included, together with proposals permitting the pretrial detention of dangerous offenders, sections governing the disposition of insane or incompetent defendants, and the extension of wiretap authority.[75]

The sentencing regime approved by the 98th Congress in 1984 required the abolition of the U.S. Parole Commission and the ending of the discretionary power, exercised since 1910, to determine the suitability for release of selected inmates from federal prisons on license. In its place, a commission appointed by the President was charged with devising and promulgating a system of sentencing guidelines binding on trial judges in the federal courts. At least three of its members had to be federal judges selected from a list of six judges recommended by the Judicial Conference of the United States. Both the judicial and the nonjudicial members of the U.S. Sentencing Commission required confirmation by the Senate. Although the Department of Justice maintained that the executive functions of an independent sentencing commission set up in the judicial branch of government violated separation-of-powers principles, and others argued that Congress had granted the Commission excessive legislative discretion, the Supreme Court upheld the constitutionality of its location in the judicial branch. In a rare claim that Congress had improperly delegated its powers to an agency composed in part of federal judges, the Court decided that in creating the Sentencing Commission, an unusual hybrid in structure and authority, Congress had neither delegated excessive legislative power not upset the constitutionally mandated balance of powers among the coordinate branches. Judges served on the Commission not in their judicial capacity, but because of their appointment by the President under the terms of the Act.[76]

Consequent upon the 1984 reforms, sentences would be calculated on a graduated scale according to the gravity of the offense and the offender's prior criminal record. The discretion of the trial judge would be limited to selecting a sentence within a range in which ordinarily the maximum would not exceed the minimum by more than the greater of twenty-five percent or six months. The period of time spent in custody would no longer be susceptible of being shortened by discretionary release on parole, all sentences in future being basically determinate. A prisoner would be released at the end of the sentence passed by the court, reduced only by any credit earned by good behavior while in prison.

VII

Few of the original proponents believe that events since the commencement of the system of guidelines in 1987 have brought the benefits they had hoped to see. Judicial discretion has been curtailed, but the disparities and uncertainties in sentencing that the reforms sought to eliminate have been replaced by other and less obvious sources of disparity and uncertainty. Plea bargaining

transfers power to the prosecutor and determines the offense for which the offender is actually sentenced, and hence the penalty.[77] Although the guidelines are almost universally unpopular amongst federal trial judges, some follow them scrupulously while others, regarding them as unjust, treat them with less reverence. The operation of the system has been criticized as harsh, mechanistic, and excessively rigid. It has led to widespread judicial distress, some outspoken opposition, and a rising level of noncompliance.[78] Both the legislation and the U.S. Sentencing Commission have been blamed for an outcome that is plainly unsatisfactory to all parties. By February 1992, at a symposium held at Yale Law School to deliberate upon what should be done, there can have been no room for dissent from the proposition that when a penalty structure offends those charged with the daily administration of the criminal law, causing tension between the judge's duty to follow the written law and the judge's oath to administer justice, it is time for corrective action to be taken by the judiciary, the Sentencing Commission, and Congress.[79]

The problems encountered in devising a workable framework for sentencing guidelines were compounded in the later 1980s by an over-reliance on the part of legislators on fixed sentences for persons convicted of possessing drugs as well as dealing in them. The mandatory minimum terms of imprisonment prescribed by statute filled the prisons with relatively low-level drug offenders. For example, in 1993 approximately 3,500 defendants were sentenced to terms of imprisonment in the federal system under mandatory minimum laws for the possession of crack cocaine. The average sentence was more than five years.[80] The sentences for trafficking were longer than the median penalties for armed robbery, kidnapping, or extortion and were hard to reconcile with the painstakingly constructed mathematical matrix relating offense seriousness and previous record to a scale of penalties across the whole range of criminal offenses.[81] Nor did the politically mixed parentage of the sentencing reforms in Congress help to make remedial action on agreed lines a realistic possibility.

In the early stages of policy formulation the desire to reduce disparities between sentences for similar offenses in the interests of fairness and justice was impeccably liberal in origin. That impetus carried through to the idea, pioneered by a federal judge for the Southern District of New York, Marvin E. Frankel, of a sentencing commission to make rules or guidelines that would confine the discretion of individual (and often highly individualistic) judges.[82] A few liberal Democrats took up the cause in the Senate, and support for legislation began to grow in the late 1970s and early 1980s. Bills introduced by Senator Edward Kennedy (Dem. Massachusetts) were linked at first to the codification project being promoted by McClellan and other senators more conservative in outlook than Kennedy. It was this that led Kennedy into an improbable alliance with his successor as chairman of the Senate Judiciary Committee, the veteran Republican (originally Democrat) senator from South Carolina, Strom Thurmond. When the Republicans took control of the Senate in 1981, it was Thurmond who sponsored an omnibus anti-crime measure which included the Sentencing Reform Act.[83] The contents were virtually identical to a separate bill introduced by Kennedy. After some unorthodox maneuvers in the closing stages, the Senate bill, with the sentencing provisions attached, was passed by the House of Representatives and signed into law by President Reagan on October 12, 1984.[84]

Before then a series of compromises with conservative opinion had been made over four successive Congresses. None of them was destructive of the original idea, but taken cumulatively they were hostages to fortune. As was so noticeable in the proceedings on the later crime bill in 1993–94, there is an ingrained reluctance in the legislative process to abandon accommodations previously reached by hard bargaining. In this way, the finishing point in one session of Congress tends to be the starting point for the same issue in the next.[85] Over a nine-year span, sentencing reform had begun its congressional life as a free-standing measure; had been joined to the bill intended to reform and codify federal criminal law; had been detached from it to stand alone once more; and finally had been joined to the Reagan administration's anti-crime proposals enacted in 1984.

It was an ominous portent that the expectations of the two most prominent backers of sentencing reform should have been so far apart in their aims. Whereas Kennedy insisted that guidelines were needed because federal sentencing practices, arising out of untrammeled judicial discretion, had become "a national disgrace," Thurmond was looking forward to a commission that would issue guidelines and policy statements that had teeth and would not necessarily approach offenses and offenders from "the lenient perspective."[86] Looking back a decade later, Michael Tonry encapsulated the underlying cause of the travails of the Sentencing Commission and the guidelines it promulgated in a lapidary sentence: "[T]he federal sentencing commission legislation was formulated and agreed on in one political era, in which Judge Frankel's ideals were widely shared, but implemented in a different political era in which they had little influence."[87]

VIII

During the Reagan and Bush years at the White House the penal climate became progressively more punitive. The Republican takeover of the Senate and the subsequent passage of the Comprehensive Crime Control Act began a process that was to be repeated many times: the introduction of a crime bill, pushed by Republicans and resisted, although out of political caution not usually killed, by Democrats in Congress. Whether manipulated by politicians or for other reasons, there were visible signs that popular opinion was hardening. Debates about whether or not harsher penalties deterred were superseded by the demand for retribution. An ideology, encouraged by the administration, took hold that the public would be safer and better protected from the risk of victimization by incarcerating those who had offended against them for as long a time as possible. A single statistic bears out the results in this era of the "get tough on crime" policy. Between 1975 and 1989 the average prison time per violent crime tripled.[88] And yet, in spite of a record number well in excess of one million people in prison or jail,[89] the incidence of violent crime stuck obstinately at levels that were not only the highest in the Western world but, more relevant to domestic politics, beyond the tolerance of the American public and their elected representatives.

Thus a self-perpetuating cycle was established. To be tough on crime was a political necessity. Toughness on crime meant embracing demonstrably punitive measures, without differentiating between dangerous and nondangerous offenders. It meant disregarding public opinion research findings indicating significant potential support for programs of prevention, treatment, and alternative sentencing. It meant building more prisons and ensuring that more offenders were sent to them for longer periods as a consequence of mandatory prison sentences. Some were career criminals and repeat violent offenders who were seen as an evident threat to the public. Others caught in the net, low-level drug offenders being an obvious and numerous example, were not.

The attraction of mandatory minimum penalties for legislators was clearly apparent. Politicians were powerless to affect the actual sentences imposed on particular offenders, although they could and did influence by their rhetoric policy decisions on levels of penalty set by sentencing commissions. Where there were no sentencing guidelines in state courts, political rhetoric served to condition the environment in which judges across the nation, having seen the defendant in court, heard the evidence, and considered any relevant reports, duly passed what they judged to be the appropriate sentence to match the seriousness of the offense, but seldom disregarding the expectations of the public. Yet the legislators in Congress felt that they had to respond more decisively to the public mood. They had to act as well as talk. In criminal justice, as in much else, the only positive action open to legislators is to legislate. But even that is hard to achieve and uncertain in outcome. Once adopted, the yardstick of toughness imposes inelastic constraints on the scope for legislative change in the future.

The powerful imagery of the incorrigible criminal committing further violent offenses soon after being released into the community, having served only a fraction of the sentence imposed for his previous crimes, inspired the Armed Career Criminal Act of 1984.[90] If a person was caught in possession of a firearm and had three prior convictions for robbery or burglary or both, the minimum sentence would be enhanced from ten years to not less than fifteen years' imprisonment up to a maximum of life without eligibility for parole. The qualifying offenses were widened by the next Congress to include any violent felony or serious drug offense.[91] Although the legislation may have fulfilled for a time its political purpose of reassuring the public that Congress wanted to see violent offenders incarcerated until they were no longer dangerous, unforeseen difficulties soon emerged. The definition of what constituted the qualifying prior convictions and the grounds for challenging them in the courts were not settled until cases decided by the Supreme Court several years later.

Once in operation, the Armed Career Criminal Act was open to criticism as being overinclusive, creating unwarranted prosecutorial discretion, and failing to target actual career criminals since multiple offenses committed in a single day might establish a "career" for the purposes of the statute.[92] Overinclusiveness was seen in the lack of any requirement of recency in prior convictions;[93] the separate counting of related cases; the range of comparatively minor crimes included as predicate offenses; and the absence of serious misconduct to trigger the statute's application.[94] These flaws were a good example of the consequences of adopting stratagems with insufficient regard to their policy implications in order to achieve popularly accepted aims.

IX

In the Anti–Drug Abuse Act of 1986[95] Congress decided upon a sentencing approach that linked the punishment to the quantity and harmfulness of the narcotic substance. Mandatory minimum penalties were related to the amount of the drugs, rather than to the offender's role in the offense and degree of culpability. The justification for such an inflexible policy was that the punishment should reflect the damage done to society caused by the drugs handled by a particular defendant, irrespective of any personal or other circumstances. In short, the sentence was directed at the offense rather than the offender and his or her individual responsibility. Five- and ten-year minimum mandatory penalties were set for drug distribution or importation based on the quantity of any mixture or substance containing a detectable amount of the prohibited drug.[96]

Two years later, another Anti–Drug Abuse Act in 1988[97] tightened the screw, adding further mandatory minimums including one that was to cause the greatest of all sentencing disparities: a five-year minimum sentence on first conviction for the possession of crack cocaine exceeding five grams in amount.[98] Simple possession of other dangerous drugs including heroin and powder cocaine, as well as less than five grams of crack cocaine on first conviction, remained a misdemeanor with a mandatory penalty of no more than fifteen days imprisonment for a second offense. At the other end of the scale was a twenty year mandatory minimum for drug offenses forming part of a continuing criminal enterprise, or using a weapon during a violent or drug-trafficking crime.[99] Mandatory sentences of imprisonment for life would be the fate of any offender with two or more prior state or federal drug felony convictions.[100] Attempts and conspiracies were made subject to the same mandatory penalties as completed offenses.[101]

Federal judges complained that district courts were being flooded with minor drug cases formerly prosecuted in state courts where the penalties were generally lower for comparable offenses.[102] In individual cases mandatory minimum sentences could be unjust and disproportionate, while the removal of all discretion from the court merely transferred its exercise from a public courtroom to the privacy of a prosecutor's office. Judicial opinion could not have been expressed more plainly, nor more forcibly, than when two Supreme Court Justices, Kennedy and Souter, were invited to comment on the application of mandatory minimum sentencing at a hearing before a subcommittee of the House of Representatives Committee on Appropriations. Choosing his adjectives with precision, Justice Kennedy said that most judges in the federal system were of the view that mandatory minimums were an "imprudent, unwise and often unjust mechanism for sentencing." They took away from the judge the ability to differentiate among a group of defendants involved in a crime according to their degrees of culpability and responsibility.[103] Similarly the Chief Justice of the United States, William Rehnquist, told a conference that mandatory minimums frustrated "the careful calibration of sentences, from one end of the spectrum to the other, that the guidelines were intended to accomplish."[104]

As a child of Congress, the U.S. Sentencing Commission was more restrained in its language. But the message was the same. In 1990 the Commission had been formally directed by Congress[105] to respond to a series of questions on the compatibility between guidelines and mandatory minimums, the effect of mandatory minimums, and the options for Congress to exercise its power to direct sentencing policy through mechanisms other than mandatory minimums. After a thorough review of all the available data, the Commission submitted a special report to the Congress in August 1991.[106] It noted that whereas over sixty criminal statutes contained mandatory minimum penalties applicable to federal offenses, only four frequently resulted in convictions. Each of these related to drugs and weapons offenses.

The report stated bluntly that despite the expectation that mandatory minimum sentences would be applied to all cases that met the statutory criteria of eligibility, the available data indicated that this was not the case. The lack of uniform application created unwarranted disparity in sentencing and compromised the potential of the guidelines to reduce disparity. In 35 percent of cases where the defendant's behavior "strongly suggested" that a mandatory minimum was warranted, defendants had pleaded guilty to offenses carrying either non-mandatory or reduced mandatory penalties. Since the charging and plea negotiation processes were neither open to the public nor reviewable by the courts, honesty and truth in sentencing was compromised.

The data "strongly suggested" that the disparate application of mandatory minimums appeared to be related to the race of the defendant, with whites more likely than non-whites to be sentenced below the applicable mandatory minimum, and to the circuit in which the defendant was sentenced. The differential application on the basis of race and circuit reflected the very kind of disparity and discrimination that the Sentencing Reform Act had been designed to reduce. Whereas the structure of the federal guidelines differentiated between defendants convicted of the same offense by a variety of aggravating and mitigating factors with a view to providing just punishment and proportional sentences, mandatory minimum sentences lacked any such distinguishing characteristics. Under the guidelines, offenders classified as similar received similar sentences. Under mandatory minimums, offenders seemingly not similar nonetheless received similar sentences. The effect was unwarranted sentencing uniformity. The resort to mandatory minimums had generally been "single-shot efforts at crime control intended to produce dramatic results."[107]

The Commission concluded the summary of its findings with this comment:

> Congress has ultimate authority over sentencing policy. The question is how Congress can best translate its judgment as to appropriate levels of sentence severity into sentences imposed. Our analyses indicate that the guidelines system established by Congress, because of its ability to accommodate the vast array of relevant offense/offender characteristics, and its self-correcting potential, is superior to the mandatory minimum approach. Congress has effectively communicated its policies on sentencing through the provisions contained in the Sentencing Reform Act and subsequent legislation. It has continuing oversight of the work of the Sentencing Commission through the statutory requirement that proposed guidelines and amendments to guidelines be submitted to Congress for 180-day review before they become effective. The Sentencing Commission is always open to guidance from the Congress through its established oversight mechanisms.[108]

It was not without irony that some of the criticisms, notably of inflexibility and prosecutorial discretion, were the same as those which had been directed at the Commission's own sentencing guidelines. Unlike the guidelines, however, mandatory minimum penalties lacked any mechanism for evaluating their impact or making adjustments. The result had been to magnify the existing weaknesses in the process of federal sentencing still further. There was no rational answer to the Commissioners' critique. The reality was that mandatory sentencing had been taken up not as a consequence of any rational consideration of its likely effects, but as a symbolic gesture.

X

One of the most telling objections to the policies aimed at countering the far-reaching evils of drug abuse in America in the 1980s and early 1990s is that the reduction of demand, accepted by a large majority of specialists in the field, as well as by law enforcement officers, as the most practical solution, should have been dismissed as too soft an approach to have any hope of winning anything more than token political support. Hence the concentration on reducing the supply of drugs, within the countries of origin and at the points of entry to the United States, and by stringent law enforcement.

The manner of enforcing the laws was to have profound implications for the entire system of criminal justice. Between 1980 and 1993 the number of persons in custody nationally for drug offenses grew by a factor of ten, from about 24,000 to nearly 240,000 prisoners. About 40 percent of those arrested for drug offenses, and 60 percent of those imprisoned, were black.[109] Since African-Americans constitute between 12 and 13 percent of the U.S. population, the discrepancy calls for some explanation. It may be that the police are more inclined to stop a young black man for questioning than a young white man. On occasion they may lack civility in doing so. It may be that in the interests of crime prevention certain neighborhoods of cities are more intensively patrolled by law enforcement officers than others. It may be that the urban cultures in which many young black males grow up are more susceptible to drug-related offending than the cultures of their white counterparts. Not all of the explanations involve conscious racial discrimination, although its existence cannot be denied.

In acknowledging that black rates of criminal offending in many areas are substantially higher than those for whites, even so moderate and fair-minded an analyst as Randall Kennedy concludes that by permitting the police to use race too easily as "an indicia of suspiciousness," the courts have derogated from the fundamental idea that individuals should be judged on the basis of their own particular conduct, and not on the basis, partly or wholly, of racial generalizations.[110] The result of police use of race-dependent criteria, he writes, has been that "the current permissive regime nourishes powerful feelings of racial grievance against law enforcement authorities that are prevalent in every strata of black communities."[111]

Although less openly visible, the available evidence suggests that in the early 1990s the actual use, and abuse, of prohibited drugs by whites was about the same as by blacks. But white people were much less likely to be arrested or charged. It has been argued that "if white people were imprisoned for drug offenses at the same rate as black people, there would be nearly one million white drug offenders in custody—with a million white mothers, a million white fathers, and millions of white friends and relatives. Don't you think that might force a change in drug policies?"[112]

Chapter 2

Organized Interests and Populist Beliefs

I

The prologue to some of the most dramatic events of the 103rd Congress was set in the Rose Garden of the White House on August 11, 1993. During the presidential campaign Clinton had decided that, if elected, it would be a priority for his administration to bring forward an early crime bill. His strategy was to combine support for crime prevention measures, toward which he was sympathetic, with stronger penalties and more effective law enforcement. Such a combination, Clinton believed, would have popular appeal as well as being politically attractive to Democrats and their supporters in the urban areas where the needs were greatest, and it was contended that too few resources had been directed toward the roots of the problems of crime before the harm occurred. Once installed at the White House, the President lost no time in telling the chairmen of the Judiciary Committees of the Senate and the House, Senator Joseph Biden (Dem. Delaware) and Representative Jack Brooks (Dem. Texas), both battle-hardened veterans of previous crime bill initiatives, that he wanted a bill drafted as soon as possible, building on the compromises reached in the conference report on the Bush administration's crime bill, which had been blocked in the Senate in its final stages. With this as a starting point, he envisaged the addition of some new elements to give greater emphasis to policing and prevention.

On several occasions in the first six months of 1993 Clinton reminded Biden of his desire to see a draft without delay. From the outset he preferred the legislation to originate from the congressional leadership rather than the alternative of a bill drafted by the Department of Justice and sent by the President to Congress by way of executive communication. The reasons lying behind this tactic will be explored later in the narrative when the scenario has become more familiar.

The President was accompanied at a 9.30 A.M. news conference by the Attorney General (Janet Reno), Biden, Brooks, and members of Congress from both parties. Representatives of state attorneys general, district attorneys, and police organizations were also present. The first duty of any government, Clinton said, was to try and keep its citizens safe. But clearly too many Americans were not safe. There was no longer the freedom of fear for all citizens that was essential to security and prosperity. When it was not possible to walk the streets of the cities without fear, then an essential element of civilization had been lost. To restore the rule of law on the streets it was necessary for the administration to work with thousands of law enforcement officials who risked their lives every day, with the mayors and the governors, and the people who dealt with children before they became criminal. Politicians in Washington had to work together too. "For too long, crime has been used as a way to divide Americans with rhetoric. . . . It is time to use crime as a way to unite Americans through action." Thanking the Republican members of Congress who were present, the President called on Democrats and Republicans to work with the administration and the law enforcement community to craft the best possible crime legislation.[1]

One of the few specific policies announced was a community policing initiative. This meant having more police officers on the streets, patrolling the same neighborhoods, and making relationships with the local community in ways that would help to prevent crime. A first installment to honor a campaign pledge to put 100,000 additional police officers on the streets would be the provision of $3.4 billion to make federal grants to state and local governments to increase police presence by up to 50,000 new officers. Already $150 million had been made available to hire or rehire police officers, and the Labor Department was allocating funds to retrain newly discharged troops from the United States armed forces to become police officers.

The second policy, to which strong emphasis was given, was gun control: "We must end the insanity of being able to buy or sell a handgun more easily than obtaining a driver's license."[2] The Brady bill, which required a waiting period while checks were made on the intending purchaser of a handgun, was simply common sense. It was long past time for Congress to pass it, and if and when it did, Clinton would sign the bill. There was no conceivable reason, he said, to delay action one more day. Nor would the effort against crime be complete if it did not eliminate assault weapons from the streets. No other nation would tolerate roving gangs stalking the streets better armed than police. "Why should we do it? We shouldn't, and we ought to stop it."[3] Finally, the President spoke about community boot camps for young people, which he had worked on in Arkansas. He believed young people who were not yet hardened criminals deserved a second chance and that the discipline, training, and treatment that they would receive would help them to build a good life.

As governor and a former attorney general of a largely rural southern state, Clinton needed no reminders of the risks he was taking, or the constituency to which he was appealing, with his outspokenness on gun control. Together with habeas corpus reform, by means of limiting petitions from prisoners on death row, which he also wanted to resuscitate, restrictions on the availability of firearms had been a prime cause of the failure of the Bush crime bill to pass the previous Congress. The Brady bill, named after James Brady, a former White House press secretary who had been wounded and severely incapacitated in an assassination attempt on President Reagan in 1981, had gained widespread public sympathy. But it was opposed furiously by the NRA and its allies, becoming one of the most contested of all political issues. Bills had been introduced in the 100th, 101st, and 102nd Congresses, but none had succeded.[4] As a presidential candidate in 1992, Clinton had endorsed the attempts to pass the Brady bill. On his election, the gun control movement had a sympathetic president in the White House for the first time since Johnson, who unexpectedly had come to office through the fatal shooting of his predecessor, John Kennedy.

Where Clinton had executive authority to act, he did. On August 11, in an announcement timed to coincide with the launch of the anti-crime initiative, he issued two directives under existing powers. The first was a memorandum addressed to the Secretary of the Treasury that opened the way to a ban on the import of assault-type pistols.[5] This action stemmed from proposals submitted to the administration by the Center to Prevent Handgun Violence, the research, legal advocacy and education affiliate of Handgun Control, Inc., outlining a number of regulatory steps that could be taken to reduce gun violence by the Bureau of Alcohol, Tobacco, and Firearms (ATF) pursuant to the Bureau's broad regulatory authority.[6] The Center had argued that assault-type pistols did not qualify for exemption from the ban on the importation of firearms under the Gun Control Act of 1968 as they were not "suitable for or readily adaptable to sporting purposes."[7]

The opening sentence of the second presidential directive, also addressed to the Secretary of the Treasury, was "A major problem facing the Nation today is the ease with which criminals, the mentally deranged, and even children can acquire firearms."[8] Gun dealer licensing, which encouraged a flourishing criminal market in guns, was open to abuse. The memorandum stated that there were in excess of 287,000 federal firearms licensees, a great number of whom should probably not be licensed. The ATF estimated that only about 30 percent were bona fide storefront dealers. Probably 40 percent of the licensees conducted no business at all, and were simply persons who used the license to obtain the benefits of trading interstate and buying guns at wholesale rates. The remaining 30 percent engaged in a limited level of business, typically out of private residences. While the federal statute created no level of business activity to qualify for a license, many of the licensees were operating in violation of state and local licensing, taxing, and other business-related laws.[9] The administration was committed to doing more to prevent the criminal market in illegal guns from continuing to flourish. Since all new firearms used in crime at some point had passed through the legitimate distribution system, federal firearms licenses represented the first line of defence. The ATF was instructed to improve the thoroughness and effectiveness of background checks in screening applications for dealer licenses, including more reliable forms of identification such as fingerprints in order to assist in identifying any criminal or other disqualifying history. Six further requirements were specified with the aim of ensuring that only legitimate gun dealers were in the business of selling guns or holding licenses.

A third proposal submitted by the Center to Prevent Handgun Violence was put into effect by the Secretary of the Treasury, Lloyd Bentsen, on March 1, 1994. On that date Bentsen announced the reclassification by the Treasury Department of combat shotguns, including the Streetsweeper, Strike-12, and USAS-12, as destructive devices, thereby restricting their future sale.[10] Then, on May 27, 1994, as part of the grant of most-favored-nation status in trade negotiations with China, the administration was able to stop the import of Chinese-made guns that had been modified slightly in order to avoid the ban on the import of assault weapons, but which permitted certain nonsporting long guns.

II

In the week before the White House lawn party the Republican leadership in Congress had announced its own program. Some of the proposals were broadly bipartisan, such as increased federal aid for local law enforcement, while other policies, more punitive in intent, were familiar enough from the past: a greater emphasis on prison building; mandatory minimum penalties for crimes by gang members; and a restriction on the recourse to habeas corpus petitions by prisoners on death row challenging the lawfulness of their sentences under the Constitution, having exhausted appeals against their conviction in the state and federal appellate courts.[11] Unlike the Democratic version, the Republican proposal did not include any qualification standards for defense counsel in capital cases. Two features of the Republican plans stood out. There was no mention of any need for gun control, while a new nostrum, life imprisonment for three-time convicted felons, popularly known as "three strikes and you're out," made its first appearance on stage at Capitol Hill.

With the aim of passing an omnibus anti-crime bill by Thanksgiving, parallel bills were introduced in the House of Representatives (H.R. 3371) and the Senate (S.1488) on September 23, 1993. Brooks and Biden were the sponsors. Much of the content of the two bills was similar, although there were some variations. Each authorized expenditure to enable states and local government to employ fifty thousand more police officers; to develop local education and training programs to prevent crime, violence, and drug abuse in the schools; and to phase in drug treatment at federal prisons. The minimal, but nonetheless worthwhile, attempts to get to grips with the demand side of the drug problem were matched by authorizing expenditure to allow the Drug Enforcement Administration to take on more agents and staff to keep up the pressure on restricting the supply of narcotics.

Both measures extended the list of federal crimes punishable by death, including the murder of federal law enforcement officials, murder by federal prisoners or escaped prisoners, killings by terrorists, and rape, child molestation and sexual exploitation of children if the death of the victim resulted. The House bill extended the death penalty to sixty-four crimes and the Senate bill to forty-seven. In each case, death was to be a maximum, and not a mandatory, penalty. For some of the new capital crimes there was no requirement that the death of one or more victims should have resulted from the criminal act.[12]

The thorny issue of the long-drawn-out series of collateral appeals by death row prisoners, which had divided liberals and conservatives within both parties, was whittled down to the compromise of permitting a single federal petition of habeas corpus to be filed within six months of exhausting regular appeals. In view of the evidence that such a substantial proportion of wrongful or unconstitutional convictions in capital cases were due to errors made by incompetent counsel, indigent defendants would be provided with legal representatives meeting rigorous qualifications at all state proceedings. The compromise had been hammered out in several months of negotiation between Reno, Biden, and the state attorneys general and district attorneys. Some defense lawyers had also seen parts of the proposed legislative language.

Even before its publication, the formula had been sharply criticized as institutionalizing the diminution of civil rights for condemned prisoners, which had resulted from a number of Supreme Court decisions. At the White House launch on August 11, Biden spoke confidently and, as it turned out prematurely, in describing the habeas issue as "[s]omething the American public does not have much interest in, but has divided us. And we settled it."[13] Another procedural controversy, which had been before Congress on previous occasions, the admissibility of evidence obtained illegally, was omitted altogether.

Neither of the original bills authorized expenditure to add to the capacity of the federal prisons to house more convicted felons, although money would be provided to assist states in building additional prison places for violent offenders. The Senate version encouraged states to develop military-style boot camps,[14] at one-third of the cost of traditional prisons, for younger nonviolent offenders, so releasing space in the prisons.[15] Other provisions included drug court programs, new offenses of terrorism, sexual violence and child abuse, kidnapping by parents, and action against youth gangs. Gun control was played in a low key. The House bill contained a waiting period for the purchase of handguns, and authorized expenditure to help states set up an instant check system to replace the period of waiting while checks were made on the bona fides of the purchaser.

Less demonstrative than the President's forthright statements, the Senate bill went no further than to enumerate some new penalties for gun crimes and the possession of explosives. The reason was that for tactical purposes Biden had decided the controversial issues of the Brady bill and the possibility of imposing a ban on assault weapons would be better handled in separate measures that would not jeopardize the passage of the main crime bill. The Republicans' enthusiasm for a three strikes law, a novelty not previously considered by Congress, met no response at this stage. In fact many states already had enacted recidivist statutes, which called for life imprisonment after multiple convictions. Under federal law mandatory life imprisonment after two or more convictions was the penalty for certain serious drug violations and firearms offenses. The novelty lay in the breadth of some formulations of the three strikes policy, and the popular appeal of the link with baseball.

The legislation proposed lacked any reference to racial justice, an issue of great concern to the Black Caucus and to some other liberal Democrats in the House. Several months later, their insistence that the law must include provisions to counter any racial discrimination in the imposition of the death penalty was one of the two key issues that brought the crime bill to the edge of the abyss into which Bush's previous attempts had fallen. The other was a non-retrospective ban on certain assault weapons, also delayed for tactical reasons until the forces in Congress could be assessed and the necessary bargains forged to get the votes.

III

On introduction the anti-crime legislation was already a compromise. It was constructed from elements that previously had passed one or both Houses, or where the congressional leaders believed the capacity for interparty agreement existed. Yet significant policy differences existed between the mainstream Democrats, the Congressional Black Caucus and its sympathizers, and the conservative Democrats. On the Republican side, too, there were cross-currents. Both the Senate and the House contained Republican moderates whose support would be crucial to the passage of the legislation. Democrats had not abandoned faith in the potential for preventive programs, for young people and drug abusers in particular, although care was taken to associate them with policies such as community-oriented policing to avoid the categorization of "soft on crime." The Republican leadership continued to press for stronger penalties, including mandatory minimum sentences and the building of new prisons, although the body politic did not seem any more secure as a result of the dominance of these policies during twelve years of Republican administrations.

Real as they were, such differences had not prevented coalitions from being formed before between moderate Republicans and the mainstream Democrats in the House, while in the more evenly balanced Senate tacit understandings had been reached on a variety of issues. But consensus between relatively like-minded pragmatists in the two parties would not be enough. Concessions unwelcome to the administration would have to be made to Republican hard-liners, as well as to Democrat liberals, and to those in either party whose vision had been narrowed by the pursuit of special interests. Gun control was a rock on which the whole initiative could be wrecked.

Within weeks of the launch there was a divergence between the House of Representatives and the Senate over tactics. While Senator Biden continued with a broad-brush bill, working to gain sufficient support in the Senate for its main proposals, Representative Brooks took another course. Unable to persuade liberals on the Judiciary Committee to adopt the omnibus bill, which they regarded as too harsh, he switched to the device of moving a series of smaller bills, including the Brady bill and ten other less contentious subjects. Action was deferred on the most controversial items, such as extensions to the federal death penalty and revising habeas corpus procedures, on the grounds that both liberal and conservative lawmakers needed more time to debate those issues. Brooks was not willing, he said, "to see important, innovative crime prevention programs like cops on the beat be deferred at a time when the American public is clamoring for us to provide more protection against violent acts."[16]

By the end of November 1993, the House of Representatives had approved eleven single-subject bills. These covered federal drug treatment, youth gangs, state drug treatment, community policing, the Brady bill (H.R. 1025), prison alternatives, a youth handgun ban, crimes against women, crimes against minors, kidnapping by parents, and control over child care providers. The last two (H.R. 3378 and H.R. 1237) quickly passed the Senate and were signed into law by the President on December 2 and December 20.[17]

The slow rate of progress in the House meant that the objective of getting the main legislation enacted before the end of the first session of the 103rd Congress could not be realized. There were two main causes: liberal disillusion with the direction in which the legislation was developing, and obstruction by the Congressional Black Caucus (CBC). Penal reformers had been encouraged earlier in 1993 by the overtly pro-prevention stance taken by Janet Reno, and expounded in a series of high-profile speeches around the country during her first months in office as Attorney General.[18] Public reaction generally had been positive and, although previously little known, she had become recognized as a popular member of the administration, respected for her integrity. As described in the opening chapter, the federal judiciary, many of them Republican appointees, were highly critical of the disparities and injustices resulting from mandatory minimum sentences in practice, while corrections officials, state legislators and a cross-section of criminal justice professionals were questioning the penal rationale and heavy burden of financial cost of continuing to build prisons as a solution to crime. To liberals it seemed that the ground was prepared and the climate receptive for the consideration of alternative policies to ever-harsher penalties and the reliance on incarceration as the main planks of anti-crime policy.[19]

If the administration's initial approach, with the accent on policing, additional funds for prisons, the death penalty, boot camps, and drug treatment was a disappointment, it was soon eclipsed by the reaction to the bill by members of Congress. In each House, but the Senate especially, legislators vied to out-do each other and to impress their intended audiences with demonstrations of the toughness of their attitudes. Speech after speech, amendment after amendment, called for more punitive policies, without regard to their likely effect. The Senate held no hearings, although a number of the proposals had been the subject of previous testimony. It was when Brooks attempted to impose the same procedure in the House that Democrats belonging to the CBC demanded a slowing down to allow a fuller public review of the proposals before any floor votes were scheduled.

The CBC was a cohesive force in the House of Representatives, and one to which the Democratic leadership had to pay close attention. Positioned on the party's left wing, its membership and influence had expanded steadily since its formation in 1970 with a membership of thirteen. The numbers had grown to about twenty by the mid-1980s, mainly concentrating on civil rights issues and sanctions against South Africa. The 1992 elections, which brought Clinton to the White House, increased the strength of the Caucus from twenty-six to thirty-eight Democrat representatives. The nominal congressional membership was forty, including a lone Republican, who seldom agreed with the Caucus and was often shut out of its meetings,[20] and one Democrat senator.[21] Described by its chairman, Kweisi Mfume (Dem. Maryland), as "[o]nce simply a loyal rubber stamp of the Democratic Party," the Caucus had evolved into a group of "tough-minded activist legislators" willing to challenge everyone from Bill Clinton to Louis Farrakhan. "It was," declared Mfume, "our time to shine."[22]

The intersection of race, economics, and criminal justice policies[23] subjected black congressmen to electoral pressures that were not shared by other legislators. While there was some awareness on Capitol Hill that the increased rates of incarceration had led to a costly quadrupling of prison populations over the two decades since the early 1970s, special-interest pressures on elected representatives in their districts for the lesser use of imprisonment were minimal. But in the mainly black districts the situation was markedly different. Whereas in the decade 1973–82 the proportions of African-American males in custody moved in step with the increase in custodial populations overall, a sharp escalation occurred in the mid-1980s. During that period drug offenders began to account for a progressively larger share of prison admissions, with African-Americans making up an ever larger share of drug convictions.

Between 1983 and 1993 the number of incarcerated drug offenders rose by 510 percent, the majority of them being low-income African-Americans.[24] In 1990 the remarkable statistic had been published, and attracted much comment, that one in four African-American males in the age group twenty to twenty-nine was under some form of criminal justice supervision (in prison or jail, or on probation or parole) on any given day. Five years later, the situation had worsened still further. From an examination of the data for 1994, and using the same methodology, it was calculated that almost one in three (32.2 percent) of young black men in the same age group was under criminal justice supervision on any given day. The cost of criminal justice control for these 827,440 young African-American males was about $6 billion per year.[25] The fact that firearm-related injuries were the leading cause of death among young black men has already been noted in the previous chapter.

It was not only penal reformers who identified a vicious cycle with no clear resolution in sight. As Marc Mauer has pointed out, with the decline of manufacturing jobs in many parts of the country, the urban economy and opportunity structure changed for the generation reaching adulthood. The limited availability of economic opportunities, combined with the lure of the drug trade and its financial rewards, resulted in unprecedented levels of criminal justice control over young black males.[26] The resulting polarities of opinion were equally ominous, with many African-Americans regarding the system of justice as irremediably prejudiced against them, and many white Americans believing that crime is linked to race and ethnicity.

In the spring of 1993, at a time when the Democrat and Republican leaderships were working on their crime bills, staff from the offices of several members of the CBC began to meet to develop an alternative bill. Advisers were called on to assist, and a comprehensive 280-page bill "to prevent crime and to reform the criminal justice system to make it more fair" (H.R. 3315) was introduced in the House of Representatives on October 19, 1993. The declaratory findings printed at the start sounded several themes that were to be reiterated throughout the coming months. It was stated that

> 6. many measures included in what is usually called a crime bill (more penalties, more Federal crimes, longer prison sentences) do nothing to reduce crime and polarize and shift the focus and resources away from strategies that have proven to be more effective in addressing crime and violence;
>
> 7. law enforcement professionals agree that the solutions to the Nation's crime and drug problems will be found in crime prevention measures that include drug treatment, early childhood intervention programs, full funding for Head Start programs and the Women, Infants and Children Program, rehabilitation and alternatives to incarceration, community policing, and family support programs, as well as in programs to rebuild communities through education, employment, and housing; . . .

9. there is a sense of distrust and a widespread perception in many communities, particularly among people of color, that the criminal justice system values victims differently and is at times fundamentally unfair to criminal defendants of color;

10. the perception and reality of racial bias in the workings of the criminal justice system is deeply corrosive of one of the most important institutions in our society and the perception of unfairness robs the criminal justice system of the respect and credibility it must have to achieve its goal of keeping the public safe and maintaining law and order;

11. reform of the criminal justice system is necessary to restore the credibility and respect that have been undermined by racism, excessive and disproportionate prison sentences, abusive police practices and civil forfeiture practices;

H.R. 3315 placed a greater emphasis on prevention and alternatives to incarceration than did the Brooks/Biden versions. It aimed to reduce the much-criticized disparity in sentencing for crack cocaine and powder cocaine drug offenses; it abolished minimum mandatory sentences; and put forward less restrictive habeas corpus reforms. A substantial part of the bill dealt with firearms, incorporating a waiting period to enable checks to be made on the intending purchaser before the sale of a handgun; and a nonretrospective prohibition on the sale or possession of certain semiautomatic assault weapons. Licensed dealers would be subjected to more effective regulation. The bill contained no new death penalties, concentrating instead on measures to counter racially discriminatory capital sentencing, which would narrow the grounds for implementing the death penalty. The latter proposals were cited as the Racial Justice Act of 1993.

The bill attracted twenty-four named sponsors, not all of whom were members of the CBC. It was well received in the press; the *Washington Post* commenting in an editorial that it was a counterweight for those who had reservations about the leadership proposals.[27] With the endorsement of the Congressional Hispanic Caucus, the combined caucuses represented almost sixty votes, a sizable proportion of the Democratic majority in the House. The CBC bill became a rallying point for organized opposition to much of the content of the Brooks bill and to the fast-track treatment sought by the Democratic leadership. The chairman of the Subcommittee of the Judiciary Committee on Crime and Criminal Justice, Representative Charles Schumer (Dem. New York), initially opposed holding hearings on the bill. But ultimately he acceded to the CBC's request, which culminated in two full days of hearings on February 22–23, 1994.

Over the entire period that the anti-crime legislation was before the 103rd Congress, the most significant positive achievement of the supporters of the CBC bill was to sustain a level of funding devoted to prevention programs higher than would otherwise have been enacted. Their influence was crucial during the early negotiations on the Democratic proposals, and later in maintaining programs that might otherwise have been eliminated or cut back more than they were. While the most publicly visible opposition to the leadership bill in the final post-conference stages, which divided members of the CBC, centered upon the absence of the racial justice provisions, there remained until the end some who refused to abandon their objections of principle to what they regarded as the too heavily punitive orientation of the legislation taken as a whole.

<h1 style="text-align:center">IV</h1>

On one issue at least, the CBC, the mainstream Democrats in the House of Representatives, and the administration saw eye to eye. The Brady bill had been passed by the House on November 10, 1993, the voting being 238 yeas to 189 nays.[28] The result was almost identical to a floor vote on a slightly different version of the bill in the 102nd Congress, which had passed the House by 239 to 186.[29] Then, as later, the problems lay in the Senate. Although in somewhat altered form the bill was passed by the Senate in June 1991,[30] it had been obstructed when there had not been enough votes to end the debate on the report of the House-Senate Conference Committee reconciling the differences between the respective bills.[31]

Once again, having passed the House with relative ease, the Brady bill had run into a determined filibuster on the floor of the Senate in November 1993. The administration made strenuous efforts to break the impasse: the Attorney General, accompanied by Sarah Brady,[32] lobbied senators in person on Capitol Hill, backed up by Vice-President Gore with telephone calls. The NRA, arguing that the bill posed no threat to criminals while inconveniencing the law-abiding, was engaged simultaneously in intense lobbying. On Friday, November 19, after a vote approving the main crime bill package, opponents of gun control twice defeated motions to close the debate on the Brady bill,[33] and the prospects looked bleak. Over the weekend the indications of public sentiment in support of the measure began to undermine the resolve of some of the congressional opponents to the imposition of a period of delay while inquiries were made to establish if the intended purchaser was prohibited from buying a handgun. Although the conference report was passed by the House on Monday, November 22, by 238 votes to 188,[34] it was stalled again in the Senate. By then tense negotiations were taking place behind the scenes between Biden and Robert Dole (Rep. Kansas), the Senate minority leader. A majority of Democrats and a smaller number of Republican senators wanted to see the bill passed, but the Republican leadership continued to obstruct.

Dole finally dropped his opposition when the Democratic leadership agreed to let the Senate consider legislation to modify the bill the following year. This modest, and essentially face-saving, concession would make possible the phasing out in two years of the waiting period while checks were made, provided that by then the national computerized checking system had reached a certain level of accuracy. With one further refinement,[35] the conference report was accepted and the bill passed after some brief remarks on November 24. Few senators were present in a chamber emptied by the Thanksgiving holiday. The two leaders, George Mitchell (Maine) for the Democratic majority and Dole for the Republican minority, pronounced the measure adopted by unanimous consent on a voice vote. Dole was magnanimous: "After a long, long, hard fight, Jim Brady has won. . . . I believe all of us will feel better to have this issue behind us. There will be other issues, maybe other gun issues, but at least as far as the Brady bill is concerned it has now passed."[36] The Senate then adjourned until January 25, 1994.

The following week, in the East Room at the White House, the President signed the bill into law on November 30. It was a genuinely poignant ceremony, far removed from the normal run of reportable happenings orchestrated by the administration or its opponents. Seated in a wheelchair beside Clinton was James Brady, who all those years ago had stood beside another president when both were shot. "How sweet it is; how long it took" was Brady's subdued comment. Clinton was more forceful. Thumping the lectern for emphasis, he recalled his own upbringing:

> I come from a State where half the folks have hunting and fishing licenses. I can still remember the first day when I was a little boy out in the country putting a can on top of a fencepost and shooting a .22 at it. I can still remember the first time I pulled a trigger on a .410 shotgun because I was too little to hold a .12-gauge. I can remember these things. This is part of the culture of a big part of America.
>
>   . . . We have taken this important part of the life of millions of Americans and turned it into an instrument of maintaining madness. It is crazy. Would I let anybody change that life in America? Not on your life. Has that got anything to do with the Brady bill or assault weapons or whether the police have to go out on the street confronting teenagers who are better armed than they are? Of course not.[37]

Exacerbated by the unremitting hostility of the NRA, gun control had become one of the most enduring and highly politicized of all crime policy issues. The 1993 Act[38] only delayed and did not ban, the purchase of handguns, allowing up to five working days for law enforcement authorities to check the background of intending purchasers for evidence of a criminal or mentally unstable past, or disqualification under the other prohibitions of the U.S. Code.[39] It did not mandate the duration of a fixed waiting period, only setting a maximum time for making the checks. Even with such limited scope, it was the first restriction of the general availability of firearms to be enacted by Congress for twenty-five years.[40] In 1968, the year of the assassinations by shooting of Martin Luther King and Robert F. Kennedy, the administration had tried to introduce a ban on the sale by mail order of rifles and shotguns. The proposal was not acceptable to Congress, neither House being willing to go further than prohibiting the shipment or transportation of handguns and ammunition in interstate or foreign commerce, other than by licensed importers or dealers, and the purchase over the counter of handguns by nonresidents of the state. Rifles and shotguns were exempt.

The Omnibus Crime Control and Safe Streets Act[41] was signed by President Johnson on June 19, 1968. Public opinion was so shocked, however, at the murder two weeks before of Robert Kennedy, a senator and presidential aspirant at the time of his death, that within a few months a second and more restrictive law was enacted. The Gun Control Act of 1968[42] removed the exemption of rifles and shotguns and prohibited the sale of handguns or ammunition to young people below the age of twenty-one. The Act also specified certain high-risk categories of person, including drug abusers, who were declared ineligible to purchase firearms. In his remarks on signing what he described as ''the most comprehensive gun control law ever signed in this Nation's history,'' Johnson added that Congress had not carried out all the requests made of them by the administration. He had asked for the national registration[43] of all guns and the licensing[44] of those who carried them.[45] He continued:

> If guns are to be kept out of the hands of the criminal, out of the hands of the insane, and out of the hands of the irresponsible, then we just must have licensing. If the criminal with a gun is to be tracked down quickly, then we must have registration in this country.
>
> The voices that blocked these safeguards were not the voices of an aroused nation. They were the voices of a powerful lobby, a gun lobby, that has prevailed for the moment in an election year.
>
> ... We must continue to work for the day when Americans can get the full protection that every American citizen is entitled to and deserves—the kind of protection that most civilized nations have long ago adopted. We have been through a great deal of anguish these last few months and these last few years—too much anguish to forget so quickly.[46]

In his sixth and last annual message to Congress on the State of the Union, President Johnson repeated the same message with a vehemence that was not heard again from an occupant of the White House for more than two decades. As he left the Office of the Presidency, he said that one of his greatest disappointments was the failure to secure passage of a licensing and registration act for firearms. If such an act had been passed, he believed that it would have reduced the incidence of crime.[47] Although Johnson, so experienced in the ways of Congress,[48] had looked forward to further restrictions on the availability of firearms at ''not too distant a date,'' the next action taken by Congress did not come until 1986. When it did, the legislation amended, and for the most part weakened, the provisions of the Gun Control Act. The Firearm Owners' Protection Act of 1986[49] restored the exemption of rifles and shotguns from the interstate trade prohibition, although retaining the ban on interstate sales of handguns. It also narrowed the definition of who needed to obtain a license to sell firearms and relieved ammunition dealers of record-keeping requirements.

As its name implied, the 1986 Act stood as a monument to the NRA. In many ways it marked the high point of its influence. For years the NRA had campaigned against the hated Gun Control Act. By its own account, it spent an estimated $1.6 million working to overturn the Act, a figure that excluded campaign contributions. The money was spent on advertisements, direct mailing, lobbying, and other expenses. In addition, Federal Election Commission records showed that through its Political Victory Fund the NRA spent a total of $1.7 million on the congressional elections to the Senate and House of Representatives in 1986.[50] Although there were other and deeper factors at work besides campaign finance, an independent analysis of the voting on the legislation indicated that 80 percent of those legislators who voted with the NRA position had received campaign contributions from the Association or its affiliated organizations, while 80 percent of those who voted against had not received any NRA support.[51] The legislation in 1986 was signed by President Reagan, a lifetime member of the Association, who symbolized in his own person and political ideology many of the values to which it appealed so evocatively.

The disabled James Brady and his wife, Sarah, a skilled campaigner and former worker for the Republican Party, had crusaded persistently throughout the 1980s, and a waiting period was incorporated in the 1988 drugs and anti-crime bill. It did not succeed in getting the approval of the House, although the Anti–Drug Abuse legislation in 1988,[52] which contained some general criminal and law enforcement provisions, required the U.S. Attorney General to develop a felon identification system. Another enactment in 1988, the Undetectable Firearms Act,[53] aimed to regulate plastic guns by banning the manufacture, import, possession, and transfer of firearms not detectable by security devices. The following year, the Brady bill was reintroduced by Democrats in both chambers, only to see it founder in Senate Judiciary Subcommittee hearings. In 1990, the gun lobby beat back three separate attempts to enact further restrictions on firearms, including a ban on assault weapons and a seven-day waiting period to enable checks to be made before a handgun could be purchased.

Financial contributions to candidates in the 1990 congressional elections were thought likely to have strengthened the hand of the NRA in the 102nd Congress, although the proponents of gun control were making some headway. According to the Federal Election Commission's figures, the NRA spent $916,135 on 1990 campaigns. By comparison, the fledgling, but increasingly effective, counterlobby, Handgun Control, Inc. (HCI), spent $178,882.[54] Both chambers voted for the handgun waiting period in 1991, and by comfortable majorities: 239–186 in the House on May 8 and 72–32 in the Senate on June 28.[55] Yet when the anti-crime bill of which it was part reached the final stage, it was lost when the Senate failed to adopt the conference report. Further efforts were blocked twice more in the Senate the following year, in March and October 1992.

V

Although polls consistently indicated that the advocates of gun control had the majority of public opinion on their side, HCI and others had a hard task in competing with the relentless political pressures generated by the gun rights activists. Fear of political intervention in elections by the NRA or its supporters against legislators who had advocated gun control in Congress was well founded, as was to be demonstrated in the mid-term elections in November 1994. There was also an authentic populist strain of opinion upholding the NRA campaign. As crime, above all violent crime, became so pervasive, a deep-rooted commitment to what was proclaimed as the inalienable right of Americans to keep and bear arms was strengthened. Arguments about the ownership, and if called for, the use of guns to protect persons and property merged with a righteousness attached to the possession of firearms for farming, hunting, and sporting purposes.

None of this had much to do with the postcolonial right, indeed duty, of the organized citizen militias to keep and bear the few arms that were available to avoid the dangers of depending on a standing army for the defense of the new states.[56] But the assertion of a constitutional right, however remote the connection with modern life, added a sense of legitimacy to a personal need keenly felt. More than that was the conviction lodged in the minds of some of the true believers that their constitutionally conferred right justified holding firearms in order to check the excesses of an arbitrary government if its actions encroached on the fundamental freedoms of the populace.[57] Claims of the ultimate right of an armed citizenry to overthrow an oppressive and tyrannical government read better in the pages of law journals than they appeared after the emergence into public view of a very different style of citizen militia following the bombing of a federal office building in Oklahoma City on April 19, 1995. The death toll of 168 victims including nineteen children, with many more injured, was the highest resulting from any act of domestic or international terrorism ever to have taken place on American soil.

A rare glimpse of the mentality of the far Right was disclosed in a strategy paper, purporting to be a war plan for paramilitary groups around the country, which came to light when twelve people in Arizona were arrested in July 1996 and charged with conspiracy to blow up federal buildings. It was reported that those arrested called themselves the Viper Militia and trained in the desert with explosives for what one member said was an "upcoming war" with the federal government.[58] The strategy paper, titled "Operation American Viper," outlined a scenario in which United Nations troops occupy the United States. It called on the various paramilitary groups to wage guerrilla war against a vague conglomeration of "globalists," international bankers, United Nations officials, and "rogue" elements of the federal government—the Central Intelligence Agency, the FBI, and the Bureau of Alcohol, Tobacco, and Firearms.[59]

Two hundred years after the Bill of Rights the constitutional reality can be stated quite briefly since it is a matter of settled law. The wording of the

Second Amendment of the Constitution reads: "A well regulated Militia, being necessary to the security of a free State, the right of the people to keep and bear Arms, shall not be infringed." Relying on the last part of the amendment, the NRA and other opponents of legal restrictions on the availability of firearms claim that gun control legislation is unconstitutional because it violates a fundamental right to keep and bear arms conferred by the Second Amendment. The courts have taken a different view. As long ago as 1876 in *U.S. v. Cruikshank*[60] the Supreme Court held that the right to keep and bear arms was not a right granted by the Constitution; that it was not dependent on the Constitution for its existence; and that the right of the citizen was protected only to the extent that the right to hold a firearm was necessary for the states to maintain well-regulated militias.[61] Eschewing selective quotation, in *U.S. v. Miller* the Supreme Court decided in 1939 that the obvious purpose of the Second Amendment was "to assure the continuation and render possible the effectiveness" of the militia. The Amendment "must be interpreted and applied with that end in view."[62] In 1980, upholding a federal statute prohibiting a felon from possessing a firearm, the Court in *Lewis v. United States* found no constitutionally protected liberties infringed by the law.[63]

In two other cases, not involving the Second Amendment, the Court affirmed that the modern equivalent of the eighteenth-century militia is the National Guard.[64] In more than thirty cases since *Miller* was decided, lower federal and state courts have found that the Second Amendment guarantees no right to keep and bear a firearm that does not have some reasonable relationship to the preservation or efficiency of a "well-regulated militia." There has been unanimity in rejecting the contention that the amendment relates to the use of firearms for sporting purposes or self-defense. In summary, as the U.S. Court of Appeals for the Eighth Circuit has written, the courts "have analyzed the Second Amendment purely in terms of protecting state militias, rather than individual rights."[65] That the constitutional interpretation of the Supreme Court has not changed was shown as recently as October 1996 when the Court declined to review a decision by the Ninth Circuit of the U.S. Court of Appeals in *Hickman v. Block*.[66] In that case, standing to bring an action had been denied to a licensed arms dealer claiming a Second Amendment right to carry a concealed handgun. In a brief and unanimous decision the Court of Appeals held that the Second Amendment did not protect the possession of a weapon by a private citizen,[67] and therefore no lawsuit alleging denial of personal constitutional rights could go forward.

If any further extrajudicial authority is needed it can be found in a letter from the retired Chief Justice of the Supreme Court, Warren Burger, to Sarah Brady. On December 2, 1994, he wrote:

> I would like to take this opportunity to applaud the tireless efforts of the Center to Prevent Handgun Violence to educate the American public on the true meaning of the Second Amendment to our Constitution. Your battle to shatter the myth, perpetrated by the National Rifle Association and other groups, that

gun control laws violate the Second Amendment's right "to keep and bear Arms" is a worthy cause. I wish you well in your continued efforts.[68]

VI

Recent historiographical research on the origins of the American gun culture[69] has established that many of the traditional beliefs upholding the right to bear arms are as insecurely based as are the legal ones. Contrary to an "imagined past," where frontiersmen "with guns in their hands and bullets on their belts"[70] conquered the wilderness and so created modern America, it transpires that gun ownership was rare throughout the eighteenth and early nineteenth centuries. Hunters depended on trapping for their food, and firearms were in short supply. Meat came from domesticated, rather than wild, animals. The militias were poorly armed and took little care of the few muskets that were stored in their armories. Well into the nineteenth century the indifference with which militiamen treated their weapons was a constant source of complaint by their commanders. In the first official inventory of arms carried out in 1793, 37 percent of the muskets owned by the government were found to be unusable, and an additional 25 percent were either archaic or in serious need of repair and cleaning. In the following year, the Secretary of War estimated that of the 450,000 militia members in the United States no more than 100,000 either owned or had been supplied with guns.[71]

Michael Bellesîles, whose critical examination of original sources is summarized here, argues convincingly that public indifference to firearms, most of which had to be imported from Europe, continued until industrial production took off in the late 1840s and early 1850s. The active participation of the federal government was crucial. It provided capital, protected patents, encouraged technological development, and constituted the largest market for gun manufacturers. In the forefront of the new entrepreneurs was Samuel Colt. With his invention of the revolver, a lethal weapon became available for the first time which was relatively inexpensive, easily portable, and capable of firing several rounds rapidly. Colt's flair was as a salesman as well as an inventor. He made skillful use of newspapers as vehicles for some of the cleverest advertisements yet seen. The romance of the West, a man armed only with his Colt six-shooter protecting his terrified wife and child from savage Indians, was a powerful message, if one to which the majority of potential purchasers at first was apathetic.[72] The growth of hunting as a leisure pursuit, and the determined efforts of the federal government to provide arms for volunteer companies to supplement the ineffective and often mocked state militias, were additional factors in the gradual arming of a larger proportion of the population.

The climax came with the outbreak of the Civil War in 1861. The thesis is convincing that the origins of the gun culture are to be found not in the American Revolution and its immediate aftermath, nor in the imperatives of survival on the Western frontier, but in nineteenth century industrialization and the Civil War. Bellesîles identifies the true sources of an enduring culture which has bedeviled American society ever since:

> The Civil War dramatically accelerated the slow cultural shift that had been instigated by the increase in arms production in the 1840s. By 1865 it would seem that most Americans believed that the ability to use a gun made one a better man as well as a patriot more able to defend the nation's liberties— they certainly showed a willingness to act on that assumption. Technological innovation coupled with government support had powerfully altered the national character and sensibilities within a single generation. The Civil War established these attitudes permanently.[73]

When the war ended Union soldiers were allowed to take their firearms home with them, and many Confederates did the same. An industry by now geared to the manufacture of firearms continued with high levels of production, and prices fell. The antebellum advertising linking the possession of guns with manly security was expanded with new and uplifting themes. Encouraged by the government, the idea took root that "individual ownership of guns served some larger social purpose; for instance, that they preserved the nation's freedom or the security of the family. The advertising campaigns of all the gun manufacturers played up those two angles."[74] With the added incentive of low prices a market was created, not at first a mass market, but one which grew rapidly in size as the gun culture spread.

In modern times the lack of any national system of registration or licensing, as exhorted by President Johnson, has permitted the accumulation of a vast arsenal, estimated at nearly 200 million guns in private hands[75] and an ease of access to them unknown elsewhere. The average number of victimizations in which firearms were stolen was estimated at 340,700 per year over the period 1987–92.[76] Hence the dismal catalog of aggression, fights, violent settlement of disputes, robberies, woundings, and above all killings of individuals or whole groups of people, which so often involved the use of guns. Clinton did not exaggerate in castigating the lack of effective restrictions on the availability of firearms as "an instrument for maintaining madness."

Violent crimes involving firearms inevitably are more likely to be fatal than those involving other weapons, or no weapon at all. Very many crimes of violence are impulsive and committed on the spur of the moment. If a loaded firearm is to hand, or readily available, the consequences are incomparably more serious. In the previous chapter it was noted that in 1993 nearly 70 percent of the murders, 42 percent of the robberies known to law enforcement, and a quarter of the reported aggravated assaults were committed with firearms; 16,189 Americans were murdered with guns that year, and in 13,252 of these crimes a handgun was the weapon used. The total number of gun murders had increased every year between 1988 and 1993.[77] Nor are firearm deaths confined to unlawful homicide. Legal intervention, suicides, and accidents take the totals higher still. In 1993, deaths caused by firearms were estimated to include 19,590 suicides, 1,740 accidents, and 460 of unknown provenance.[78] People living in households in which guns are kept have a risk of suicide that is five times greater than people living in households without guns.[79] Some telling comparative statistics illustrating the enormity of the difference in homicide and other gun-related deaths between the United States, Great Britain, Australia, and Canada are set out in the final chapter (see table 4).

No one who has studied the statistics, or who has firsthand experience of the actuality of criminal offending and crime control policies, can doubt that the strikingly disproportionate level of homicide and nonfatal violent crime suffered by the United States is directly related to the possession and availability of guns.[80] Over and over again the President drove the message home, often in its most vivid form. ''We cannot renew this country,'' he declared in his State of the Union Address in January 1994, ''when 13-year old boys get semiautomatic weapons to shoot 9-year-olds for kicks.''[81]

Chapter 3

Symbolism and Reality

I

One of the single-issue House bills (H.R. 3355), authorizing the provision of federal funds for community policing, became the vehicle for the comprehensive legislation that was enacted many months later. Although stemming from a Clinton campaign pledge, the community policing initiative had won all-party support in Congress. It was, however, the most expensive element in the package and raised the question of how the extra money was to be found. The funding of costly new programs is a perennial problem for legislators, never more so than when, as in late 1993, Congress had just put in place caps on appropriations in endorsing the administration's five-year deficit-reduction plan.

H.R. 3355, passed by voice vote of the House on November 3, was sent to the Senate and placed on its calendar the following day. Senators meanwhile had been zealous in amending their omnibus bill, by now renumbered S.1607, which they preferred to the piecemeal approach. In passing H.R. 3355 on November 19 the Senate struck out all after the enacting clause and inserted the text of S.1607 in lieu. The extent of bipartisan support for this tactic, and for the contents of the big bill, was shown in the vote of ninety-five yeas and only four nays. By then the question of financing the anti-crime proposals, in particular grants to the states and units of local government for additional police, had been resolved, also to bipartisan satisfaction, by an unorthodox proposal in the course of a debate on the Senate floor on November 4 put forward by the chairman of the Appropriations Committee, Senator Robert Byrd (Dem. W. Virginia). Although normally critical of the practice of dedicating public expenditure for specific purposes, such as the "fire walls," dismantled only shortly before, that had protected defense and foreign aid spending, Byrd had been persuaded by the majority leader, George Mitchell, with the support of the Budget Committee chairman, to allocate the savings anticipated from the administration's plan to reduce the size of the federal workforce to a trust fund that could be used solely to finance the programs contained in the crime bill. The costs were substantial. Originally estimated at $5.9 billion, the total cost of the bill had risen with enlargements to $9.6 billion over five years, before more than doubling to $22.3 billion once the unexpected largesse had come into view. The final cost of the bill as enacted was approximately $30.2 billion over six years.

A trust fund earmarked to provide federal aid for employing more police and law enforcement officers, to make grants to states to expand their correctional facilities for the confinement of violent offenders, to experiment with boot camps, and to provide drug treatment and prevention programs for young people and soon-to-be-released prisoners, was an unforeseen development.[1] From then on, it was to be the adhesive holding together the diverse groups in the Congress on the crime bill. What had made it possible? Although never spelt out, the explanation had more to do with fiscal than criminal policy. In the plan to cut back the scale of federal government masterminded by Vice President Gore, savings in excess of $20 billion had been identified as a result of reducing the numbers in the federal work force by 252,000 over a five-year period.

Nothing had been said about how to handle the savings. The general assumption had been that they would be used to reduce the deficit, another prime aim of the Clinton administration, but no commitments had been made. Some observers, it was reported, thought this somewhat casual. "It's like leaving a $20 bill out there on the counter expecting it will be there when you come back tomorrow. Somebody's going to pick it up" was the reported comment of one Senate aide.[2] The main reason it was picked up so swiftly by the Democratic leadership in the Senate was a fear that the recently approved caps on appropriations might be cut still further. The idea of the trust fund had three attractions. It would keep the spending caps where they were; it would ensure that the savings were directed toward domestic spending, always advantageous for the party in power; and it would thwart Republican taunts that although the Democrats were now talking tough on crime, it was only talk and they were not prepared to find the money needed to fight crime more effectively.[3]

The crime bill absorbed much time on the floor of the Senate in November. Amendments to strengthen the laws on child pornography and enhance the penalties for hate crimes were agreed on November 4. On November 5, 8, and 9, the next three working days, the Senate approved a long list of amendments and rejected or held over others. Carjacking (the use of force to obtain control over a motor vehicle being operated by another person) would be subject to prosecution as a federal crime whether or not a gun was used, and the death penalty would be available if death resulted from the commission of the offense. Federal penalties would apply to persons involved in the criminal activities of street gangs, to the possession of a handgun or ammunition by juveniles, and to the sale or transfer of a gun or ammunition to a juvenile. Juveniles with parental permission to use guns for ranching, farming, hunting, target practice, or a course of instruction in the safe and lawful use of a handgun, were exempted, as would be juveniles who defended themselves with a handgun against an intruder to their home. From the age of thirteen, juveniles prosecuted for serious crimes,[4] or in possession of a firearm during the commission of the offense, would be tried as adults. If found guilty they would build up criminal records in adult courts.

At a distance from Capitol Hill, informed observers concerned with the rationality of the criminal law, and where responsibility should rest between the states and federal government for its content and enforcement, despaired at the absence of coherent principle in the selection of new offenses for inclusion in the federal criminal code. Zimring and Hawkins, deriding the proposals for new federal crimes in the Senate's version of the crime bill as ranging from the typical to the preposterous, used "the sad and shabby history" of the passage of the legislation by Congress in 1993–94 as a case study to support their arguments for jurisdictional principles.[5] The proposal to create a new federal crime of carjacking was typical because it derived from, and was a legislative response to, expressions of intense public concern. Yet the behavior constituting carjacking was already punishable in all fifty states, and increasingly it was being defined as a separate offense. There was no structural incapacity standing in the way of enforcement by the states, and no reason to suppose that federal law enforcement resources were better suited to the apprehension of carjackers than state and local law enforcement. The fundamental reason for federalizing the offense was to recognize its seriousness, and to demonstrate a commitment on the part of national government to deal with a problem that was arousing fear on the part of citizens.[6]

Political symbolism hung over the proceedings. Periodically it was acknowledged openly, as when the chairman of the Judiciary Subcommittee on Juvenile Justice, Senator Kohl (Dem. Wisconsin), whose amendment on the underage possession of handguns was agreed by a unanimous vote of one hundred to nil,[7] said that only a small number of young people would be affected because the provision was limited to offenses tried in federal courts, and not to the large majority tried in the state courts. Nevertheless, he believed there was "a strong symbolism in the vote that says that kids are responsible for their action," adding "It's more symbolic than it is real."[8] Although such a frank recognition of the indicative quality of federal lawmaking was refreshing, the juvenile gun ban was a stronger example than carjacking, and some of the other new offenses, of a law designed to curtail potentially harmful conduct that was inconsistent with the policy of the federal government. Moreover, since gun control was such a controversial issue, there could be no certainty about the effectiveness of enforcement in states where comparable restrictions already existed. The following year, the day after signing the Violent Crime Control and Law Enforcement act into law, Clinton singled out the juvenile gun ban as the main topic for his speech to the United States Attorneys (the chief federal prosecutors) at a White House gathering:

> One of the most important provisions of this crime bill is one which has been largely over-looked. . . . I want to discuss it with you today because I think it can make a huge difference. And that is the ban on juvenile possession of handguns. Except when hunting or target shooting with a parent or other responsible adult, young people simply shouldn't be carrying guns. Period. This provision is critical to our ability to make our schools and neighborhoods safer. It is so critical that I am directing you today, each of you, to prepare a plan in your districts for enforcing this law over the next 100 days. We need to work with local law enforcement officials and other local officials as you have been doing. . . . If this law turns out to be just a law on the books that is widely ignored and never enforced, it will be a terrible shame, because this law can save our children's lives. . . . [W]e obviously have to have a strategy to enforce it, and the means by which it is enforced may not be the same, as a practical matter, in every district in the country.[9]

II

In another Senate vote, also with symbolic appeal, although to a different constituency, an amendment by the liberal Senator Paul Simon (Dem. Illinois) to prohibit the death penalty for all young people under the age of eighteen failed on November 8 by forty-one votes to fifty-two. Under federal law no person may be sentenced to death who was less than eighteen years of age at the time of the commission of an offense punishable by death. The federal exemption, however, did not affect the overwhelming majority of prisoners on death row who had been sentenced to death according to state law. Only 5 out of the total of 2,848 prisoners under sentence of death on April 20, 1994, had been sentenced under federal statutes.[10]

Earlier, in 1988, the Supreme Court ascertained that nineteen states had a statutorily authorized death penalty that did not include any minimum age, and that eighteen states had statutorily authorized minimum ages varying between sixteen and eighteen, below which no defendant could be executed. In fourteen states there was no statutorily authorized death penalty. In *Thompson v. Oklahoma*[11] the Court decided by a majority of five to three that a capital sentence imposed on a defendant younger than sixteen years at the time the crime was committed violated the Eighth Amendment prohibition of cruel and unusual punishments. Simon's amendment was aimed at prohibiting capital sentences being passed by state courts on defendants between the ages of sixteen and eighteen at the time of the crime, so achieving parity in the administration of the death penalty between the federal and state jurisdictions.

At this stage in the Senate the habeas corpus reform proposal, on which Biden, a supporter of capital punishment, and Reno, who was opposed to the death penalty on principle, had worked together, was abandoned. Although a majority of legislators believed that the procedures allowing so many prisoners condemned to death to spend ten years or more on death row were in urgent need of reform, there was insufficient consensus on the nature of the reforms that were necessary to remedy the situation. The formula included in the bill was to allow a state-sentenced capital prisoner a single federal habeas corpus petition to be filed within six months of final adjudication in the state courts. Secondary petitions would be limited to extraordinary circumstances involving the establishment of innocence or a constitutional defect in the sentence. States would be required to provide indigent capital defendants with qualified counsel at all stages of state proceedings, and federal grants would be made available to assist states with the extra costs of fulfilling the counsel requirements.

These were the main features of the settlement that had been arrived at in consultations earlier in the year with the National District Attorneys Association and the National Association of Attorneys General. But as the months passed, and the hopes of speedy enactment faded, second thoughts came to the surface. Some of the states' representatives, mainly those who feared that the agreed formulation was going too far in a liberal direction, began to express reservations. At the same time, the libertarian view was articulated in a series of editorials in several of the leading newspapers that the proposal was regressive and failed to leave adequate procedures in place to avoid the possibility of miscarriages of justice occurring. An articulate strain of purist opinion wanted to see the decisions of the Supreme Court in narrowing the scope of habeas corpus reversed, and was critical of any measures which would codify in statute law a restricted application of the "great writ."

Biden's chosen ground, on this as on other issues, was center left. But by the time the bill was under consideration in the Senate, and before going into conference, he was not sufficiently confident of the result to put the proposal to the test of a floor vote. Nor could he afford to risk the possibility of a more conservative, Republican-inspired version, passing. In negotiation, therefore, he dropped habeas corpus reform. In return for an agreement not to bring it back during the 103rd Congress, he obtained an undertaking from the Republican leadership that they would not obstruct the passage of the bill as a whole. Recalling the fate of the previous crime bill, this was a valuable objective to have secured. Biden's aim was to maintain the momentum and get the bill into conference without allowing the Republicans and sectional interests time to regroup. In the outcome the tactic was unsuccessful, not because of undue delays in the Senate, but because of the slower pace dictated by the Congressional Black Caucus and its allies in the House of Representatives.

Some of the amendments passed by the Senate in the two-and-a-half week, tougher-than-thou bidding war in November[12] had heavy cost implications. Replying to criticism that the criminalization of gang activities would increase the burden on the federal courts, Dole pointed out that the amendment of which he was the sponsor authorized $100 million over five years to be spent on recruiting additional federal prosecutors. A further $100 million would be made available for a grant program to work with juveniles and gang members. By the time his amendment was debated Dole, as minority leader, was fully aware of the potential of the trust fund proposal that had been agreed by an overwhelming majority the previous week.[13] Other successful Republican amendments included the extension of the death penalty to drug "kingpins," that is, those engaged in continuing criminal enterprises dealing in large quantities of illegal drugs. This provision had been added to the 1991 crime bill by the populist Senator D'Amato (Rep. New York), but had been omitted from the Biden bill. On its introduction in September, D'Amato had committed himself and other Republican supporters of the policy to pressing it again. The flavor of his rhetoric comes through even in the printed record:

> I am outraged that despite all the talk of getting tough on crime, the administration has shown itself, in fact, to be soft on crime. By deleting two provisions that I added to the 1991 crime bill, the new bill will not be one that cracks down on crime, but one that gives criminals a break—a break they do not deserve and should not get . . . [I]t cannot be wrong to require the death penalty for large-scale drug enterprises. Those who sell death, should receive death. How many people have to die before we come to the realization that we need a greater sanction against those who head the criminal drug enterprises. . . . Killing people by selling them drugs has the same result as killing them with a gun. The death penalty for drug kingpins . . . provides the ultimate sanction. This is right and this is just. We should do no less.[14]

Two of the other amendments affected prisons and prisoners. In future all prisoners held in federal, state, or local prisons would be subject to the statutory ineligibility for Pell grants for higher education which hitherto had applied only to death row and life prisoners. It was an early sign of a shift in opinion, becoming more pronounced in the 104th Congress, whereby deserving students in the general community were contrasted with undeserving prison inmates. A second amendment, potentially of far-reaching importance, aimed to restrict the power of the federal courts to set population caps in prison-overcrowding lawsuits, barring class actions in such cases, and limiting the remedies that a federal court might impose for conditions caused by overcrowding in violation of the Constitution.

III

The proper role of federal judges in litigation over prison conditions and overcrowding had been a matter of controversy for several years. The power to intervene, and the prudent use made of it by certain judges, Morris Lasker in the U.S. District Court for the Southern District of New York being an outstanding example, had been instrumental in ameliorating the total degradation in many state-run prisons and local jails that resulted from the rapidly escalating populations in custody. Even the opponents of judicial intervention did not deny that in most cases basic standards of amenity, regulation, and service had been improved as a result of federal court orders.[15] In one of the most conspicuous instances, the New York City jails (amongst the largest, most politically complicated, and distressed of all detention facilities), it was a paradox that a majority of the inmates, numbering more than thirteen thousand out of a total of over fifteen thousand inmates in 1990,[16] was made up not of convicted and sentenced prisoners being punished for their wrongdoing but of accused persons awaiting trial in detention. During two decades following a notorious outbreak of inmate riots and staff protests at the Manhattan House of Detention for Men, then, as now, popularly known as the Tombs,[17] it was the sensitive handling of a potentially explosive situation by Judge Lasker that led to the intervention of the federal district court in New York being declared "an almost unqualified success."[18]

By the late 1980s judicial activism in cases of overcrowding had become commonplace throughout the United States. A survey published in 1988 found that there were major court orders on prisons and jails in forty states,[19] a total that had declined to thirty-one by 1993.[20] Limits on capacity were set to check overcrowding, and a wide range of orders made to change and improve specific administrative practices. To oversee the implementation of the court orders, judges appointed special masters, monitors, or compliance coordinators. One unusual solution to the problems of enforcement came when a Republican judge who had taken control of the entire Alabama prison system appointed the governor of the State as temporary receiver, and ordered the Board of Corrections to transfer all its authorities and functions to the governor. The state legislature then passed a law dissolving the board and replacing it with a Department of Corrections directly under the governor's control. When the governor left office in 1983, the court set up a four-member expert committee to oversee the system.[21]

It is not hard to see why the intervention of federal judges was often resented, and sometimes resisted. The main practical objection was that additional capacity in the shape of building new prisons and jails, and making improvements at existing penal establishments, cost money. All of the money, in the early years before federal grants became available, had to be found by state and local governments from budgets that were committed already to fund more electorally attractive services. If the extra capacity needed to meet the requirements of a court order was not forthcoming, then some existing prisoners might have to be released to reduce the pressure of overcrowding and to allow for the admission of newly sentenced offenders. Such a resort was an even less popular course of action than finding the money for building more prisons and jails. Moreover it was argued, with some truth, that by training, background, and outlook, judges were not qualified to supervise and manage prisons. The orders they made, and the officers they appointed to supervise compliance with their orders, might make things worse rather than better by destabilizing precarious prison cultures. Some critics believed that once institutional authority was undermined by external intervention, tension increased, leading to prisons becoming more unruly and violent. Other studies, however, indicated that while short-term disruption might result, court decrees did not lead to continuing problems of inmate unrest and violence.[22]

At another level, leaving practical issues to one side, there were the rival claims of judicial activism and judicial restraint. The conflict was not confined to intervention in the prisons and jails, but was part of a wider ideological clash of opinion over the constitutional propriety of judges making and implementing public policy. The breadth and detail of the involvement of the federal judiciary in initiating and supervising changes in penal administration was recognized as being on a scale that some commentators regarded as second only to the courts' earlier role in dismantling racial segregation in the public schools.[23]

The legal basis for intervention was the prohibition against the infliction of cruel and unusual punishments in the Eighth Amendment to the Constitution. While only the most extreme would argue that the protection against cruel and unusual treatment should not extend to prisoners, there were some large and unresolved questions. First was the status of class actions, aimed at obtaining relief not confined to an individual plaintiff, but extending to a group of inmates subject to similar conditions at a particular institution. Then there was the provision of remedies. Where a court found that conditions had violated the Eighth Amendment was it entitled to prescribe a ceiling on the size of the inmate population? And did the need to see that court orders were complied with justify the intrusive assumption of a management role?

These were questions which in due course were bound to be considered by Congress. In 1989 a fruitless attempt was made in the Senate to limit judicial intervention in prisons and jails by means of restricting judicial remedies for prison overcrowding. In the debates on the crime bill in November 1993 some of the proponents tried again, this time successfully. One of the most conservative members of the Senate, the Republican Jesse Helms of North Carolina, supported by Senator Gramm (Rep. Texas), moved an amendment in the course of the general floor debate on November 16. It provided that a federal court should not hold prison or jail crowding unconstitutional under the Eighth Amendment, except to the extent that an individual plaintiff inmate proved that the crowding caused the infliction of cruel and unusual punishment on that inmate. The relief in such a case should extend no further than necessary to remove the conditions that were causing the cruel and unusual punishment of the plaintiff inmate. As to inmate population ceilings, the amendment stated that ''[a] Federal court shall not place a ceiling on the inmate population of any Federal, State, or local detention facility as an equitable remedial measure for conditions that violate the eighth amendment unless crowding is inflicting cruel and unusual punishment on particular identified prisoners.''[24]

The short debate on remedies for prison overcrowding did not show the Senate at its best. Helms's rhetoric was addressed directly at the voters in his home state without any acknowledgment of the wider constitutional implications. All over America, he declaimed, innocent citizens were being murdered, raped, robbed, and beaten by violent felons who had been turned loose on society by federal judges after they had served only a fraction of the prison terms received for their crimes. In North Carolina, more than twenty-six thousand prisoners had been given early release the previous year, including eighty-eight felons convicted of murder and thirty-seven rapists. They had been "set free because prison cells were not quite large enough to suit some Federal judge."[25] He cited examples of two young police officers and other victims from his state "whose lives had been snuffed out by violent felons returned to the streets by the Federal courts."[26]

Senator Graham, a centrist southern Democrat and former governor of Florida, with greater knowledge of release procedures, was more restrained in his language, but he too asserted that the effect of judicial intervention had been to return serious offenders to the streets in order to find bed space for those admitted to the institution. His concern was that the pattern of federal court orders relative to prison construction, operation and population had been setting higher and higher standards that went far beyond those necessary to ensure that the constitutional standard of cruel and unusual punishment was not violated. He particularly objected to the fact that the federal government was using the Eighth Amendment to impose standards on state prisons and local jails that were higher than those maintained in its own penal institutions.[27]

It was left to Biden, opposing the amendment, to point out that it would introduce novel changes in the relationship between Congress and the courts that required a more thorough airing. Thirty minutes of debate on the Senate floor was not an appropriate airing.[28] Although opinion amongst constitutional scholars was not unanimous, he believed that the weight of authority supported his contention that the amendment might be an unconstitutional encroachment on the separation of powers. It aimed to restrict the authority of the federal courts to interpret a part of the Constitution, and limited the courts' remedial powers. In his view, the amendment was infirm in both respects. The drafting meant that courts presiding over class action lawsuits would not be permitted to hold that prison overcrowding violated the Constitution, unless the court made particularized findings of cruel and unusual punishment respecting an individual plaintiff. If the Senate adopted the amendment, in effect it would be stating that the federal courts, which since *Marbury v. Madison* in 1803[29] had been considered to be the final arbiters of what the Constitution requires, might not make determinations of what is or is not constitutional with respect to Eighth Amendment litigation over prison crowding.

As its promoters intended, the Helms amendment would prevent a court that made a finding of system-wide constitutional violation from remedying the infirmity, even if the court believed that to be the correct result. In doing so, Biden said, it flew in the face of national history and understanding of the courts' role in the constitutional system.[30] The proposal did more than merely tell the courts that they might not fashion a specific remedy for a constitutional violation; it sought to define the limits of the law under the Constitution. It prescribed that a federal court might not hold that certain prison conditions violated the Constitution unless the claim was brought by an individual plaintiff, even where other aspects of the case were properly before the court. If a class of plaintiffs demonstrated pervasive unlawful prison conditions, the court would be prevented from finding such conditions unlawful and providing a remedy. The effect of the amendment would be to restrict the ability of the federal courts to remedy cruel and unusual punishment caused by prison overcrowding. "Deny the remedy, you deny the right."[31] Congress had never granted a federal court subject-matter jurisdiction over a particular class of claims, and then stripped it of its right to fashion a particular remedy. Consequently, the Supreme Court had not ruled on the question of whether Congress improperly encroached on the judicial power by restricting the ability of the federal courts to provide appropriate remedies for constitutional wrongs.

Elegant and powerful as it was, Biden's reasoning, paraphrased above, failed to convince. Electoral politics, the attraction of seemingly tough and decisive measures, rooted in what was perceived by the sponsoring senators as the weight of populist resentment toward "activist federal judges" were against him. The next morning, November 17, a motion to table the amendment, thereby blocking it from making progress, was defeated by sixty-eight votes to thirty-one.[32] The amendment survived in conference, having passed the remaining stages in both Houses. The following year it became law as section 20409 of Public Law 103-322. The section proved to have a short life, failing to accomplish its sponsors' intention to make it more difficult for prisoners to succeed in overcrowding cases.[33] The reasons leading to its early repeal and replacement by more stringent provisions in the 104th Congress[34] belong later in the book.

IV

A turning point in the long drawn-out controversy over firearms came on the floor of the Senate on November 9. Republican hard-liners had proposed increased mandatory minimum penalties for the use of a gun in the commission of a crime of violence or drug-trafficking crimes. They wanted mandatory terms of not less than ten years' imprisonment for the possession of a firearm during the commission of such a crime; twenty years for discharging it with intent to injure another person; and life imprisonment or the death penalty for murder involving a firearm. To this amendment was attached another proposal, that the federal penalties specified, including the death penalty, should apply also to offenses committed within state jurisdictions where the firearm involved had moved at any time in interstate or foreign commerce. In such cases, state prosecutors would decide whether to seek federal jurisdiction. Biden warned the mover, Senator D'Amato, whose emotive rhetoric already has been noted, that this could lead to clashes with U.S. Attorneys, and the federal death penalty being sought in cases where the law of the state in which the killing occurred did not allow capital punishment. Six hundred thousand handgun crimes were committed each year, and under the amendment they would all be federalized.[35] Ignoring the objections by the federal judiciary, on record since a similar attempt had been made in the 102nd Congress, the amendment was approved by a majority of fifty-eight voting yea to forty-two voting nay, with the underlying amendment agreed by voice vote.[36]

On September 19, 1991, the Chief Justice, William Rehnquist, in his capacity as presiding officer of the Judicial Conference of the United States, had written to Brooks to convey the opposition of the Judicial Conference to legislation that would provide for federal jurisdiction over offenses traditionally reserved for state prosecution. He enclosed a statement summarizing the objections, and the reasons for expressing them. During the proceedings on the crime bill in the 103rd Congress, both Rehnquist and the chairman of the Executive Committee of the Judicial Conference, Chief Judge John Gerry, reiterated the misgivings of the judges toward the proposed expansion of the role of the federal courts in the administration of criminal justice. The statement read:

FEDERALIZATION OF STATE PROSECUTIONS: POSITION OF THE JUDICIAL
CONFERENCE OF THE UNITED STATES
The Judicial Conference of the United States opposes legislation adopted by the Senate which would expand federal criminal law jurisdiction to encompass homicides and other violent state felonies if firearms are involved. Such expansion of federal jurisdiction would be inconsistent with long-accepted concepts of federalism, and would ignore the boundaries between appropriate state and federal action.

The addition to federal jurisdiction of virtually any crime committed with a firearm that has crossed a state line will swamp the federal courts with routine cases that states are better equipped to handle, and will weaken the ability of the federal courts effectively to deal with difficult criminal cases that present uniquely federal issues.

Not only will bona fide federal criminal prosecutions suffer if the Senate's expansive firearms provisions are adopted, but federal courts, overburdened by criminal cases, will be unable to carry out their vital responsibilities to provide timely forums for civil cases.[37]

With the furies gathering, the omens were hardly auspicious when, later on November 9, Senator Dianne Feinstein (Dem. California) moved to amend the bill to include a ban on the manufacture, transfer, or possession of nineteen specified types of assault weapon. Although the policy was fervently supported by Clinton, and had been raised in Congress before, the ban had not been included in the original bills introduced in either chamber. Unlike his counterpart in the House, Representative Brooks, Biden was a staunch supporter of gun control. But he was apprehensive lest the fierce controversy surrounding the assault weapons proposal should imperil the chances of the main bill being agreed. Moreover, the Brady bill was still outstanding, having been passed by the House, and was currently awaiting action by the Senate. Mrs. Feinstein, a long-time campaigner against crime in California, remained resolute and would not be put off. Her proposal was confined to military-style weapons that could have no legitimate sporting or hunting use and were ill-suited for personal protection. It was estimated that as many as one million were in circulation. The ban, which had a life of ten years, did not apply to existing weapons lawfully possessed before the date of enactment. It also specifically exempted 670 types of manual and semiautomatic guns used for sports and hunting, as well as the use of semiautomatic weapons by police officers and other law enforcement officials. The naming of the actual weapons that would be included or excluded was an effective counter to the allegation that the legislation would deprive law-abiding citizens of their favorite guns.

Feinstein began her speech with a reference to the state of general public opinion, and later listed the names of fifty-three organizations that endorsed a ban on assault weapons. They included the National Association of Police Organizations and the Fraternal Order of Police, as well as the American Bar Association, the National Association for the Advancement of Colored People (NAACP), the U.S. Conference of Mayors, medical associations, labor unions, and religious bodies.[38] The amendment, she said, dealt with

> a problem that 66 percent of all American citizens want addressed. Asked in a recent poll, ''Would you favor a law banning the manufacture, sale, and possession of semiautomatic assault guns such as the AK-47,'' 66 percent said yes; only 30 percent said no. There is no reason for weapons of war to be used freely on the streets of America—where they are weapons of choice for every assassin, terrorist, gang member, drug syndicate, drive-by shooter, Mafioso, or grievance killer.
>
> The most troubling of these categories is the grievance killer, someone who takes out their wrath on anyone who happens to be around—children in a school yard or a swimming pool or walking down a street; workers in offices or post offices; innocent people eating hamburgers in a restaurant; or the grandmother watching television in the privacy of her own living room, when a high velocity bullet from a semiautomatic assault weapon comes through the wall and pierces her chest. I believe it is time to stop the sale, the manufacture, and the possession of more semiautomatic assault weapons on the streets of America.[39]

Each of the examples was based on a factual incident, several of them having occurred in the senator's home state. A lone gunman had gone to a law firm in San Francisco earlier in 1993 carrying two assault weapons and more than 500 rounds of ammunition. He opened fire and killed eight people. Six others were wounded. At a McDonald's outlet twenty-one people eating burgers had been killed, and nineteen more wounded, by a man armed with an assault weapon, a shotgun and a pistol. Another gunman, described as a "dangerous drifter with an assault weapon," had walked into a schoolyard in northern California and fired 106 rounds of ammunition. Five small children were killed, and twenty-nine injured.[40] What in the past, said Feinstein, had been regarded as shocking episodes because of their randomness and multiple victims, were becoming the norm.

Some senators argued that because more people might have been killed by the shotgun than by the assault weapon in the McDonald's shooting, the incident bore out their maxim that it was people who killed, not guns. Feinstein replied eloquently. While semiautomatic weapons were not in themselves responsible for the large number of deaths, their availability for sale over the counter in all save four states offered to the deranged killer or the grievance killer the possibility of taking out a whole room of people without having to reload. Yes, it is true, she admitted, "Guns do not fire themselves, nor however, do they thrust themselves into the hands of the distraught, the deranged and the disaffected. They have to be bought or stolen."[41]

Later in the debate, a condescending put-down by a speaker opposed to the amendment, that the senator of California needed to become "a little more familiar with firearms," gave Feinstein an opening for a devastating riposte. "I am quite familiar with firearms. I became mayor as a product of assassination. . . . They found my assassinated colleague and you could put a finger through the bullet hole."[42]

Passionate emotions were expressed on both sides of the argument and little quarter given. When the vote came it was taken not on the merits of the issue, but on a procedural motion to table the amendment that would prevent it making any further progress. The result was bound to be close. In the end a tie was averted only when one Democrat, who had opposed an assault weapons ban in 1991, switched his vote, so keeping alive Feinstein's ability to offer her amendments.[43] After much tactical maneuvering behind the scenes, the Senate resumed its consideration of the Feinstein amendment on November 17. There was no debate, but five Republicans changed sides to support the ban. This time the amendment was agreed by fifty-six votes to forty-three, with one senator absent.[44] The contest was not over, for the reaction of the House of Representatives could not be forecast with any confidence, but a significant step toward sanity had been taken.

V

Of all the diverse proposals that eventually found a place in the 355 pages of Public Law 103-322, none was more genuine a product of the demands of populist sentiment than mandatory sentencing to life imprisonment for repeat offenders on their third conviction, if they had been convicted previously on separate occasions of two or more serious felonies, or one or more serious felonies and one or more serious drug offenses. Whereas the first two convictions could be either in a federal or state court, the third conviction, which activated mandatory life imprisonment, had to be in a federal court only. That outcome lay ahead. By November, the Senate bill as amended contained some mandatory penalties for repeat offenders convicted of certain serious crimes that were variants of the three strikes policy. But they were limited to specified offenses, as were the penalties up to imprisonment for life to which recidivists were liable under existing federal and state law. The tidal wave from the West, sweeping all before it with the slogan borrowed from baseball, "Three strikes and you're out," had not yet reached the administration and Congress.

The origins were located far away in the State of Washington on the West Coast. It was rumored that an advertising agency had come up with the catchy slogan linking the punishment of criminals, for which the public craved, to the sport which the public loved. At first the campaign was localized and in a low key. The aim was to get the policy on repeat offenders onto the ballot as an initiative. That objective, which had failed in 1992, was achieved by a 76 to 24 percent margin the following November when the NRA and the Washington Citizens for Justice stepped in to help. The result was proclaimed by the NRA as a people's victory and a defeat for soft-on-crime politics.[45]

It was California, however, a seedbed for regressive penal policies leading to a population of 200,000 adults confined in state prisons and local jails,[46] which provided the springboard to a national audience. In the autumn of 1993, a campaign had been launched to put a version of the three strikes law on the ballot at the elections the following year as an initiative for popular vote. Political support initially was at a relatively low level, being limited to the NRA and some of the state's more conservative politicians.

The catalyst that transformed the situation was a dreadful event: the abduction in October from her mother's home in a middle-class neighborhood and subsequent murder by strangulation, of a twelve-year-old girl, Polly Klaas. The man charged with her killing had a record of violent offending and had been released from prison only three months earlier. He had served eight years of a sixteen-year sentence for kidnapping and robbery, being released under state rules as he had worked well and been of good behavior while in prison.[47] The public outrage was made up of a mixture of anger, fear of victimization, sympathy for the victim and her family, and incomprehension that such a potentially dangerous repeat offender should have been allowed out of prison after serving no more than half the sentence imposed by the court. In the same way as with the murder the following year of another child, Megan Kanka, it was the personal circumstances of a tragedy attracting massive national media coverage that was the stimulus for an unstoppable surge of opinion carrying far beyond the boundaries of the state.

Before continuing the narrative, two short digressions are worth making. The first is to trace the successive stages of the course of justice in the case of Richard Allen Davis, the man charged with the abduction and murder of Polly Klaas. Although he had been arrested within weeks of the crime, and charges against him had been filed on December 7, 1993, two years later the trial still had not begun. After efforts had been abandoned to empanel a jury in Sonoma County where the killing had occurred, protracted negotiations took place to agree on an alternative location offering a greater prospect of a fair trial. In November 1995, a Sonoma County Superior Court judge ordered both sides to appear in court in Santa Clara County on February 5, 1996. In June, Davis was convicted on ten counts, including murder, kidnapping and robbery, after a jury trial at the Santa Clara County Superior Court in San Jose. Then came a separate sentencing phase when the same jury, having deliberated for twenty-one hours, over five days, recommended the death penalty on August 5. The next month, the trial judge formally pronounced the sentence of death which under California law is automatically appealed to the State Supreme Court of California. Further appeals to the federal courts were to be anticipated. In the reported opinion of the official in charge of capital cases for the State Attorney General's Office it would be reasonable to conclude that the appeals could not be completed in less than five or six years.[48]

This extended sequence, estimated to last for some eight or nine years from the date of the crime, illustrates some of the reasons for the very long drawn-out procedures that lead to the delays that are endemic in capital cases. Since California reinstated the death penalty in 1977, only four men had been executed, with the result that well over four hundred were on death row. At the time he was sentenced, Davis became the 444th death row prisoner in the state. What was more unusual, and unlikely to have earned him a friendly welcome on arrival at St. Quentin prison, was the fact that many of the inmates who had been sent there were serving life or enhanced terms of imprisonment, having already been sentenced under the three strikes law, which the public reaction to the murder of Polly Klaas had precipitated.[49]

The second digression is institutional rather than individual. Throughout most states of the Mid- and Far West, California amongst them, a system of direct legislation coexists alongside the more familiar processes of representative government. Access to the electorate by way of legislative initiatives and popular referendums on laws or policies, especially if there are any constitutional implications, goes back to the Progressive Era at the turn of the nineteenth and twentieth centuries. The notion was that the citizens themselves should have the opportunity to participate directly in the lawmaking process, unmediated by elected representatives. During the last two decades, direct legislation has become an important feature in more than fifteen states and can influence the political agenda-setting for the entire nation.[50] Since the 1970s California has been one of the most initiative-prone states. A new industry has grown up, with initiative campaigners spending large sums in employing professional managers, petition circulators, media consultants and pollsters. Over two decades the industry has expanded to include litigation, direct mail fundraising, and petition signature collection.[51]

Because of its size, its wealth, and the heterogeneous nature of its vast and ethnically mixed population,[52] California has acquired many of the characteristics of a nation within a federal union. Its political culture and way of life are quite distinct from the neighboring states. The high proportion of immigrants from other parts of the United States, as well as across the Mexican border and the Pacific, has meant that there is little sense of shared history or tradition. In its eagerness to embrace new ideas California has invigorated, but also at times irritated, the American body politic. Directly, through the presence in Congress of fifty-two elected members of the House of Representatives, as well as its two senators, and indirectly, through popular ballots, the media, and business, professional, intellectual, and special interest channels, ideas germinated in California tend to be radiated more widely, and taken up more readily, than those from elsewhere.

So it was with three strikes, a paradigm of populist policy appearing to offer a simple and clear-cut solution to an intractable problem of high visibility. By May 1, 1994, the National Conference of State Legislatures reported that ten states had adopted variants of California's three strikes law, rising to fourteen by the end of 1994. After much foaming water had flowed under the bridge, when the votes on the initiative were counted in the California ballot, coincident with the midterm November elections to Congress, the three strikes law, which had been effective since March 1994, was endorsed by a majority of almost three to one. Seventy-two percent of the voters were for and 28 percent against.

The fact that populist policies should be supported by popular votes is scarcely surprising, although not necessarily inevitable; miscalculations can be made of the public mood. There is a critical distinction, however, to be drawn between the condition of latent opinion, as measured by a ballot of all the voters, and its political effect when mobilized. As already noted, public opinion was consistently favorable toward gun control, although not overwhelmingly so. The proportion of two to one claimed by Senator Feinstein reflected the findings of numerous opinion polls. More relevant to direct legislation was a successful initiative in Maryland in 1988 prohibiting the manufacture and sale of certain handguns, despite a campaign by the NRA, which spent $6 million in opposing it.[53] Although there were other statewide referendums on gun control before and after the Maryland vote,[54] the result was supportive of the analysis that the influence of the NRA in national politics derived less from widespread majority support, than from its effective mobilization of the minority, and the pressure applied by its strongly motivated supporters on elected politicians. Organization, money, and the intensity of commitment can count for as much or more than numbers in influencing legislators.

Unlike the confrontation on gun control, where the battle lines had been drawn many years before, three strikes, although essentially not a new policy, had the appearance of novelty. Its appeal suited it to the NRA's diversionary strategy to deflect public attention away from the gun issue toward penal policy, leading to a contribution of $90,000 to the campaign in support of the California initiative. The California Correctional Peace Officers Association, which stood to gain from the creation of an estimated increase of eighteen thousand prison officers jobs by 2027, gave $101,000. The largest sum of all came from a wealthy individual running for election at the same time as the

November ballot on the three strikes initiative, Proposition 184. Michael Huffington, a freshman member of the House of Representatives and Dianne Feinstein's Republican opponent to represent California in the U.S. Senate, donated $300,000.[55] Apart from the correctional officers, there were few vested interests involved, and it is noticeable that most law enforcement officials were less ardent than legislators in their enthusiasm for the policy. The criminals had no say, and while the voices of criminologists and policy analysts were raised, they were drowned by the hubbub, and their warnings ignored. The reality was that the message conveyed by three strikes, apparently so simple a formulation, was an extraordinarily powerful one. It offered, simultaneously, a strong political response to the moral outrage of many voters while holding out the potential for greater personal protection. As a combination, it was to prove irresistible to the majority.

VI

The governor of California, Pete Wilson, never slow in responding to the demands of public opinion and with reelection looming in 1994, had already taken up the crime issue as an integral part of his appeal to the electorate. He exhorted voters to adopt the three strikes proposal as a memorial to Polly Klaas. On March 7, the governor chose the broadest of five different versions of three strikes offered by the legislature, discarding a proposal drafted by the California Association of Prosecutors, which he regarded as being too soft on crime. Sources as diverse as the Los Angeles district attorney and the Earl Warren Legal Institute at the University of California at Berkeley estimated that the resulting law would increase the sentences of some twenty-five thousand offenders a year, 70 percent of them convicted of nonviolent crimes,[56] and a majority not multiple recidivists. In contrast, the federal version passed by Congress later in the summer was expected to affect no more than a few hundred convicted offenders each year.[57]

While the first two strikes under the 1994 California law accrued for serious or violent felonies only,[58] the offense that triggered the life sentence could be any felony. The new law also doubled the minimum required sentence for the second strike. For second- and third-time offenders, the sentences had to be served in prison, rather than in jail, low-security rehabilitation centers, or on probation. The "good time" credit that prisoners could earn for good behavior was reduced to 20 percent of the total term of imprisonment imposed, having been raised from a third to a half in 1983. Presented as a technical change, and attracting little notice at the time, the increase to 50 percent "good time" made a mockery of the boasted punitiveness of determinate sentencing. The reason for its introduction had been the sharp rise in the state prison population, which had reached 130 percent of capacity in 1982.[59] Although three strikes rhetoric implied a life sentence without possibility of parole, the wording of the statute mandated an indeterminate term of imprisonment in a state prison for life, with prescribed minimum terms. A three-times convicted felon would have to serve a term not less than the greatest of three times the term otherwise provided as punishment for each current felony conviction subsequent to the two or more prior felony convictions, with a minimum of twenty-five years imprisonment in a state prison, or the term determined by the court for the underlying conviction, including any applicable enhancement or punishment provisions.[60]

The fact that the third offense included such nonviolent and frequent crimes as the possession of hard drugs, auto theft, or house burglary opened the way for widespread criticism on financial as well as penal grounds. Even the Klaas family publicly questioned the governor's judgment in signing a law that shifted the focus away from violent crime, and the girl's father became a public critic of the policy. But crime control was a bitterly contested partisan issue in the coming electoral campaign, and Wilson could not afford to let his opponent claim to be as tough as he was in speech, attitudes, and policies. When the November elections were held in California, not only Governor Wilson, a Republican, but Senator Feinstein, a Democrat and the victor in persuading Congress to impose the ban on assault weapons, were candidates for reelection. Both were politicians of stature. They stood their ground, fended off vituperative abuse from those antipathetic toward them, and both were reelected.

Also on the ballot, as Proposition 184, was the original initiative that had provided the California legislature with the impetus to take up the three strikes proposal. The text of the initiative and the law passed in the wake of the killing of Polly Klaas were very similar. If the voters approved the initiative they would be ratifying the legislature's action; whereas if they rejected it, they would be sending a message that the law should be reconsidered, and possibly amended in favor of one of the competing alternatives.[61] An impartial and comprehensive analysis of the benefits and costs of the three strikes law carried out by researchers at RAND and published in September 1994[62] indicated that certain alternatives could reduce crime almost as much, but at lower cost. Benefits were expressed in terms of quantifiable crime reduction, and costs defined as the expenditures required to implement the new law by the component parts of the criminal justice system. As a glimpse of the future it was disturbing.

The findings of the RAND study derived from analytical models predicting how populations of offenders on the street and in prison would change under the new law and under various alternatives. From these populations future crime rates and costs were estimated.[63] The most impressive finding was that if fully implemented the new law would reduce serious felonies committed by adults in California to between 22 to 34 percent below what would have occurred had the previous law remained in effect unchanged. About one-third of the felonies eliminated would be violent crimes, such as murder, rape, and assaults causing great bodily injury. The other two-thirds would be less violent, but still serious, felonies, including less injurious assaults, most robberies, and burglaries of residences. The qualification that the forecast applied only to serious felonies committed by adults was significant, since juveniles, who were excluded from the three strikes law, accounted for about one-sixth of all violent crime in the state.[64]

The benefits to society of a reduction in crime on this scale called for no elaboration. But what would the financial cost be, and how did it compare with alternative policies? The RAND study estimated the extra costs of the three strikes law, if implemented in full, at between $4.5 billion and $6.5 billion per year in current dollars above what would have been spent had the previous sentencing law remained in effect. Some police and court costs would be saved by closing the revolving door on repeat offenders, but they would be outweighed by the far larger costs of additional prison construction and operation. Over most of the twenty-five-year projection period, the full three strikes law would require more than double the available number of prison places.[65]

From a public resource, the California Department of Corrections, came a population and fiscal estimate of the scale of the increased operating and construction costs for the state prison system. By the turn of the century, it was estimated that at least 81,628 repeat offenders would be incarcerated in prison as a result of the initiative, and that at least 17,549 fewer felons would be on parole. Total operating costs in the fiscal year 1999 were estimated at about $1.6 billion, and prison construction costs estimated at about $1 billion in the same year. The full impact would not be achieved until the fiscal year 2027, when it was estimated that there would be 275,621 added inmates, 3,183 fewer parolees, and operating costs totalling $5.7 billion. Cumulative capital outlay costs due to the initiative would total an estimated $21.4 billion by fiscal year 2027.[66]

Were there any alternatives that would achieve a substantial part of the benefits, but at lower cost? Four were postulated by the RAND researchers. They were to eliminate the third strike provision but leave the other elements undisturbed; to confine the third strike to violent offences only; to be harsher on violent felons but more lenient on others; or to abandon the three strikes approach entirely and guarantee instead that offenders convicted of serious felonies would serve the full term of a prison sentence, without any discount for work time or good behavior. Each of these alternatives would be less costly than the three strikes law, but all save the last also would be less effective in reducing crime. In each case, the cost would decrease more steeply than the effectiveness. The limitation to a second strike would be 85 percent as effective, so establishing that only 15 percent of the total crime reduction attributed to the three strikes policy would come from the third strike, the feature that had so dramatically caught the imagination of the public. The guaranteed full-term alternative, again with the crucially important, and possibly unattainable, caveat "if implemented in full," would be just as effective as the three strikes law, but at substantially lower cost. A facility for convicted prisoners to earn remission of part of their sentence for good work and cooperation with disciplinary regulations, however, is regarded by many prison administrators as an essential management tool if order is to be maintained.

The very high cost of the California three strikes law, and the wasteful use of resources in locking up older offenders, many of them convicted of less serious felonies, until well after the time when they might be expected to have retired from their criminal careers, put a question mark against whether the policy would ever be implemented in full. Where was the money to come from? On the basis of the RAND calculation that over the next twenty-five years the new sentencing law would prevent something of the order of 340,000 serious crimes being committed each year, the additional cost would be roughly $5.5 billion annually. This expenditure represented about $16,000 per serious crime prevented. The guaranteed full–prison term alternative could prevent the commission of a similar number of serious crimes for an additional expenditure of about $4.4 billion annually, representing a lesser cost per crime prevented of about $13,000.

Unusual as it is to have the cost of crime prevention quantified with such precision, it was beyond the capacity of a computerized model to reconcile imponderable social values and financial cost. Neither did the survey find it possible to make any projections of economic savings resulting from lower medical costs and insurance premiums, nor reduced property losses from businesses and domestic residences. What was brought into the balance, however, was those publicly funded services that would have to be given up, or cut back, to find $5.5 billion annually from the state budget. The assumptions made in the RAND research were that tax increases of the order of $300 per year from the average working person to finance the three strikes policy were unlikely to be forthcoming, and that borrowing as a long-term source of revenue on this scale would be impractical. Once the focus is directed toward current spending it becomes immediately evident how little flexibility there is for reductions.

The largest heading of state expenditure in California, on K–12 education (kindergarten through 12th grade), is mandated as a result of a popular initiative written into the state constitution by the voters. Minimal levels of funding are required and, because school enrollments are forecast to grow at a faster rate than the tax base, the percentage of the state budget devoted to K–12 education by the year 2002 is estimated to increase from 36 to 47 percent. Also under pressure are health and welfare, amounting to 35 percent in 1994; higher education at 12 percent; corrections at 9 percent; and other government expenditures, also at 9 percent. Of these headings the two most vulnerable are those that have been declining as a proportion of overall expenditure in recent years: higher education, down from 17 percent to 12 percent over the last twenty-five years; and other government services, including pollution control, park, and other natural resource management, workplace safety assurance, and insurance industry regulation, which have fallen from a proportion of 12 percent of state expenditure in 1980 to 9 percent in 1994. Corrections, which have

risen threefold since 1980 to 9 percent of the total budget in 1994, are estimated to double again to 18 percent by 2002 to pay for the cost of three
strikes.

It would be a dispiriting outcome, to say the least, if the only practical
way to finance the theoretical maximum level of crime reduction was to cut
back on total spending on higher education, including the internationally renowned University of California, and other services by more than 40 percent
over the next eight years. Yet this was the prospect held out by the RAND
study. If the three strikes law remains in force unamended, by 2002 the state
government will be spending more money keeping people in prison than putting people through college. The probability, however, is that the legislators
who voted so fervently for three strikes will find it far less attractive politically
to fund its implementation in full. Developments yet to emerge may avoid the
most drastic outcomes, but only by accepting a lesser degree of crime protection than public opinion has been encouraged to anticipate. After the party
comes the reckoning.

VII

One of the recurring themes of this book is how often unintended effects
elsewhere in the criminal justice system follow hard on the heels of the implementation of populist-inspired legislation. Some of the trends take time to
identify and measure; others are more immediately apparent. In the early
months of 1995 two reports emanated from public sources in California. Both
told the same story. A survey by the Legislative Analyst's Office of the State
of California reviewed information collected over the first eight months of
operation of three strikes from local prosecutors, public defenders and defense
counsel, county jails, the State Board of Corrections, judges and trial court
administrators, the State Judicial Council, and the Department of Corrections.[67]
The survey indicated that large numbers of cases were being prosecuted under
the three strikes provisions. At the end of August 1994, six months after enactment, more than 7,400 second- and third-strike cases were filed. Los Angeles County, which generally accounted for up to half of the state's criminal
justice workload, indicated that at the end of November more than 5,000 sec-
ond- and third-strike cases had been filed with the courts.

The usually hidden significance of plea bargaining was starkly revealed
by the statistic that prior to the enactment of the three strikes law about 94
percent of all felony cases statewide were disposed of through plea bargaining.
Given the much longer sentences that defendants would face if convicted of a
second- or third-strike offense, public defenders and criminal defense attorneys
were advising their clients to refuse to plea bargain and take their cases to jury
trial, on any appearance in court on felony charges. As a result of the drop in
plea bargaining in many jurisdictions, a steep increase was forecast in the
number of jury trials. In Los Angeles County the District Attorney estimated
that jury trials would increase from 2,410 in 1994, roughly the number handled

annually since 1992, to 5,875 in 1995, an increase of 144 percent. More than half of the increase was expected to be third-strike cases. Unlike some other prosecutors, Gil Garcetti, the District Attorney for Los Angeles County, issued a directive that prosecutors pursue all eligible three strikes candidates.[68] In San Diego County the estimated increase in jury trials was 300 percent, and in Santa Clara County nearly 200 percent. Because so many more cases were going to trial there was an accumulation in the backlog of cases. This meant that some district attorneys were prosecuting fewer misdemeanor cases.

The impact on civil cases was even more marked. In October 1994 no civil cases were being tried in three of Los Angeles County's ten Superior Court districts. In addition, more than half of the fifty courtrooms in the central district that were normally used for civil cases were being diverted to criminal trials. By early 1995 the Los Angeles Superior Court anticipated that 60 of the 120 judges currently hearing civil cases would be redirected to criminal cases. The County estimated that in 1995 two-thirds to three-fourths of all courtrooms would be devoted to criminal trials. The displacement of civil litigation is likely to have far-reaching effects on the institutions of civil justice, accelerating the trend toward alternative forums for resolving disputes, such as arbitration or private judging, for those who can afford them.

More criminal cases coming to trial meant more pretrial detention in county jails. Because offenders charged under the three strikes law faced long prison sentences, most counties had set bail for second-strike defendants at twice the usual amount, and refused bail altogether for third strike defendants. By the end of 1994 Los Angeles County estimated that more than 1,000 three strikes inmates were housed in its jails awaiting trial. Other counties were forecasting the need for additional accommodation to house three strikes defendants in local jails pretrial. Since third-strike offenders faced the possibility of life in prison if convicted, they were treated as high-security inmates who had little to lose by assaulting staff or other inmates, or attempting to escape. High-security inmates called for closer supervision at greater cost than the general jail population. As a result of court-ordered population caps or federal mandates limiting jail overcrowding, the amount of available space in the jails was strictly limited.

In 1994 the institutions containing 70 percent of California's total supply of jail places were capped by court order. The only way to keep populations down and make room for the new arrivals was to release sentenced inmates. Before the enactment of three strikes, sentenced offenders in Los Angeles County generally served about two-thirds of their sentence before being released. After implementation, the percentage of the sentence served fell to about 45 percent. Before three strikes the County's jail population consisted of roughly 60 percent sentenced offenders and 40 percent pretrial inmates. After, the proportions reversed to 30 percent sentenced offenders and 70 percent pretrial offenders. This outcome was one that was directly contradictory to the intentions of those stentorian advocates of "truth in sentencing" who had so enthusiastically supported the policy of three strikes.

What were the criminal and personal characteristics of the offenders so far convicted and sentenced under three strikes law? The data in the survey showed that at the end of November 1994 there were 2,912 persons in state prisons having been convicted of a second-strike offense, and 63 convicted of a third strike. The low number of third-strike offenders was attributed to the large group of offenders going to trial and the backlog in those cases reaching the courts. Approximately 17 percent of the second-strike offenders had been convicted of violent offenses including robbery and first-degree burglary, and the remainder of lesser offenses, the main categories being possession of a controlled drug or petty theft with prior intent. The majority were male, 48 percent were in their twenties, 33 percent in their thirties, and 9 percent aged less than twenty. Thirty-seven percent were black, 33 percent Hispanic, and 26 percent white or another race. The report commented that these proportions were roughly comparable to the state's overall prison population. Of the third strike offenders, who faced a minimum sentence of twenty-five years to life in prison, only twenty of the sixty-three had been convicted of a serious or violent offense. The largest category was possession of a controlled drug.

And so it went on. What seemed on the political platform to be a straight-forward increase in penalties for the most dangerous and persistent of criminals had consequences that ran right through the system of justice. Another report, in March 1995,[69] came from the Three Strikes Impact Subcommittee to the County of Los Angeles Countywide Criminal Justice Coordination Committee. It confirmed that although the law had been in effect for only one year, the data showed that the justice system was "seriously out of balance" and that the primary cause was the number of strike cases that were going to trial. They were staying in the system longer and costing more to handle. Virtually every level of criminal justice from the point of arrest to completion of sentence was being impaired. In his covering letter the chairman of the subcommittee[70] said that "As strike cases increasingly demand greater and greater resources, the system's capacity to handle other workload, such as the processing of civil cases, minor felonies and misdemeanors, will dramatically decline. These collateral impacts of three strikes may be almost as significant as the direct impacts."

In November 1995 the subcommittee produced its final report on the impact of the three strikes law in the County of Los Angeles. Despite early concerns that the justice system would suddenly burst from the pressure of a rising floodtide of felony cases, the system had not collapsed or self-destructed. Nevertheless, the report made it "inescapably clear," that "the structure was weakening and that major cracks were leading to serious and unacceptable breaches in the system of justice." Without some level of relief in the immediate future, the chairman of the subcommittee forecast, there would "continue to be a rapid decline in both the quantity and quality of justice system services."[71] The effects of shifting resources to criminal trials at the expense of civil justice was again brought out. Civil litigation was not exclusively about money matters. Personal injury cases and orders restraining harassment and violence were also the subject of civil litigation. The Superior Court had constitutional statutory obligations to provide a civil justice system for the citizens of Los Angeles County that it could not fulfill if the criminal trial workload continued to reduce the availability of civil courts.[72]

VIII

Although it is inevitable that there will be an element of special pleading in reports of this nature in order to justify the allocation of a greater share of shrinking financial resources in competition with other publicly funded services, their authors were entitled to draw to the attention of the public to the practical consequences of the three strikes law. Once in force the new sentencing regime exemplified the always precarious triangular relationship between politics, law, and justice. As usual, politics first commanded the front of the stage. Coinciding with trends becoming apparent elsewhere in the United States, violent crime in California showed a welcome downturn, which supporters of the three strikes policy were quick to attribute to the effects of the new law. "There is just no way to ignore the positive impact of the Three Strikes law," said the Attorney General, Daniel Lungren, one of its strongest proponents. "California's drop in crime (a decrease of 6.6 percent in reported offenses of violence over the first six months of 1995) is outperforming similar downward trends in other parts of the nation."[73] Only later did more detailed research findings establish the inconvenient pattern that in 1994–95 violent and overall crime rates dropped more steeply in states without three strikes than in those that had adopted the policy. Of the thirteen states that had three strikes laws in place in 1994, California was by far the most significant because of its size. In eight of the others increases rather than decreases in violent crime were reported over the same period.[74]

Apart from the typically barren exchanges on causes and effects, a conflict arose when the priorities accorded by the governor and the California legislature to a generalized view of the measures necessary to protect the safety of the public, supported by the outcome of the referendum on Proposition 184, collided with the circumstances of individual defendants and the principles of proportionality in sentencing. The major weakness of the formulation that had been adopted was that the third strike, which triggered a mandatory sentence of twenty-five years to life in prison, could be for a lesser offense if prosecuted as a felony. The theft of a slice of pizza, or a pound of meat, or a shirt from a store, all actual cases, were examples often cited. Unlike the prior two strikes, the third felony did not have to be either violent or serious.

Plea bargaining, the oil that previously had kept the wheels of justice turning, was not available, either on the second strike activating a sentence of double the normal for the offense, or on the third strike. For over a century, however, the California Penal Code had contained a relatively unnoticed judicial power for the trial court to dismiss an action "in furtherance of justice," either on the motion of the prosecutor or at the discretion of the court. The power did not sit easily with the earlier manifestations of mandatory sentencing in the state, and its scope had been narrowed by the legislature in 1986.[75] But it had survived, emerging into public view in June 1996 when the California Supreme Court upheld a decision of the Superior Court in San Diego striking two prior felony convictions that otherwise would have led to the automatic imposition of a sentence of twenty-five years to life on a man who had been charged with being in possession of a very small amount of a controlled substance, namely 0.13 grams of cocaine base.[76]

Jesus Romero, the defendant, had the characteristics of a minor recidivist. He had been convicted of second-degree burglary in 1980, of the attempted burglary of an inhabited dwelling in 1984, and of first-degree burglary of an inhabited dwelling in 1986. He also had prior convictions of possessing a controlled substance in 1993 and 1994. Two of the burglary offenses made him eligible for the automatic third strike penalty of twenty-five years to life if he reoffended. On its own, the instant drug offense would have been punishable by sixteen months, two years, or three years in a state prison. Under current sentencing law, the three prior burglaries or attempted burglaries, for which he had served prison terms, would have resulted in three consecutive one-year enhancements being added to the basic term for the drug possession offense.

At his trial Romero pled not guilty. The trial court at a subsequent hearing indicated its willingness to consider striking the prior felony convictions if the defendant changed his plea to guilty. The prosecutor objected, arguing that the court had no power to dismiss prior felonies in a three strikes case, unless the prosecutor asked the court to do so. The court disagreed, reasoning that to interpret the three strikes law in this way would violate the constitutional doctrine of separation of powers by leaving the power solely in the hands of the executive. Having warned the defendant that the court was making no promises, it permitted him to change his plea and struck the two prior felonies. After considering the prosecutor's arguments, the defendant's criminal history, and the scale of punishment in similar cases, the court imposed a sentence of six years in state prison. The District Attorney successfully appealed the decision to the Court of Appeal, which concluded that the trial court had no power to dismiss the prior felonies on its own motion in a three strikes case. A writ was issued requiring the trial court to vacate the sentence and permit the defendant to withdraw his plea. The California Supreme Court then granted Romero's petition for review.

After a lengthy discussion on the separation-of-powers issue, the Supreme Court decided unanimously that because the three strikes statute did not contain a clear legislative direction to the contrary, the trial court retained its discretion under the furtherance of justice power to dismiss alleged prior felonies. While broad, the power was by no means absolute. In the absence of any statutory definition, the courts had been faced with the task of establishing the boundaries of judicial power, and had been guided by a large body of useful precedent. The concept of furtherance of justice required consideration both of the constitutional rights of the defendant and the interests of society represented by the people. A court would abuse its discretion if it dismissed a case, or struck a prior conviction, solely to accommodate judicial convenience or because of court congestion. Nor could it do so simply because a defendant pled guilty, or because of a personal antipathy on the part of a judge to the effect of a sentencing policy on a defendant, ignoring the defendant's background, the nature of the offenses charged, and other individualized considerations. Reasons had to be given, and they were subject to appellate review.

The decision of the Supreme Court in *Romero* was immediately repudiated as a weakening of the three strikes law by its original sponsors and advocates. Governor Wilson stated his intention to find a way either to amend the law or to seek a referendum to restore its teeth. "Those who repeatedly assault our citizens, terrorize our elderly and prey on our children must pay a severe price for their crimes," he said. "I intend to keep faith with the people of California who have every right to demand protection against career criminals and predators."[77] The Secretary of State, Bill Jones, a cosponsor of the original law (AB 971), and the Assembly Speaker, Curt Pringle, lost no time in announcing their plans to find a legislative way to plug what they saw as a new and dangerous hole in the three strikes law. "The justices showed that they are more interested in defending the turf of the bench than they are about protecting the safety of Californians," Jones proclaimed, indifferent to the reputation of a majority of the justices on the state Supreme Court as being generally sympathetic toward law-and-order approaches.[78] "By granting judges the unilateral ability to impose weak sentences," he continued, "the justices have ignored the mandate from the voters that repeat felons be held accountable for their entire criminal careers."[79]

The supercharged politics of instant response continued when supporters of the original three strikes law began to draft legislation to undo the Supreme Court's decision on the same day it was rendered.[80] The resulting amendment to limit judicial discretion was passed by the Assembly without any difficulty, and arrived in the Senate early in July 1996. The aim of the legislation (SB 331) was to prohibit a court from striking a defendant's prior serious or violent felony convictions for the purposes of avoiding sentencing enhancements under three strikes, either on its own motion or upon application of the prosecuting attorney unless certain conditions were fulfilled. These followed some general declaratory propositions, including the intent of the legislature in amending and reenacting three strikes not to acquiesce in, nor to adopt, the holdings or reasoning of court decisions interpreting the existing provisions of three strikes statutes.

Once the largely rhetorical preliminaries had been got out of the way, the bill moved in the direction of ameliorating some of the problems occurring in the administration of the three strikes law that had come to public notice as a result of the *Romero* decision, and other cases of clearly disproportionate punishment. Under the terms of the bill, a court would have discretion to strike a defendant's prior serious or violent felony conviction, upon motion of the prosecuting attorney or upon its own motion, only if three requirements were met. They were that none of the defendant's prior convictions were for a violent felony, as defined; that the defendant's current conviction was not for a serious or violent felony; and that the current offense occurred more than five years after the defendant's release from custody for, or conviction of, a serious felony, whichever was the later.

Although under this formula it was likely that some less serious offenders would have been spared from the inflexible inequities of a sentencing law designed to penalize the more serious and violent offenders, the bill became mired in controversy from which it had not escaped by mid-1997. An extra impediment to enactment was that because the bill would amend the three strikes initiative statutes, it required a two-thirds vote of the membership of each house before it could be passed into law. Unless and until the legislature musters sufficient votes to change the law, discretionary action by the courts "in furtherance of justice" lives on in California.

Chapter 4

Partisanship and Compromise

I

By the time that the legislators returned to Washington for the Second Session of the 103rd Congress in late January 1994, they had seen concern about crime climb in the polls and had been reminded of its compelling importance to their electorates. In the House of Representatives, congressmen were vocal in declaring that legislation on crime was a top priority.[1] The President embraced the popular sense of urgency. In his State of the Union Address, Clinton characterized the problem of violence as an American problem without any partisan or philosophical element. He admonished members of Congress "to find ways as quickly as possible to set aside partisan differences and pass a strong, smart, tough crime bill."[2] In endorsing the three strikes law, and mentioning Polly Klaas by name, he drew the longest ovation for his speech. The rapidity of Clinton's conversion to the policy of three strikes owed more to the promptings of his private pollsters than the caution of the Department of Justice.[3] Biden for one was taken by surprise, having only shortly before dismissed the three strikes policy as "wacky."

Despite the stirring language, what was smart and what was tough were linked only in rhetoric. In practice there were bound to be conflicts. The dilemma was illustrated with embarrassing clarity by the Deputy Attorney General, Philip Heymann, an experienced criminal lawyer and administrator who had served four previous Attorneys General at the Department of Justice.[4] On the day before the State of the Union speech, Heymann announced his resignation, citing differences in management style with the Attorney General, Janet Reno. But, as became only too clear at a news conference called when vacating office on February 15 and in later public statements, he had become disenchanted with the way the administration had responded to public pressures and the legislative compromises required by Congress. Accepting that the omnibus crime bill passed by the Senate and awaiting consideration by the House had many useful provisions, he said that the ones getting most attention showed a legislature "swept far from common sense by the heavy winds of political rhetoric about crime." In an article for the *Washington Post* Heymann wrote:

> The reason the Congress does these things and President Clinton supports them is, of course, straightforward. Fear is a powerful emotion in constituents. Pretending to retaliate fiercely against the source of fear has been politically popular in every country for a very long time. There is less of a market for real remedies than for patent medicines. Thus, there are dozens of new death penalties in the Senate bill, but they are largely irrelevant to any realistic law enforcement effort. They sound tough, and we as a nation are very sick of violence. The only problem is that the prescription won't improve the patient's condition.[5]

He was equally scathing about the populist motivation behind three strikes; the unintended effects of previous congressional attempts to control drug abuse by setting minimum mandatory sentences of imprisonment in federal prisons for drug dealing; and the D'Amato amendment for blurring the lines between state and federal law enforcement. In a press interview the previous week Heymann had elaborated on the conflict between toughness and smartness:

> Crime is one of the great political issues in most Western democracies. It generally breaks down along partisan lines. We're seeing a time when it's being handled in a nonpartisan way, with both parties competing to be as firm and tough on crime as they can be. I don't have any objection to that, but you can't be both the toughest and the smartest.
>
> President Clinton said he wanted to be tough but smart. If you want to be decently smart and exercise some common sense, you can't be tougher than anybody who's competing for toughness. The toughest guy will say one strike, and you're out. Or the toughest guy will say, build 10 times more prisons.
>
> So the difficult trick is how to be smart as well as tough in a political environment that rewards toughness more than smartness. The reason for that is it takes a little while to explain why one thing's smart and the other thing isn't. It doesn't take any time at all to explain why one thing's tougher than the next.[6]

Heymann spoke generously of Reno's ability to change the way people talked about violence by adding the prevention dimension, instancing her interest in child development. But at the Justice Department she had been hampered by lack of familiarity with the workings of the federal system of government. She had come in as and, in his opinion, continued to think like, the chief prosecutor of a major urban area.[7] On matters of criminal policy, communications between the White House and the Department of Justice were too informal, without any clearly established structure at either end. The Associate Attorney General, Webster Hubbell, another outsider who had been brought to Washington by Clinton,[8] acted as the main point of contact, but he was no substitute for the regular consultation needed to ensure that policies were developed in a systematic way in the Department with an awareness of the views of the White House at each stage. The delay in getting an Attorney General into post inhibited further the Department's role at the formative stage when decisions were being taken on the scope of the legislation. Reno had not been the President's first choice, two earlier nominees having withdrawn.[9] As a consequence, there had been a two-and-a-half-month interregnum until her confirmation by the Senate on March 11, 1993. During this period the Department was left in the hands of Stuart Gerson, a Republican appointee of the Bush administration.[10]

Even without these organizational and personal weaknesses, it is unlikely that the Department of Justice would have been able to accomplish much more than fine tuning in the preparation of the legislation. Many of the detailed provisions had been a long time in the making and were the product of previous compromises. Bargains had been struck between competing interests and alliances forged. As already noted, Clinton had made known to Biden and Brooks his intention to depart from the practice of his Republican predecessors, who had sent draft bills prepared by the administration to Congress by way of an executive communication. The alternative of a single crime bill or, if that was not feasible, broadly similar bills sponsored by the two Judiciary Committee chairmen, building on the report of the conference on the Bush crime bill, which had failed to pass the Senate in October 1992, appeared to hold out the promise of swift passage of an electorally attractive measure by a Congress in which the Democrats had a majority in each chamber.

Clinton was not the first, or last, election winner to feel a compulsion to produce quick results. The Republicans, after gaining control of both Houses in the midterm elections in November 1994, similarly had as their immediate priority bringing ten bills to the floor of the House of Representatives for a vote in the first hundred days of the 104th Congress, so honoring a pledge by 367 candidates in their manifesto, the *Contract with America*. The subsequent course of events is the topic of chapter 6.

The President's strategy averted the prospect of lengthy and potentially divisive prelegislative negotiations between at least four participants. In addition to the White House and the Justice Department, with inadequate coordinating machinery in place, there were two powerful factions in the Democratic

Party in Congress: the moderate mainstream, with Senator Biden in the lead, and the more ideologically committed liberals such as Senator Howard Metzenbaum of Ohio and Representative Don Edwards, dean of the California delegation in the House. On the liberal wing, the Congressional Black Caucus stood as a cohesive and influential grouping, and one with its own agenda. Although personally respected, the Attorney General, with her reserved style and deliberative cast of mind, had little time to make her mark on Capitol Hill. In any event Reno was awkwardly placed being on record as pro–gun control, opposed to the death penalty, and supportive of social programs aimed at addressing the root causes of crime. To a legislature so attentive to special interests and populist opinion, such clear-cut beliefs could too easily be caricatured as liabilities. However improbable it seemed, she secured an early tactical advantage by striking up a cordial working relationship with the influential chairman of the House Judiciary Committee, Jack Brooks.

The reasons for the lack of progress in the House of Representatives and the substantial additions made by the Senate in the autumn of 1993 were described in the previous chapters. By the opening of the Second Session, members of the Democratic Caucus in the House were still at odds on several of the key issues after the President had addressed the joint session of both Houses of Congress at the end of January 1994. Keenly aware of the expectations of their constituents, most of them wanted to make progress, although not at any price. Brooks was in no hurry. A crusty and irascible Democrat of the old school from Texas, he was in his forty-second, and as it turned out last, year in Congress. At the age of seventy-one and in failing health, he was no great enthusiast for crime control legislation, having seen so many attempts founder in the past, and was accustomed to moving cautiously. Moreover, he was out of step with a majority of Democrats on the Judiciary Committee in being opposed to gun control on which he wanted a vote on a separate bill later. Brooks was sceptical of the Senate's proposal for a trust fund to pay for community policing and other programs and ensured that it was omitted from the House bill. Although his seniority, second in a House of 435 representatives, conferred power, by March the effective leadership on the bill had come to be shared in an uneasy partnership with the chairman of the Crime and Criminal Justice Subcommittee of the Judiciary Committee, Charles Schumer.

Representing an inner-city congressional district, Brooklyn, in New York, Schumer was a contrast to Brooks in almost every sense. At forty-three he was energetic, ambitious, and keenly publicity conscious. He was more liberal in outlook, although prepared to compromise when necessary to achieve results. He also had the benefit of being a close friend and political ally of Leon Panetta, named as chief of staff at the White House at the end of June. Although some of the larger issues, such as grants to states or multistate alliances to help them build prisons or expand existing facilities, and racial justice and death row appeals, were the province of other subcommittees, the lion's share fell to Schumer's subcommittee to mark up.

The agenda was formidable: the extension in the number of federal crimes to which the death penalty would apply; mandatory sentencing and three strikes; the trial of juveniles aged thirteen and older as adults for certain violent crimes; community services to reduce crime; and, most controversial of all, the ban on assault weapons. On March 10 and 11 the three House Judiciary subcommittees tackled the main proposals. Several of the key features were approved, although often in an amended form, including more than fifty new federal death penalty offenses, aid from federal funds for state prison construction, the prosecution of juveniles as adults in certain circumstances, and a range of youth and community programs designed to prevent crime.

II

That potentially so bothersome an issue as three strikes was resolved with so little difficulty owed much to the improved liaison between the administration and the Congress. Responding to representations by the Democratic leadership, Clinton had sent a member of the White House staff to the Justice Department with a mandate to coordinate the administration's position on the new issues that continued to arise over the crime legislation. Although only in his early thirties, Ronald Klain was ideally fitted for the job.[11] Two years' clerking for Justice Byron White at the Supreme Court had been followed by appointment at the unusually early age of twenty-seven as chief counsel to the Senate Judiciary Committee. There, under Biden's chairmanship,[12] he had a hand in the evolution of the crime bills of the early 1990s, which had come to nothing. Joining Clinton's campaign staff for the presidential election, Klain had helped to develop the community policing project. At the White House he was put in charge of judicial appointment evaluations in the office of the Counsel to the President. His keen political instincts, firsthand knowledge of Clinton's methods, access to the President and his advisers, and experience of congressional lawmaking, were exactly the qualities absent from the Attorney General's Office.

At the Department of Justice, Klain was located strategically in Reno's office with the title of counselor. They had established a constructive understanding dating from the time of her confirmation, and Reno had invited him to join her staff soon after. At that stage he could not be spared from his judicial selection duties. By February, with discontent growing over the handling of the crime bill, the President was ready to agree to Klain's transfer "to have a voice singing off our song book."[13] The impact was immediate. "Before [Klain] came over," one House Democrat was quoted as saying, "you couldn't get the Administration to move on any of those issues. Justice and the White House weren't talking and didn't trust each other. Everyone would 'yes' you. Nothing would happen."[14]

Three strikes was an issue well suited to Klain's presentational and political skills. It chimed with his mission to associate Clinton with a strong anti-crime position. It had attracted widespread public support. But officials at the Justice Department were aware that in its more extreme manifestations three strikes had the capacity to backfire on the administration. The unintended consequences of mandatory sentencing in terms of nonselectivity of offenders, cost, and the effects on prosecutors, courts, and prisons were only too familiar. As the California experience had shown, the crucial decisions turned on the definition of a strike. Should it include offenses against property, or should it be confined to offenses involving drugs or violence? If violent offenses only, should all offenses against the person qualify, or only the most serious offenses? What should be the definition of seriousness? Would the public perception permit the exclusion of drug offenses? How was a repeat offender, the "career criminal" of popular legend, to become eligible to play in this game of criminal baseball? Apart from drug offenses, relatively few crimes are tried in the federal district courts. But recidivism pays little regard to the jurisdiction under which the defendant is prosecuted. If the legislation was to have any practical meaning was it necessary to treat as strikes previous convictions in state courts, and if so, for what offenses? Should there be a provision allowing the release from prison of convicted three strikes inmates over the age of sixty who were sick or no longer dangerous?

Heymann was quoted as saying that he did not think anybody in the Justice Department knew about the three strikes proposal before Clinton mentioned it in the State of the Union.[15] Klain came to the Department determined to prioritize action on the President's announcement. He was fortunate in that there were no existing decisions to endorse or repudiate. The objective was straightforward and expedient: to gain for the administration the political kudos without paying an undue price. With the support of the like-minded Schumer, whose subcommittee would need to endorse the President's proposal, and working closely with his old colleague, Cynthia Hogan, by now chief counsel of the Senate Judiciary Committee,[16] Klain evolved a minimalist approach. So long as the White House language was preserved, the three strikes law could be narrowly defined, concentrating on incarcerating the genuinely dangerous and incorrigible offenders, safeguarding federal resources, and respecting the right of states to prosecute and sentence those convicted of committing crimes within their jurisdictions. It was a remarkable indication of the skill and political judgment represented in the drafting that, once the preferred formulation had been agreed by the House subcommittee, the three strikes proposal, for all its high profile, attracted so little controversy or even debate in Congress.

The wording that was enacted in due course as section 70001 of Public Law 103-322[17] provided that a person convicted in a court of the United States (i.e., a federal court) of a serious violent felony should be sentenced to life imprisonment if the person had been convicted on separate prior occasions either in a federal or state court of two or more serious violent felonies, or one or more serious violent felonies and one or more serious drug offense. A serious violent felony was defined as meaning a federal or state offense of murder, manslaughter other than involuntary manslaughter, assault with intent to commit murder or rape, aggravated sexual abuse and some other serious sex crimes, kidnapping, aircraft piracy, robbery involving the use or threat of a firearm or other dangerous weapon, extortion, arson posing a threat to human life, firearms use, and certain offenses of carjacking. Attempts, conspiracy, or solicitation to commit any of the designated offenses would qualify as strikes.[18]

Robbery, where no firearm or other offensive weapon was used or threatened and the offense did not result in death or serious bodily injury, or arson, where the offense posed no threat to human life and the defendant reasonably believed that his or her act posed no such threat, were specifically excluded.[19] Serious drug offenses, which did not qualify for the third strike, were those defined in existing federal or state law of manufacturing, distributing, or dispensing certain quantities of drugs, or possessing them with the intent to do so; or committing a narcotics felony that was part of a continuing series of narcotics crimes in which at least five persons engaged in drug dealing were supervised and substantial revenue was derived. Although no one could forecast with any confidence the total number of persons likely to be sentenced to mandatory life imprisonment by federal courts under this carefully drawn formulation, the estimate of the Justice Department, based on statistics maintained by the U.S. Sentencing Commission, was in the region of two hundred per year.[20] The Bureau of Prisons could breathe again.

Despite the political imperative of making a gesture on three strikes, the impact of mandatory sentencing was a mounting cause of concern within the Department of Justice, as well as to some members of Congress. In February 1994, a report prepared by the Deputy Attorney General's office, with the assistance of the Bureau of Prisons, analyzed in detail the effects of mandatorily sentenced low-level drug offenders in the federal prisons. The work had been completed the previous August, but release of the findings had been delayed, in Heymann's belief because of apprehension in the White House that its contents might be misconstrued.[21] Since 1980 the population in the federal prisons had more than tripled, from 24,000 in 1980 to more than 90,000 in December 1993. Much of the increase was due to far longer mandatory minimum sentences for drug law violations and offenses involving firearms. Sixty percent of inmates in federal prisons were drug offenders compared with 18 percent in 1980.

The report showed that 16,316 prisoners, amounting to 36.1 percent of all drug law offenders in the federal prison system, and 21.2 percent of the total sentenced population, could be considered as low-level drug offenders. The criteria were no recorded current or prior offenses of violence, no involvement in sophisticated criminal activity, and no prior commitment.[22] The average sentence of this group of prisoners with relatively low levels of criminality was 81.5 months. Under federal sentencing guidelines that meant the individuals would serve on average at least five and three-quarter years before release from prison. Among low-level drug offenders, 42.3 percent were couriers or played peripheral roles in drug trafficking.[23] Drug quantity was the dominant determinant of sentence lengths, and defendants with minor functional roles received sentences that overlapped with defendants with much more significant roles.[24]

In the Senate a bipartisan coalition formed between Democrats and Republicans, on grounds of fairness (Senators Simon and Kennedy) and pragmatism (Senator Thurmond) to promote the notion of a "safety valve." This was a device to leave existing mandatory sentencing laws in place, but to allow low-level, nonviolent, and first-time offenders to be sentenced under the federal sentencing guidelines rather than the mandatory drug laws. Schumer, adept at the interplay of politics and substance in lawmaking, was attracted by the idea. He proposed a variation to the House Subcommittee on Crime and Criminal Justice that would waive the mandatory minimum sentencing requirements for first-time, low-level drug defendants if they had cooperated with the government in providing information about the offense or offenses with which they were charged.

Initially the White House was uncertain whether to give the proposal its backing, but shortly after Klain's arrival at the Justice Department the administration came out in favor of the safety valve. By June, a detailed commentary containing the views of the Department sent to Brooks and Biden by the Attorney General urged the conferees to adopt an exception to drug law mandatory penalties for certain low-level, nonviolent offenders without serious records. Although not going so far as agreeing that the proposal should be retroactive, and applied to inmates already serving a prison term, the House proposal was commended as "a sound step toward insuring that our limited Federal prison space is used to incarcerate violent and dangerous offenders for the long sentences they deserve."[25] If the language used was closer to that of Thurmond than Kennedy, the two former Senate Judiciary Committee chairmen who had worked together on the sentencing guidelines ten years before, the change was a first step toward a reform that was overdue on grounds of principle as well as practicality.[26]

To qualify for sentencing under guidelines promulgated by the U.S. Sentencing Commission without regard to any statutory minimum sentence, five requirements would have to be satisfied. They were that the defendant had no more than one criminal history point; that no violence had been used or threatened, nor had any firearm or other dangerous weapon been in the defendant's possession in connection with the offense; that the offense did not result in death or serious bodily injury to any person; that the defendant was not an organizer, leader, manager, or supervisor of others involved in the offense, nor engaged in a continuing criminal enterprise; and that the defendant had truthfully provided the government with all information and evidence concerning the offense or offenses. Although never publicly acknowledged, there was a tacit understanding that the safety valve was a counterweight to give something to those liberal Democrats who were unhappy about the extension of mandatory sentencing implicit in three strikes.

III

The full House Judiciary Committee met on March 14 and approved thirteen separate anti-crime bills dealing with death penalty sentencing and appeals, insurance fraud, violence against children, sexual abuse of children, community crime prevention programs, crime victim protection and compensation, repeat offenders (the three strikes policy), mandatory minimum sentencing, and trying juveniles as adults. Subsequently these bills were combined into a single bill (H.R. 4092). The debate on the floor of the House began on April 13 and continued over two weeks. Most of the provisions in H.R. 4092 were retained, with the exception of the habeas corpus reforms that had been dropped already by the Senate. The bill was passed on April 21 by 285 to 141 votes, renumbered H.R. 3355, and sent to a conference of representatives of each chamber to resolve the differences between the versions passed by the House and the Senate.

One outstanding issue was omitted from H.R. 3355. The ban, accepted by the Senate in November, on the manufacture, transfer, and possession of nineteen semiautomatic assault weapons had been held over for fear it would jeopardize agreement being reached on the other provisions of the House anticrime package. Two weeks later, on May 5, in an atmosphere of high drama, the House of Representatives voted on a bill incorporating a similar prohibition (H.R. 4296). Brooks had given prior notice of his intention to throw all his weight against the bill. He expressed the reasons forcefully:

> I am strongly opposed to H.R. 4296 . . . because it misidentifies the causes of violent crime in the United States; diverts national priorities away from meaningful solutions to the problem of violent crime; punishes honest American gun owners who buy and use firearms for legitimate, lawful purposes such as, but not necessarily limited to, self-defense, target shooting, hunting, and firearms collection; fails to focus the punitive powers of government upon criminals. Most fundamentally, a prohibition on firearms violates the right of individual Americans to keep and bear arms, protected by the Second Amendment to the Constitution of the United States—a stark fact of constitutional life that the proponents of H.R. 4296 conveniently overlook in their zeal to abridge the rights of law-abiding citizens.[27]

Many other Democrats shared Brooks's doctrinaire dissent, as did a majority of Republicans. On an issue that polarized opinions as sharply as gun control there was limited scope for persuasion. Unusual as it is for a senator to lobby members of the House, Feinstein and her staff had been hard at work. An agonized handful of Democrats remained undecided until the very last moment. One of them, Andrew Jacobs of Indiana, had cast his vote against the ban, but then reversed it while the vote was being taken on the floor, explaining that his original vote had been based on a misunderstanding. He thought that he would have another chance to vote against the large magazines on assault weapons, but when he realized he was mistaken he switched his vote. Another representative did the same. Moments afterward, the last three undecided members cast their votes: two were in favor and one against. Seventy-six Democrats joined Brooks in voting against the bill, while Schumer, after intense lobbying, won the support of 177 Democratic representatives.

Republican members of the House were divided: 137 voting against the measure, with 38 Republicans and 1 independent supporting it. The outcome could hardly have been closer: 216 voting for the bill and 214 against, with 2 members not voting.[28]

The result had been impossible to predict. Even as he watched the voting, Schumer expected to lose. In his comments immediately afterward he said that Clinton's support had been invaluable. The President had telephoned members until midnight the previous day, and had resumed his calls in the morning, continuing until the vote was taken. Clinton himself told reporters of a conversation with a Democrat who had been a longtime supporter of the NRA: "After I hung up the phone—that was right at the beginning of the vote—I said: You know, we might just pull this off." He recognized that it had taken "extraordinary courage" by the members of the House who had stood up for the national interest.[29]

The President was not the only Cabinet member to put his shoulder to the wheel. The Treasury Secretary, Lloyd Bentsen, formerly a senator from Texas and Democratic nominee for the vice presidency in 1988, was recruited after his services had been offered by his chief of staff, one of the same cohort as Klain. As a gun owner well-known and respected in Congress, Bentsen was able to provide cover for other gun owners who wanted to vote for the ban, but feared political repercussions from the NRA. In the pursuit of wider exposure in the press for their chief than he was receiving, his staff saw a role for Bentsen in helping to sell the administration's crime package. No longer dependent on electoral support in Texas, where to be pro–gun control was regarded as certain death at the polls, the former senator agreed. A coordinated public relations initiative was then mounted to portray the old congressional warrior in a new light, making sure that he had an assault weapon in his hand, and was accessible to photographers, every day for a week. "It would really be very useful," his chief of staff ruminated, "for Bentsen to be seen going up the stairs of the Capitol, flanked by police officers. We ended up bringing in a group of police officers to line the steps of the Capitol. Bentsen and Schumer came down, shaking hands and schmoozing. It made for great visuals on TV. It made the front page of *US Today*."[30]

Apart from the impact of media-oriented politics, it was direct electoral intervention, the NRA's strongest card, that may have lost them the vote. Douglas Applegate (Dem. Ohio), previously one of the Association's firmest backers, had voted for the Brady bill the previous year. After eighteen year's membership, he was retiring from the House of Representatives at the end of the 103rd Congress. When his chief aide sought to replace him, the NRA endorsed his opponent in the primary, who won. Applegate was reported as telling his friends in his home state that the gun lobby had distorted his record after years of loyalty, and that his vote for the ban on assault weapons was partly in protest.[31] From a different quarter, the Congressional Black Caucus put pressure on another past supporter of the NRA, a Democrat from Georgia, to vote with them for the ban, and eventually he did.

IV

Throughout June and July the CBC occupied center stage in the proceedings on the crime bill. The wrong done to African-Americans, as seen by the Caucus, that most urgently needed righting in the legislation was racially discriminatory capital sentencing. Although previously raised in debates on the 1988 legislation, no proposals had been brought forward by the administration, nor did they feature in the original bills introduced in either chamber. But racial justice was one of the foremost components of the alternative crime bill (H.R. 3315 introduced in the previous October by the CBC, with support from some influential nonblack Democrats.[32] At a later stage, as a result of pressure from the Caucus, it was incorporated in the House version of the bill that went to the conference. For many black and Hispanic representatives it was the top priority. To them, as to other legislators, symbolism was all-important.

Resentment over the imposition of the death penalty, especially in the Southern states, had been building up for a long time. The argument advanced by some scholarly critics as well as by black activists, was that sentencing for homicide was unduly influenced by the race of the defendant and/or the race of the victim. Statistics on disparities in sentence were marshaled to support the contention that capital sentencing, in Georgia at least, was administered in a way that was racially discriminatory and in violation of the Eighth and Fourteenth Amendments of the U.S. Constitution. The issue came to a head in 1986 when the Supreme Court considered a petition from a death row prisoner named McCleskey.[33] The statistical disparity between the treatment of whites and nonwhites had been before the Court in a different context in 1976.[34] In a case brought by unsuccessful black applicants for employment as police officers by the District of Columbia, the Supreme Court held that although invidious discrimination on the basis of race was unconstitutional, it did not follow that a law or other official act was unconstitutional solely because it had a racially disproportionate impact, regardless of whether it reflected a racially discriminatory purpose.[35]

In its finding on McCleskey's petition the Court rejected the constitutional significance of racial disparities in the imposition of the death sentence, upholding Georgia's death penalty statute, and finding that the statistics alone were not sufficient to show purposeful discrimination in the adoption, maintenance, or administration of the death penalty statute. McCleskey's defense was handled by the NAACP Legal Defense and Educational Fund, which had enlisted Professor David Baldus and a team of his colleagues from the University of Iowa to undertake a methodologically sophisticated study of death sentencing in Georgia. The study was funded by the Edna McConnell Clark Foundation of New York.[36]

Delivering the opinion of the court, Justice Powell accepted the existence of a discrepancy that appeared to correlate with the race of the victim, and assumed the statistical validity of the study used in support of McCleskey's claim.[37] But he observed, "our assumption that the Baldus study is statistically

valid does not include the assumption that the study shows that racial considerations actually enter into any sentencing decisions in Georgia.''[38] The court
held that the statistics did not prove, nor did they claim to prove, that race
entered into any capital sentencing decisions, or that race was a factor in
McCleskey's particular case.[39] Despite a widespread perception to the contrary,
especially in black communities, the study did not show any markedly disproportionate link between a defendant's race and the likelihood of his being
sentenced to death.

To circumvent the requirement of proof that a legislature, prosecutor,
judge, or jury had acted with racially invidious and discriminatory motives the
CBC drafted the racial justice title which formed part of H.R. 3315. Finding
words to express in law the strength of their conviction, and of others who
shared it, had not been easy. There was a conceptual difficulty to be overcome
in that the circumstances of each case were different and that no one case
could be compared with another. The drafting of what was cited as the Racial
Justice Act was amended over the months that it was in the House of Representatives, but the aim was to recognize the need for justice to be done by
providing a remedy for a defendant who could show that the facts of his case
fitted a pattern of racial disparity. Prosecutors, some of the more vocal of
whom lost little time in declaring their opposition to the proposal, would have
a chance to rebut claims of racial bias, with the decision being made by the
judge on the preponderance of the evidence. The provision would apply to
past as well as future cases.

In the final version, the opening section stated that ''[n]o person shall be
put to death under color of State or Federal law in the execution of a sentence
that was imposed based on race.'' An inference that race was the basis of a
death sentence would be established if valid evidence was presented demonstrating that, at the time the death sentence was imposed, race was a statistically
significant factor in decisions to seek or impose the sentence of death. Evidence
relevant to establish such an inference might include evidence that death sentences were being imposed significantly more frequently in the jurisdiction in
question upon persons of one race than on persons of another race. If statistical
evidence was presented to establish an inference that race was the basis of the
sentence of death, the court would be required to determine its validity and
whether it provided a basis for the inference.

The evidence would have to take into account, to the extent it was compiled and publicly made available, evidence of the statutory aggravating factors
of the crimes involved, including comparisons of similar cases involving persons of different races. In seeking to rebut an inference the prosecution would
have to show that the death penalty was sought in all cases fitting the statutory
criteria for the imposition of the death penalty. It could not rely on mere
assertions that it did not intend to discriminate, or that the cases in which death
was imposed fitted the statutory criteria. An additional procedural precaution
had been designed to reinforce the protection against discrimination in the
imposition of the death penalty. The effect would be that in a hearing before

a jury, having been instructed by the judge before returning their finding, each juror would be required to sign a certificate that no consideration of the race, color, religious beliefs, national origin, or sex of either the defendant or any victim had influenced him or her in reaching a decision.

On April 20, the day before the House omnibus bill (H.R. 3355) was passed, an attempt to strike out the Racial Justice Act was narrowly defeated by five votes. The voting was 212 for the amendment, 217 against, with 9 not voting.[40] Over the previous months opposition to the racial justice provision had been spreading. The National Association of Attorneys General, the National District Attorneys'' Association, and the American Legislative Exchange Council, an educational and research organization for state legislators, had all come out against it. Most Republicans and a sizeable group of Democrats supported the amendment by Representative Bill McCollum (Florida), the ranking Republican on the International Law, Immigration and Refugees Subcommittee of the Judiciary Committee, who argued that the Racial Justice Act would create an inference of racial discrimination on the basis of death penalty statistics. That inference was one the prosecutor would have to overcome. He forecast that the result would be to undermine the death penalty, establish racial quotas for capital punishment, and lead to more litigation and delays in death row cases. During the floor debate, some speakers offered evidence of disparity in sentencing that suggested that if the racial justice provision passed, no state would be able to inflict the death penalty, either upon those already on death row or upon those subsequently convicted, because of the statistical significance of the race of the victim. Once the taint had been established how could it ever be purged? Thus in the minds of many, inside the Congress and outside it, the specific issue of racially discriminatory capital sentencing became joined to the wider controversy over the morality and constitutionality of the death penalty.

The lack of voting power of the Black Caucus in the Senate (one senator) meant that its direct influence was minimal compared with the House. The Democratic leadership, Mitchell and Biden, was skeptical and had other more pressing priorities on the crime bill. Nor had the President given any indication of his own position, beyond repeating his campaign statement that he supported capital punishment, and as governor of Arkansas had on occasion implemented the death penalty. Thereafter the White House remained silent. On May 11 it came as no surprise when senators passed a resolution, by fifty-eight votes to forty-one with one not voting, urging their conferees to reject the racial justice provision.[41] In conference the Racial Justice Act was the major bone of contention, taking up much time. In June the CBC received some mild encouragement when Reno and other administration officials, who had been noncommittal hitherto, said they favored a compromise that would counter any racial bias in sentencing without impairing the implementation of the death penalty. But that was a circle that could not be squared. On the other side was such indomitable opposition as Thurmond, who threatened to filibuster the entire bill if the racial justice sentencing provision remained in the House-Senate conference report.

As time began to run out if the bill was to complete its passage by the August recess, a realization took hold that several other important items were being held hostage to the Racial Justice Act. Although a majority of the CBC members remained adamant that they would not vote for a crime bill that omitted the racial justice title, some cracks began to appear in its united stand. By July some Caucus members found that they could after all support the total crime package, even without racial justice, because it contained substantial money for prevention programs in the urban areas that they represented. Others cited their outright opposition to capital punishment as a reason why they could not vote for the overall bill, with its extension of the death penalty to many more offenses, whether or not it included racial justice provisions. Race and politics are an explosive mixture and the situation, by now becoming critical, called for delicate handling.

Who was going to tell the Black Caucus that the Racial Justice Act was doomed and would have to be dropped? The House leadership was apprehensive, with good reason as events were to show, that the CBC might join forces with the Republicans to block the procedural vote necessary to take the conference report to the floor of the House. If this happened, the bill would be held up, and possibly lost owing to the limited amount of legislative time remaining. The President, too, was awkwardly situated. He had come to Washington with the support of many black voters and to an extent stood for their aspirations. Moreover, he badly needed the votes of the CBC and the Hispanic Caucus for his health care legislation and other issues. Clinton had said that he would sign a crime bill with or without a racial justice provision, but he could not afford to put at risk the entire legislation. So it was Biden who was left holding the short straw. He conveyed the message to the CBC, courteously but firmly, that there was no prospect of the racial justice provisions passing the Senate, however modified. It was time to move on if the remainder of the bill, by now dangerously delayed, was to become law. If it did not, and it failed as the Republican efforts had failed, they would all be the losers.

Shortly after the deed was done, and an unsuccessful appeal had been made to the White House, the mournful chairman of the CBC, Kweisi Mfume, informed a news conference on July 14 that the administration had given up efforts to find an acceptable version of the proposals on which his members had set such store. The tone was one of disillusion: 'We have negotiated in good faith. I'm afraid I cannot say the same for all the negotiations we have had with the White House.'[42]

The unmistakable signal that the Racial Justice Act would be jettisoned cleared the outstanding impediments to reaching agreement in the conference. Some major unresolved issues remained, the ban on assault weapons being nonnegotiable for some, but not all, Democrats in the Senate, and the practical imperative of deleting the sweeping Republican amendment federalizing gun crimes and drastically increasing the mandatory penalties for drug trafficking and violent crimes where a firearm was involved (the D'Amato amendment).

V

Conflicting attitudes toward crime prevention, and the political patronage that can accompany the distribution of federal grants, constituted another stumbling block to reaching agreement. Conservative ideology was suspicious of crime prevention programs, which were looked on as a branch of a prodigal system of social welfare on which successive governments had spent lavishly and to little effect. The liberal assumption that potential or actual offenders could be steered away from a life of crime by targeted government initiatives aimed at altering their environment was subjected to caustic analysis by conservative think tanks that related the huge expenditure on welfare spending, an increase of 800 percent in real terms between 1960 and 1990, to a tripling in the number of felonies per capita over the same period.[43] The fact that the same criticism could be made of incapacitation as a penal sanction was left unsaid.

The extremes of opinion were displayed in the House floor debate on H.R. 4092 on April 21. Democrats warmly commended innovative prevention programs that were devoted to providing youth with employment, education, and recreation as alternatives to crime and violence. The bill authorized a total expenditure of about $7 billion in federal grants to fund a variety of programs intended to prevent crime. An ''Ounce of Prevention'' Council was to be set up, comprising in its membership several cabinet officers and other officials of the executive branch of government nominated by the President. The new body would make grants for certain specified purposes including summer and after-school programs, mentoring and tutoring programs, substance abuse treatment, and job placement. If requested by the relevant council member, it could coordinate other programs and advise communities and community-backed organizations seeking information about the development of crime prevention, integrated program service delivery, and grant simplification.

Representative Bruce Vento (Dem. Minnesota), a conscientious legislator first elected in 1976, was the coauthor of some provisions on urban recreation and at-risk youth that had passed the House as a free-standing bill on March 22 before being added to H.R. 4092. In the floor debate he said that his proposal to amend and strengthen existing legislation had attracted the support of over fifty national organizations. In 1978 Congress had enacted a program to help distressed urban areas develop recreational opportunities. Matching grants were made to economically distressed cities for repair of park and recreational facilities, and for innovative recreation based programs for youth. It had been proven to be effective, but in recent years the available funds had fallen well short of the number of applications from cities that had matching funds and were ready to go. The new provisions were intended not only to provide more adequate federal funding, but to maximize cost efficiency and program effectiveness. They recognized the important role that urban recreation played in developing positive values in young people and keeping them away from crime. Grants would be authorized to urban areas with a high prevalence of crime to expand park and recreation facilities for at-risk urban youth. They would enable facilities to be rehabilitated and improvements to be made to increase the security of urban parks, and to support successful existing programs.

Vento claimed that urban recreation had been grossly neglected as a national priority over the previous decade. Ironically, opportunities for low- and middle-income urban residents had declined at the same time that private health clubs had proliferated for higher income residents. Urban dwellers, especially those in economically distressed communities, were the most dependent on public parks and recreation programs. Testimony had been provided by the police as well as by city park directors and Boys and Girls Clubs organizers about the effectiveness of urban recreation programs as a crime prevention measure. He stressed that 50 to 60 percent of all crime in the United States was committed by young offenders between ten and twenty years of age. If they could be reached before turning to a life of crime, dollars and lives would be saved.[44]

This speech, bringing into relief the operation of a program in which a congressman had a particular interest, was matched by other advocates of the crime prevention proposals contained in the bill. In his final words spoken before the bill as amended was read a third time, Vento went wider. Thoughtfully articulating the liberal outlook, he said:

> Some provisions in the measure and the votes of the House concern me. They demonstrate that significant misunderstandings exist regarding the antisocial behavior and the criminal justice system. Federalizing a crime is not an automatic solution. The death penalty in my view is an admission of frustration not a solution. So often our society in modern America is insulated and isolated. There does not appear to be much empathy or understanding of the social conditions and plight of significant populations and sectors of our society. The dehumanizing, antisocial behavior of the criminals and inexplicable actions should be met by the reason of law deliberation not retribution.[45]

However virtuous the purpose, the reality is that the diversion of federal funds to particular localities also confers political advantage upon those who can take the credit. Naturally this is unwelcome to their political opponents who are seldom slow to invoke the idiom of the pork barrel, so enduring a feature of American political life. A histrionic passage in a speech during the same debate by a confrontational conservative, Jim Bunning (Rep. Kentucky) used colorful language to bring out the degree of patronage the bill would confer on the Democratic sponsors of the many funding programs:

> The bill before us is still far too soft and full of pork. In fact, it is so full of pork that I am surprised that it did not squeal and run out of the Chamber when it was brought to the floor. Once again, Members with pet projects that

could not pass on their own have larded on the pork in a bill that they are certain will pass because it carries the "crime bill" label.[46]

At a later stage, the same charge was to be directed at Brooks when it emerged that a proposed criminal justice center at his alma mater, Lamar University in Texas, was to be established with the aid of a federal grant of $10 million. In his speech, Bunning declared that even the pork would not be so bad if the rest of the bill "truly returned deterrent power to the justice system." Criminals and victims alike should be fully certain that the justice system would provide a sure, swift, and severe punishment for criminal behavior. The American people were fed up with a system of justice that was kinder to criminals than to the victims of crime, and so was he. When he had gone home to Kentucky for the district work period at Easter, the people who had come to his open-door meetings told him that they did not think they should have to wait for a violent criminal to get a third conviction before he was locked away for good. They were right. The average law-abiding citizens of Kentucky, and of the nation, deserved to be protected from the human predators that the criminal justice system had consistently returned to the streets to commit more and more criminal acts. Bunning urged the House to defeat the bill, and come back with one that would let the people know that "we are on their side, not the criminals."[47]

VI

By the time the conference produced its report on July 28 there were warning signs that the final version of the bill could not expect an easy acceptance by the House of Representatives. The racial justice provisions had been eliminated, as had the D'Amato amendment extending federal jurisdiction over almost all crimes involving the use or threat of force against a person or property in which the offender had a firearm. In a covering letter forwarding the comments of the administration on the crime bill, Reno had strongly opposed these provisions. If put into effect they would largely obliterate the distinction between federal and state criminal jurisdiction. She continued:

> They represent a false promise of action in fighting violent crime—a promise that will not be realized, given limited Federal resources—and divert attention from our critical Federal role in the fight against violent and drug crime. Extending Federal jurisdiction over hundreds of thousands of local offenses, which state and local law enforcement is generally best-situated to deal with, will not increase the public's security against these crimes. At best, these provisions would be ineffectual—at worst, they would divert Federal resources from dealing with the distinctively Federal matters and interstate criminal activities that Federal law enforcement is uniquely competent to handle.[48]

Despite the overwhelming volume of criticism that the federalization of violent crimes involving firearms had attracted, on grounds of principle as well as practice, the proposal was one that touched a responsive chord in the hearts of the more conservative Republicans inside and outside the Senate. Rejection by the conference was not to be the last that was heard of it. The ban on assault weapons survived unchanged, with a majority of the elements making up the House crime prevention package being accepted, although their total cost was $7.6 billion (including drug courts and violence against women), compared with the Senate prevention programs amounting to about $4 billion. Conversely, the conference accepted the higher Senate figure of $8.8 billion for hiring 100,000 extra police officers in preference to the original House proposal of 50,000 extra police at a cost of $3.5 billion. The combined effect of these changes, together with some other additional items, was to drive up the overall cost of the bill to $33.5 billion. This figure compared with the preconference cost of the Senate bill passed in November 1993 at $22.3 billion, and the House bill that followed in April 1994 at about $28.0 billion.

Deep as were the divisions between members of the House on the merits of the more controversial provisions, there was a wider political perspective against which the next scene was to be played. Clinton's plan to reform health care, the centerpiece of his administration's legislative priorities, was in serious trouble and unlikely to make further progress before the mid-term congressional elections in November. The Republican leadership was determined to exploit to the full every legislative issue to demonstrate that they had now obtained the upper hand, despite the Democrats much vaunted triumph in gaining control of the presidency, as well as retaining a majority in both Houses of Congress in 1992. If the Republicans could win on crime control, as well as thwarting health care, they could ridicule the President as weak and ineffective, so boosting their campaign platform for the November elections. Thus to deny Clinton the credit he might derive from signing the crime bill was a prime objective of national politics.

The conflict of loyalties facing the Republicans who supported the bill was acute. For some, the motivation was a nonparty conviction of the need to grasp the first real opportunity for a quarter of a century to make a start down the long road of restricting the availability of firearms that so fatally had aggravated the intolerable level of violent crime in America. Feeble as party discipline normally is in Congress, intense pressure was applied to prevent Republican defections in the House. On August 9, the Republican National Committee hand-delivered copies of a proposed resolution condemning any Republican representatives who backed the assault weapons ban and threatening to deny them electoral funding. One of the few who continued to stand firm on the need for gun control was Christopher Shays (Rep. Connecticut). A moderate Republican representing an urban district on the East Coast, and cochair with Mfume of the Congressional Urban Caucus, Shays cited a barrage of negative calls in his district which he believed were orchestrated by the NRA.[49]

The Speaker, Thomas Foley (Dem. Washington), deferred by one week the procedural vote needed to bring the conference report on the bill to the floor of the House. His foreboding was born out when on August 11, beyond the date when members of Congress had expected to depart for their summer recess and the anniversary of Clinton's first unveiling of the legislative proposals in the Rose Garden at the White House, the motion was defeated by 210 to 225 votes.[50] Every House member cast a vote; a rare occurrence. The normally low-key Foley, leaving the chair to make a speech from the floor closing the debate, had pleaded: "Let us not be a helpless giant in response to the demands and concerns of our people. Let us respond to their most deeply felt needs and concerns. The society that cannot protect the physical security of their citizens is a pretty useless society whatever else it can accomplish."[51] It was, he said, unusual for the Speaker to vote. It was a tradition of the House. But, like everyone else, he had the right to vote and intended to exercise it in voting for the rule and for the bill.

As at the previous critical stages in the bill's progress, the White House took an active part in lobbying for support. The chief of staff, Leon Panetta, who had been a long-serving congressman before joining the Cabinet as Director of the Office of Management and Budget in 1993,[52] was on hand to cajole his former colleagues, and a command post was set up by the Democratic Whips in a room off the chamber with an open line for the President to speak personally to any waverers. Republicans who had voted for the assault weapons ban, and for the House version of the bill, were contacted direct. According to White House staff, Clinton called more than fifty members of the House on August 10 and 11. One of them, a freshman from New York,[53] said that he had received a telephone call on the afternoon of the vote. The President did not offer any deals or inducements, but had stressed the importance of preserving their common stance on assault weapons.[54] At the same time, the congressman was conscious of the insistence by the Republican leadership for a unity vote which they argued could be justified, in part at least, as a protest against the way in which the Democratic majority had manipulated procedural rules to their advantage in the past. In the end he, and all save eleven Republican supporters of the bill, voted with their party.

More ominous for the administration was the total of fifty-eight Democrats who defied their leadership by preventing the bill from coming to the floor. Most of the dissentients were rural conservatives opposed to the ban on assault weapons. To take any other political position, said one of them, would be "just like putting a gun in your mouth in rural Texas."[55] Eleven others were members of the CBC, acting on principle in withdrawing their support from a bill that extended the death penalty to many additional offenses, while omitting the Racial Justice Act.

In the immediate aftermath of the defeat there was no unanimity amongst the Democratic leadership on the action necessary to save the bill. As Schumer put it, "[T]here is no Plan B."[56] All were agreed that the political stakes were too high to let the bill die, but time was running out, and it would have to be brought back within the next two weeks at the outside if there was to be any chance of reversing the vote. The White House was in favor of trying again with the same bill after a few days' drumming up public support. But the House leadership felt that concessions would have to be made, if unavoidable, even on the hard-fought ban on assault weapons. To those accustomed to the ways of Congress nothing was sacrosanct in the pursuit of compromise. After a postmortem on August 12 the House Majority Leader, Richard Gephardt (Dem. Missouri), indicated that Democrats would probably not return to the floor with an identical package. "My sense is there need to be adjustments in the bill," he said. "[I]t would not be sensible to go back with the same bill."[57]

At one remove from the setback, Biden was confident that the Senate would accept the conference report and pass the bill. The course he advocated was not to change the bill, but to change eight votes in the House. Both Biden and Brooks rejected the idea of reopening the conference. After the vote, Brooks commented "I don't think the conference can meet any more. It's too fragile."[58] Schumer took the same line, warning that even on minor issues reopening the conference could open up the whole bill to renegotiation and probably doom it.[59] The unpalatable choice had to be faced of making compromises with the conservative Democrat rebels, mainly from the South and West, which would almost certainly mean abandoning the assault weapons ban, or trying to find the extra votes from among the ranks of the moderate Republicans.

VII

Clinton himself decided the issue. Foley and Gephardt, the two most experienced and influential Democratic members of the House, called on him to urge that assault weapons be taken out of the main bill and voted on separately. The President was stubborn in his response. He refused to compromise on the ban, which to him was an indispensable part of the bill. In a statement after the vote he stressed that majorities had been won in votes in both Houses on all of the separate elements in the bill, including gun control. It was, he said, "especially disheartening to see 225 members of the House participate in a procedural trick orchestrated by the National Rifle Association, then heavily, heavily pushed by the Republican leadership in the House and designed with only one thing in mind, to put the protection of particular interests over the protection of ordinary Americans."[60] The opposition of the NRA was not confined solely to the issue of gun control. Their lobbyist was quoted as saying that the administration had failed to get the legislation passed because "Americans want precisely the opposite of what politicians offered them. We want prisons, not pork; police, not empty promises; crime fighters, not social workers."[61]

The priority to be accorded to the protection of individual citizens rather than the furtherance of particular interests was the theme of Clinton's appeal in a barnstorming campaign to rally public opinion to his side. The following morning, August 12, the President was up early. Speaking to reporters on the South Lawn of the White House at 8.12 A.M., he said:

We are going out now, the Cabinet, mayors of both parties, citizens of both parties all across this country, to say that this crime bill cannot die. Congress has an obligation to the American people that goes way beyond politics and way beyond party. The American people have said over and over this is their first concern. If we can't meet this concern, there is something badly wrong in Washington. And we are going today, starting now, to the National Association of Police Officers [*sic*] conference to carry this battle back. We are going to fight and fight and fight until we win this battle for the American people.[62]

The assault weapons ban consolidated the support of the representative police organizations behind the bill and was to be a critical factor in outmaneuvering the NRA. At about 1.30 P.M. Clinton appeared on the platform of the National Association of Police Organizations convention in Minneapolis. In a spectacular coup de thèâtre he was flanked by the Republican mayor of New York and the Democratic mayor of Philadelphia. Rudolph Giuliani and Edward Rendell were both former U.S. Attorneys, and as prosecutors were only too well aware of the fatal consequences of the unlimited access to automatic weapons, which could leave the police outgunned on the streets. Their cities, moreover, stood to benefit substantially from the enhanced law enforcement and crime prevention measures and funding in the bill. For Giuliani it was a courageous gesture to agree to join the President in a public display of bipartisan support for his counteroffensive.

Shortly after Clinton had appeared on television the previous evening, Giuliani had telephoned the White House to ask if he could do anything to help get the legislation restarted.[63] The next day he was aboard Air Force One en route for Minneapolis, accompanying the President and discussing the prospects for lobbying some Republican congressmen. Senator Wellstone and Representative Vento, both Democrats of Minnesota, also joined the presidential party, while on the West Coast another Republican Mayor, Richard Riordan of Los Angeles, made up a trio of big-city mayors who lost no time in coming out in support of the bill. Joined by the mayors of Chicago, Seattle, Kansas City, and Louisville, Kentucky, they formed an important element in a strategy designed to subject legislators in Washington to the pressures of local opinion.[64]

Clinton used the police convention platform,[65] and the national television and media exposure it attracted, to claim that never before had there been a bill that had been endorsed by every major law-enforcement group in the United States. It would put 100,000 more police on the streets, make "three strikes and you're out" the law of the land, and provide more funds for prisons to house serious offenders. Handgun ownership by juveniles would be banned, as would the assault weapons that gangs and thugs deployed to outgun the police. But the bill also protected 650 specifically named hunting and sporting weapons, something the American people too often had not been told. There were tougher penalties for violent crime, including the death penalty for killing an officer of the law in his line of duty. In addition, the bill contained prevention funds. It made his blood boil to hear people talking about pork when he had seen first-hand the impact of prevention programs on children. To applause, he dared his audience to find one person who knew anything about crime who was not for tougher punishment and more prevention.[66] That the police organizations were solidly behind his stance was demonstrated in the introduction by the convention chairman. "The police of this country," he assured the President, "are completely outraged by the House action. . . . Without the aid and resources contained in this bill, we will be forced to continue to fight the war on crime with limited manpower, substandard equipment and outdated laws."[67]

As Clinton kept up the pressure on public opinion, the search for votes continued in Washington. At first the target of winning over eight Republicans, or persuading some of the Democrats who had rebelled against their party leadership to change sides, seemed attainable. The President had been careful to respect the "principled opposition" of the ten Democratic members of the CBC who had voted against the bill because of their conviction that the use of the death penalty was racially discriminatory. On Sunday, August 14, after making a national radio address from Camp David on the Saturday,[68] Clinton spoke at a morning service at a nonconformist church in a poor and racially diverse suburban area of Maryland. Always effective in addressing a predominantly black congregation, his secular message was unchanged: that the American people had made it clear to Congress they wanted the crime bill, and he intended to see that they got it.[69]

Early in the following week two members of the CBC, after a meeting at the White House, announced that, while still opposed to the extension of the death penalty and the omission of the racial justice provisions, they had decided to vote to allow the House to take up the crime bill as a whole. One of them, Representative John Lewis (Dem. Georgia), a veteran civil rights leader, was influential in the House as a deputy Whip and member of the Democratic leadership. Later the same day a third black Democrat, as a result of a meeting with Reno, said that while he could not vote for the bill itself, he would support the procedural motion to move it to the floor.[70]

The balance of five votes needed to reverse the decision remained elusive. Nor could it be assumed that the eleven Republicans who had voted to get the bill to the floor would be willing to do so again. Their spokesman, Christopher Shays, like the Democratic leadership in the House, was convinced that the administration would have to consent to some concessions. Once the first flush of victory had subsided the Republican leadership took a more conciliatory attitude and was open to negotiations. Some Republican congressmen, in the same way as their Democratic counterparts, were uneasy about returning to their constituents with an empty knapsack. The vote had been on a little understood procedural rule, and there was sensitivity toward the force of public criticism that Congress was so rule-bound, and so in debt to special interests, that it was incapable of legislating to meet the evident concerns of the people. Although each side would blame the other for the failure to end a stalemate on crime that had prevailed for six years, Clinton's media blitz had established irrefutably in the public mind that it was he and his administration who were doing everything in their power to get the crime bill passed, and the Republicans in Congress who were obstructing it. Moreover, Republican leaders were uncomfortable about being depicted as the tools of the gun lobby.

For these reasons, as the quest for individual votes continued, being directed especially toward certain Republican representatives from New York where the influence of the gun lobby was weak and that of Giuliani was strong, the objective of working toward bipartisan compromise began to take shape in the minds of the less committed on each side of the barricades. The Republican leadership, in the shape of Robert Dole in the Senate, and Newt Gingrich (Rep. Georgia), then minority whip in the House, while not themselves instrumental in initiating attempts to bridge the gap, had indicated they were willing to talk if the President wanted to meet them. They insisted, however, that the overall levels of spending, particularly on crime prevention and social programs would have to be cut back drastically if there was to be any hope of making progress. At this stage they would have been aware of the signs of a growing number of potential defectors within their ranks. By the middle of the week, about forty Republican moderates in the House had coalesced around a newcomer, Michael Castle, first elected to Congress as recently as 1992, but experienced as a former governor of Delaware.[71] It was this group that hammered out a compromise with the Democrats to save the bill.

In its original form the plan was for an across-the-board cut of $3 billion, representing rather less than ten percent of the overall cost of the bill, which was estimated at $33.5 billion. The reductions would not eliminate any program in full, and would fall equally on social spending, the cost of additional police officers, and grants for prison building. The plan averted the main burden of the cuts falling on crime prevention projects in the urban areas, where the support of their Democratic sponsors (including some members of the CBC) was needed to maintain the voting strength for the bill. At a news conference on August 19 Clinton indicated that he was willing to accept the plan. The bill that had come out of conference, he said, met all his criteria: the assault weapons ban, the ban on handgun ownership by kids, tougher penalties, longer imprisonment, more prevention.[72] But the total cost amounted to more than could be accommodated in the trust fund resulting from reducing the size of the federal bureaucracy.

To Clinton a cutback of 10 percent had the advantage of bringing the cost to a level that could be contained in the trust fund, while maintaining the bill's fundamental integrity. The plan did not, however, satisfy the Republican leadership. Dole's blunt comment was that they wanted the focus to be "on cutting pork, not on cutting prisons or the police," with the main cuts being made from the social spending account.[73] Gingrich, more hawklike, was calling for reductions amounting to $5.5 billion, with a similar emphasis, as well as the reinsertion of Republican-backed sentencing measures.[74]

The even-handedness of the bipartisan approach toward the imperative of cutting back the overall cost of the bill did not survive an all-night bargaining session between the various interest groups, which was hurriedly convened with representatives of the Senate on August 19. While the willingness of the moderates to trim as much as $3.3 billion from the total was maintained, the sources from which the savings would have to come were changed pointedly. Hard-line Republicans succeeded in pushing up to $2.5 billion the reductions in social spending from the conference cost of $7.6 billion, with a far smaller saving of $800 million coming from reduced expenditure on prisons.

Fifty percent of the total funds authorized to be appropriated for prison construction, expansion or improvement, amounting to $7,895 million over six fiscal years, 1995–2000, was to be made available to states in the form of truth-in-sentencing incentive grants. To be eligible to receive such a grant a state would have to demonstrate that it had in effect laws that required that persons convicted of violent crimes served not less than 85 percent of the sentence imposed, or was moving in that direction. The criteria specified in section 20102 of Public Law 103-322 included increasing the percentage since 1993 of convicted violent offenders sentenced to imprisonment; increasing the average prison time to be served in prison by convicted violent offenders; and increasing the percentage of the sentence served in prison by violent offenders.

Other controversial issues continued to delay agreement being reached on a package that had a realistic chance of success in getting the bill relaunched onto the floor. A Democratic proposal that large numbers of low-level drug offenders, estimated at between 10,000 and 16,000 prisoners serving mandatory minimum sentences for possession and dealing, should become eligible for early release to make room for violent offenders, was strenuously resisted. Republicans argued that many of those who would be eligible for release were drug dealers and not merely users convicted of possessing small amounts of drugs. A compromise was reached whereby the "safety valve" was preserved, but it was to be prospective and not applicable to those who were already serving prison sentences. Where the statutorily prescribed minimum sentence was five years, and the conditions were met, including cooperation in providing information to law enforcement about the offense or offenses, the sentencing guidelines and any amendments to them should call for a guideline range in which the lowest term of imprisonment was at least twenty-four months. Another last-minute initiative was a Republican attempt to amend the bill to enable judges to order the deportation immediately on their release from prison of illegal aliens who had been convicted of criminal offenses. Democrats were apprehensive that this proposal would imperil the support the bill needed from the nineteen-strong Hispanic Caucus. Although it made no progress in the 103rd Congress, the proposal did not die. In the 104th Congress a bill on deporting criminal aliens was one of six anti-crime measures passed by the House of Representatives in the first hundred days, being enacted in omnibus legislation the following year.[75]

Chapter 5

Ending the Insanity

I

The winds of compromise blew back into contention some proposals that had not won sufficient support in the earlier stages. While there had been little dissent to the bulk of the measures designed to combat violence against women: on the streets, in public transit and public parks, and as victims of domestic violence, there had been a lack of unanimity over the approach toward repeat sexual offenders. The final version of the bill included provisions increasing the level of federal penalties for sex crimes, instructing the U.S. Sentencing Commission to review and promulgate amendments where appropriate to the sentencing guidelines in cases of aggravated sexual abuse or sexual abuse. The guidelines should also be reviewed and amended to take account of the general problem of recidivism in cases of sex offenses, the severity of the offense, and its devastating effects on survivors. On penalties for repeat offenders it was more specific, providing that after one or more prior convictions for an offense punishable under the relevant chapter of the United States Code, as amended by the Act, or under the laws of any state relating to aggravated sexual abuse, sexual abuse or abusive sexual contact, the penalty would be a term of imprisonment up to twice that otherwise authorized.

A further proposal directed toward so-called sexual predators[1] had been added to the Senate bill (S. 1607) by Senator Gorton (Rep. Washington) modeled on a similar law in his home state.[2] There had been no opposition and the amendment had been accepted by the managers of the bill on both sides of the Senate.[3] The intention was to require a person who had been convicted previously of a sexually violent offense to register a current address with a designated state law enforcement agency.[4] A comparable proposal to promote the establishment by states of registration systems for convicted child molesters was included in the House bill. In its detailed comments prepared for the conference, the Department of Justice supported the enactment of the child molesters registration proposal, and favored the concept of registration systems for violent sex offenders who preyed on adult victims. But it wanted to see more definite criteria concerning the class of offenders who would be covered and the duration of registration requirements.[5] In addition to these reservations, vexatious questions arose in conference over privacy, the conditions for the release of information collected under a state registration program, and the risks of excessive community vigilance and informal sanctions.

Gorton's amendment would have enabled the designated state law enforcement agency to release information that was "necessary to protect the public" from a specific sexually violent predator who was required to register. By a large majority (407 to 13) the House instructed its conferees to accept the Senate language. Instead, what emerged from the conference was a composite section covering both child molesters and sexual predators, narrowing the release of information to law enforcement purposes and the notification of victims of the offender. Once again, as with the murder of Polly Klaas in California, another emotive and highly publicized killing of a child led to a demand for the substitution of stronger wording, which would allow notification to local communities of the address of sexual predators. This provision became known as Megan's Law, after a seven-year-old girl, Megan Kanka, who had been sexually assaulted and murdered, allegedly by a neighbor, in July 1994. Unknown to the residents of the New Jersey suburb in which he was living, the man charged with her death had been twice convicted of other sex crimes.

During the final stages of negotiation, a potential swing voter, Representative Susan Molinari (Rep. New York), pressed for a fundamental change in the judicial process. She wanted evidence of previous charges of sexual offenses to be admissible in evidence in court, even if the defendant had not been convicted of the offense. Democrats objected both on grounds of civil liberties and because a procedural change on these lines would have little effect as so few sexual crimes were tried in the federal courts. One of the most experienced city prosecutors, Linda Fairstein, director of the Sex Crimes Unit in Manhattan,[6] commented that sex crimes committed within the federal jurisdiction accounted for only between 3 and 5 percent of all sex crimes that go to court. It would be more important, in her view, to finance programs to train investigators and prosecutors in this field.[7] In the meantime Molinari had obtained an encouraging response from a surprising quarter. She said that when she had talked to Clinton on the telephone, he had expressed his disappointment that two items had been dropped from the bill—the sexual predator notification provision and the provision that would make admissible in court, at the discretion of the judge, a defendant's prior charges of sexual offenses. According to Molinari, Clinton had said that he would try and get them back.[8]

The Safe Streets for Women title contained some new grant programs intended to combat violent crimes against women and to make federal funds available to increase security in public transportation systems and reduce the incidence of crime in national parks. Community programs on domestic violence, and preventive and educational programs, were included in another title on Safe Homes for Women. After the uproar over pork had subsided, it became apparent that of all the multifarious provisions on violent crimes and prevention, women and children were the quiet winners.[9] First introduced six years earlier, the Violence Against Women Act had been regarded initially as a radical package and a political hot potato. It had been backed consistently by Biden, its original sponsor in the Senate, but had been unable to gain majority support. With the passage of time, Republican as well as Democratic congressmen began riding the wave of changing attitudes, seeing in it another issue where each could demonstrate their toughness on crime.[10] In this way, sufficient bipartisanship was generated to enable the proposals to be passed into law with little resistance.

II

The expectation of a vote on the bill on Saturday, August 20, drew an estimated six thousand people to the Capitol.[11] Throughout the day batches of visitors were ushered into the Gallery of the House where they sat patiently overlooking an empty chamber. But the culminating stages of the negotiations over the compromises needed to attract the forty Republican moderates without losing a significant number of Democrat votes were not yet complete. The bargaining between the leadership of both parties and those with particular interests, which had begun in earnest at 2.00 P.M. on Friday, did not end until 3.15 A.M. on Sunday, August 21. During a disorderly series of meetings between different groups in different rooms the main impediments to reaching agreement were eliminated one by one. The criminal justice center in Brooks's district in Texas had become a symbolic sacrifice demanded by even the most moderate Republican. It was of little or no importance to the administration, but to the House leadership Brooks's seniority as chairman of the Judiciary Committee, and his influence with conservative Democrats, remained factors that could not readily be overlooked. In vain it was argued, by Foley among others, that two studies had verified the necessity for the center. It would be a training academy for federal, state, and local corrections officers. The prisons and jails in the region housed a total of twenty thousand inmates, and the proposed center would provide training for more than seven thousand corrections officers. But to Republicans, and even to some Democrats, it was seen as pure pork that had to go. Gingrich had made it abundantly clear that he would not agree to any negotiated settlement whatever until it was removed.

By then Brooks was alienated from the process of negotiation and compromise. A prickly character, who had seen countless bills obstructed before, he had lost any remaining appetite for seeking consensus, either within his own party or with the Republicans. Did he, perhaps, have a premonition of what was to come, for him, and for other Democrats, in the congressional elections only eleven weeks away?[12] Biden, although senior in the Senate, was a younger man who treated Brooks respectfully, whenever possible making a point of coming to see the congressman at his House Office Building to discuss business on the bill. The same tactfulness had not been displayed by Schumer. Relations between Brooks, as chairman of the Judiciary Committee, and the most energetic of his subcommittee chairmen, had been strained from the start. In the final stages, they broke down completely. Brooks retired to his room, a brooding presence who ceased to play any decisive role as the political drama neared its climax. After the defeat over the vote on the rule, the Democratic leadership on the handling of the bill passed to Foley, the Speaker of the House; Gephardt, the majority leader; Biden, from the Senate; and Schumer. For part of the time they were joined by Panetta from the White House. Of this group, it was the last named who broke the news to Brooks that the $10 million federal grant to the Lamar University project would have to be abandoned.

Another Texas program, also labeled as pork by suspicious Republicans, was a $1 million authorization for a center to retrain laid-off military workers for new careers in substance abuse treatment. Inoffensive as this seemed, it was only when it was noticed in the febrile atmosphere of the negotiations at about 2.00 A.M. on the Sunday morning that it was to be located at Huntsville, Texas, that hackles were raised. Huntsville was in the district of another Democratic representative, Charles Wilson, adjoining that of Brooks, who had been responsible for its insertion into the bill. It too was deleted peremptorily from the slimmed-down bill that the exhausted legislators strove to achieve.

Once all the interested parties had reached final agreement on the changes, two votes took place during the afternoon and early evening of Sunday, August 21. The first was a procedural motion to bring the bill to the floor of the House. This time it was agreed by 239 to 189 votes, with 7 not voting.[13] Forty-two Republicans, 196 Democrats, and one Independent voted yea; with 134 Republicans and 55 Democrats voting nay. After more than two hours of further debate, a second vote followed in which the House defeated a motion to recommit the conference report to accompany the bill to the committee of conference. The number of Republican supporters held in the forties, with the total number of Democrats voting against their party increasing to 64. Nevertheless, the eventual result was clear enough a demonstration of the collective desire of the House of Representatives to pass a crime bill that had seen such expenditure of time, effort, speech-making, and arduous negotiation. On the bill itself the voting was 235 for, 195 against, not voting 5.[14] Of these, 188 were Democrats who voted yea, joined by forty-six Republicans and one Independent. Sixty-four Democrats and 131 Republicans voted nay.

The ban on military-style assault weapons and copycat versions was preserved unchanged in substance, with ammunition clips for existing weapons being limited to ten bullets. The extension in the number of federal crimes punishable by death and the procedures for carrying out the death penalty were maintained, but unaccompanied either by the habeas corpus reforms so dear to the conservative Right, or the racial justice provisions sought by liberals and the Black Caucus. No last-minute challenge emerged to three strikes. Once accepted by Clinton as part of the balanced package he wanted to present to the American public, soon to be voters in the November elections, it had become a shared orthodoxy.

The total cost of the provisions authorized by the bill was cut back to $30.2 billion over six years, representing about 10 percent less than the bill which had been reported by the conference of both Houses. The cumulative and unschematic approach to the legislation had led to a five-fold increase on its original cost when introduced the previous year which had been estimated at about $5.9 billion. In the final tally, prevention programs totaled $6.9 billion, law enforcement $13.5 billion, and prisons $9.8 billion. The discrepancy between the monetary amounts authorized by legislators in one Congress, and the actual amounts appropriated in the next, was brought out pointedly in the Republican-controlled 104th Congress.

The late run of enthusiasm for countermeasures aimed at sexual offenders was sustained. The wording of the title on crimes against children and the registration of sexually violent offenders was amended to give access to community groups as well as law enforcement officials to the criminal histories of repeat offenders. Persons classified as sexually violent predators would have to register with state law enforcement officials for the rest of their lives, or until declassified as a sexual predator,[15] notifying officials of their address at regular intervals. The information could then be shared with community officials at the discretion of the registration agency. This concession to Republican opinion, fanned by the public outrage at the death of Megan Kanka, was described by Senator Gorton's colleague from Washington, Representative Jennifer Dunn, in the House of Representatives in these words:

> Ten days ago I rose to complain about bogus language that supposedly allowed local police to notify a community when a sexual predator was released into their midst. After nearly 4 hours of tough negotiations, we conferees finally succeeded in reinserting true community notification language that should have been there in the first place—language that had been approved by 407 Members of the House, and unanimously accepted in the Senate. No question, this is one small victory for the women and families in this nation.[16]

As we shall see in a later chapter, this was far from being the end of the story of Megan's Law. Another last-minute addition sailed even closer to the rocks marking the outermost boundaries of justice. Molinari's energetic lobbying, unexpectedly made easier by the President, resulted in a provision that when a defendant was accused in a federal court of an offense of sexual assault or child molestation, evidence of the commission of any similar offenses in the past would be admissible, whether or not a conviction had resulted in a federal or a state court. Evidence of the commission of similar acts would also be admissible in civil cases concerning sexual assault or child molestation.

The only justifications for such a radical change in criminal procedure, described by Biden as turning on its head eight hundred years of Anglo-Saxon jurisprudence,[17] were put forward by Molinari in the course of the all-inclusive Sunday afternoon debate preceding the crucial votes in the House. Offenses of sexual assault were different from others, she argued, because of the need to detect a propensity to commit such offenses; to test the probability or improbability that a defendant had been falsely or mistakenly accused; and the compelling public interest in admitting all significant evidence that would assist in the difficult credibility determinations that arise in rape cases.[18] Given the pressing need for haste in reaching a final resolution on the bill as a whole, it is understandable that no contrary, or indeed supporting, views were expressed.

The Judicial Conference of the United States, to which the necessary amendments to the Federal Rules of Evidence were referred, was forthright in its criticism. In a report submitted to Congress in accordance with section 320935 of Public Law 103-322,[19] it said that the provisions would apply both to civil and criminal cases. Accordingly, they had been reviewed by the separate Advisory Committees on criminal and civil rules of evidence. Having solicited comments, the report stated that "the overwhelming majority of judges, lawyers, law professors, and legal organizations who had responded"[20] were opposed to the new rules. The principal objections were that the rules would permit the admission of unfairly prejudicial evidence and contained numerous drafting problems not intended by their authors. The Advisory Committees agreed, adding that the new rules were unsupported by empirical evidence, and could diminish significantly the protections that safeguard accused persons in criminal cases and parties in civil cases against undue prejudice. These protections formed a fundamental part of American jurisprudence and had evolved under long-standing rules and case law.

A significant concern was the danger of convicting a criminal defendant for past, as opposed to charged, behavior or for being a bad person. Because prior bad acts would be admissible even though not the subject of a conviction, mini-trials within trials concerning those acts would result when a defendant sought to rebut such evidence. Many of the comments received had argued that as drafted the rules were mandatory, that is, that such evidence would have to be admitted regardless of other rules of evidence such as the hearsay rule. If the critics were right, the new rules would free the prosecution from rules that applied to the defendant, giving rise to serious constitutional implications.[21]

The Advisory Committees, unanimous except for the representatives of the Department of Justice, their hands tied by higher authority, concluded that the new rules would permit the introduction of unreliable but prejudicial evidence, and would complicate trials by causing mini-trials of other alleged wrongs. The Standing Committee endorsed the conclusion, and recommended Congress to reconsider its decision on the policy embodied in the new rules in section 320935. In its formal report, the Judicial Conference drew attention to the "highly unusual unanimity of the members of the Standing and Advisory Committees, composed of over forty judges, practicing lawyers, and academicians" in taking the view that the new rules were undesirable. Indeed, the only supporters were the representatives of the Department of Justice. If Congress would not reconsider its decision on the policy questions, an alternative draft of the rules had been prepared which would correct ambiguities and possible constitutional infirmities, yet still effectuate congressional intent.

Despite the strength and uniformity of the judicial recommendation no action was taken by Congress within the prescribed period, with the result that the new rules of evidence as set out in section 320935 became effective on July 9, 1995. Although representatives of the Judicial Conference continued to try and persuade Congress to adopt the alternative rules that had been recommended,[22] their ability to achieve changes when faced with a resistant, or disinterested, Congress was limited. The constitutional position is that whereas Congress has authorized the federal judiciary to prescribe the rules of practice, procedure, and evidence for the federal courts, such authority is subject to the ultimate legislative right of the Congress to reject, modify, or defer any of the rules.[23]

III

The closing scene could have been portrayed as the finale of a compelling action-drama were it not for the somber realities of the context in which the elected representatives of a great democracy were in the throes of arriving at a positive or negative conclusion. It was fitting that the decision lay with the United States Senate, where a hundred senators, some far-sighted and others with their gaze directed single-mindedly toward the imminent midterm elections, had the last word on the legislative measure that had consumed so much time over two sessions.

The President sensed that the Senate was more than simply a final fence to be surmounted in the steeplechase that lawmaking in Washington had proved to be for his administration. Senators needed to be treated with respect and encouraged to take a statesmanlike view. As the 103rd Congress neared its end, he urged them to reach agreement without delay on the remaining issues, giving less weight to the specific provisions of the crime bill, to be accepted or rejected as part of the give and take of partisan politics, and more to the need for a demonstrable response by President and Congress alike to the heartfelt desires of millions of Americans to see the power and wealth of the nation's government purposefully directed toward combating the destructive antisocial forces that affected so adversely the quality of their lives. It was true that Clinton badly needed the bill to pass for his own standing; especially as health care, his other main legislative priority, was foundering and unlikely to become law. But such factors did not conflict with the persuasive appeal of his wider democratic message.

The day after the House vote, these considerations found expression in a letter sent personally on August 22 by the President to each Senator. The text is reproduced in full.[24]

Dear——

This week, the Senate has an historic chance to move us beyond old labels and partisan divisions by passing the toughest, smartest Crime Bill in our nation's history.

I want to congratulate members of Congress in both houses and both parties who have reached across party lines and worked in good faith to produce this Crime Bill. This isn't a Democratic Crime Bill or a Republican Crime Bill, and it will make a difference in every town, every city, and every state in our country.

The Crime Bill produced by House and Senate conferees and passed yesterday by Democrats and Republicans in the House achieves all the same objectives as the bipartisan Crime Bill which the Senate passed last November by a vote of 95 to 4.

Many of the central provisions of this Crime Bill were included in the Senate bill:

• Nearly $9 billion to put 100,000 new police officers on our streets in community policing;

• An additional $4.6 billion for federal, state and local law enforcement (a 25% increase above the Senate bill);

• $9. 9 billion for prisons (a 30% increase above the Senate bill), coupled with tough truth-in-sentencing requirements that will shut the revolving door on violent criminals;

• Life imprisonment for repeat violent offenders by making three-strikes-and-you're-out the law of the land;

• Federal death penalties for the most heinous of crimes, such as killing a law enforcement officer;

• A ban on handgun ownership for juveniles;

• Registration and community notification to warn unsuspecting families of sexual predators in their midst;

• A ban on 19 semiautomatic assault weapons, with specific protection for more than 650 other weapons; and

• Innovative crime prevention programs, such as the Community Schools program sponsored by Senators Danforth, Bradley, and Dodd, and the Violence Against Women Act sponsored by Senators Biden, Hatch, and Dole.

One of the most important elements of this Crime Bill is the creation of a Violent Crime Reduction Trust Fund, which ensures that every crime-fighting program in the bill will be paid for by reducing the federal bureaucracy by more than 270,000 positions over the next six years. The idea for the Trust Fund came from Senators Byrd, Mitchell, Biden, Gramm, Hatch, and Dole, and the Senate approved it by a vote of 94 to 4. The Trust Fund will ensure that the entire Crime Bill will be fully paid for, not with new taxes, but by reducing the federal bureaucracy to its lowest level in over 30 years.

The Senate led the way in passing these important anti-crime proposals last November, and I urge you to take up this Crime Bill in the same bipartisan spirit that marked that debate. The American people have waited six years for a comprehensive Crime Bill. It's time to put politics aside and finish the job. After all the hard work that has gone into this effort by members of both parties acting in good faith, we owe it to the law-abiding citizens of this country to pass this Crime Bill without delay.

Sincerely
Bill Clinton

A new procedural challenge faced the bill in the Senate. The device of setting up a trust fund, financed by savings made in the reduction of the federal workforce, had not been approved by the Senate's Budget Committee as required by the Congressional Budget Act of 1974. There was power to waive the rule, but the Act provided that such a waiver required sixty votes out of the total membership of one hundred. Although the Democrats had a majority in the Senate, they held only fifty-six seats. Thus the procedural hurdle was far more formidable than the simple majority needed to accept the conference report. Over four hot Summer days, well into the normal vacation period, Republican obstructionists mounted a last assault. The ranking Republican on the Judiciary Committee, Senator Hatch of Utah, led the charge, backed by Senator Gramm, a dedicated opponent of the administration's economic policies and a leader on budget issues in the Senate. They were reinforced by Senator Domenici (Rep. New Mexico), another strong critic of what he condemned as the Democrats propensity to high spending and the escalating federal budget deficit. As a member both of the Appropriations and Budget Committees, it was Domenici who raised the crucial point of order against the conference report on the ground that it contained matters within the jurisdiction of the Senate Budget Committee, which had not been considered as required by section 306 of the Budget Act. George Mitchell, the majority leader, then moved to waive the Budget Act to allow consideration of the conference report.[25]

The previous day the minority leader, Robert Dole, had objected to the inaccuracy of a *New York Times* headline "Dole Seeks Measure without Weapons Ban, Asserting He Has Votes to Block Bill."[26] Mindful of the sensitivity of national public opinion on gun control, he maintained that the argument was not about guns, but about unjustified discretionary spending. Republicans were looking for changes and he had given a list of proposed amendments to the majority leader. They were not set on wrecking the bill or preventing the Congress legislating on crime. The American people, he said, expected senators to protect their interests in crime and their interests in the way their money was spent.

Behind these high-flown sentiments lay a straightforward power struggle embracing the familiar ingredients. At this late stage, any further delay, caused by reopening the bill to amendments likely to be unacceptable to the House, meant that it would be lost. An undeclared subplot was that if the point-of-order tactic was successful, and the version of the bill currently under consideration was invalidated as a result, it would be substituted by an earlier version before the trust fund device had been added. The text of that bill did not contain the ban on assault weapons which had been inserted by Feinstein's amendment on November 17, 1993. The opponents of gun control realized they could not win on that issue alone. Delay offered the only chance of averting the prospect of defeat.

As an experienced and skillful manager of legislative business, Dole had taken care to omit assault weapons entirely from a list of ten amendments that he offered to the Democratic leadership. The Republican amendments concentrated on cutting expenditure further on prevention programs and toughening penalty provisions. Mitchell and Biden, having obtained by then indications of support from three Republican senators, retaliated with the counteroffer of a single amendment of their own. This would have stripped the bill of all prevention programs, except those involving domestic violence and antidrug treatment in prisons. Knowing that it would fail on a floor vote, and noting the absence of any mention of penalties, the Republican leadership rejected it out of hand. This was enough to win over an independent-minded Republican, Nancy Kassebaum, Dole's colleague from Kansas. In a written statement shortly after the leadership's decision was announced, she expressed her disappointment that the offer of an additional $5 billion cut in social spending had been rejected. On balance she now believed that the positive aspects outweighed the negative.[27] Soon afterward, she was joined by another Republican senator, John Chafee of Rhode Island. With five out of the total of forty-four Republicans ready to change sides, it looked as though Mitchell had the votes needed to beat off the challenge on the Budget Act waiver, provided there were no defections on his own side. Both factions were aware of the urgency to reach a decision, and the Senate voted on August 25 to accept a motion to waive the requirement of the Budget Act. The necessary sixty votes were gained, with one to spare. Sixty-one senators voted for the motion, and thirty-nine against.[28] The necessary three-fifths majority having been obtained, the point of order fell.

An analysis of the vote by party allegiance reveals the cross-currents that often characterize the key congressional decisions on legislation. Fifty-five of the fifty-six Democrats voted for Mitchell's motion, and one against. Richard Shelby of Alabama, a wayward conservative Democrat, joined thirty-eight Republicans in opposing the waiver.[29] But six Republicans, including Arlen Specter of Pennsylvania, who within months was a candidate to seek the Republican nomination for the next Presidential election campaign, voted with the Democrats. On a second vote to close the debate later in the evening, a consistent opponent of the death penalty, Russell Feingold (Dem. Wisconsin), joined Shelby in voting against the bill, while a seventh Republican senator broke ranks to support it. Another Republican did not participate in the final vote. The outcome was that the Senate approved the conference report on the bill, as amended by the House of Representatives, by sixty-one votes to thirty-eight.[30] It then adjourned for a foreshortened recess until September 12.

The eventful passage of the legislation launched a full year earlier was complete at last. After the procedural vote, Mitchell and Biden praised the courageousness of the dissident Republicans and credited Clinton's steadfastness on the assault weapons ban as a key factor in preserving the most politically hazardous of the bill's provisions. Off the floor, dismissing Republican protestations to the contrary, Biden insisted that the issue had been "guns, guns, guns, guns and guns."[31] Mitchell added a cautionary rider. Despite the NRA's defeat, he said, it should not be assumed that it had lost its clout: "An organization that can wield such enormous power with such an unpopular issue cannot be discounted."[32] To comprehend how the NRA came to nail its colors to such an extreme example of defending gun owners' rights as retaining the right of private individuals to possess deadly weapons designed for military purposes, it is necessary to have some insight into the origins, beliefs, and methods of one of the most politically assertive of all single-issue interest groups in America.

IV

The intensity of belief that typifies so many NRA activists is rooted in habitual populist fears that the government is set on taking away basic freedoms. This belief transcends the traditional objectives of the NRA, which were to encourage accurate rifle shooting, both as a competitive sport and as training for military reservists, and to further the legitimate use of firearms for hunting and farming purposes. In the early years, following the formation of the Association in 1871, it concentrated on sponsoring target-shooting competitions on its own rifle range on Long Island and elsewhere, in order to provide riflemen with an incentive to improve their skills and foster military preparedness.[33] Connections, never to be entirely severed, were forged with arms and ammunition manufacturers, and it was political lobbying that secured funding from the New York state legislature for the purchase of the land and the construction of the Long Island range. After a decline of interest in target shooting during the latter part of the nineteenth century, Congress established a National Board for the Promotion of Rifle Practice at the instigation of the NRA in 1903. One-third of the Board's officers were trustees of the National Rifle Association, and following a change in the law in 1905 surplus military firearms and ammunition were made available at cost, or later given away free, to rifle clubs sponsored by the NRA.[34]

Between the two World Wars, NRA members continued to enjoy the exclusive privilege of purchasing weapons at cost. The membership flourished, tripling between 1945 and 1948 as a result of servicemen joining the Association on postwar demobilization. By the mid-1950s, with a national membership of about 300,000, the goal had shifted away from military preparedness to preserving the interests of sportsmen and hunters. In 1958, the aims of the NRA, as boldly stated for all to see on the façade of its new headquarters building in Washington, were "Firearms safety education, marksmanship training, shooting for recreation."[35]

The politicization of the NRA, although always present in its culture, did not become the dominant strain until after a palace revolution in 1977. In that year the old guard previously in control of the Association was summarily displaced. Its policy had been to consolidate the strength and reputation of the NRA as the national representative body for hunters and target shooters. A future was envisaged in which the NRA would expand its role beyond the encouragement of safe shooting to teaching outdoor skills such as camping, survival training, and environmental awareness, for which 37,000 acres of land had been purchased in New Mexico. The ambitious plan for a national outdoor center was the last straw for the militant wing of the NRA. The 1968 gun control legislation, described earlier in this narrative, had strengthened the hands of an activist group of hard-liners who were convinced that the priority should be the resolute lobbying of legislators to prevent the erosion of the cherished right to bear arms. Not for them the boy scout–like activities of the leadership they overthrew. What mattered above all else was to curb the menace of federal regulatory control of firearms.

The ideology of the Reagan era helped the militants of the NRA. The accent on self-reliance, personal responsibility, and less government chimed with the fundamentalist message they preached. The imagery of rugged individualism, the pioneer striding westward toward the setting sun, with his dog at his heels and his gun on his shoulder, unhistorical as it was, appealed alike to a fast-growing NRA membership and to the voters who flocked to the Republican standard. In 1983, for the first time in its history, a serving President of the United States came to an NRA Annual Convention. Speaking at the annual members banquet, with one thousand more people watching on closed-circuit television in an overflow hall, Ronald Reagan expressed his "pride and pleasure" at being the guest of his fellow members of the NRA. It did his spirit good, he said, "to be with people who never lose faith in America, who never stop believing in her future, and who never back down one inch in defending the constitutional freedoms that are every American's birthright."[36] Remarking on the "great respect" in which the "fine, effective leaders" of the NRA were held in Washington, the President continued:

Being part of this group, you know that good organizations don't just happen. They take root in a strong body of shared beliefs. They grow strong from leadership with vision, initiative, and determination to reach great goals. And what you've accomplished speaks for itself—more than 2 million members, and the NRA's getting stronger every day.[37]

The references to never backing down one inch in the defense of constitutional freedoms and the bond of shared beliefs illustrated Reagan's knack of putting into words what his audience felt deeply and wanted to hear from their President. Fortified by the reassuring presence of a soulmate at the White House, the NRA stepped up its political activities during the 1980s. National advertising campaigns were launched to boost the total membership and improve the Association's image by portraying its members as decent and upright citizens, dedicated to responsible gun use. The underlying message throughout was that to confiscate the weapons of such wholesome persons (which had never been proposed) would be unthinkable, an abuse of power, and a step down the road to an authoritarian state.

The lobbying wing, known as the Institute for Legislative Action, maintained the pressure on legislators, reinforcing voluntary persuasion with sanctions. Intervening directly in congressional, state, and local elections, the NRA and its allies supported selected candidates, either by contributing money directly to their campaigns or by providing advertising, mailings or organizational resources. Candidates unsympathetic to the cause were virulently opposed. Although empirical evidence was hard to come by, exit polls and the firsthand experience of elected representatives tended to verify the ability of the NRA to influence the results of certain contests by bringing the single issue of the rights of gun owners to the forefront. Thus it was more than NRA self-promotion that had caused it to become renowned for the effectiveness of its lobbying, and feared for the potential consequences of its electoral intervention.

The fervor of the activists' beliefs left little or no room for compromise. In their minds there was no middle ground. Congressmen and senators were either with them or against them. Those in the first category could look forward to electoral support and were encouraged to obstruct all attempts to restrict the availability of firearms. Those in the second category were treated as enemies, lacking in determination to stand up for fundamental freedoms, and unfit for the responsibilities of lawmaking. As the NRA was fond of reminding waverers, no politician mindful of his or her career would want to challenge its legitimate goals.[38]

V

A combination of factors came together in the early 1990s to weaken the grip of the gun lobby on the levers of power. The widespread revulsion from violent crime, so often aggravated by the use of firearms, continued to grow. Horror story after horror story was featured in the headlines and the electronic media. The public memory may have been short, but the cumulative impact was more enduring. The repeated assertion of the NRA that it was criminals who killed, not guns, failed to explain some of the most notorious incidents. Like much else in populist culture, the claim was based on a stereotype, in this connection a person living off crime, which did not correspond with the reality of many of the deranged, disaffected, or intoxicated individuals who had killed, sometimes on a mass scale, with firearms legally purchased. The point was made succinctly by the judge appointed to carry out a public inquiry and to make recommendations on further safeguards against the misuse of firearms after a mass shooting at a Scottish school in March 1996. A man without any criminal record had entered the school armed with four handguns and 743 rounds of ammunition. He fired 105 rounds with a 9 mm self-loading pistol over a space of three to four minutes, killing sixteen children aged five and six, and one teacher, and wounding ten other pupils and three more teachers. He then shot and killed himself. In reporting to the British Parliament, the judge wrote: "There is no certain means of ruling out the onset of a mental illness of a type that gives rise to danger; or of identifying those whose personalities harbor dangerous propensities. On this ground alone it is insufficient protection for the public merely to tackle the individual rather than the gun."[39]

The frequency of accidental and nonaccidental deaths and other injuries in the home involving firearms caused the medical profession to become increasingly vocal on the need for preventive action. The American Academy of Pediatrics cooperated with the Center to Prevent Handgun Violence to publicize the alarming fact that every day fourteen children under the age of twenty were killed, and many more wounded, by guns. The risk of suicide was five times higher, and of domestic homicide three times higher, if a firearm was available in the home.[40] A survey of eight hundred adult gun owners residing in the United States, carried out in 1994 for the Harvard Injury Control Center and published in the *Journal of the American Medical Association*,[41] found that one-fifth kept loaded weapons in their homes and did not lock them up. One in seven of gun owners with children kept firearms loaded and unlocked. After a review of the literature, the authors concluded that many firearms fatalities were not premeditated. Lethal assaults frequently occurred during arguments, often domestic, when one or both parties had ingested alcohol. Individuals who had taken their own lives had often done so when confronting a severe but temporary crisis. Morbidity and mortality associated with unintentional shootings involving children were often the result of spontaneous happenings that occurred when children found and played with a loaded gun.

Further data established that a high proportion of homicides were killings by family members or friends in the course of quarrels or violent altercations. Disputes between persons who were family members or intimates in New York City were twenty-three times more likely to result in death if a firearm was present at the scene.[42] Firearms were the cause of death for 49.6 percent of all homicides occurring in the home in New York City in 1990 and 1991, and 80.3 percent of those on the streets.[43] The fact that nearly half of all domestic homicides were the result of shooting supported the results of a previous study that showed that guns kept in the home increased the risk of homicide by a family member or intimate acquaintance rather than conferring protection against intruders.[44]

Domestic homicides failed to fit the caricature of the career criminal, nor did the instinctive resort to firearms as a way of resolving some of the most mindless disputes outside the home. In vivid form this was seen in the number of young men roaming city streets armed with semiautomatic weapons ready to shoot each other if provoked by behavior they regarded as disrespectful, or because of gang affiliations. Sometimes strangers were killed accidentally. The relevance of the public health data, and the extent of the heightened risks of domestic homicide, suicide, and unintentional injury to children and adults, was brought home by the Department of Justice statistic that in 1993 nearly half of all U.S. households (49 percent) contained one or more firearms.[45]

In an effort to counter this situation, one of a set of national health promotion objectives adopted for the year 2000 by the U.S. Department of Health and Human Services was a 20 percent reduction in the proportion of people who possess weapons that are ''inappropriately stored and therefore dangerously available.''[46] The unambiguous wording of this official publication aimed at improving national standards of public health is worth noting:

> The impulsive nature of many homicides and suicides suggests that a substantial portion of those events might be prevented if immediate access to lethal weapons was reduced, in particular through appropriate storage of guns and ammunition. More than half of the 20,000 homicide victims in the United States each year are killed by persons they know. In many instances, these homicides are committed impulsively and the perpetrators are immediately remorseful. Similarly, a substantial proportion of the Nation's 30,000 suicides each year are committed impulsively. Impulsive suicide without concomitant clinical depression appears to account for a particularly large proportion of youth suicides. Homicide and suicide attempts are more likely to result in serious injury and death if lethal weapons are used. Firearms are both the most lethal and the most common vehicle used for suicide and homicide, accounting for approximately 60 percent of these violent deaths each year.[47]

While safer storage of firearms would certainly reduce the risk of misuse, some gun owners, female as well as male, might fear that it would inhibit the immediate access to their weapon needed for purposes of self-defense. Here the evidence was contradictory. A comprehensive study, based on National Crime Victimization Survey data between 1987 and 1990, showed that crime victims used firearms for self-defense very rarely.[48] Only in 0.18 percent of all crimes recorded by the NCVS and 0.83 percent of violent offenses was a gun used against an offender. While firearms should not be ruled out as a protection against crime, the conclusions of the study were that criminals faced little threat from armed victims. The probability of armed resistance was not zero, but given that about half of all U.S. households owned a gun, armed self-defense was extremely uncommon. Compared with the risks of wrongful or accidental use of guns kept in the home by family members or acquaintances, the findings of the survey raised questions about the crime-related costs and benefits of civilian firearm ownership.[49]

The NCVS methodology was challenged by the findings of some other studies, which indicated that defensive gun use by victims against criminal perpetrators had been underestimated, and that victims who resisted with guns were less likely to be injured than those who were unarmed.[50] Behind the arguments over the statistics, in particular the way NCVS questions were framed and reservations about the situations in which the replies were obtained, lie important policy implications. It was claimed that prohibitionist measures, whether they included all firearms or were limited to handguns, would result in disarming noncriminal gun owners as well as criminals. This would discourage, and presumably reduce, the defensive gun use that might otherwise save lives, prevent injuries, thwart rape attempts, drive off burglars, and help victims to retain their property.[51]

Apart from the merits of the dispute, a fact of political life is that policy making is conditioned by public attitudes to a far larger extent than by the findings of detailed research surveys. Whatever the actuality, there can be little doubt that the perception of guns in the home or in the street as providing a valuable means of self-protection is widespread. Although it may be unquantifiable, it is a factor that policy makers are unlikely to ignore. This truism was brought out in the relaxation of many state laws regulating the carrying of concealed firearms by civilians. A long list of states followed Florida, which in 1987 had adopted a "shall issue" statute requiring law enforcement agencies to issue a permit to carry concealed firearms to any adult eligible to own guns who had taken a firearms safety course. Persons with a history of drug or alcohol abuse, a felony conviction, mental illness, physical inability, or who were not Florida residents were disqualified from obtaining a license.[52]

Mississippi and Oregon adopted broadly similar statutes in 1990, changing from discretionary "may issue" to mandatory "shall issue" systems. In 1985 the NRA had announced that it would lobby states strongly for this change which it believed would both prevent crime and reduce homicides.[53] While the new policy was intended to, and did, increase the number of people lawfully permitted to carry concealed weapons, the effect on crime was less obvious. Two outcomes were possible. "Shall issue" licensing might reduce crime by deterring potential criminals wanting to avoid victims who might be carrying guns for their own protection. Alternatively, it might raise levels of criminal violence by increasing the number of people with easy access to guns. Since assaults are often impulsive acts involving the most readily available instrument, and guns are the most deadly weapon, more guns might lead to more assaults causing death or serious injury to the victims.[54] Either way, the NRA had admitted a Trojan horse into its camp by conceding the principle of compulsory licensing.

In a before-and-after analysis carried out in the three largest urban areas in Florida, and the single largest urban area in both Mississippi and Oregon, a research study found that there had been a statistically significant enlargement in firearms homicides in three of the five cities, and insignificant changes in the other two.[55] The study was carried out by members of the Violence Research Group and Department of Criminology and Criminal Justice at the University of Maryland, College Park, supported by a grant from the U.S. Public Health Service, Centers for Disease Control and Prevention (CDC). As in the past, the findings were challenged by some academic critics,[56] and rejected angrily by the NRA.

In August 1995, it was reported that the NRA was calling on Congress for the CDC research programs on firearms injuries and deaths to be "disbanded, defunded, and taken completely apart." Its director of federal affairs fulminated that there was nothing important about the research, nothing objective about the analysis, and that the mission was to distort issues relating to firearems. Violence should be treated as a criminal justice issue and not a public health problem.[57] In the next Congress NRA allies sought to reduce the Department of Health and Human Services Appropriations by the amount of the research spending on firearms-related deaths and injuries. The 1997 Appropriations act for the Departments of Labor, Health and Human Services, and Education, went further in specifically providing that none of the funds made available for injury prevention and control at the Centers for Disease Control and Prevention might be used "to advocate or promote gun control."[58]

VI

To take advantage of the emerging signs of climatic change, the incoming tide of opinion had to be channeled and directed toward specific targets if the thrust of public policy was to be intensified. The agent of change, gathering in public opinion and bringing it to bear on legislators, was Handgun Control, Inc. (HCI). From modest beginnings in 1974, HCI had enrolled a membership of some 8,000 across the country by 1980. In the belief that legislation alone would be insufficient to curb gun-related violence, a Center to Prevent Handgun Violence was set up in 1983 to promote education and research. A legal advocacy component was added later, and came to have a high priority as a means of bringing about the most rapid changes. In 1985, Sarah Brady joined the organization, subsequently becoming chairman both of HCI and the Center. By 1994, when the crime bill was before Congress, HCI had a paid-up membership of 450,000 and claimed over one million supporters. The latter total was made up of members past and present, and others who had expressed their support in a variety of ways.

At election time, which had seen the NRA's influence at its peak in the past, HCI also began to campaign vigorously. Receipts for the 1991–92 electoral cycle amounted to $1,101,072 with an expenditure of $938,210. Campaign contributions amounted to $154,862 of which $135,112 went to Democrats and $19,750 to Republicans.[59] Comparable statistics in the same year for the NRA showed a stated membership of 2.8 million (the basis of the calculation not being disclosed), with receipts of $5,971,253. Expenditure totaled $5,708,327, with contributions from its Political Victory Fund amounting to $1,738,446. Of this $1,098,354 went to Republican candidates, and $635,142 to Democratic candidates. Besides contributing directly to candidates for federal, state, and local office, the NRA Political Victory Committee also engaged in independent expenditure activities on behalf of candidates it supported. A candidate's position on gun control was the sole basis for determining an NRA endorsement and NRA/Political Victory Fund campaign gift.

As the statistics quoted above indicate, HCI although smaller and less wealthy than the NRA, was by no means an insignificant competitor. By 1993, the published annual financial statement for HCI showed total revenues reaching $8,055,830 of which $5,553,105 was spent on program services (legislation and adjudication, public education, membership services, and political action), and $2,645,796 on supporting services (management and general, membership development, and fund raising). Equally important was the powerful symbolism of the crippled James Brady, campaigning from a wheelchair often pushed by his indomitable wife. Republicans both, the Bradys were not merely figureheads, but skilled and determined publicists to whom the media responded positively. With an active and highly motivated leadership, HCI established national headquarters in Washington D.C., with offices in New York, Los Angeles, Chicago, San Francisco, and San Diego. By the time the crime bill was introduced in Congress in 1993, the NRA no longer had the field to itself on the gun issue. A formidable opponent, using the techniques of political activism, applying pressure to the same legislators and, ominously for the NRA, with access to the White House, had entered the arena from the other side.

The inability of the NRA to make any move that could be interpreted as an ideological softening of its position, the "not an inch" strategy that had been commended by Reagan, accelerated the pace of its declining support amongst those who might be expected to have been counted amongst its natural allies. To the police and many law enforcement officers the outright refusal by the NRA to contemplate any restrictions on the availability of military-style assault weapons was unacceptable and indefensible. Worse still, on the streets and in other emergency situations, it left policemen at a disadvantage in the firepower at their disposal. The remarks of Robert Morgenthau, District Attorney for Manhattan, were symptomatic of prosecutors and big-city law enforcement officers across the nation:

> [W]e must enact strong Federal gun control legislation. By itself, no state or city can control the spread of illegal guns. Federal leadership and laws are required. Current law bans the importation of assault weapons, but not their manufacture or distribution within our borders. It is small solace to police officers that the weapons overpowering them are made in America.[60]

Nearly a year after its introduction, with many hesitations and compromises, the Congress had enacted the most extensive gun control legislation for quarter of a century. The Brady Handgun Violence Protection Act of 1993 and the Violent Crime Control and Law Enforcement Act of 1994 contained between them six substantive changes in the law restricting the availability of firearms or ammunition, as well as enhanced penalties for a number of crimes involving firearms or explosives. The laxness in the licensing procedures for gun dealers, which already had attracted executive action by the administration, was tightened up. The firearms provisions contained in Title XI of Public Law 103-322 ran to twenty-five pages and are summarized at pp. 227–28 below.

The delay of up to five days to enable checks to be made on the intending purchaser of a handgun (the Brady bill), had by 1991 won the public support of all living former presidents of the United States: Nixon, Ford, Carter, and Reagan; the last named being a great prize won over by Sarah Brady. In addition to the restrictions on the manufacture, transfer, and possession of certain semiautomatic assault weapons,[61] the 1994 Act made four other important changes. They were a ban on large-capacity ammunition-feeding devices;[62] a prohibition against the possession of a handgun or ammunition by, or the private transfer of a handgun or ammunition to, a juvenile (subject to certain exemptions);[63] a prohibition against the disposal of firearms to, or the receipt of firearms by, persons who had committed certain offenses of domestic abuse;[64] and a prohibition against transactions involving stolen firearms which had moved in interstate or foreign commerce.[65] The gun dealer licensing provisions of the Act[66] went further and gave the force of statute law to the directive issued by the President the previous year in an effort to cut down on the number of persons dealing in firearms who should not be licensed. In future, all applications for federal licenses would have to be accompanied by photo identification and fingerprints. It would be a condition of the license to conduct the business in compliance with the requirements of state and local law.[67]

Another straw in the wind, indicative of changing attitudes amongst manufacturers, came in November 1993 when Black Talon handgun ammunition was withdrawn from sale to the public. This bullet, which with others had come to the critical notice of Senator Moynihan (Dem. New York), was designed to split open into six prongs on entering the body. These then spun and were specifically destructive of the organs in the area of the body entered.[68] According to the manufacturer, the decision had been taken because Black Talon ammunition was becoming a focal point for broader issues that were well beyond their control. The controversy threatened the good name of Winchester, which had stood for the safe and responsible use of arms and ammunition for 125 years.[69]

Moynihan's campaign, pursued for several years, differed from other protagonists of gun control in that it was based on a single causative factor which he encapsulated in a parody of the NRA slogan: guns don't kill people; bullets do. Unlike firearms which had a long life measured in decades, generations, or even centuries, ammunition had a far shorter finite life. Moreover, while the supply of handguns in existence could last for two centuries, there was only a four-year supply of ammunition. Since 1918 manufacturers of ammunition had been taxed, and since 1938 the Bureau of Alcohol, Tobacco, and Firearms required a license to manufacture. In supporting the efforts to control access to handguns, Moynihan recognized that with an estimated 200 million in the United States, and between one million and 1.7 million handguns in the City of New York alone, guns were not going to go away.[70] His argument that the availability of ammunition, particularly in its most lethal forms, should be subjected to greater restriction and higher taxation was convincing, as well as persistently maintained.

By the time the crime bill was signed into law by the President in September 1994, public health and epidemiological approaches[71] toward counteracting the epidemic of gun crime had conjoined the more familiar approaches to the rational formulation of policy. But, as we have seen, policy toward gun crime was dictated less by rational considerations than by an irrational belief, deeply held, that the federal government wanted to confiscate people's guns. It was this dogma, cultivated by the NRA, and rooted in mistrust of a distant and interfering government, that had facilitated political mobilization.

The controversy over abortion is another issue on which feelings run deep. The findings of a large-scale citizen participation survey published in 1995 showed pro-choice and pro-life views polarized at the extremities of a scale indicating degrees of intensity of opinion. Although opinion on abortion was clustered at the ends of the issue continuum, it was not balanced. More than twice as many respondents registered extremely pro-choice views as registered extremely pro-life views. Yet the impact of those holding pro-life attitudes on political activity was more than twice as great as those holding pro-choice attitudes. The effect of education was to bring in an activist population that was more pro-choice, whereas the effect of religious factors was to enhance the number of pro-life activists.[72] The survey did not measure attitudes toward gun control, although there appear to be parallels between the intensity with which pro-life attitudes toward abortion are held and the rights of gun owners.

Elections are when political activists come into their own, relishing the opportunities to demonstrate their strength. At the termination of the 103rd Congress, it was still the special interest groups dedicated to preserving the rights of gun owners that set the parameters beyond which legislators strayed at their peril. Senator Mitchell's forecast that the NRA had not lost its clout as a result of its defeat in Congress was soon borne out by events. Only weeks later, the NRA sought retribution at the polls. "This year," the NRA's chief lobbyist, Tanya Metaksa, proclaimed, "it's payback time—time to reward our friends and punish our enemies."[73]

Democratic casualties in the mid-term congressional elections on November 8 included Jim Sasser, chairman of the Senate Budget Committee, in Tennessee,[74] and two of the most prominent members of the House of Representatives. Thomas Foley in Washington was the first Speaker of the House to be defeated in the twentieth century, and in Texas Jack Brooks went down to defeat after forty-two years in Congress. In each case there were other factors besides the hostile intervention of the NRA, notably the compelling forces that swept the Republicans to a victory of landslide proportions nationally.[75] Yet the NRA and its associates, such as Gun Owners of America, which opposed Brooks, were adept at picking contests where they could make a difference. For Brooks, more than anyone else, there was cruel irony that his political career should have ended in this way, since he had long been an outspoken opponent of gun control. Nevertheless, the fact that he had voted, however reluctantly, for the crime bill containing the ban on certain assault weapons and other restrictions on firearms was enough to condemn him in the eyes of the unforgiving zealots who were determined to make a public display of undiminished strength.

No accurate measure exists of the impact of the gun control issue on the results of individual elections in 1994. But at the heart of government there were no doubts. In his State of the Union Address in January 1995 the President said:

> The last Congress passed the Brady Bill and the ban on 19 assault weapons. I think everybody in this room knows that several members of the last Congress who voted for the assault weapons ban and the Brady Bill lost their seats because of it. Neither the bill supporters (nor) I believe anything should be done to infringe upon the legitimate right of our citizens to bear arms for hunting and sporting purposes. Those people laid down their seats in Congress to try to keep more police and children from laying down their lives in our streets under a hail of assault weapons' bullets. And I will not see that ban repealed.[76]

VII

Below the surface of the legislation, ideological currents ran strongly. Apart from gun control, the mechanism by which a large part of the additional federal funding was to be made available to the states for prison construction and operation was conditional on the acceptance of the so called truth-in-sentencing objective that violent offenders should serve 85 percent of their sentence in custody. Whether or not this policy would lead to a reduction in the incidence of violent crime, and if so what the projected costs and savings would be, mattered less than its appearance as a seemingly tough approach in tune with the public mood. In other parts of the Act, for example the intention to curtail the power of the federal courts to regulate overcrowding in state prisons and local detention facilities; the notification requirements of the addresses of released sex offenders; and the admissibility in evidence of the commission of previous alleged offenses of sexual assault where no conviction had resulted; long-standing case law and procedural rules designed to protect accused, but not convicted, persons in the criminal process were abruptly swept aside.

With the exception of the prevention programs, there was little display of concern during the passage of the 1994 Act for the traditional American values of fairness, economic efficiency and the social consequences of governmental action. Such an outcome may have resulted as much from a lessening in the hold of liberal idealism on the center ground of politics and the law as a deliberate move to the political Right. Taken as a group, few lawmakers would have been able to agree on where to place the Act on a graduated ideological spectrum. Appearances were all-important. The practical application of such a varied collection of largely self-contained provisions would depend less on the intentions of the legislators in Congress than on the myriad factors, predictable or otherwise, that would bear on their implementation.

It is commonplace for legislators to overlook the proposition, elegantly expressed by Judge Posner, that the criminal justice system is a machine comprising a set of interrelated and interacting parts, each of which has a function in maintaining the system. The parts are in the hands of different branches of government, and the American commitment to separation of powers keeps it that way.[77] Congress may pass laws, and the President may use his executive authority, but it is for the courts to decide on the constitutionality of their actions. The subsequent course of events on the Brady Act, including a successful challenge in the Supreme Court to the way it was implemented, and the crime policies enacted in the 104th Congress, are described in the chapters that follow.

At the end of the day, the new public law represented the sum of a series of political decisions, connected loosely by the requirements of compromise, on issues that had been propelled into the federal legislative arena by the force of special interests or their perceived popular appeal. As in the previous Congresses, some issues remained gridlocked, habeas corpus reform and the racial impact of capital sentencing being foremost amongst them. While the 103rd Congress did succeed in passing a comprehensive bill, which its immediate predecessors had failed to do, it was unlikely in practice to live up to its title of controlling violent crime. Despite the substantial extra funding that was authorized for state action, subject to the prescribed conditions being met, the vast bulk of criminal offenses, when and if detected, would continue to be prosecuted, tried, sentenced, and punished under state law by the individual states.[78]

Of all the provisions in the 1994 crime legislation, the most important, functionally, symbolically, and as an expression of the national mood, were those related to gun control. For the NRA and the gun rights lobby, it was a battle lost. Other voices, less strident and apparently more reasonable, criticized the emphasis on gun control as a panacea that was bound to fail because of Americans' love of guns and their utility for the purposes of deterrence and self-defense.[79] The world-weary resignation implicit in this view came close to accepting the fallacy promulgated sedulously by the NRA: that the aim of the Administration's policy was the outright prohibition, rather than the regulation, of firearms held for legitimate purposes. Unschematic and unpredictable as had been the passage by Congress of the individual regulatory provisions, each of them so patently justified on their merits, there had been a consistency of purpose from the outset: to restrict the ease of access to deadly weapons. The degree of restriction was related to ascertainable risk factors such as the intrinsic dangerousness of certain firearms, for example, assault weapons, or the age, state of mind, or previous misconduct of would-be purchasers of handguns.

For his handling of the issue, credit must go to President Clinton. In the short term at least, it seemed that this verdict was shared by the public. During the final stages of the crime bill, when Clinton had refused to compromise on the assault weapons ban, a *USA Today* poll indicated that confidence in the President's handling of crime jumped from 29 to 42 percent.[80] Unlike his tactic on some other issues, of which three strikes was an example, intervening at a critical juncture to move ahead policy proposals that had their origin elsewhere, on firearms he had marked out his position at the start and saw it through to the end. The same determination was evident in his commitment to 100,000 more police officers on the streets. In his approach to the treacherous terrain of gun control, the President showed political courage in positioning himself one step ahead of the general public, articulating and acting in harmony with their latent wishes in defiance of the demands of a louder, more politically active minority. On August 11, 1993, when first announcing the anti-crime initiative, Clinton had spoken of ending the insanity of being able to buy or sell a handgun more easily than obtaining a driver's license. The same day he signed two presidential directives aimed at reducing gun violence. He had stated explicitly that the effort would not be complete if assault weapons were not eliminated from the streets: "No other nation would tolerate roving gangs stalking the streets better armed than the police officers of a country. Why do we do it? We shouldn't, and we ought to stop it."[81] Twelve months later, in one of the most fiercely controversial of all policy areas, and with the equivocal consent of the Congress, those legislative objectives had been achieved.

VIII

The 1994 Act, representing an investment in excess of $30 billion over six years, was claimed to be the largest federal anti-crime legislation in the nation's history.[82] One feature, which attracted little notice, was the comprehensiveness of the research agenda mandated by Congress in an attempt to assess the effects of many of its programs. Policing, sentencing and corrections, substance abuse treatment and drug courts, violence against women, law enforcement family support, and DNA forensic testing, were each to be subjected to research and evaluation. The list did not stop short of the assault weapons ban. Subtitle A of Title XI required the Attorney General to investigate and study the effect of the prohibition, with particular reference to its impact, if any, on violent crime and drug trafficking. The study was to be conducted over a period of eighteen months, commencing twelve months after enactment. The findings and determinations were to be reported to the Congress not later than thirty months from the date of enactment.[83] To satisfy these directions the National Institute of Justice, the research and development arm of the U.S. Department of Justice,[84] commissioned an evaluation from the Urban Institute. The final report containing the findings was published in March 1997.[85]

Between 1994 and 1995, the criminal use of assault weapons, as measured by law enforcement agency requests for ATF traces of guns associated with crimes, fell by 20 percent. This statistic compared with an 11 percent decrease for all guns. While ATF requests for traces were acknowledged to be an imperfect measure, since they reflected no more than a small percentage of guns used in crime, similar trends were identified in an analysis of all guns recovered in crime in two cities, Boston and St. Louis. The conclusion of the study was that although the potential impact of the assault weapons ban was limited by the fact that such weapons were never involved in more than a modest fraction of all gun murders, the best estimate was that the ban had contributed to a 6.7 percent decrease in total gun murders between 1994 and 1995, beyond what would have been expected in view of ongoing crime, demographic, and economic trends.[86] The proportion of police murders involving assault weapons was higher than that for civilian murders.[87]

In the context of the notorious mass killings that had been such an influence on the votes in Congress, the study found good reasons for believing that assault weapons were more prevalent in mass murders than in events involving smaller numbers of victims.[88] Two hypotheses put forward were that the characteristics of assault weapons, especially their high magazine capacities, enabled a rational but intent killer to shoot more people more rapidly with an assault weapon than with many other firearms, whereas deranged killers might tend to select assault weapons to act out commando fantasies.

The thirty-month timeframe meant that the storm over the assault weapons ban had blown itself out before the publication of the research findings on its effects. An ill-judged attempt by the House of Representatives in the 104th Congress to repeal the ban proved to be damagingly counter-productive for the NRA and its allies on the Hill. The police organizations remained resolutely supportive of the legislative restrictions. The verification of the extreme dangerousness of assault weapons in the commission of lethal crime, however cautiously expressed in the conclusions of the study, could not be dismissed. The volume of gun-related homicides in the early 1990s was so high that the estimated reduction of 6.7 percent on the 1994 total of 15,456 gun murders[89] indicated that over a thousand lives may have been saved.

Chapter 6

———

Processing the Contract

I

With the main legislative controversies settled, for a time at least, relatively meager public attention was directed toward the postenactment outcomes of the 1994 law on violent crime and law enforcement. The attention span of the mass media, matching the hectic pace of political life in Washington, is usually short. There is a rhythm to national politics and its reporting. Specific legislative issues get lifted up by waves generated by the interaction of the administration's objectives and tactics, the ambitions of elected representatives, the pressures of lobbyists on Congress, and the value judgments made by the media. Sooner or later the moment comes when interest switches to other targets and the waves subside. Although the almost universal public concern at the prevalence of crime showed no signs of abating, the sense of relief that a massive 355-page act on crime control at last had reached the safe haven of the Statutes at Large seemed to have stifled any disposition on the part of legislators to scrutinize what happened to its provisions in the very different political environment of the 104th Congress.

The starting point for the next phase of the narrative must be the Contract with America.[1] This bold and original plan was unveiled in Washington by Representatives Newt Gingrich of Georgia, Dick Armey of Texas, and other

124

House Republican leaders on September 27, 1994. More than three hundred Republican candidates for election to the House of Representatives in the forthcoming elections assembled on the West Front of the U.S. Capitol for a mass signing ceremony on an unusually warm and sunny autumn day. The skillfully staged and widely publicized rally bolstered the confidence of those who would be facing the voters in six weeks' time. They set off on the campaign trail furnished with a remarkable document, a detailed manifesto presented in the novel guise of a contract between the House Republicans and the American people. A list of reforms to the internal procedures of the House, to be introduced on the first day of the 104th Congress, was backed up by ten bills on carefully selected issues to be brought to the floor for debate and put to a vote during the first hundred days of the new Congress.

The reforms set out in the Contract were aimed at "restoring the faith and trust of the American people in their government."[2] They rested upon what were claimed to be the basic principles of American civilization, but were more readily identified as the hallmarks of current conservative ideology: individual liberty, economic opportunity, limited government, personal responsibility, and security at home and abroad.[3] The eventual total of 367 members and candidates who signed the Contract with America pledged themselves to honor the terms of the pact. Despite strenuous efforts to enroll Republicans in the Senate, they stood aloof and were not bound by the Contract. Three current members of the House,[4] and three other Republican candidates for election, did the same.

The consciously populist appeal of the document meant that some of the most cherished causes of the radical/religious Right were omitted lest they alienated the moderate voters whose support would be needed if the Republicans were to gain control of the next Congress. Although the Democratic 103rd Congress had been portrayed as arrogant, free-spending, and out of touch, a favorite theme of right-wing radio talk-show hosts, and the President's personal popularity was at a low ebb, disillusionment had to be converted into votes at the election that would mark the middle of the term won by Clinton in 1992. Thus there was no mention of abortion, prayer in schools, or repeal of the assault weapons ban.

Of the ten bills, or more accurately commitments to bills, which found a place in the Contract, one was an anti-crime package. It comprised such familiar Republican themes as strengthening the policy of truth in sentencing, good-faith exemptions from the exclusionary rule barring the use of evidence improperly obtained, and more stringent death penalty provisions. Prevention programs would be cut back or eliminated, both because of skepticism as to their effectiveness and to make possible additional prison construction and law enforcement spending without jeopardizing the fundamental strategic aim of a balanced budget by 2002. The crime proposals were evocatively titled the Taking Back Our Streets Act (H.R. 3). Also resurrected was the proposal, dropped from the 1994 Act, to federalize large numbers of state violent or drug crimes that involved the possession of a gun.

When the votes were in and counted the magnitude of the Republican victory at the polls on November 8 became apparent. In the Senate, Republicans won eight seats to gain control by 53 to 47 members. Far more significant was their victory in the House of Representatives. There Republicans won 52 seats from Democrats, increasing their numerical strength from 178 to 230 members. The Democrats retained 204 seats. Thirty-four Democrats standing for reelection were defeated, compared with not a single Republican incumbent. For the first time in forty years the Republicans had majorities in both Houses. As an analysis of the election results in the *Congressional Quarterly Almanac* pithily commented: "A Democratic president held in disfavor and a Democratic-controlled Congress held in disrepute gave Republican candidates a target they could not miss."[5] At a deeper level was the continuing shift toward the Republican Party brought about by the changing political demography of the southern states.

The same trend, if not so dramatic, was shown in the elections for state governors and legislative seats held on the same day. No incumbent Republican governor was defeated, and no legislative chamber changed hands to the advantage of the Democrats. Eleven state governorships were won by Republicans from Democrats, increasing their total of governorships to thirty, their first majority since 1970. Among the fallen were such prominent governors as Mario Cuomo of New York and Ann Richards of Texas.

Once elected, the first priority of the House Republicans was to deliver on their prospectus. Although each of the legislative commitments presented to the voters in the Contract was accompanied by a brief description, the actual bills were not drafted until after the election. Little detailed preparatory work had been done in advance, and the hundred-day mandate imposed a sense of urgency. The work of drafting, hastily carried out by committee staffs and others, was supervised by the new majority leader, Dick Armey, and his aides. In places the resulting bills contained some items that had not been forecast in the Contract, while others were omitted.

Out of necessity, as one perceptive observer noted, the Contract metamorphosed from a campaign document into something else.[6] Not only did it set clear legislative goals for the first months of the new Congress, but it provided the leverage to enable changes to be made in the ingrained culture of the House of Representatives. Committees and subcommittees were merged, some being renamed, others having their jurisdictions varied. Committee staffs were cut back by a third. Three main committees and 31 out of a total of 115 subcommittees were abolished. The strict application of the seniority rule, which conferred status and power on committee chairmen according to their length of service, was abandoned, the power surrendered being diverted toward Speaker Gingrich and the committee members who owed their nominations to him.

The chairmanship of the Committee on the Judiciary, previously the preserve of the Democrat Jack Brooks, went to a seventy-year-old Republican, Henry Hyde of Illinois. Despite the length of his service in Congress, having been first elected in 1974, Hyde was not the ranking Republican on the committee, but neither was there any likelihood that he would act as a placeman of Gingrich. "If you were casting Newt's inner circle," one of his colleagues on the Judiciary Committee volunteered, "Henry Hyde would not be in the front row."[7] Although a staunch conservative on some issues, and a leading anti-abortionist, Hyde had demonstrated his independence from the leadership in the 103rd Congress by voting both for the Brady bill and the safety valve for the sentencing of nonviolent first-time drug offenders. Still more pivotal had been his role as the only Republican member of the Judiciary Committee to vote for the ban on assault weapons. The example set by such a senior and respected member served to fortify the moderate group of Republicans who were instrumental in retaining the ban in the 1994 Act.

While readily acknowledging the success of the Contract strategy in wresting control of the House from the hands of the Democrats, Hyde was apprehensive that too much was being attempted too quickly. But he accepted the political imperative of accomplishing the highly publicized goal of bringing the promised bills to the floor of the House within the stated time limit. There was no delay in bringing forward the Taking Back Our Streets Act, but neither was there any delay in the reaction of the administration. The Department of Justice had been hard at work, and on January 26 a comprehensive and detailed critique of the bill's contents was sent to Hyde by the Assistant Attorney General for Legislative Affairs, Sheila Anthony. In part the letter, which ran to twenty-seven pages, was conciliatory in tone, referring to certain provisions that would supplement the 1994 Act. Most of these related to matters left aside the previous year: the strengthening of federal death penalty procedures, habeas corpus and exclusionary rule reform; mandatory victim restitution; the deportation of criminal aliens; and limiting abusive prisoner litigation. As the course of events was to show, there was ample room for controversy over the scope and detail of changes in these areas, yet the broad policy objectives were not at issue. Much sterner in tone was the language of the letter referring to the efforts to undo or repeal key elements of the crime legislation passed by the previous Congress:

> [W]e strenuously oppose provisions of H.R. 3 that would fundamentally alter the Public Safety Partnership and Community Policing Act ("COPS") program and the prison funding program, and that indiscriminately repeal most of the crime prevention programs in the 1994 Act. It would be a tragic mistake to repeal a program to put 100,000 new police officers on the streets, and replace it with a plan to pass out $10 billion of taxpayers' funds with *no assurance that any specific improvement in public safety will result.* . . .
>
> Similarly, it would be foolish to slash virtually all of the bipartisan crime prevention programs included in the 1994 Act. It is mystifying why anyone would advance an ill-advised proposal to repeal wholesale programs supported by police, prosecutors, and parents that implement common sense measures to protect our children from crime—such as keeping schools open after hours and on weekends as safe havens, or getting tough on drug abusing offenders

through coerced abstinence and mandatory drug-testing. While these programs account for about one-fifth of the Act's funding, in the view of police officers around the country, they are a critical aspect of the Act's comprehensive attack on crime. The proposals to repeal or fundamentally revise these programs in H.R. 3 are in many respects illogical and ineffective, and would disserve anti-crime objectives. *Passage of these aspects of H.R. 3 would mean fewer police officers on the streets, fewer violent criminals behind bars, and significantly less assistance to state and local governments that are trying to take proactive measures to prevent crime.*[8]

To avert an outbreak of the trench warfare that could result from a frontal assault by the victorious majority, the leadership decided to split H.R. 3 into a series of shorter single-issue bills. There were two reasons for this tactic. The first was a calculation to keep a stream of bills moving rapidly through the House in the opening hundred days at a pace that denied Democrats the opportunity to marshal effective national opposition. It takes time to put coalitions together, to identify and agree on the messages to be communicated to the public, and for the public or the interest groups to respond by putting pressure on elected representatives in Washington.[9] Opposition usually builds up slowly, whereas the cascade of legislative initiatives, combined with the stringent timetable, meant that there would be insufficient time for opposition forces to be mobilized.

The second reason was more prosaic, but it furnished a shield against unwelcome intervention from an ominous quarter. With the original bill broken into separate parts, only amendments germane to the respective part could be offered. By narrowing the scope of the anti-crime measures the risk of an NRA-sponsored attempt to repeal the ban on assault weapons was averted. A hostage to fortune was left behind in the shape of an undertaking given by Gingrich and Armey to the NRA that once the Contract items were out of the way they would take up the assault weapons ban. For the time being the NRA and its allies in Congress regarded the prospect of overturning the Brady Act as unattainable.

The danger of escalating the controversy over the assault weapons ban also provided the justification for abandoning the most far-reaching of the titles of H.R. 3. The proposal in Title II to federalize drug trafficking and violent felonies under state law where a firearm which had crossed state lines was involved in the commission of a violent or drugs offense (the D'Amato amendment that had caused such consternation to the Judicial Conference of the United States when it was passed by the Senate before being eliminated from the 1994 Crime Act) would open the way to prosecute several hundreds of thousands of gun-related crimes in the federal courts each year. Apart from the enormous practical implications in terms of cost and resources, it would have represented the largest, and least carefully thought out, expansion of the federal criminal jurisdiction in modern times. The appeal to the public was intentionally rhetorical. Because gun crime was so prevalent and so serious in its harmful effects, it was contended that elected representatives in Congress should recognize the strength of public feeling by prescribing severe punishment for the perpetrators instead of wasting time with restrictive and possibly ineffective bans on the private possession of firearms. Yet in practice it was hard to see how the policy could amount to anything more than a false promise of action, adding no perceptible degree of security against offenses that were already strictly prosecuted and penalized by state and local law enforcement. There was irony too in the espousal of so sweeping a measure of federalization by members of a party wedded to the doctrine that the reach of federal authority should be reduced, and states encouraged to make their own laws to govern their own citizens.

Each of the six bills embodying the provisions on crime, described as constituting the "toughest crime package approved by the House of Representatives in decades,"[10] won the consent of the House within the hundred-day deadline. Under the heading "Promises Made, Promises Kept," they were summarized as set out below in *Restoring the Dream,* the sequel to the *Contract with America.*[11]

- *Mandatory Victim Restitution* [H.R. 665], Approved: 431–0.

No longer will victims be the forgotten casualties of violent crime. Our bill requires criminals to pay full restitution for damages caused as a result of federal crimes.

- *Additional Spending for Prison Construction* [H.R. 667], Approved: 265–156.

This bill authorizes $10.5 billion of funding for new state prison construction, up from $8 billion in Clinton's bill. A condition of these funds is that states keep their violent criminals behind bars. To receive funds, states must now comply with truth-in-sentencing guidelines, which require convicted felons to serve at least 85 percent of their sentence, before being released from prison. Studies show that 40 percent of crimes are now committed by convicts released early from prison.

- *Law Enforcement Block Grants* [H.R. 728], Approved: 238–192.

This bill eliminates the social spending in the Democrats' bill and allows states and localities to use these funds for genuine law-enforcement programs, such as putting more cops on the street or buying new crime-fighting equipment. This approach saves $1.4 billion over five years.

- *Good Faith Exemptions to the Exclusionary Rule* [H.R. 666], Approved: 289–142.

This bill allows prosecutors to use evidence in court gathered by law-enforcement officers acting without a warrant, but in good faith and not unreasonably. This will help prevent violent criminals from avoiding conviction based on minor technicalities.

- *Limitations on Death Penalty Appeals for Capital Crimes* [H.R. 729], Approved: 297–132.

This bill places a one-year limitation on the filing of death penalty appeals. This act will facilitate the swift execution of convicted cold-blooded

murderers, such as those responsible for the bombing of the federal building
in Oklahoma City.
• *Deportation of Criminal Aliens* [H.R. 668], Approved: 380–20.
States today spend hundreds of millions of dollars imprisoning illegal aliens
convicted of violent crimes. This bill facilitates the deportation of criminal
aliens who are in the United States without a green card.

II

The obligation incurred by the Contract was limited to bringing the original
list of bills to a vote on the floor of the House, not that they would be passed
into law. The distinction was an important one, if little understood by the
general public, made necessary by the inability of House Republicans to speak
for their colleagues in the Senate, let alone a Democratic President in the White
House. Nevertheless, the achievement in getting all save one of the ten published commitments approved by the House of Representatives within ninety-
three days was an exceptional feat of sustained motivation and cohesion. The
sole failure was a forlorn attempt to replace career politicians with citizen
legislators. The bill, titled the Citizen Legislature Act, imposed term limits of
twelve years service or less on members of the House of Representatives and
the Senate. As a constitutional amendment it required a two-thirds vote of
approval. On March 29, 1995, four different versions of an amendment were
put to the vote, but each fell short of the two-thirds majority needed to make
the change.

The ideal of curtailing the length of time that elected representatives could
serve in the Congress of the United States epitomized the populist appeal and
practical weakness of the Contract's approach. The policy of term limits, according to Gingrich writing on the opening day of the debate, was at heart a
statement on how the country had been run and how it should be run in the
future. In an article contributed to the *Washington Post* he asserted that the
overwhelming public support for the proposal (nearly 80 percent according to
some polls) was more than a brief feeling of disgust with government on behalf
of the American people. The Speaker continued grandiloquently:

> Rather we understand what our citizens know in their hearts: This is an
> America standing on the doorstep of the 21st century, which no longer needs
> or desires a class of permanent career politicians who are there to solve each
> and every problem....
> [T]he 21st century America will benefit more from having regular turn-
> over in its elected leaders; the 21st century America will gain insight from
> the influx of new ideas; the 21st century America will thrive with continual
> waves of new leaders with fresh alternatives. Upon doing their period of serv-
> ice, these citizen-statesmen will return to their private-sector lives and remain
> productive resources for their own communities.[12]

Rousing as it might be on the campaign trail, such a message was less
attractive to the totality of largely career politicians elected to membership of

the 104th Congress. As a constitutional amendment it needed 290 votes to pass if all members voted (a two-thirds majority). Since the full Republican roll-call numbered 230, it was evident that a substantial addition of Democrat votes was needed to have any chance of succeeding. Yet the confrontational style of the new Republican ascendancy had alienated many of those who might have been well-disposed toward the principle. Moreover, there were waverers, and some forthright opponents, Hyde among them,[13] in the Republican ranks.

The reality of the failure to persuade the House to impose term limits on itself may have owed something to self-interest, but insufficient weight was given to the value of experience and judgment, at times maturing into wisdom, enabling some longer-serving congressmen to stand back from the pressures of the day and ruminate on where the true national interests lay. Shorn of their presence, it was at least a plausible thesis that power would be tilted away from Capitol Hill to the executive branch. Reelection every two years, more frequent than for most other directly elected national legislatures, was a continuing antidote to the possibility of losing touch with electors and becoming insensitive to their interests.

After failing in 1995, Gingrich promised to make term limits the subject of the first vote of significance on the floor of the House in the 105th Congress. He kept his word, and on February 12, 1997, the House of Representatives voted again on a constitutional amendment limiting terms to a maximum of twelve years in each House. This time the main vote of 217 to 211 not only fell far short of the required two-thirds majority, but the amendment won the support of ten fewer representatives than on the previous occasion.

The subsequent progress of the six crime bills that were passed by the House was fitful. All were held up in the Senate, and none became law as a freestanding act. But the device of omnibus legislation enabled the core portions of five of the six bills to be included in more far-reaching legislation passed by both Houses and signed by President Clinton, before the close of the second session in the fall of 1996. Only the renewed effort to amend the exclusionary rule (H.R. 666) failed to build up enough of a head of steam to carry it through into law. Under this rule, evidence that had been discovered as a result of improper police action could not be introduced in a federal or state criminal trial. Critics argued fervently that its application suppressed evidence of unquestionable reliability and led to the acquittal of many who were obviously guilty.[14] The contrary view was that the Fourth Amendment protection against unreasonable searches and seizures[15] was a right guaranteed by the Constitution that should not be diluted. Not only did it serve as an essential bulwark to resist the undermining of due process and the supremacy of the rule of law, but more pointedly it was the single constitutional provision that governed police conduct more directly than any other.

In 1984 the Supreme Court had modified the rule to allow the introduction of evidence that had been obtained in good faith relying on a search warrant that subsequently was determined to be invalid.[16] Despite the fact that warrantless searches or seizures are presumptively unreasonable, and so unlawful, in practice many are carried out in the absence of a warrant. The courts have recognized a number of exceptions to the warrant requirement including searches incident to lawful arrests; searches conducted under "exigent circumstances" where delay would impose an unacceptable risk of flight or the destruction of evidence; seizures of evidence in "plain view"; and seizures of persons in "hot pursuit." In such cases the probable cause requirement is tested after the fact, usually in the context of a motion by the accused to exclude the evidence.[17]

The Republican reformers were not content to let the courts nibble away at the practical application of a rule dating from the high tide of decisions of the Supreme Court safeguarding individual liberty and privacy in the 1960s.[18] They wanted to go further by amending the law to permit evidence to be introduced that had been obtained during a search or seizure conducted with the objectively reasonable belief that it was in accordance with the Fourth Amendment, regardless of whether or not a search warrant had been granted or applied for. Persons whose rights were violated by federal law enforcement officers would have expanded rights to sue offending agencies for damages in civil actions.

In a statement of administration policy (SAP) the Executive Office of the President said that the administration supported the passage of H.R. 666, with the all-important proviso that it was amended to apply the good-faith exception to the search-and-seizure exclusionary rule only when a search warrant had been obtained. The SAP said that with this modification the Act would be consistent with the current prevailing approach of most courts and state legislatures that had not recognized a good-faith exception for nonwarrant cases. The approach would provide an appropriate incentive for officers to obtain warrants before carrying out searches and seizures.[19]

The floor debate on the Exclusionary Rule Reform Act, although ending in a comfortable majority of 289 to 142 members voting for the passage of the bill,[20] revealed cross-currents of opinion that did not augur well for its future progress. As illustrated by their speeches, it was not so much the potential for misconduct by the police that worried some of the more vociferous legislators as the allegedly high-handed practices of certain federal enforcement agencies, notably the Bureau of Alcohol, Tobacco and Firearms (ATF) and the Immigration and Naturalization Service (INS). Speaker after speaker roundly denounced instances of illegitimate intrusion into private homes and arbitrary searches by federal agents. Whereas the purpose of the reform was to make it easier for law enforcement authorities to investigate wrongdoing, by bringing evidence necessary to obtain convictions before trial courts, an improbable alliance linking liberal Democrats with supporters of the NRA voted to exempt searches and seizures carried out by, or under the authority of, the ATF from the provisions of the Act.[21] As a result, ATF agents would have to operate under a stricter standard than other officers. A similar amendment to exempt INS searches and seizures failed by 330–103 votes.[22]

Another multisided controversy, the locus of even more passionate convictions, was over repeated habeas corpus petitions to the federal courts by prisoners who had been condemned to death in state courts and exhausted their appeal rights. Although there was widespread dissatisfaction with the long drawn-out procedures that had resulted in more than three thousand inmates as of mid-1995 being held on death row for periods of ten years or more after being sentenced to death, there was no general agreement on how best to reform the complex system of appeals and postconviction review that had grown up. In Georgia, Florida, Alabama, and Texas, four states with an active death penalty, the average length of time between the original conviction for murder and sentence of death, and the ultimate execution, was eleven and three-quarter years. Giving testimony on H.R. 3 before the House Subcommittee on Crime in January 1995, a Senior Assistant Attorney General for the State of Georgia said that the period was often extended to fourteen or fifteen years. One case, where the defendant pled guilty, had been litigated for over fifteen and a half years, being reviewed by 132 judges on fourteen or fifteen different occasions.[23]

During the 1960s and 1970s the scope of federal relief by way of the writ of habeas corpus had been transformed by decisions of the Supreme Court. Together with the due process clause of the Constitution, and the other guarantees contained in the Fourth, Fifth, and Sixth Amendments, the case law had evolved into an unwritten national code of criminal procedure.[24] Habeas corpus provided the judicial machinery to enforce federally guaranteed constitutional rights against state power in noncapital as well as in capital cases. But the return of the death penalty in the mid-1970s, and the growing number of states reinstating capital sentencing, made federal habeas corpus the primary battleground for death penalty litigation.[25]

The burden on the Supreme Court was heavy and when, after years of legal argument, stays of execution came to be considered, the urgency was acute. Although the elements of a procedural code were in place, the accumulated mass of case law failed to yield any generally accepted principles. To impartial and well-informed observers the Court appeared to be fractured, with no one able to predict what would happen next.[26] Whereas some decisions significantly restricted access to the writ, others declined to impose similar restrictions. Of the six habeas cases cited in the Supreme Court Yearbook for the 1994–95 term,[27] all save one resulted in split decisions. In each of the two death row cases the decision was reached by a bare majority of five to four.[28] In both cases, lower court rulings imposing stricter standards for granting habeas corpus review were reversed.

However protracted in duration and unsure in outcome, the value of the process as a protection against possible miscarriages of justice was demonstrated by the fact that relief was granted in a meaningful, if declining, proportion of capital petitions reviewed in the federal courts. Estimates varied between 17 and 42 percent, depending on the yardstick employed for measurement.[29] Another analysis, published by the Department of Justice, estimated that between January 1, 1973, and May 30, 1990, 558 death sentences had been vacated by federal courts as being unconstitutional.[30]

From a different quarter came a cri de coeur, reverberating from one state capitol to another, that in any jurisdiction where the death penalty existed the consequent litigation was a black hole absorbing "as much time, and as much money and as much lawyering, as judges will permit."[31] With a procedure that was so slow, expensive, and inefficient, and caught between irreconcilable beliefs, each of the prior legislative initiatives to reform habeas corpus had foundered. An earlier chapter described how the compact reached by Reno and Biden with state prosecutors on changes in habeas corpus procedures came unstitched when subjected to congressional pressures during the passage of the Violent Crime Control and Law Enforcement Act in 1994.

III

While the remainder of the House anti-crime package in the spring of 1995 was delayed in the Senate, with Republicans undecided about how far and how fast to follow their colleagues in the House, an opportunity occurred to take up once again the vexatious issue of habeas corpus reform. A bill, titled the Habeas Corpus and Death Penalty Act (H.R. 729), implementing the Contract with America commitment, had been passed by the House on February 8, 1995, but there was a distinct possibility of it going the same way as its predecessors, were it not for the device of linking it to a larger, more urgent, and less controversial measure. Such a vehicle was available in the shape of legislation (S. 735) aimed at countering terrorism, which was currently before the Senate. This was the major criminal justice initiative of the 104th Congress and one which had the support of the President and the leadership of both parties.

The original bill was a bipartisan response to the evident threats posed by international terrorist activity and had been in the making since the bombing of the World Trade Center in New York City by Islamic extremists in 1993. The preparation of legislation in such a novel and sensitive area had taken time, with the Department of Justice handling the drafting, supplemented by input from the FBI and other agencies, and a keenly interested White House. Eventually a bill was ready, and in February 1995 it was introduced in the Senate (S. 735) and the House. As with the 1994 crime legislation, the sponsor in the Senate was Biden, although by now the ranking member, rather than chairman, of the Committee on the Judiciary. Schumer sponsored a similar bill in the House (H.R. 896). Despite the concern of the White House to avoid treading on civil liberties[32] it was only a matter of weeks before a coalition of advocacy groups had mobilized opposition to several of its provisions. The sharpest criticism was directed toward a provision allowing the government to use evidence in deportation proceedings that had been obtained from secret sources in cases where an alien was suspected of terrorist involvement. In such circumstances, the government would not be required to disclose the source to the person it wanted to deport. Biden was unpersuaded of the merits of the provision, and he was not alone.

A neat headline in the *New York Times,* "Blast Turns a Snail into a Race Horse,"[33] captured the immediate congressional import of another outrage, the bombing on April 19 of the Murrah Federal Building in Oklahoma City. After initial uncertainty, the evidence strongly indicated that terrorism on such a large scale could have a domestic as well as an international face.[34] Gruesome as were the after-effects, with a final toll of 168 dead and more than 400 injured, the Oklahoma City incident not only inspired further measures aimed at domestic terrorists, but gave the existing proposals the impetus that was needed to overcome the resistance of those, both on the right and left of the political spectrum, who shrank from what they saw as conferring more power on federal law enforcement agents.

An example of the changed climate of opinion was a statement by the White House, only days after the blast, that President Clinton intended to seek new authority for federal agents to monitor telephone calls and check the credit, hotel, and travel records of suspected terrorists. The President also wanted funding to put into effect recent legislation that required telephone companies to assure access for court-ordered wiretaps of new digital computer lines, which were harder to monitor than conventional lines. Improved electronic surveillance remained a high priority for the FBI, and for Clinton personally, but aversion to wiretaps was deeply ingrained in the House of Representatives, which deleted the provisions from the final version of the antiterrorist legislation the following year.

A week after the bombing, at a meeting of the congressional leadership of both parties with the President at the White House on April 26, Senator Hatch (Rep. Utah), chairman of the Senate Committee on the Judiciary, suggested that limitations on habeas corpus should be added to the antiterrorist legislation. Now, it was said, more than ever before there was a compelling need to show that swift execution would be the fate of those convicted of mass killings that attracted the death penalty. Although Biden had misgivings, and was later to oppose the inclusion of habeas reform in the bill, both the Senate and House concurred. Under the House bill deadlines would be imposed allowing state prisoners who had been sentenced to death to challenge their convictions in the federal courts within one year. Federal prisoners would have two years. In states that provided competent counsel at the appellate stage of capital cases, prisoners would have shorter deadlines and generally be limited to one petition.

Some of the more liberal Democrats maintained that the federal appeals process, although long drawn-out, acted as an essential check on wrongful executions and that the Supreme Court had already done more than enough to limit such appeals.[35] But the White House, backed by most of the mainstream Democrats in the Congress, was in favor of making changes to curb what was described by the Department of Justice as the abuse of habeas corpus and to shorten the acute problems of delay and prolonged litigation in capital cases.[36] Adequate legal representation for capital defendants facing capital sentences was a touchstone of the administration's support. Reno, who was not in the forefront of the reform faction, regarded this as a condition not open to compromise.

The question of the competence of counsel was crucial because an estimated 99.5 percent of prisoners on death row are indigent and most of them do not have attorneys.[37] Since the decision of the Supreme Court in *Powell v. Alabama* in 1932,[38] any person facing the death penalty is entitled to a court-appointed lawyer at trial. In *Gideon v. Wainwright*[39] the Court extended the right to counsel to all state felony prosecutions. Sensitivity toward the disjuncture in legal principle between criminal proceedings in the state courts and the civil procedures for postconviction review in the federal courts seems to have caused the Supreme Court to hesitate before acknowledging that there was a need, if not a right, for adequate legal assistance to petitioners who had been sentenced to death.

The balance of opinion in the Court was moving toward acceptance of the view that the unique seriousness of the death penalty, and the complicated nature of the litigation to establish its constitutional propriety in individual cases, justified a departure from the purist doctrine that proceedings for collateral relief in the federal courts stood apart from the criminal process ''as a civil action designed to overturn a presumptively valid criminal judgment.''[40] But the need for further heart-searching before reaching a conclusion was overtaken by events when Congress decided the matter by legislation. In 1988 the Anti–Drug Abuse Act[41] not only extended the death penalty to continuing criminal conspiracies and other serious drug-related offenses, but at the same time created a statutory right to qualified legal representation for indigent capital defendants in any postconviction proceedings in the federal courts.[42]

Notwithstanding the recognition of these entitlements, the standard of legal representation continued to raise doubts. Empirical research and judicial experience alike verified that poor people accused of capital crimes were often defended by lawyers who lacked the skills, resources, or commitment to handle such serious matters. Indeed, it was often not the facts of the crime but the quality of legal representation that distinguished a case where the death penalty was imposed from similar cases where it was not.[43] Augmenting the demands of fairness and equity were some practical considerations set out in the Justice Department letter of January 26:

> Competent representation at trial and on appeal not only provides essential safeguards of fairness for defendants, but also constitutes a critical element in ensuring the integrity and finality of judgments. Effective counsel at the primary stages of litigation promotes error-free proceedings, and reduces the likelihood that reversible error will be found at later stages, potentially after years of protracted litigation. Conversely, a failure to provide effective representation for the defendant at the initial, critical stages is a false economy that complicates and undermines the proceedings, and jeopardizes the finality of any resulting judgment on review.[44]

Few states could match an Indiana initiative to improve the quality of representation in death penalty cases. By virtue of a rule of its supreme court, which became effective as Criminal Rule 24 in 1993, Indiana required two experienced attorneys, a lead counsel and a co-counsel, to be appointed in all death penalty cases. Their qualifications and levels of compensation were specified in the rule, which also required the provision of "adequate funds for investigative, expert, and other services necessary to prepare and present an adequate defense at every stage of the proceeding, including the sentencing phase."[45]

When, following the defeat in the congressional and gubernatorial elections of November 1994 of Governor Cuomo, a resolute opponent of the death penalty, capital punishment was reintroduced in the state of New York,[46] the courts were anxious to adopt similar standards in cases where the death penalty might be imposed. A new section was added to the Judiciary Law, effective April 1, 1995, applicable only to offenses committed on or after that date.[47] Two attorneys, one to be designated lead counsel and one associate counsel, would be appointed by the court to represent the accused at the trial and separate sentencing procedure, to be paid at rates approved by the court of appeals. Minimum standards of competence for counsel would be set, again subject to judicial approval. Compensation and expenses would be paid for expert, investigative and other reasonably necessary services. Any compensation, fees, or expenses would be a state charge. On appeal from a judgment, including sentence of death, lead counsel only would be assigned, but for good cause, the court could assign associate counsel.

The inadequacy of public funds to pay defense counsel in capital cases is frequently part of the problem, but it is not the whole explanation. A rare opportunity for legislators to hear from a Supreme Court Justice occurred in 1994. Once confirmed, Justices do not normally appear before congressional committees. But each year, as part of the appropriations process, one or more of the Justices appears before either a House or a Senate Appropriations Subcommittee to address the budget requirement of the Supreme Court for the coming fiscal year. In a perceptive comment at a hearing before an Appropriations Subcommittee of the House of Representatives, Justice Kennedy said this:

> In many cases, it is difficult to get an attorney to undertake an appeal or a collateral review of any death penalty case. These cases are very, very difficult for the practitioner. The records are huge.
>
> In California . . . the record in a capital case will run to over 20,000 pages. If, perchance, the attorney ultimately loses in that case, he or she feels a burnout factor, and never wants to take another one. The crime is often very heinous to begin with, because only the most serious crimes call for that penalty, and so it is difficult to get qualified attorneys to do this. And we need a qualified attorney in our court to represent the condemned person.

So the problem of getting adequate counsel in criminal cases, both at the trial level and at the appellate level and at the collateral review level, is a persistent, serious problem.

Of course, delay is built into the system. It is, in part, one of the objectives of the counsel to keep his client alive. We have made very clear in our habeas corpus filings that if capital punishment is to be effective, it must be swift, and that is not happening.[48]

In answer to a question on the percentage of habeas petitions alleging ineffective counsel, Justice Kennedy, supported by Justice Souter, replied that it was a very substantial number. It was a common ground to include in a petition for habeas relief.[49]

IV

At the later stages the House and Senate proposals on habeas corpus reform came together, so that by the time the conference on the Antiterrorism and Effective Death Penalty Bill was reached they were identical. In their report on the Senate bill (S. 735) the managers of the legislation in the two Houses stated that there had been no need to modify any of the proposals in the conference committee.[50] When he signed the resulting act into law on April 24, 1996, President Clinton said that while presidents could advocate and the executive branch could enforce the laws, the new provisions on antiterrorism and the death penalty would not have happened but for the remarkable convergence of Republicans and Democrats in the Congress.[51]

The language of the joint explanatory statement by the Committee of Conference was that of the Republican majority. The title on habeas corpus reform, it said, was intended to curb the abuse of the statutory writ of habeas corpus, and to address the acute problems of unnecessary delay and abuse in capital cases. It set a one-year limitation on any application for a habeas writ, and revised the procedures for the consideration of a writ in a federal court. It provided for the exhaustion of state remedies and required deference to the determinations of state courts that were neither contrary to, nor an unreasonable application of, clearly established federal law. Time limits were set within which the district court must act on a writ, and provided the government with the right to seek a writ of mandamus if the district court refused to act within the allotted time period.

Successive petitions would need to be approved by a panel of the court of appeals for the circuit in which the proceedings were held, and were limited to those petitions containing newly discovered evidence which would seriously undermine the jury's verdict, or which involved new constitutional rights that had been retroactively applied by the Supreme Court. In capital as well as noncapital cases the ineffectiveness or incompetence of counsel during federal or state collateral postconviction proceedings would no longer be a ground for relief. This limitation did not preclude the appointment by the court in capital cases of different counsel at any phase of state or federal postconviction proceedings on the grounds of the ineffectiveness or incompetence of existing counsel. The substitution could be made either at the request of the prisoner or on the court's own motion.[52]

In capital cases, applications by prisoners in state custody who were subject to a capital sentence would have to be filed within six months of the final affirmation of their conviction and sentence in the state courts, or the expiry of the time for appellate review. In such cases procedures were established for the appointment of competent counsel for indigent prisoners, the conduct of evidentiary hearings, and the application of the procedures to state unitary review systems.[53] As enacted, the legislation did not make any provision for trial representation of indigent capital defendants. This was one of the crucial differences between the Republican initiative and the habeas corpus reforms promoted by the Democrats in the 103rd Congress, which provided for representation by qualified counsel at all state court proceedings. Biden's earlier version also would have recognized a right to relief, even on a successive petition, if a capital defendant could present sufficient new evidence of innocence or ineligibility for the death penalty.

Courts were directed to give priority to habeas petitions in capital cases and to decide them within specified time periods. The procedures applied to both state and federal capital cases and were intended to make it difficult for prisoners who had been sentenced to death to get a second round of federal review. The purport was that federal judges would be expected to defer to the rulings of state judges on constitutional and other issues, unless the rulings were clearly unreasonable.

Since the start of his presidency, Clinton had sought to cut back on repeated applications for relief by prisoners who had been sentenced to the death penalty. In a written statement made on signing the Antiterrorism and Effective Death Penalty Act, he said that for too long and in too many cases endless death row appeals had stood in the way of justice being served.[54] But in a cautionary rider, echoing the views of the Department of Justice, where the Attorney General had strong reservations about the final form that the reforms had taken, he emphasized the importance of the federal courts' interpreting the new provisions in such a way as "to preserve independent review of federal legal claims and the bedrock constitutional principle of an independent judiciary." The statement continued:

> Section 104(3) provides that a Federal district court may not issue a writ of habeas corpus with respect to any claim adjudicated on the merits in State court unless the decision reached was contrary to, or involved an unreasonable application of, clearly established Federal law, as determined by the Supreme Court. Some have suggested that this provision will limit the authority of the Federal courts to bring their own independent judgment to bear on questions of law and mixed questions of law and fact that come before them on habeas corpus. . . . Section 104(3) would be subject to serious constitutional challenge if it were read to preclude the Federal courts from making an independent determination about "what the law is" in cases within their jurisdiction. I expect that the courts, following their usual practice of construing ambiguous

statutes to avoid constitutional problems, will read section 104 to permit independent Federal court review of constitutional claims based on the Supreme
Court's interpretation of the Constitution and Federal laws.

Section 104(4) limits evidentiary hearings in Federal habeas corpus cases
when ''the applicant has failed to develop the factual basis of a claim in State
court proceedings.'' If this provision were read to deny litigants a meaningful
opportunity to prove the facts necessary to vindicate Federal rights, it would
raise serious constitutional questions. I do not read it that way. The provision
applies to situations in which ''the applicant has failed to develop the factual
basis'' of his or her claim. Therefore, section 104(4) is not triggered when
some factor that is not fairly attributable to the applicant prevented evidence
from being developed in State court.

Preserving the Federal courts' authority to hear evidence and decide questions of law has implications that go far beyond the issue of prisoners' rights.
Our constitutional ideal of a limited government that must respect individual
freedom has been a practical reality because independent Federal courts have
the power ''to say what the law is'' and to apply the law to the cases before
them. I have signed this bill on the understanding that the courts can and will
interpret these provisions of section 104 in accordance with this ideal.[55]

As the newly set limits applied to all capital cases pending on or after the
date of enactment (April 24, 1996) the Supreme Court lost no time in granting
an expedited hearing to the first case to reach it that afforded an opportunity
to rule on whether the new provisions unconstitutionally restricted the Court's
jurisdiction. The case was *Felker v. Turpin*.[56] After being convicted of murder
and other crimes and sentenced to death by a Georgia court in 1982, Wayne
Felker had not succeeded in obtaining relief on direct appeal, nor in two rounds
of state collateral proceedings, nor in a first round of federal habeas corpus
proceedings. While awaiting his execution, Public Law 104-132 was signed
into law. On May 2, Felker filed a motion in the Court of Appeals for the
Eleventh Circuit for stay of execution, and a motion for leave to file a second
federal habeas corpus petition. Both motions were denied on the same day they
were filed. An immediate petition to the Supreme Court followed to review
the circuit court's decision and to stay Felker's execution. The stay application
and petition for certiorari were granted by the Supreme Court on May 3, and
briefing ordered on the extent to which the provisions of the Act applied to a
petition for habeas corpus filed in the Supreme Court; whether application of
the Act suspended habeas corpus in the case before the Court; and whether
the Act constituted an unconstitutional restriction on its jurisdiction.[57] Two
weeks only were allowed for the preparation and filing of briefs, with the oral
argument being scheduled for two weeks after that.

Despite protests of unseemly haste from four of the Justices (Stevens,
Souter, Ginsburg, and Breyer) the Court was unanimous when its decision was
given on June 28, shortly before the end of the term that had begun in October
1995. The route by which the conclusion was reached was not that foreseen
in the President's statement, although broadly consistent with the thrust of his

remarks. Delivering the opinion of the Court, Rehnquist, C.J. held that while the Act did impose new conditions on the authority of the Court to grant relief, it did not deprive the Court of its jurisdiction to entertain habeas petitions filed as original matters. Since the Judiciary Act of 1789 the Supreme Court had been empowered to grant the writ of habeas corpus to petitioners who had not gone through the lower federal courts. The "gatekeeping" requirement of the Act, that no second or subsequent petition could be filed in a federal district court unless authorized by the court of appeals for the circuit, did not prevent the exercise of the Supreme Court's jurisdiction to entertain original habeas corpus petitions. The Act did not by implication repeal the two-hundred year-old power, nor did the restrictions on successive habeas corpus petitions amount to an unconstitutional suspension of the writ.[58]

A year later, on June 23, 1997, the Supreme Court ruled on another element of the legislation. Whereas the terms of the Act specifically covered pending capital cases, it made no express provision indicating whether or not the limitations applied to pending noncapital cases. In *Lindh v. Murphy*[59] the same four Justices who had wanted more time to consider the issues in *Felker v. Turpin* won over O'Connor, J. to decide by five to four that the statute did not govern applications by petitioners in noncapital cases that were already pending when the Act was passed. In delivering the opinion of the court, Souter, J., having grappled with the arcane problems of statutory construction and congressional intent, remarked judiciously that "in a world of silk purses and pigs' ears, the Act is not a silk purse of the art of statutory drafting."[60]

V

A less contentious component of the Contract with America was mandatory victim restitution. The bill to give effect to this intention (H.R. 665) was the only one of the six to be passed unanimously by the House of Representatives. It was then taken up by the Senate in the fall. On November 16 the Senate Committee on the Judiciary approved the bill by fifteen votes to one, having amended it to allow judges more latitude than did the House version. A court order of restitution would be mandatory, but for exceptional circumstances, on conviction for crimes of violence, offenses against property including any offense committed by fraud or deceit, or certain other offenses that resulted in an identifiable victim or victims suffering a physical injury or pecuniary loss. The order would be in addition to, or in lieu of, any other penalty authorized by law. Once an effective tracking system was in place no compensation would be due to the victims of crimes under federal law who had failed to pay any outstanding fines, other monetary penalties, or restitution arising out of their own criminal convictions.[61] The Senate passed the amended bill by voice vote on December 22.[62] Senator Hatch, who gave the bill his unqualified support, noted it was the third time that the Senate had passed bills in substantially similar language, but that none of them had reached the stage of being presented to the President.[63] Biden pointed out that the violence against women provision of the 1994 Crime Act, in which he had a strong personal interest, had mandated restitution for victims of sexual abuse and child abuse. He was proud to be the cosponsor with Hatch of the latest bill and urged his colleagues to support it.[64] In the second session of the 104th Congress, under the heading of Justice for Victims, mandatory restitution joined the habeas corpus provisions as another addition to the antiterrorism bill, being enacted on April 24, 1996, as Title II of Public Law 104-132.[65]

Whether by coincidence or otherwise, the week in which the bill was signed into law had been proclaimed as National Crime Victims' Rights Week by the President. The gesture recognized the phenomenal growth of the victims movement over two decades, and the shift that had occurred in the orientation of the criminal justice system away from the civil rights of the accused toward the victim who had suffered injury, loss, or damage. The previous twenty years had seen significant developments: victims' bills of rights, once a novel idea, had become a reality in most states, with victim assistance programs, dating from 1972, multiplying fast.

The presidential proclamation noted that every state had a compensation program to help reimburse victims for mental health, medical, or other expenses resulting from the crimes committed against them. In 1995, the Crime Victims Fund in the U.S. Treasury, which supported many of the state programs, surpassed the one-billion-dollar mark in funds distributed to the states.[66] Restitution is distinguished from compensation in that restitution is the payment from the offender to the victim and compensation is the payment from the state to the victim. If the state has already made compensation to the victim, part of the restitution to the victim may go to the state to reimburse the original outlay of compensation.

The pronounced move toward reparative or restorative justice was brought in by one tide of public opinion as an earlier one receded. The rights of suspects, on arrest and when charged, of defendants at trial, and of appellants at postconviction review, were subject at each stage to the forces of erosion. Liberal ideals of justice remained deeply embedded in the criminal process and were articulately and consistently defended, not least in the influential columns of the *New York Times* and much of academia. But politicians, in state legislatures as in the Congress, were sensitive to the pressures of their electors, and in general voters had shown themselves increasingly prone to identify with the victims of violent crime, especially women and children. As the incidence of life-threatening personal violence became more common, so the numbers grew of those who had experienced directly or indirectly the painful consequences of crime. Potential votes lay waiting to be harvested by declarations of support for victims at the same time as demands for more severe punishment for convicted criminals. If proof was needed that events could change the course of public policy, it was unnecessary to look any further than the murders of Polly Klaas and Megan Kanka.

Restitution was not a new concept in American criminal justice. In almost every culture and legal system the principle has been recognized that whatever penal sanctions may exist to punish wrongdoers for their criminal acts, the law should provide for the wrongdoer to make amends by restoring so far as possible the victim to his or her prior state of well-being. Hitherto honored more in the abstract than in practice,[67] restitution moved closer to the forefront of legislative policy with the enactment of the Victim and Witness Protection Act of 1982[68] by the 97th Congress. For the first time this Act empowered the federal courts when sentencing a convicted offender to order the defendant to make restitution to any victim of the offense in addition to, or in lieu of, any other penalty authorized by law. If the court did not order restitution, or ordered only partial restitution, it was required to state its reasons on the record.[69]

Two other Acts followed, the Victims of Crime Act of 1984,[70] which enabled fines and the proceeds of other court-imposed penalties to be used to encourage states to expand their compensation programs and victim assistance networks, and the Victims Rights and Restitution Act of 1990.[71] The Violent Crime Control and Law Enforcement Act of 1994 went further in providing mandatory restitution in federal cases of sex crimes and the sexual exploitation or other abuse of children.[72] It also extended and strengthened restitution in cases of domestic violence,[73] and made it a requirement for eligibility for Violent Offender Incarceration and Truth in Sentencing Incentive Grants that the state had implemented policies providing for the recognition of the rights and needs of crime victims.[74] States were not required to adopt any mandated set of victims'' rights measures, but were encouraged to adopt measures that were comparable to or exceeded the rights recognized in federal proceedings.

While Congress had demonstrated a sustained interest in victims we should not lose sight of the fact that about 95 percent of all felony convictions typically occur in state rather than federal courts.[75] Of the totality of those crimes that are tried in the federal district courts, a large proportion consists of offenses of drug dealing that are the least likely to result in orders of restitution being made, owing to the difficulty in identifying victims deserving to be put back into their prior state. In the fiscal year 1994 federal courts used their discretion to order restitution in no more than 20.2 percent[76] of criminal cases. By this time twenty-six states had laws in force that provided that restitution to the victims of violent crime should be mandatory, although several of them permitted exceptions.[77] The main problem in practice was that, on the statistics reported by the Judicial Conference of the United States, some 85 percent of criminal defendants were indigent at the time of their conviction[78] and lacked any funds that could be directed toward financial compensation.

Here again symbolism vied with reality. Sympathy with the plight of victims was increasingly vocal, and in America as elsewhere the relevance of restitution as a central element of penal policy was widely accepted. Practical considerations apart, restitution was seen as having a demonstrative value in helping to make the victim of crime ''whole'' again, while holding the offender liable for the damage caused by his or her criminal act. But what if laws required judges to order restitution in cases where the likelihood was that it would never be paid? What if an order for full restitution would result in undue hardship for the dependents of the offender? Was there a danger of it being the victim who would suffer yet again if hopes were raised only to be dashed when no restitution was forthcoming?

Unlike Britain, where the main nationwide service organization, Victim Support, did not press for mandatory restitution in the belief that while compensation orders were important they were too often unsatisfactory in practice because payments were uncertain and spread out over a lengthy period, in America the National Organization for Victim Assistance (NOVA), reflecting the views of the victims movement as a whole, had come out firmly in support of efforts to introduce mandatory restitution legislation. After an initial period of doubt, it was found that when the nature of the restitution order and the feasibility of full collection were clearly explained, victims understood the situation and most preferred that an order should be made so that it stood as a record of the damage done and the offender's culpability.[79]

Restitution is an instance of where in the formative stages of national policy experience within the states paved the way for subsequent federal legislation. The budding victims movement of the 1980s was not persuaded that judges were using their authority to order restitution with sufficient readiness, too often relying on the excuse of inability to pay when the offender in fact had adequate means to pay compensation. Two questions dominated the dialogue in private and in public. If an offender was incarcerated, how could he or she pay? And what should happen when the offender was indigent?

California was a pioneer in enacting a mandatory restitution statute in 1983.[80] It provided that in any case where a defendant was convicted of a felony, the court shall order the defendant to pay a restitution fine in addition to any other penalty or fine imposed, regardless of the defendant's present ability to pay. If the court found there were "compelling and extraordinary" reasons, it could waive imposition of the fine. Whenever such a waiver was granted, the court was required to state all of the reasons on the record.[81] At first the lack of enforcement procedures made these provisions ineffective. After further legislation in the 1990s, effective enforcement was achieved to the extent that in 1996 the state of California was collecting some $434,000 each month from incarcerated offenders. State law provided that inmates should work in prison, with the wages they earned being divided into one-third for direct restitution to the victim, one-third for the upkeep of the prisoners and their incidentals, and one-third into a general victims fund.[82]

Responses varied to the second question, What happens if the offender has no means? The experience of state systems suggested that many more offenders than most people think actually had sufficient means to pay some restitution, particularly if they did so by installments. Moreover indigence was sometimes temporary rather than a permanent condition. In several states, including California, the practice was introduced for a restitution order, once made, to become simultaneously a civil judgment against the offender. If not paid during the probationary period, it would remain in force as a civil judgment so that if the offender came into money at any time in the future the victim could collect without further court action.

An indication that practice in the states was developing at a faster pace than in Congress can be found in the guarded wording of the Victims Rights and Restitution Act of 1990. Section 506, conveying the sense of Congress with respect to victims of crime, declared that the states should make every effort to adopt a number of goals. Item (7) read: "Victims of crime should be compensated for the damage resulting from the crime to the fullest extent possible by the person convicted of the crime."[83] Although the inclusion of mandatory victim restitution in the Contract with America confirmed the strength of its appeal to Republican voters, it was a policy that enjoyed bipartisan support. The unanimous acceptance of the mandatory provision by the House of Representatives, and its unchallenged passage through the Senate, was evidence of the shift that had occurred in orthodoxy on Capitol Hill since the sense of the Congress resolution in 1990.

VI

The third Contract item to be taken into the Antiterrorism and Effective Death Penalty Act of 1996 could be regarded as having a closer identification with the original subject matter of the legislation than the two other additions. The move to make deportation procedures more rigorous was an active issue even before the World Trade Center bombing concentrated public attention on the dangers of terrorist acts committed by aliens. Like mandatory victim restitution, criminal alien deportation was not a policy that most Democrats had any stomach to oppose. Savings in cost combined with an apparent enhancement of public safety to give it an irresistible appeal to voters. To all save a small minority of legislators, any prickings of conscience about the restricted application of the rule of law to aliens were best concealed from the public gaze. The prevailing view, within the Congress as outside it, was that those who had entered the country illegally had forfeited the full protection of law accorded to American citizens, or those who had been granted permanent residence.

The bill (H.R. 668) passed the House easily, by a majority of 380 to 20, on February 10, 1995. The populist nature of the message was unvarnished: to relieve states to the greatest extent feasible of the hundreds of millions of dollars spent in holding illegal aliens who had been convicted of serious crimes while in the United States. Some estimates put the total number of criminal aliens on probation, in prison, or on parole as high as 450,000 with an overall cost to state and county criminal justice systems in excess of $500 million per year.[84] The legislative intent, as succinctly stated in the Contract with America, was "the prompt deportation of any alien without a green card who has been convicted of an aggravated felony and is deportable."[85] The designation as aggravated felonies of a number of offenses common to organized illegal immigration was intended to counter the activities of rings that preyed on illegal immigrants, extorting large sums for fraudulent documents and unsafe transportation. The bill also tightened up the defenses to deportation.

The Contract contained a more detailed and considered set of proposals for the judicial and nonjudicial removal of deportable aliens than for any of the other crime items. Definitions were given of aggravated felony, categories of aliens designated as deportable, appeal rights, and defenses based on permanent residence or witholding of deportation. The latter ground reflected an international obligation accepted by the United States not to deport or return aliens to their native countries if they could show that their life or freedom would be threatened on account of race, religion, nationality, or political dissent. Proof of the likelihood of maltreatment if an alien was deported was seldom readily established, and it was this aspect of the bill that attracted the sole critical speech during the floor debate in the House.

Jerrold Nadler (Dem. New York), a member of the Judiciary Committee and a habitual advocate of liberal causes, with a sizable Jewish immigrant population in his Manhattan district, opposed the legislation because it was written so broadly that he believed it to be inevitable it would be used to send back political and religious refugees to their oppressors. As such, it was at odds with the nation's highest traditions and went well beyond what was needed to protect the American people from criminals.[86] If the bill had provided simply for the deportation of violent felons, there would be no debate. But it went much further, he claimed, providing "near-summary deportation of people without so much as a hearing to determine whether the individual is a legitimate refugee, that is someone who has fled his or her homeland because of a well founded fear of persecution."[87]

Each of the remaining speeches concentrated on the need to strengthen the existing laws to ensure the swift deportation of noncitizens who had committed serious crimes and to crack down on alien smuggling. Although John Conyers (Dem. Michigan), the ranking member on the Judiciary Committee, had made a low-key speech echoing the general tenor of the debate, he joined fifteen other members of the Congressional Black Caucus in voting against the passage of the bill. Apart from the 380 who voted yea, and the 20 who voted nay, 34 representatives were listed as not voting.[88]

The following week, all six elements of the House crime package reached the Senate. In a statement on February 15, Dole, still the majority leader, commended the action taken by the House as moving one step further toward the kind of tough on crime legislation that the American people deserved.[89] Noting with approval the changes to facilitate mandatory victim restitution, the deportation of criminal aliens, and a narrowing of the exclusionary rule, he praised the more effective death penalty procedures as preventing "convicted criminals from exploiting the system with more frivolous appeals, more unnecessary delays, and yes, more grief for the victims of crime and their families."[90] The remaining two Contract items were increased funds for prison construction and block grants intended to give states and localities greater flexibility to determine their own law enforcement priorities. Both had significant budgetary implications and became part of the struggle between the Clinton administration and the Republican Congress which dominated the political scene over the next twelve months.

The shadow cast by the Oklahoma City bombing muted the criticisms that might have been expected of the new counterterrorism laws. The restrictions on individual liberty, freedom of speech and association, privacy, and due process, were duly denounced by the American Civil Liberties Union (ACLU)[91] and other organizations dedicated to the protection of civil rights. The extension of police powers, and the enhanced opportunities for abuse by federal law enforcement officers, with vivid examples fresh in the public mind as a result of congressional hearings on the debacles at Waco and Ruby Ridge, led to the formation of an unusual coalition between the ACLU and a variety of groups including the Gun Owners of America, the Irish National Caucus, the National Black Police Association, the National Association of Criminal Defense Lawyers, and the Electronic Privacy Information Center. The breadth of the political spectrum was underlined by the support of conservative organizations such as the Cato Institute and Frontiers of Freedom.[92]

The campaign against the further expansion of powers that were subject to abuse, and that had been abused in the past, was running against the grain of public opinion and had a limited impact. When the Senate approved the antiterrorism bill in June 1995, only eight senators voted against it. In the House there was a greater degree of opposition, mainly from the more conservative Representatives, including the persistent right-wing critics of government and advocates of the alleged right to bear arms.[93] While their hostility dictated a slower pace and some compromises, the omnibus bill was considered and passed by the House the following March, and signed into law by the President on April 24, 1996. Although Hyde had supported certain provisions that did not make it into the law as enacted, including wider wiretapping authority in terrorism cases, he believed that members of the House should be proud of the final product. "It maintains the delicate balance between law and order," he declared, but added that it would be necessary to confront the skepticism about federal law enforcement before passing more effective measures: "We've got to rehabilitate law enforcement and government, but right now it's in the basement with a lot of people."[94]

Chapter 7

Money and Ideology

I

The critical nexus between the levels of federal spending authorized by legislation for specified purposes and the actual amounts subsequently appropriated by Congress is heightened if in the interval party control of one or both Houses changes hands. Although initially the Republican leadership in the 104th Congress had talked expansively about "fixing Clinton's crime bill,"[1] what this came down to in practice was a protracted and acrimonious conflict over the method and purposes of federal funding for community policing, prevention programs, and prison construction by states. In addition to these issues, a cluster of more sharply defined amendments were made to the 1994 Crime Act. Three direct responses to surges in public opinion were compulsory notification to protect local communities from previously convicted sexual offenders or child abusers;[2] prison litigation reform;[3] and an amendment to the U.S. Code clarifying the intent of Congress regarding the new federal crime of carjacking.[4] The mainline provisions on gun control, the death penalty, three strikes, and violence against women, were preserved intact.

The prime thrust of Republican radicalism as it affected crime was directed at shifting the balance, so laboriously negotiated during the passage of the

148

1994 Act, away from prevention programs toward a greater reliance on incarceration. Not only did this tactic reflect the punitive preferences of many Republican congressmen, strengthened by a militant cohort of freshmen, but it coincided with the overriding objectives of cutting taxes and reducing the size and scope of federal government. Thus money and ideology came together to accentuate the clash on the remaining crime items of the Contract with America.

At the center of the dense thicket of programs, projects, or activities contained in the 1994 Crime Act was the unorthodox means of funding them by way of the Violent Crime Reduction Trust Fund (VCRTF). The eventual compromise had resulted in the authorization of a total expenditure of $30.2 billion over six years, including $6.9 billion for prevention programs, $9.8 billion for expenditure on prisons, and $13.8 billion for enhanced law enforcement including matching grants of up to 75 percent to states or units of local government to recruit and train 100,000 additional officers for community policing. The monies to sustain the VCRTF were to come from the projected savings realized by the elimination of over 250,000 federal jobs as required by the Federal Workforce Restructuring Act (Public Law 103-226). Amounts could be appropriated from the fund only for purposes authorized by the 1994 Crime Act, which placed limits on the extent to which authorized appropriations from the fund might be spent. Authorized outlays not appropriated, or not fully appropriated, could be carried over into succeeding fiscal years covered by the Act.[5]

Unlike other public trust funds, such as the Highway Trust Fund and the Social Security Trust Fund, with continuing sources of revenue from gas and payroll taxes, the VCRTF was finite. Its income would be derived from savings accruing from a one-time reduction in the federal payroll, which might or might not be achieved in full, and in any event would end by the fiscal year 2000. For the implementation of anti-crime policies the fund was a pot of gold, not inexhaustible but protected by the same firewalls that Congress had so recently dismantled around defense spending and foreign aid. But while safe from outside predators, the appropriations process permitted the 104th Congress to negate numerous programs in the 1994 Act, transferring the funds authorized for those programs to alternatives more in tune with Republican ideals.

H.R. 728, passed by the House together with the other crime items of the Contract with America in February 1995, was a forerunner of what was to come. It amended Title I of the 1994 Crime Act to confer upon local government entities a discretion to decide how to allocate lump sums granted from federal funds to support any crime reduction purpose, including but not limited to police staffing, overtime, equipment, school security measures, neighborhood watches, and citizen patrols. In addition H.R. 728 would eliminate virtually all of the crime prevention programs authorized by the 1994 Act. Model intensive grants, family and community endeavor schools grants, assistance for delinquent and at-risk youth, prevention-related matching payments to local governments under the Local Partnership Act, and urban recreation and at-risk youth grants were among the casualties.

When the House bill was referred to the Senate, many leaders of local police departments came forward to express their support for the "Cops on the Beat" program of community policing. This provision had required the states and localities to spend a specified proportion of their grant money on hiring new police officers, so allaying concern that local politicians would divert federal funds toward projects other than putting more police officers onto the streets. The Senate did not pass H.R. 728, but it endorsed the block grant policy in a bill of its own, the Violent Crime Control and Law Enforcement Improvement Act of 1995 (S. 3). Adversarial politics being what they are, the fact that President Clinton was deeply committed to fulfilling a pledge made when campaigning for his first term, to put 100,000 more police on the streets of America's communities by the year 2000, and often referred to it in his speeches, served only to fortify the resolve of his Republican opponents in the Congress to prevent him reaching that goal.

The considered objections on the part of the administration to block grants were set out in detail in the Assistant Attorney General's letter of January 26 to Chairman Hyde.[6] It pointed out that a policy change would destroy a highly successful program that already was in the early stages of implementation. To replace it with a poorly conceived and designed grant program would not guarantee any gains in public safety. The lesson to be drawn from the experience of the Law Enforcement Assistance Administration (LEAA) in the 1970s[7] was that too often unrestricted funds such as the proposed block grant are dissipated by scattering them widely or applying them to "unwise, frivolous, or routine expenditures." The result was that their impact was "scatter-shot, short-term, and diluted." In the absence of clear statutory guidelines about priorities, untargeted block grant funding had resulted in many dollars spent with no discernible impact on crime or the administration of justice. Limited federal resources should be directed toward the critical objective of promoting community policing. Under the existing spending program the vast majority of funds was employed in putting more police officers on the street, with the remainder of grant funds designed to promote and strengthen police presence in the community, and the ability of police officers to work effectively with their communities to prevent crime. The letter continued:

> This is an absolutely fundamental feature of the existing program. Crime cannot be effectively abated if the nation's communities view the police at best as outsiders who appear briefly in the aftermath of particular criminal incidents, or at worst as an occupying army that becomes the target of racial, ethnic, and class antagonisms.
>
> The experience of community policing—stationing police *in the communities they serve, on the beat*—offers enormous benefits from every perspective. On the side of the community, it enables citizens to learn to know and trust the police, to assist them in carrying out their mission, and to acquire

the sense of security that comes from the regular presence of familiar officers in their neighborhoods and the knowledge that those officers are personally committed to protecting them and their families from crime. Similarly, it enables police officers to know the members of the communities they serve as human beings, to obtain specific intelligence from their community contacts concerning criminal activities, and to develop an understanding of the general nature and causes of a community's crime problems and the ability to devise proactive strategies to mitigate or eliminate these causes.[8]

The continuing high profile of the community policing issue meant that sooner or later it would be the subject of a hearing by the Crime Subcommittee of the House Judiciary Committee.[9] When the moment came, Bill McCollum (Rep. Florida), who had succeeded Charles Schumer as chairman, displayed a conciliatory attitude toward the principal witness, Joseph Brann, director of the Office of Community Oriented Policing Services (COPS) at the Department of Justice. The program had been established shortly after the signing into law of the 1994 Crime Act, and by the time of the subcommittee hearing in December of the following year Brann was able to report that grants had been authorized to put an additional 23,913 police officers, sheriffs' deputies and state troopers onto the streets. With 2,020 officers funded under a 1993 police hiring supplement program, a total of 25,933 more officers were serving small and large, urban and rural, and Native American communities across the country. Seventy-five percent of the officers funded had already been hired.[10]

The timing of the subcommittee's hearing was fortuitous, for only the previous day the House had adopted the conference report on the Commerce, Justice, and State Appropriations Bill for 1996, which eliminated the COPS program and replaced it with the block grant system of payments to local government. Once the Senate had adopted the report, the bill would be sent to the President who had made clear that he would not sign into law any Appropriations Act that did not fund the COPS initiative as a distinct grant program, as authorized in the 1994 legislation. Speaking with the authority of a former police chief, Brann assured the subcommittee that the President's firmness had the support of the entire law enforcement community, as well as the nation's mayors.

Expanding on some remarks he had made in the floor debate in the House the previous day,[11] McCollum challenged Clinton to take a closer look at the block grant proposal and reconsider his veto threat. The insistence on continuing the COPS program amounted to an argument of form over substance. He cited a letter received from the president of the National League of Cities who believed that the Republican alternative could lead to initiatives and programs that would put more, not fewer, officers on the streets. It would permit cities to purchase equipment and move trained personnel onto the streets and take other actions to ensure more effective and efficient responses.[12]

McCollum agreed with his correspondent that supporters of the COPS program had created a false dichotomy. They argued that a choice must be made between more cops on the beat or block grants. In his judgment that was not the choice. The real choice was between more cops and more cops at a lower cost to localities with more flexibility. Block grants were a better way of assisting localities in their battles against crime. Many jurisdictions would get more money, needing to spend less of their own funds with a 10 percent match than the 25 percent required under the COPS program. Large numbers of localities had not applied for the current grants, or not taken up grants offered, because they could not afford them. Under the Republican proposal everyone would participate with grants being distributed on the basis of a formula that favored localities in which violent crime rates were the highest. McCollum ended his remarks by saying that his criticisms in no way reflected on "the fine efforts" of the witnesses in administering the COPS program, nor his respect for the way they were doing their jobs.[13]

Schumer followed, relishing the irony that having shot the program the previous day the House was now turning its attention to how it was working. There was no doubt that a hearing that might seem moot, or even bland on the surface, was charged with high voltage politics.[14] He agreed with McCollum that the COPS program illuminated the fundamental differences between how Republicans and Democrats wanted to fight crime on America's streets. Democrats were convinced that community policing was the best and most certain return for the taxpayer's dollar. The cop on the beat could stop violent crime on the street before it happened. For their part, Republicans thought a better way was simply to write a blank check to local politicians. They might indeed decide to hire cops. Or they might decide something else was needed. Always fluent, Schumer declared that the real choice between the two sides was "real cops versus maybe cops, maybe not."[15]

Within two weeks the expected outcome occurred when on December 19 the President sent back to the House of Representatives without his approval the Departments of Commerce, Justice and State, the Judiciary and Related Agencies Appropriations Bill (H.R. 2076). It was the third time Clinton had used his veto, having vetoed two other Appropriations Bills the previous day. There were higher stakes than community policing in contention. The tug of war between the President and Congress over a balanced budget was nearing its climax, and nine unfunded departments of federal government and dozens of agencies were temporarily shut down. The refusal of Congress to accept the President's budget led to a prolonged confrontation, only contained by an unprecedented series of thirteen continuing resolutions. By holding a press conference to announce his veto on the same day as a crucial summit meeting with congressional leaders on the shutdown, Clinton publicly demonstrated the importance he attached to giving no quarter on the dispute over policing.

With the Attorney General, the mayors of Chicago and Philadelphia, and representatives of law enforcement in attendance at the White House, the President rehearsed the origins of the community policing initiative; its successful launch and the progress made during the first year; the overall reduction in rates of murder and violent crime; and the folly of replacing a program that guaranteed to put 100,000 police on the street with a block grant that had no guarantees at all. In 1992 he had given his word to work for 100,000 more police officers. In 1994, when he signed the Crime Bill into law, it had represented a solemn commitment by the United States Government to put 100,000 more police officers on the street. He intended to keep his word.[16]

II

In the course of the House subcommittee hearing on the COPS program, Schumer had not let the opportunity pass by without scoring the point that however much Republicans might talk about preserving local choice it was not an ideological straitjacket. When it came to prison money, he said, they were willing to have Washington call the shots and tell state governments what to do.[17] In doing so they were carrying on, and making more stringent, the policy enacted by the 103rd Congress which had linked eligibility for 50 percent of the federal funds available for prison construction to "truth-in-sentencing" requirements that persons convicted of violent crimes should serve not less than 85 percent of the sentence imposed.[18]

"Truth in sentencing," so emotive a phrase and one warmly embraced in the Contract with America, was neither a new concept, nor an exclusively Republican one. The Federal Sentencing Guidelines, discussed in an earlier chapter, which took effect in November 1987, had adopted "honesty in sentencing" as one of the objectives. The abolition of parole meant that the sentence imposed by the court would be the sentence the convicted offender would serve, less approximately 15 percent for good behavior.[19] This was the source of the 85 percent target for the proportion of the sentence to be spent in prison. Since then many states had implemented laws under the rubric of truth in sentencing. Some enactments sought to balance the longer terms to be spent in custody by violent offenders with treatment or community sanctions for less serious offenders.

Although, like three strikes, truth in sentencing had become part of the vocabulary of crime politics, there was a lack of certainty as to its meaning. Marc Mauer has summarized its most frequently proclaimed objectives as falling into three categories, sometimes overlapping:

　　• To restore "truth" in the sentencing process so the public knows how much time an offender will serve in prison.

　　• To increase the proportion of a sentence that is served in prison, generally to eighty-five percent, and/or to eliminate parole release as a means of reducing crime by keeping offenders incarcerated for a longer period of time.

　　• To control the use of prison space, often in conjunction with a guidelines system, so decision makers know in advance what the impact of sentencing will be on prison populations.[20]

When making his personal appeal to individual senators during the fraught final stages in the passage of the 1994 Crime act, Clinton had not hesitated to deploy the jargon of toughness in commending the authorization of "$9.9 billion for prisons (a 30 percent increase above the Senate bill), coupled with tough truth-in-sentencing requirements that will shut the revolving door on violent criminals."[21] Subtitle A of Title II of that Act had been intended to assist the expansion by states of their ability to incarcerate violent offenders. To be eligible to receive grants from federal funds, states or compacts of states would have to submit applications satisfying a lengthy list of requested assurances. Among them were that the state or states had implemented, or would implement, correctional policies and programs, including truth-in-sentencing laws, to ensure violent offenders served "a substantial portion of the sentences imposed," that were designed to provide "sufficiently severe punishment" for violent offenders, including violent juvenile offenders; and that the prison time served was "appropriately related" to the determination that the inmate was a violent offender and the period of time deemed necessary to protect the public.[22]

Seeking assurances rather than laying down statutory requirements did not obscure the legislative intent of the 103rd Congress to specify certain conditions that would have to be fulfilled by states wishing to obtain federal grants to "construct, develop, expand, modify, operate or improve" their correctional facilities to ensure that prison space was available for the confinement of violent offenders. Not all of the conditions looked for greater severity in punishment. Applications would need to include assurances that the state or states had implemented policies providing for "the recognition of the rights and needs of crime victims,"[23] and had developed a "comprehensive correctional plan" showing an integrated approach to the management and operation of correctional facilities and diversionary programs. Included in the latter category were drug diversion programs, community corrections programs, professional training for corrections officers in dealing with violent offenders, prisoner rehabilitation and treatment programs, prisoner work activities and job skills programs, educational programs, and postrelease assistance.[24]

Once eligibility had been established, two types of grants would be available. Fifty percent of the total amount of funds authorized under the subtitle would be allocated to truth-in-sentencing incentive grants, and the other 50 percent to violent offender incarceration grants. In each case applicants would need to meet the qualifying conditions set out in the 1994 Act. Still more conditions were listed to establish eligibility for the truth-in-sentencing grants, the most important of which was that a state was able to demonstrate that either it had in effect laws requiring that persons convicted of violent crimes serve not less than 85 percent of the sentence imposed, or it could meet criteria showing that since 1993 the state had increased the percentage of convicted violent offenders sentenced to prison and the amount of prison time served by violent offenders.[25] Different formula allocations procedures would apply to the two programs, but both were subject to a matching requirement that the federal share of any grant received under the subtitle could not exceed 75 percent.[26] At the end of each fiscal year, unused funds in the more restrictive truth-in-sentencing incentive grant program would be transferred to the violent offender incarceration program.

Complicated as it is to describe the distribution mechanism for prison grant monies concisely and accurately, applicants barely had time to familiarize themselves with the intricacies of the procedure when the Violent Criminal Incarceration Act of 1995 (H.R. 667) bid to change it. The division into truth-in-sentencing incentive grants and grants to increase the prison capacity to provide for the confinement of offenders convicted of a serious violent felony[27] was maintained. A crucial difference, however, was that the truth in sentencing eligibility requirements were applied to the violent offender incarceration grants as well as the truth-in-sentencing incentive grants. When eligibility had been established, grants would be awarded on the basis of two formulae, one a percentage applying to all states in proportion to their population, and the other a calculation made of the ratio between the number of violent crimes reported by a state to the FBI over the preceding five years and the average annual number of such crimes reported by all states. Once the implications were worked out, and the bill came under congressional scrutiny, it was fore-cast by Democrats in the House that under the criteria in the base bill only three states, Delaware, North Carolina, and Arizona, would be eligible to obtain federal grants to incarcerate more violent offenders.[28]

Another condition was that federal funds were not to be used to supplant state funds but were designed to increase the total amounts of spending on prisons. The federal share of a successful grant application was raised from the maximum of 75 percent in the 1994 Act to 90 percent. The condition of making provision for the rights and needs of crime victims was preserved, but the necessity for comprehensive correctional plans, and the rehabilitative programs associated with them, were deleted from the qualifying criteria. Other important differences were that grants could be used only to build or expand temporary or permanent correctional facilities and not to operate them, and that no provision was made to transfer unused funds between the two grant programs.

The House also took the opportunity to insert into the prison subtitle of the 1996 Appropriations Act a proposal that had not found a place in the Contract with America, or subsequently in H.R. 667 as originally introduced, although it had strong support from Republicans in California, Texas, Florida, and other border states. They joined forces with Democrats in arguing that the federal government had an obligation to reimburse states for the cost of in-carcerating undocumented criminal aliens[29] who were taking up space in state prisons and local jails as a result of failures in border controls. One hundred and thirty million dollars had been appropriated for that purpose in the fiscal year 1995, but the chief proponent, a Democrat representing a congressional district in southern California, Howard Berman, claimed that the actual cost was closer to $650 million. In the previous Congress a sum of approximately

$330 million a year had been authorized under the Immigration and Nationality legislation to help meet these costs, but that still left a balance of the order of $320 million to be found by the states.

During the committee consideration of the Deportation of Criminal Aliens Bill (H.R. 668) Berman had succeeded in passing an amendment to provide an entitlement of $650 million each year to guarantee to state and local governments that they would be reimbursed for the properly expended costs submitted to the Justice Department. His amendment, however, had fallen foul of the Rules Committee. Although Gingrich was sympathetic, Hyde and other Republican heavyweights from nonborder states were antagonistic on grounds of cost. Refusing to be put off, Berman raised the issue again during the floor consideration of H.R. 667 on February 9, offering a similar amendment to the Violent Criminal Incarceration bill.

This time the attempt met with more success, coinciding with an amendment introduced by McCollum reserving funds to make payments to eligible states for incarcerating criminal aliens. Apart from his influential chairmanship of the House Subcommittee on Crime, McCollum represented a congressional district of Florida, a state that like California had much to gain. Although Berman would have preferred his own amendment, which did not link reimbursement directly to the structure of truth-in-sentencing and violent offender incarceration grants, he accepted McCollum's version as recognizing the "preeminent priority of funding"[30] it accorded to compensating states for such heavy additional costs arising from factors outside their control. McCollum said that the Congressional Budget Office (CBO) had confirmed an overall cost estimate of $650 million per year, and that unlike the prison grants the additional payments could substitute for state spending.[31] Nor would the truth-in-sentencing requirements apply, a question raised by several speakers. After a disjointed debate, ranging over procedural considerations as well as the substance of the proposal, the Committee of the Whole House agreed to the McCollum amendment without objection.[32]

What went unmentioned in the floor debate was the high proportion of the funds provided by Congress for prison building and expansion that would be taken up by a prior charge consisting of the balance between the money appropriated under the Immigration and Nationality Act and the total of $650 million. The separate funding sources were preserved in the Appropriations Act for 1996. Three hundred million dollars, a reduction on the $330 million authorized, was appropriated for the State Criminal Alien Assistance Program under the Immigration and Nationality Act as amended, with a further $200 million to be available to states for payments from the VCRTF for the incarceration of criminal aliens as a first charge on the violent offender incarceration and truth-in-sentencing grant programs.[33] Thus nearly one-third of the federal funds intended to build and enhance state prison capacity to confine violent offenders, amounting to $617.5 million appropriated for fiscal year 1996, was diverted for this purpose. Even so, the total of $500 million from both sources still left a shortfall of $150 million, if the $650 million estimate was accurate, to be found by the reluctant states from their own resources. Some further relief was provided by a $12.5 million set-aside for a Cooperative Agreement Program (CAP) to upgrade state and local facilities that held federal prisoners.

III

Throughout the odyssey of the block grant and prison funding there were inevitable shipwrecks. Electoral and congressional storms and tempests threw scores of federally funded prevention programs onto the rocks where most perished. Occasionally a doomed program was rescued by an incoming tide or was spared on the voyage. The $11 million appropriated in 1996 to the Boys and Girls Clubs of America[34] for the establishment of Boys and Girls Clubs in public housing facilities and other areas in cooperation with state and local law enforcement was a rare replacement. Grants for programs linked to violence against women, child abuse, substance abuse, and juvenile justice fared better than many others, although the funding for drug courts,[35] an important feature of the 1994 Crime Act, was cut from an authorized $150 million to a 1996 appropriation of not more than $18 million. Even that was conditional on the Attorney General requesting a transfer from the Local Law Enforcement Block Grant Program. Mounting concern about the threats to public order posed by organized gangs of violent youths preserved the authorization of an appropriation of $7.2 million for fiscal year 1996 to fund gang resistance education and training (GREAT) projects located in communities across the country and administered by the ATF.[36] Apart from the $7.2 million shared with the fifty states, $3.5 million additional funding was appropriated for the use of the ATF in connection with the program.

The Republican antipathy toward crime prevention can be traced back to two causes. The first, shown so clearly in the controversy over ''pork'' in the closing stages of the 1994 Act, was the conviction that social programs directing federal funds toward high crime areas, most of them in cities and many of them in districts represented by Democrats in Congress, were objectionable as a form of political patronage that conferred electoral advantage upon the sponsor. The second was cynicism about the potential, although unquantifiable, effectiveness of social intervention in reducing crime, compared with the apparent certainty of incarceration. Where particular local projects were regarded as doing a worthwhile job, it was argued that they should be locally funded and controlled and not dependent on financial support or policy decisions made in Washington.

The contrast between Republican and Democrat attitudes was well brought out in the two-day hearings on H.R. 3, the original Contract with America bill, held by the Crime Subcommittee of the House Judiciary Committee on January 19 and 20, 1995. A Republican freshman, Bob Barr of Georgia, insistently questioning a witness who had decried a lack of scientific evidence on the effectiveness of some forms of law enforcement, said this:

I will pose the following scientific evidence; that if you have a wife beater who is in prison, if you have a child abuser who is in prison, beyond any scientific doubt, that wife abuser will not be abusing his spouse, that child abuser will not be abusing a child while in jail, so I think building prisons is effective prevention.

. . . I have talked within the last few days with folks in my district, and they have some very innovative programs, and they weren't funded specifically though the 1994 bill. They are using them. They are effective because they are based on the views of, for example, a U.S. attorney, a local district attorney, a police chief.

They know they work and they are going to continue to implement those because they do work, regardless of whether there is a line item in this bill or any other bill that specifically funds them. And I think that it is in that marketplace of ideas in the local community where these decisions are best made, with regard to whether a particular program works.[37]

Earlier in the same session, John Conyers of Michigan, a veteran Democrat on the Judiciary Committee and a past chairman of its Crime Subcommittee, had commented that the proposal to build more prisons but cut prevention funding was the most surefire way to destabilize the crime legislation.[38] He angrily rejected Barr's arguments, saying they were the logic that was fueling the prison industrial complex that had been building up for decades, and had now become explosive. He continued:

We have decided to add to the $10 billion already allocated for building prisons, $2.5 billion more. Now, this theory, being scientific or not, the way we are going to fight crime is lock up in America everybody that commits crime and we will build prisons until we reach some—I don't know what kind of point we will reach—but I think that in itself raises a serious question about which way we want to go. And I, for one, having come from a State where we built prisons until we were so bankrupt we couldn't open them, we had to leave the prison built standing there in Michigan and in Detroit, because there wasn't any way—we ran out of money. And now we are rushing in to build prisons. And I think that this is what this issue is all about in terms of the last crime bill versus this new proposal.[39]

An open hearing of this sort was not the best place for a meaningful exchange on scientific evidence pointing one way or the other. Among the witnesses was John DiIulio, testifying in a personal capacity, but referring to his work as co-chair of a group of leading criminologists who, although often disagreeing with each other in the past, had come together to try and form a new consensus on crime policy.[40] DiIulio felt strongly enough to follow up his appearance with a letter sent later the same day to McCollum as subcommittee chairman. For the record, he wanted to pursue some matters that were either confused or left hanging during the questioning. There had been a great deal of confusion, he wrote, about the state of scientific evidence concerning prevention programs. He reiterated that none of the scholarly literature enabled criminologists to specify precisely the conditions under which given types of interventions prevent crime, or could be replicated widely, or relied upon to produce predictable and desirable outcomes in a cost-effective way. Selective references and fanciful interpretations should be avoided. There was no question that some programs worked under some conditions, but the relationships among the key variables remained ambiguous.[41]

While DiIulio was right to counsel caution, for overstated claims can easily result in disillusion and recrimination, it is shortsighted to dismiss for political or ideological reasons the contribution that well-designed and executed social prevention programs can make toward the common good of countering criminal offending. By the mid-1990s it had become clear that despite reports of declining rates of violent crime in cities across the country there was a growing, and deeply disturbing, problem of violent crimes committed by juveniles, against each other as well as against adult victims. Between 1990 and 1994, for example, when overall rates of murder were showing a slight decline, rates of murder committed by teenagers between the ages of fourteen and seventeen increased by 22 percent.[42] Over a longer period, from 1985 to 1994, the rate of murders by youths in this age group increased by 172 percent.

Guns, especially handguns, played a major part in the incidence of juvenile murder. Since 1984 the number of juveniles killing with a gun quadrupled, while the number killing with all other weapons combined remained virtually constant. The same pattern was evident for other crimes of violence. From 1989 to 1994 the arrest rate for violent crimes (murder, rape, robbery, and aggravated assault) rose by more than 46 percent among teenagers, as against 12 percent among adults. In terms of arrest rates, fourteen- to seventeen-year-olds surpassed young adults aged eighteen to twenty-four.

Most ominous of all were the demographic indicators showing that the increase in juvenile crime occurred while the proportion of teenagers in the general population was declining. It was estimated that the demographic benefit would not last, and that by the year 2005 the number of young people aged between fourteen and seventeen will have increased by 20 percent over its 1994 level.[43] Faced with this diagnosis, and the realization that most criminal careers begin in the teenage years,[44] the rationale for intervention before or at adolescence becomes overwhelming. What can be done, what is being done, to guide the next generation of teenagers toward a path leading away from the catastrophes that otherwise await so many of them in the imminent future?

IV

The concept of mentoring, in which adult volunteers act in a supportive role to individual disadvantaged teenagers and preteenagers is one approach that holds out promise. A synthesis of research over eight years from 1988 to 1995[45] estimated that by the end of the period there were approximately 350,000 men and women who had formed a one-to-one relationship with a young person through a wide variety of programs designed to build trust between mentors and at-risk youth. Most of the young people matched in these relationships had no trusted adult inside or outside the home to whom they could turn for support or guidance. Isolated, often confused, and surrounded by a delinquent peer group, many youths in distressed urban areas gravitate toward ways of life that are inherently anti-social, escalating into actions that are harmful, and sometimes lethal, to themselves and others.

Although mentoring is not specifically linked to crime prevention some of the research findings bear directly on the causes of crime. An impact study of selected mentoring programs associated with the well-established Big Brothers/Big Sisters of America (BB/BSA) showed that youth assigned to be matched to mentors were 46 percent less likely than the control group to initiate drug use, and 27 percent less likely to initiate alcohol use, during the study period. They were one-third less likely to hit someone, and missed half as many days at school as the control group. They felt more confident about their ability to do well at school, and their grades had improved slightly by the end of the study. More positive relationships were reported with friends and parents.[46]

With about 75,000 matches nationally in 1995,[47] BB/BSA is the largest and best known organization sponsoring mentoring through some five hundred local agencies. Also at a national level, but on a smaller scale, the Quantum Opportunities Program (QOP) has demonstrated that mentoring, stipends for community service, and incentives to go on to college can be effective in reducing crime, drugs use, and school drop-outs, at least for a time.[48] The financial support of the Ford Foundation, in excess of $1.1 million for the pilot projects,[49] enabled a system of incentive payments to QOP participants to be added to the more conventional tools of social work intervention. A comprehensive research study measured how a randomly selected group of adolescent participants from welfare families at each of four sites had fared compared with a control group at the conclusion of a four year experimental program. Commenting that these were rough kids from rough neighborhoods, the *New York Times* reported:

> By the end of the program, 63 percent of the Quantum Opportunities Program participants graduated from high school, 42 percent were enrolled in a post-secondary program, 23 percent dropped out of school, 24 percent had children and 7 percent had arrest records. By contrast, of the control group, 42 percent finished high school, 16 percent went on to post-secondary schools, 50 percent dropped out, 38 percent had children and 13 percent had arrest records.[50]

The fact that some of the participants did drop out, did have children, and did incur arrest records, shows the importance of not setting sights too high or inflating expectations. In assessing the impact of the program on criminal involvement, a third-party evaluation by a team at Brandeis University found that apart from the reduction in the number of arrests, the average number of criminal convictions was approximately six times higher among male controls than among male QOP participants.[51]

Despite the usual, but important, qualifications, that the results of experimental projects may depend on an inspirational leadership, strong local community support, and a scale of funding that may not be replicated in a wider setting, the U.S. Department of Labor found the outcomes of the QOP pilot projects sufficiently encouraging to launch a national demonstration replicating QOP programs at seven sites in 1995 with larger numbers of participants. The results will be evaluated in due course and compared with the findings of the original pilot projects to test whether the quantum leap up the ladder of opportunities experienced by the original samples of youngsters can be maintained and expanded.

Numerous other less organized, less generously funded, and less studied initiatives exist in local communities, which exhibit a practical desire on the part of responsible adults to work toward a more civil society, as well as counteracting the malign influences which lead to delinquent behavior. In Washington, D.C., for example, more than one hundred staff members of the United States Attorney's Office for the District of Columbia in early 1997 were regularly mentoring or tutoring each male student in grades four through six at an elementary school in southeast Washington. "This is not a program that ends at 3.15 pm," the school principal said. "The people from the U.S. Attorney's Office have become the extended families of many children."[52] In March 1997, President Clinton nominated Eric Holder, the U.S. Attorney for the District of Columbia, who had taken part in and encouraged the project, to serve as Deputy Attorney General at the Department of Justice. Elsewhere, the establishment of "safe havens" has been commended. This is the name given to sanctuaries off the street where young people can go for help with homework, recreation, social support, and, if needs be, discipline. An evaluation by researchers at Columbia University showed the effectiveness of such safe havens, particularly after school and in the early evening.[53]

The relevance of concentrating prevention programs on youth violence and the factors relating to juvenile crime was brought out in a report prepared for the Congress, in accordance with an Appropriations Act mandate in 1996, requiring the Attorney General to provide "a comprehensive evaluation of the effectiveness" of the large sums of money expended in grants to assist state and local law enforcement and communities in preventing crime. Congress had specified that the research for the evaluation should be "independent in nature" and "employ rigorous and scientifically recognized standards and methodologies."[54] A distinguished list of "scientific advisers" had been empaneled, and a detailed evaluation of the relevant literature (exceeding some five hundred program impact evaluations) was carried out on behalf of the National Institute of Justice by a team at the Department of Criminology and Criminal Justice at the University of Maryland at College Park.

In an overview, written by the lead author of the study, Professor Lawrence Sherman, the primary conclusion was that given the evidence of promising and effective programs, the effectiveness of Department of Justice funding depended heavily on whether it was directed to the urban neighborhoods where youth violence is most prevalent. The report concluded: "Sub-

stantial reductions in national rates of serious crime can only be achieved by
prevention in areas of concentrated poverty, where the majority of all homicides in the nation occur, and where homicide rates are 20 times the national
average."[55] Although this finding was far from novel, most members of Congress had persisted in voting to spread out the money available to counter
crime so that more districts were included, rather than concentrating the resources where they would have most impact. "We need to put the money
where the crime is, not just where the votes are" was Sherman's laconic
comment in a newspaper interview.[56] On the effectiveness of building prisons
as a crime prevention strategy, the most expensive option, the report confirmed
that incarcerating serious, repeat criminals did stop some crimes. But the study
found that much of the research was inadequate or flawed, making it impossible to measure how much crime was actually prevented by locking up more
criminals. The point of diminishing returns might have been reached by imprisoning people who were less-serious offenders because the most serious
offenders had already been incarcerated.[57]

The evidence validating some "promising and effective" prevention programs needs to be set against the caricatures that periodically catch the eye of
the media, and thence the interest of politicians. In 1993–94 the program most
frequently held up to ridicule by Republicans in Congress was midnight basketball. Yet in 1991 President Bush had gone out of his way to praise the idea,
including it in his 1,000 Points of Light program. "The last thing in the world
Midnight Basketball is about is basketball" he quoted at the time.[58] It was
about providing opportunities for young adults to escape drugs and get on with
their lives. He was not surprised that the crime rate had dropped in the locality
he was visiting by 60 percent since the program began. Somebody had told
him, Bush explained, that "in Midnight Basketball the only defense allowed
is man-to-man. And that's important, because our only defense against despair,
drugs, hopelessness has to happen one-to-one. You don't have to try to change
the world, just help one person. Teach one person to read, feed one hungry
child, hold one lonely hand. That's all it takes."[59]

The coincidence that sports facilities are frequently unused during peak
crime hours from 10:00 P.M. to 2:00 A.M. had created an opportunity to attract
youths and young men off the streets to a more constructive alternative. Starting in the suburbs of Washington, D.C. in 1986, a network of late-night basketball leagues had spread to fifty cities across the country. Basketball was the
magnet, but in order to play in the teams it was necessary to participate in,
and respond positively to, arduous programs of physical activity and regular
workshops designed to improve participants' motivation toward schooling, the
job market, self-control, and personal responsibility. A variety of corporate and
private sponsors underwrote the leagues, often with the enthusiastic support of
city officials, police, and local business leaders.

Yet when federal funding was proposed in the 1994 Crime Bill it was
denounced by Republican critics as the epitome of liberal social programs
whose results nowhere near justified the claims made by their proponents.
During the crucial House debate on waiving the rule to enable the report of

the conference on the 1994 Crime Bill to be taken on the floor, one Republican speaker, Lamar Smith of Texas, bracketed midnight basketball with arts and crafts programs as having been inserted into an anti-crime bill "on the theory that the person who stole your car, robbed your house, and assaulted your family was no more than a disgruntled artist or would-be NBA star." His speech ended with a rousing, but vacuous, proclamation: "Be tougher on criminals than they are on us."[60] Although not all opinions were expressed with such vehemence, the current was running so fast that midnight sports were an almost inevitable sacrifice that would have to be made in the negotiations to save the bill. Thus it was no surprise that in the final version of the legislation as enacted in 1994 the subtitle was omitted. The episode points up vividly the volatility of political opinion. As one commentator wryly observed, it takes the particular prism of Washington politics to make what appears to be a shining beacon of light one year look like a pork by-product in another.[61]

V

The long delayed Appropriations Act for the fiscal year ending September 30, 1996, was not signed by the President until April 26, 1996, four months after he had vetoed the appropriations for the Departments of Commerce, Justice, and State. Community-oriented policing was preserved as a free-standing program funded at $1.4 billion, apart from and in addition to the $503 million for the local law enforcement block grants pursuant to H.R. 728. Funding for the two prison grant programs for states amounted to another $617.5 million, including the set-aside of $200 million to reimburse states for incarcerating criminal aliens. Monies from the VCRTF increased from a total of $2.328 billion in fiscal year 1995 to $3.926 billion in fiscal year 1996.[62] As enacted, programs administered by the Departments of the Treasury, Health and Human Services, Education, Interior, and Transportation brought the total fiscal year 1996 appropriations from the VCRTF up to $4.085 billion.[63]

Federal justice–related expenditure was one of the few areas of discretionary spending to increase its share of total federal spending over the previous two decades,[64] and looked set to continue to do so in the era of restraint that would be necessary if the aim of a balanced budget was to be achieved by 2002. The marked shift toward more and longer prison sentences for convicted felons, combined with the weakened but still extant constitutional checks on overcrowding, meant that further expansion was inexorable in the capacity of local, state, and federal correctional facilities. The cost of construction and the containment of an ever expanding inmate population was seldom mentioned in political speeches dramatizing the imperatives of fighting crime with every weapon at hand. But each year, away from the platforms on which the commitments had been made, the time came when the money had to be found.

The delay in enacting the Appropriations Act meant that the Office of Justice Programs at the Department of Justice had to move quickly to implement the labyrinthine structure of the violent offender incarceration and truth-in-sentencing grants. Since the program requirements under these two headings had continued to change throughout the appropriations process, it had not been possible to disseminate guidelines in advance of the passage of the legislation. Program guidance was sent to states in mid-June, with a closing date for 1996 applications of August 15. The funds appropriated by Congress for the construction and expansion of prisons and jails for violent offenders were divided into two pools. Half of the total amount of $319.6 million available for distribution to states in fiscal year 1996 was designated for violent offender incarceration grants, and half for truth-in-sentencing incentive grants. States that met the criteria could apply for funding under both programs. There the simplicity ended.

The Violent Offender Incarceration Grant Program had three tiers. To receive a grant, a state or territory had to meet the eligibility requirements attached to each tier. The intricacies of the system reflected the legislative patchwork created by the 103rd and 104th Congresses. In order to qualify for funding under tier 1 each state was required to provide a signed assurance in its application indicating that it had implemented, or would implement, correctional policies and programs to ensure that violent offenders served a substantial portion of the sentences imposed; *and* were designed to provide sufficiently severe punishment for violent offenders, including violent juvenile offenders; *and* ensure that the prison time served was appropriately related to the determination that the inmate was a violent offender *and* was for a period of time deemed necessary to protect the public. All states and territories received funding under this tier in fiscal year 1996. The amounts were the same, $1,248,453, irrespective of the size of the state or its inmate population.[65]

To receive a grant under tier 2, a state was required to provide data demonstrating that since 1993, it had increased the percentage of persons arrested for a part 1 violent crime sentenced to prison; *or* increased the average prison time served; *or* increased the average percent of sentence served by persons convicted of part 1 violent crime. Forty-eight states, the District of Columbia, and three territories received funding under this tier in fiscal year 1996. Total awards under tier 2 amounted to $101,207,890. Award amounts to individual states ranged from $70,408 to Wyoming to $16,376,762 for California.

A tier 3 applicant was eligible for funding if it demonstrated that since 1993 it had increased the percentage of individuals arrested for a part 1 violent crime sentenced to prison, *and* had increased the average percent of sentence served by persons convicted of a part 1 violent crime; *or* increased by 10 percent or more over the most recent three-year period the number of new court commitments to prison of persons convicted of part 1 violent crimes. Twenty-eight states, two territories, and the District of Columbia received funding under this tier in fiscal year 1006. Total tier 3 awards amounted to $26,646,913.

In its implementation report, the Corrections Program Office within the Office of Justice Programs remarked that the process of determining qualified applicants under tiers 2 and 3 had been complicated by three factors: compliance with the eligibility criteria called for data that was often not readily available; definitions were not consistent across states; and no awards could be made until all qualified applicants had been identified.[66] On one requirement at least there was no room for ambiguity. The conference report that had accompanied the 1996 appropriations had directed the Department of Justice, in developing criteria for eligibility for funding to build or expand bed space, to include a requirement that states demonstrate the ability fully to support, operate, and maintain the prison for which the state was seeking construction funds. Mindful of this congressional instruction, the Department had made it an explicit requirement that each applicant state provide documentation to support its application in the form of a certificate from the governor undertaking that the state would use the grant funds to build or expand correctional facilities, and intended to complete and operate such facilities. The 1997 Appropriations Act made an exception for California to permit funds granted under the Violent Offender Incarceration or Truth-in-Sentencing Programs to be used for payments for the incarceration of criminal aliens.[67]

Another exception had been made in the 1996 Appropriations Act[68] varying the application of the original criteria to enable states that in good faith had enacted legislation complying with the federal law as enacted in 1994, but which did not meet the qualifications as set out in the 1996 version. The main beneficiary was the state of New York, which had passed a truth-in-sentencing statute requiring repeat violent offenders to serve 85 percent of the sentence imposed, whereas the changes made in 1996 required that all part 1 violent offenders serve at least 85 percent of the sentence imposed, whether or not they were repeat offenders. Although the exception opened the way for New York to be included as one of the twenty-five states qualifying to receive truth-in-sentencing incentive grants in fiscal year 1996, obtaining the second largest award of $23,370,467, the relief was limited to that fiscal year only. Thereafter, it would have to enact fresh legislation if it was to qualify under the same program in fiscal year 1997.

Generally, however, the changes made in the truth-in-sentencing language of the 1996 Appropriations Act meant that more states were able to qualify than the very small numbers predicted by Schumer and others in the House of Representatives. Thirty states applied, of which five were unable to demonstrate that violent offenders served or would serve 85 percent of their sentences. The available funds were therefore distributed to the remaining qualifying states, including New York taking advantage of the one-year transitional provision. The formula for distribution was based on each state's share of the total average annual number of Part 1 violent crimes for the preceding year for all eligible states. Several of the more populous states (Texas, New Jersey, Maryland, and Massachusetts) failed to meet the criteria. Texas, however, succeeded in obtaining an award of more than $50 million under the State Criminal Alien Assistance Program (SCAAP) designed to reimburse states and local jurisdictions for costs associated with holding criminal aliens.

The scale of illegal immigration into California, and subsequent offending by illegal aliens, the mainspring of congressional action in 1995, was shown by the size of the amount the state received from federal funds. The California award of $252,260,225 represented over half of the total award funds (50.96 percent), with additional amounts being paid to its counties. The largest of these, Los Angeles County, received $12,824,071. Next came Texas ($51,900,069), New York ($46,842,600) with a further $15,571,566 for New York City, and Florida ($17,513,577), supplemented by additional payments to county jurisdictions in each state. Together with California, these three states took up over 90 percent of the SCAAP total of $494,468,661 for fiscal year 1996. In all, 145 jurisdictions received awards, including every state apart from North Dakota. Awards were also made to the District of Columbia, Puerto Rico, and the Virgin Islands, plus 93 local jurisdictions. The number of applicants was expected to increase substantially (up to 1500) in fiscal year 1997 due to a change in the statute broadening the criteria for qualifying.[69] But the bulk of the funding under the SCAAP program was unlikely to be diverted away from the four states that had dominated the picture in fiscal year 1996.

VI

The Department of Justice budget for fiscal year 1996, and its handling by the 104th Congress, had departed from the established principles of lawmaking, exemplifying the pragmatic reality that the majority will normally get its way, particularly if it engages in preliminary negotiation and deals with the minority party. Of the various crime items, the two most costly, funding for prisons and policing and local law enforcement, had circumvented the customary two-stage process of an appropriations bill granting funds for purposes previously approved by Congress within authorized limits.[70] The 1996 Appropriations Act itself authorized the changes, some of them fundamental, from the 1994 Crime Act. The elimination of a large number of separate prevention programs included in Title III of the 1994 Act, for example, and their replacement by block grants for local law enforcement, was a deliberate and controversial change in policy. Expenditures authorized by the 103rd Congress were rescinded, and funds for the new grant programs authorized, as well as appropriated, in a single appropriations act. In places the language necessary to give legal effect to the new policies was extensive. The revised arrangements for channeling federal funds to the states for expanding their prison capacity were enacted by means of substituting a complete new subtitle of the U.S. Code, repealing the 1994 provisions.[71] Elsewhere the connecting thread of the expenditure of federal money, elastic as it was, did not stretch as far as those provisions which essentially were new legislation unrelated to the supply of public funds. The clumsy full title of H.R. 3019 (S. 1594), signed into law as Public Law 104-134, reflected its composite characteristics. To cover all of its disparate functions in a comprehensive manner it was entitled the Omnibus Consolidated Rescissions and Appropriations Act of 1996.

One provision that owed its presence in the 1996 Appropriations Act to the ease with which the rule forbidding the inclusion of new laws, or changes in existing laws, in general appropriations bills could be waived was the Prison

Litigation Reform Act.[72] This measure was the direct progeny of Senator Helms's amendment to the 1994 Crime Act, which had evoked such eloquent, although unsuccessful, opposition by Biden. No sooner had the resulting section 20409 been enacted than it became evident it was unlikely to fulfill its promoters' heartfelt objective of making it more difficult for prisoners to obtain relief in overcrowding cases. Intentionally or otherwise, the linkage to the Eighth Amendment reduced its range.

The National Prison Project, amongst others, was quick to point out that challenges to jail overcrowding, in which the plaintiffs were detained in local facilities awaiting trial or serving shorter prison sentences, were usually brought not under the Eighth Amendment, but under the Due Process Clause of the Fourteenth Amendment. Some of the largest correctional facilities in America, such as the Los Angeles County Jail and Cook County Jail in Chicago, fell outside the ambit of the new law. The same applied to challenges at juvenile facilities. Accordingly, the Helms amendment would have little, if any, impact on most jail overcrowding cases, or on juvenile cases.[73] Even in its application to cases brought by adult inmates serving longer sentences in federal or state prisons, it was improbable that the provision would be interpreted as imposing new restrictions on the remedial powers of the federal courts in overcrowding cases.

In an apparent attempt to strike down class actions, the amendment stated, "A Federal court shall not hold prison or jail crowding unconstitutional under the eighth amendment except to the extent that an individual plaintiff inmate proves that the crowding causes the infliction of cruel and unusual punishment of that inmate."[74] It was already established in case law that federal courts do not hold prison or jail overcrowding to be unconstitutional unless an individual plaintiff can prove that the crowding causes the infliction of cruel and unusual punishment on that prisoner.[75] In 1981 the Supreme Court had held that housing two inmates in a cell designed for one did not deprive a prisoner of his constitutional rights. No static test existed by which the courts might determine whether or not conditions of confinement were cruel and unusual. To satisfy the Eighth Amendment's prohibition, the conditions must not involve wanton and unnecessary infliction of pain, nor may they be grossly disproportionate to the severity of the crime warranting imprisonment. In delivering the opinion of the Court, Powell, J., said that the Eighth Amendment "must draw its meaning from the evolving standards of decency that mark the progress of a maturing society."[76]

Where a violation is found to have occurred in the situation of an individual plaintiff, it will often be shared by fellow inmates. Many cases were argued on the basis of threats to health or safety. Typically these involved contagious diseases, lack of adequate fire precautions, lack of sanitation, and threats to physical safety. Faulty plumbing causing sewage to seep into cells, the risks of physical assault, whether by other prisoners or guards, or of exposure to health risks were examples of violations that might be experienced by a class of inmates, in addition to an individual plaintiff. Other factors recognized by the courts were overcrowding, understaffing, classification, medical care, segregation, and isolation.[77]

For these and other reasons the effect of the Helms amendment was minimal. After two federal courts in suits brought in 1994 and 1995 had held that the section was no bar to class actions, its sponsors decided to try again. A new and more restrictive piece of legislation, initially known as the Stop Turning Out Prisoners Act (STOP), was drafted, this time taking greater notice of the legal context.

The perspective against which the renewed effort to limit the scope for judicial intervention was set was a diversified and grossly overburdened national system for the secure containment of offenders sentenced to terms of imprisonment, and for the detention of accused persons awaiting trial. The legal position was that if the conditions in prisons or jails were found by the courts to violate one or more constitutionally protected rights, the particular facility or the entire system of which it was a part might be placed under a court order, or be made subject to a consent decree. Facilities or systems could be required to comply with standards laid down by the courts, such as maximum population caps, sanitary conditions, procedures used to classify inmates, or ensuring access to sources of legal information. Consent decrees were court-sanctioned agreements between government officials and inmates or their representatives that laid down how and when specified problems should be resolved.[78]

As of January 1, 1995, the National Prison Project listed thirty-nine states, the District of Columbia, Puerto Rico, and the Virgin Islands that were under court orders or were the subject of consent decrees. Thirty-three jurisdictions were under court order for overcrowding or conditions in at least one of their major prison facilities. Nine jurisdictions were under court order covering their entire systems. Only three states, as well as the federal prison system, were not subject either to orders or decrees, nor were they facing challenges in the courts.[79] The relevance of further congressional action was consequently much more than academic. Large numbers of correctional facilities across the nation, and the inmates they contained, were liable to be affected by any changes in the law, if upheld in the courts, that restricted applications for relief.

VII

The Stop Turning Out Prisoners Act was introduced in the House on January 18, 1995. Although not part of H.R. 3, which was scheduled for a two-day hearing by the Crime Subcommittee that week, it attracted comment during the hearings. One of the witnesses, a detective with the Philadelphia Police Department, believed that a cap on prison population was the direct cause of the death of his twenty-one-year-old son, also a police officer, who had been shot dead by a man who had previously been released several times because of the prison cap.[80] One of America's leading penologists, Alvin Bronstein, for nearly a quarter of a century executive director of the National Prison

Project of the American Civil Liberties Union Foundation, had been called to testify on a different issue, frivolous actions or abusive prisoner lawsuits, which was part of H.R. 3. He had no prior knowledge that the STOP bill had been introduced the day before and was likely to be raised in questioning by the subcommittee, or in the testimony of Republican invited witnesses.

Although limited by his brief, some of Bronstein's remarks struck home at the stereotype image of the activist federal judge, bent on interfering with the way state authorities ran their prisons. "It just isn't true," he said, continuing:

> I have been a lawyer for 43 years. All of that time doing civil rights and civil liberties litigation in Federal courts. I believe I know more Federal judges in this country than any other lawyer living today. And I have never met a Federal judge who didn't hate prison litigation. It is their most feared, feared kind of litigation. It is cumbersome. It goes on for a long period of time. . . . It results in all kinds of mail, personal mail to the judges by prisoners. They don't like to do it. It is messy. They are forced to do it because of the oath they take to uphold and defend the Constitution. . . . Federal judges intervene in State and . . . local prison(s) and jails only . . . when the State and local prison officials and jail officials abdicate their responsibility and allow their facilities to become unconstitutional. But the judges don't like that litigation. So this activist Federal judge thing is really . . . a mythology.[81]

Bronstein's advocacy did not persuade the Committee on the Judiciary to refrain from adding two additional titles to H.R. 667, the Violent Criminal Incarceration Act, which contained the amended provisions on prison grant programs. One was entitled Stop Turning Out Prisoners and the other, Stopping Abusive Prisoner Lawsuits. In reporting the bill to the House, the committee said that the title on Stop Turning Out Prisoners addressed the problem of federal court-imposed prison population caps by limiting the remedies that could be granted or enforced by a court in a prison suit alleging a violation of a federal right.[82] Courts hearing such suits had often approved and enforced consent decrees giving expansive relief to the complaining inmates. While both state and federal courts had in some instances entered unnecessarily broad consent decrees, it was the federal courts that had used these decrees to intrude into state criminal justice systems, seriously undermining the ability of the local justice system to dispense any true justice. In the opinion of the committee, population caps were a primary cause of "revolving-door justice." The statistics alone did not reflect the incalculable losses to local communities caused by criminals confident in their belief that the criminal justice system was powerless to stop them. Detective Boyle's compelling testimony had made a deep impression on the Crime Subcommittee and was mentioned in the report to the House.[83]

An amendment in the main Judiciary Committee to strike the STOP title from the bill was defeated by twenty-five to five votes.[84] That the desire to rein back a supposedly overeager judiciary was a breeze filling the sails of popular opinion was scented by Schumer and other Democrats on the Committee who voted to retain the title, whereas Conyers was counted among the small group of dissenters.

No expert testimony was received in the House hearings from those with firsthand knowledge of administering correctional facilities. The Senate hearings were more thorough, and in a letter sent to the chairman of its Judiciary Committee the following month a former director of the Federal Bureau of Prisons went on record as saying that he regarded the STOP provisions as "extremely misguided."[85] He gave his reasons:

> No administrator wants to operate an unconstitutional facility. The community, staff and prisoners alike are better served when we assure minimally decent conditions in our nation's prisons. My experience, as well as the experience of correctional administrators around the country, is that prison conditions litigation has often helped administrators improve conditions in their facilities.
>
> I believe that the bill is extremely misguided for two reasons. First, by requiring a court to make factual findings before approving a Consent Decree, the bill essentially prevents federal, state, and other governmental entities from entering into settlement agreements in prison condition litigation. . . . Preventing states from settling, once they have determined it to be in their best interests, is bad policy.
>
> Second, the provision that requires federal courts to use Magistrates instead of special masters or monitors in prison conditions litigation is extremely impractical. Masters and monitors . . . have typically worked in the correctional field for several years and have developed expertise in correctional management. Replacing them with Magistrates who are already overworked and have no special expertise in prison management would create inordinate delays, misguided correctional policy, and an onslaught of further litigation.[86]

Prison litigation was a rolling stone in the 104th Congress. Half a dozen or so bills were introduced in the House or Senate. New proposals were brought forward and others abandoned, including the provision that magistrates rather than special masters should oversee the implementation of court orders. The emphasis changed from prison crowding to prison conditions, and the separate initiatives aimed at stopping abusive prisoner lawsuits and the release of prisoners were combined into a single measure. Unsystematic and scrappy as the process was, the momentum was maintained. Gradually the disparate elements were gathered together and refined into the Prison Litigation Reform Act of 1995 (PLRA).[87] A child of its time, the finished product was included as Title VIII of the 1996 Appropriations Act, signed into law in April 1996.

VIII

In its final form the PLRA constituted an extensive amendment to Title 18 of the United States Code.[88] Although the emotive language of the earlier drafts had disappeared, the intention was the same: to restrict the ability of the federal courts to intervene in the management of state prisons, and to make it harder for individual inmates to pursue their grievances by way of court actions. The Act prohibited prospective relief in any civil action regarding prison conditions from extending further than necessary to correct the violation of the federal rights of particular plaintiffs. The court should not grant or approve any such relief unless it is narrowly drawn, extends no further than necessary to correct the violation, and is the least intrusive means of correcting it. Substantial weight must be given to any adverse impact on public safety or the operation of the criminal justice system caused by the relief.

Temporary restraining orders or an order for preliminary injunctive relief would be available, but such orders would need to be narrowly drawn, and with some exceptions would expire automatically after ninety days. Prisoner release orders should not be entered unless a court had previously entered an order for less intrusive relief that had failed to remedy the deprivation of the federal right, and the defendant had been allowed a reasonable amount of time to comply with previous orders. A prisoner release order could only be entered by a three-judge court that finds by clear and convincing evidence that crowding is the primary cause of the violation and that no other relief will remedy it.

Greater restrictions on suits brought by prisoners in any jail, prison, or other correctional facility, had been a high priority of state attorneys general who had argued the case for action very strongly with the administration. The Department of Justice did not dissent, accepting the desirability of minimizing the burden on states of responding unnecessarily to prisoner suits which, it observed, typically lacked merit and were often brought for the purposes of harassment or recreation.[89] Again much careful drafting was needed to attain this end, including an amendment to the Civil Rights of Institutionalized Persons Act of 1980.[90] This would ensure that in future no inmate would be enabled to bring a prison conditions suit unless the available administrative remedies had been exhausted. According to the Justice Department, the provision would bring the law more into line with the administrative exhaustion rules that applied in other contexts, and would be dependent on the administrative procedures satisfying minimum standards of fairness and effectiveness.

Under the provisions of the PLRA, courts were directed to dismiss any action relating to prison conditions brought by a prisoner if the court was satisfied that the action was frivolous, malicious, failed to state a claim on which relief could be granted, or sought monetary relief from a defendant who was immune from such relief. A prisoner seeking to bring a civil action or appeal a judgment in a civil action or proceedings would have to pay the full amount of a filing fee, unless the institution in which the prisoner was confined certified that the assets possessed by the prisoner were inadequate to cover such fees and consequent costs. Other provisions included limits on the award of attorneys' fees, limitation on recovery, hearings, and waiver of reply by defendants to actions brought by prisoners.

Unlike the earlier experience with the Helms amendment, actions to test the constitutionality of several of the PLRA provisions met with a mixed reception in the courts. The National Prison Project reported that by the end of December 1996 "good orders and opinions had been issued on the retroactivity of attorneys' fees, special masterships as prospective relief, and the automatic stay provisions of the act."[91] But on the larger issues, the outlook was less favorable. Two long-standing consent decrees had been terminated, one of the best known in the country in New York City,[92] and the other in South Carolina. The Fourth Circuit of the U.S. Court of Appeals had upheld the decision of the federal district court for the Western District of South Carolina,[93] and the Second Circuit had heard an appeal against termination in the New York City case, *Benjamin v. Jacobson* in November,[94] but had not issued a decision at the time of writing the report.

In *Benjamin,* a federal judge for the Southern District of New York upheld the Act and vacated the consent decrees dating from 1978–79 in seven related cases involving facilities at Rikers Island and sixteen other jails in New York City. All of the plaintiffs were pretrial detainees. Judge Baer found that the PLRA did not dictate certain findings or results under the old law, but changed the law governing the district court's remedial powers. The termination provision did not affect the court's ability to enforce constitutional rights. "While seemingly cramped by the new legal standards . . . and the time constraints, . . . it is nonetheless fair to say that courts will continue to define the scope of prisoners' constitutional rights, review the factual record, apply the judicially determined constitutional standards to the facts as they are found in the record and determine what relief is necessary to remedy the constitutional violations."[95] The Act also served the legitimate interest of ensuring that federal courts should return control over prison management to democratically accountable state and local governments as soon as their supervision became unnecessary to remedy a constitutional violation.

Nine months later the Second Circuit upheld the constitutionality of the termination provision of the PLRA, but reversed the order of the district court vacating the consent decrees.[96] In a unanimous decision Calabresi, J.,[97] rejected claims by the plaintiffs that the termination provision violated separation-of-powers principles, or the equal protection guarantees of the Fifth and Fourteenth Amendments, or the due process clause of the same amendments. The district court had erred, however, in vacating the consent decrees. Such decrees were a hybrid between a judgment and a contract between the parties willingly entered into, with each of the parties giving good and valuable consideration for what it received, Whether they should be construed primarily as contracts, or as judgments, was a matter of heated debate, The court was not called upon to resolve the dispute. It was for the plaintiffs to decide whether to seek enforcement of the decrees in their entirety in the state courts, rather than pursuing what might in the end give rise to partial federal court relief under the PLRA, and partial state court based on local contract law principles. The choice was for the plaintiffs. Should they choose to remain in the federal court they were entitled to an evidentiary hearing of their allegations of current and on-going violations of their federal rights.

The political sensitivities were seldom far below the surface. In *Benjamin,* as in other cases, the Department of Justice had filed a brief which, while endorsing the constitutionality of the PLRA, construed some of its provisions in ways that a group of Republican senators found highly objectionable. In a letter to the Attorney General dated July 23, 1996, Senator Hatch and seventeen other Republican members of the Senate wrote to express their "deep concern" regarding the position the Department was advancing in cases involving prison litigation. Rather than urge courts to follow the clear language and intent of the PLRA that judges should cease running prisons, the construction put on some of the Act's provisions by the Department would allow, indeed encourage, the courts to perpetuate their rule indefinitely. The robust flavor of the six-page letter, complete with footnotes, can be judged from one of its closing paragraphs:

> Finally, it is difficult to see how the Department's nullifying interpretation of these provisions of the statute, ostensibly undertaken to avoid the risk that they will be found unconstitutional, is anything other than a refusal to defend the constitutionality of the provisions that the Congress actually wrote. This is despite the Department's contention in its brief that the law is constitutional if "properly construed," as the "construction" the Department advances as the "proper" one is irreconcilably inconsistent with the enacted law. In our judgment, therefore, both Houses of Congress should have been notified that you were not going to be defending the constitutionality of these provisions at the time these briefs were filed.[98]

Faced with an onslaught of this ferocity it is no surprise that the original stance of the department was hastily revised.

IX

In addition to the Prison Litigation Reform Act and the incentive grant programs to states for building and expanding prison capacity, one other prison item featured in the 1996 Appropriations Act. Buried in the list of prohibitions on the use of the federal funds provided by the Act, and juxtaposed with such weighty matters of policy as United Nations peacekeeping missions and television broadcasts to Cuba, was a restriction that none of the funds appropriated should be used to provide certain "amenities or personal comforts" in the federal prison system. It seems barely credible that the provision of in-cell coffee pots, hot plates, or heating elements should be the subject of a specific ban in an Appropriations Act allocating huge annual sums to fund the activities of three major departments of government as well as the federal judiciary and related agencies, but that is where it is to be found.[99]

The antecedents of this strange provision lay in populism at its most naked. A well-publicized special article in the *Reader's Digest* in November 1994[100] had presented a picture of prison life of laxity and an array of creature comforts unrecognizable by those with closer firsthand experience. Unrepresentative, and subsequently contested, examples were cited of "prime-rib dinners," "manicured green lawns," activities directors and counselors, overlavish sports and recreational facilities, premium cable TV and movies depicting sex, horror, and violence, and physical fitness programs from weight-lifting to aerobics to boxing that meant "today's thugs and armed robbers can return to the streets bigger, stronger and faster than ever."[101] The theme of the article, and its policy significance, was reflected in its title: "Must Our Prisons be Resorts?." As had become fashionable, the blame was laid squarely on intervention by the federal courts: "At first, judges ruled only that prisoners were entitled to nutritious meals, basic health services and protection against arbitrary discipline at the hands of guards. But a number of federal judges went well beyond such reasonable reforms and began ordering that prisoners be provided with expensive, untested treatment programs and a wide range of recreational opportunities regardless of the cost."[102]

In no time the cry was taken up in Congress. A press conference addressed by the author of the *Reader's Digest* article was held on Capitol Hill and a bill published under the title No Frills Prison Act (H.R. 663). Among the "luxurious prison conditions" to be eliminated by the bill were earned good-time credits; in-cell television viewing; the viewing of R, X, or NC-17 rated movies, through whatever medium presented; any instruction or training equipment for boxing, wrestling, judo, karate, or other martial art, or any body-building or weightlifting equipment of any sort; the use or possession of electric or electronic musical instruments, or practice on any musical instrument for more than one hour a day; the use of personally owned computers or modems; the possession of in-cell coffee pots, hot plates, or heating elements; food exceeding in quality or quantity that which is available to enlisted personnel in the U.S. Army; and dress or hygiene, grooming, and appearance other than those allowed as uniform or standard in the prison. Still more restrictive conditions were applied to prisoners serving sentences for crimes of violence resulting in serious bodily injury.

Such a bill had no chance of being passed into law, but it achieved its purpose of channeling toward Congress a relatively new and virulent strain in public opinion. The novelty lay not in the already well-rehearsed denunciation of activist federal judges, but in the belief that prison regimes should be expressly punitive. To some vengeful and vocal critics it was not enough that convicted prisoners should be punished by being deprived of their liberty; they should also be punished and suffer while in prison. The distorted picture portrayed by the *Reader's Digest,* and other exaggerated examples that were in circulation, ignored the commonplace realities of prison life: the constant danger and degradation, the brutality and sodomy, the exploitation of the weak by the strong, and the total lack of privacy. To list the provision of education and vocational programs in the catalog of luxuries[103] was perhaps the most extreme indication of retributionist prejudice and a closed mind. No awareness was shown of the effect of inmate participation either in GED programs or postsecondary education in reducing rates of recidivism.[104] Only the statutorily protected,[105] and Republican-approved,[106] exercise of religious beliefs seems to have been exempted from the desire to harshen virtually all nondisciplinary aspects of prison life.

And yet the proposal did not die in its entirety. Despite their minimal financial implications, five of the items listed above survived to be enacted in the Appropriations Acts of 1996, being repeated in the 1997 Act.[107] The scope of the prohibition was greatly narrowed by being limited to the federal prison system and excluding the far larger number of state-run penal institutions. Moreover, the restrictions related only to the use of federal funds. Since coffee pots, hot plates, and television sets are readily available consumer goods, prisoners' personal funds, or gifts from families or friends outside, unless forbidden by prison regulations, would in most cases be able to fill the void caused by the absence of any prohibited objects paid for by federal taxpayers.

The populist appeal of policies aimed at making prison life more unpleasant for inmates was articulated graphically the following year. A reporter following up a story that chain gangs were to be instituted for prisoners working outside a county detention facility, where no inmate was serving a sentence of more than eighteen months, took the pulse of local opinion: "Rehabilitation does not work, say people in Centreville. And prisoners have it too easy, they add. A convict gets free room, board, medical care and television, while they have to earn both their own keep and his. They want convicts, like welfare recipients, to work. But they also want to stigmatize and shame the people who shamelessly violate them."[108] Contrary to its ambitious-sounding name, Centreville is not a remote place, deep in the center of the continent. With a population of 2,662 it is located on the Eastern Shore of Maryland, no more than one hour's drive from Washington, D.C., or Baltimore.

X

Of the eight titles in the Taking Back Our Streets Act (H.R. 3) introduced on January 4, 1995, six had been enacted with modifications by the end of the 104th Congress in October 1996. They covered habeas corpus reform, mandatory victim restitution, abusive prisoner law suits, criminal alien deportation, truth-in-sentencing grants for prison construction and expansion, and block grants for local government law enforcement. The most important reverse suffered by the Republican majority was inflicted by the President in his insistence that the community policing initiative should be maintained as a separately managed and funded program. No action was taken on the proposal to federalize state crimes where a firearm was used in the course of a violent felony or serious drug offense, and reform of the exclusionary rule was held over for another day.

Gun regulation had been kept in a lower key than in the previous Congresses, but was a rumbling volcano waiting to erupt again. Its tremors, less threatening than in the past, are recorded in the next chapter. Overshadowing the piecemeal enactment of the other Contract with America items, the foremost criminal legislation passed by the 104th Congress was the administration's counterterrorism initiative, to which the far-reaching reforms in habeas corpus procedures had been attached. In control of both Houses of Congress for the first time in four decades the Republican majority had dictated the agenda, on crime as on other issues. But Democrats, aided by the administration, had been successful in limiting the scale of the changes made to the Violent Crime Control and Law Enforcement Act of 1994. Although the ideological divide between the parties was still deep, and the arguments over funding would not evaporate, the rancorous partisanship that had marked the start of the 104th Congress had cooled to an extent that few could have anticipated by its close.

Chapter 8

Congress and the Courts

I

What three strikes had been to the 103rd Congress, Megan's Law was to the 104th. Changes in federal law were already under consideration to protect the potential victims of further assaults by persons previously convicted of sexually violent offenses or criminal offenses against children[1] when the rape and murder by strangling of a seven-year-old girl, Megan Kanka, occurred in New Jersey. Her assailant was a twice-convicted pedophile who had come to live with two companions, also convicted sex offenders, on the same street as the Kanka family. He had invited the child over to see a puppy when the fatal assault took place.[2] As with the earlier killing of Polly Klaas in California, it was the horrifying and extensively publicized circumstances of such a dreadful crime occurring in a quiet suburban setting that caused it to enter the national consciousness. The last minute changes made to strengthen the Jacob Wetterling subtitle of the 1994 Crime Act were described in chapter 5. But the requirements of registration and discretionary notification to local law enforcement agencies were regarded by many legislators, state as well as federal, as not going far enough to meet the public demand for more rigorous safeguards against repeat sex offenders.

By March 1996, forty-seven states had enacted sex offender registration laws, and thirty of them had adopted community notification provisions. Several states also required sex offenders to provide blood samples for DNA testing and filing the profiles in the state's criminal justice data bank. Because the federal law allowed, but did not require, state or local law enforcement to disseminate relevant information in order to protect the public, states had opted for differing community notification standards. For example, whereas New York, Pennsylvania, and New Jersey had community notification laws in place by that time which required citizens to be notified when a sex offender in their community posed a danger, the neighboring states of Connecticut and Delaware offered registry information only to law enforcement agencies, employers conducting background checks, and others at the discretion of the law enforcement authorities.[3]

It was this discrepancy, and the political capital to be gained by responding positively to the gale force of public opinion in the state of New Jersey where the Kanka family lived, that caused Representative Dick Zimmer (Rep. New Jersey) to press for further action by Congress. Although some unease had been expressed that the onrush of legislation to regulate released sex offenders threatened to violate the rights of individuals who had already been punished for their crimes,[4] such criticisms based upon principle were muted in Congress. The ranking Democrat on the House Subcommittee on Crime, Charles Schumer, agreed with the Republican chairman, Bill McCollum, that mandatory notification would add to the protection of potential future victims, and Clinton had made the same point in some of his own speeches.

An easy passage for Zimmer's short amending bill, H.R. 2137, introduced in the House on July 27, 1995, was therefore assured. The following March, when the Crime Subcommittee held hearings on a clutch of smaller bills, he was one of the only two witnesses called to testify on Megan's Law. The other was a representative of the Department of Justice. Before an entirely sympathetic audience of fellow legislators Zimmer explained that the diversity of practice between states caused him to fear that sexual predators would begin to move from state to state, settling in jurisdictions where they were able to ensure their anonymity. As a result, critical information would not necessarily get into the hands of those who needed it most, namely parents, in order to take commonsense steps to protect their children. Because of this "very real possibility" Zimmer believed that Congress should strengthen the 1994 law so that community notification would be standard in all fifty states.[5]

In the short exchange that followed, the sole questioning came from a recently elected Democrat representative, Zoe Lofgren of California. She accepted that in balancing the privacy rights of convicted child molesters and the rights of children and parents to be safe from them it was necessary to come down on the side of the parents and children. Her questions were exploratory, not hostile, turning on the differing methods of community notification. She agreed with Zimmer that federal law should make notification mandatory rather than permissive, and that the way in which it was done should be for each state to decide for itself.[6]

In supporting the enactment of the legislation, the Department of Justice took a similar line, pointing out that in the Jacob Wetterling Crimes against Children and Sexually Violent Offender Registration subtitle of the 1994 Act,[7] Congress had provided a financial incentive for states to establish effective registration systems for released child molesters and other sexually violent offenders. States that failed to establish conforming registration systems would be subject to a 10 percent reduction in formula Byrne Grant funding, with the resulting surplus funds being reallocated to states that were in compliance.[8] The Department also recommended an amendment to the Wetterling Act deleting the provision that information collected under the state registration systems was generally to be treated as private data. A draft amendment to this effect was included in a letter sent by Andrew Fois, Assistant Attorney General for Legislative Affairs, to McCollum accompanied by an offer to work with interested members of Congress in strengthening the Act.[9]

While agreeing to delete the classification of information collected under state systems as private data, Zimmer was reluctant to accept any other changes. He was aware that in the Senate attempts were likely to be made to broaden the scope of the House bill, and he feared that any additions would make his bill more vulnerable to delay. If the Senate decided to take up further proposals from the Justice Department or elsewhere in a separate bill, adding such other provisions as it wished, he would be willing to sponsor it in the House. But he was not prepared to jeopardize the chances of his own bill becoming law. In this he had the support of the Kanka parents, translated by their personal tragedy into sophisticated and effective lobbyists.

Zimmer's singlemindedness prevailed and in the week of May 6, 1996, the bill was passed by both Houses. The debate on the floor of the House of Representatives on the afternoon of Tuesday, May 7, was a full one ending in a recorded vote. Despite some misgivings about possible constitutional implications, Conyers gave the bill his support.[10] So did Pat Schroeder (Dem. Colorado), a liberal member of the committee and author of a 1993 measure that established procedures for national criminal background checks on child care providers.[11] A lone representative, Melvin Watt (Dem. North Carolina), spoke in opposition. While accepting that there was a higher rate of recidivism for sex offenders and child abusers, he was troubled by the underlying assumption that once an offense of this kind had been committed the perpetrator would be assumed guilty for the rest of his life. People should not be presumed guilty unless they had committed a specific crime. Once they had paid their debt to society they should be allowed to go on with their lives. A second cause for concern was states' rights. It seemed that Congress was not willing to allow states to make their own decisions about whether they wanted a Megan's law or not: "All of a sudden, the Big Brother Government must direct the States to do something that is not necessarily a Federal issue."[12]

Although there was no question that the bill would be passed by an overwhelming majority on a voice vote, Zimmer sought unanimity, knowing full well how difficult any dissenting representatives would find it in their congressional districts to vote against a law directly aimed at increasing protection for children. He was proved right in his assumption when the only three Democrats to cast their votes against[13] changed them from nay to yea, after hurried consultation with Conyers, before the result was announced. The final tally was yeas 418, nays 0, not voting 15.[14]

In the Senate, where there was also sensitivity toward the states' rights issue, Dole had agreed with the House leadership and the bill's sponsor to take H.R. 2137 direct to the floor without being marked up by the Judiciary Committee. In some brief explanatory remarks on May 9, two days after the House vote, he called on the Senate not to wait for some other horrific crime but to pass the bill immediately.[15] The only other speaker was Senator Gorton, the original sponsor of the registration and permissive notification provisions in the 1994 legislation. That procedure had not been as tough as he would have liked and was now improved by the requirement of community notification. Even with that mandate, he said, state and local law enforcement officials would retain a substantial discretion on what information to release and how best to inform the community.[16] There being no objections, the bill was deemed read three times and passed.

Megan's Law was signed by the President at a White House ceremony on May 17, 1996, attended by Zimmer and others in Congress who had been active in promoting the legislation.[17] Not only were Megan's parents, Richard and Maureen Kanka, present, but so too were the mother of Jacob Wetterling and the father of Polly Klaas. Each had lived through the greatest pain that a parent can know, Clinton said, "a child brutally ripped from a parent's love." And yet they had borne a further burden, to take up parents concerns for all children's safety and dedicate themselves to answering that concern.[18]

Later in the session, the Senate brought forward its own bill (S. 1675) to provide for the national tracking of convicted sexual offenders. The measure authorized the Attorney General to establish a national database at the Federal Bureau of Investigation to track the whereabouts and movement of each person who had been convicted of a criminal offense against a victim who was a minor, or of a sexually violent offense, or had been classified as a sexually violent predator. Other sections covered registration requirements, the length of the period of registration, verification, notification to local law enforcement, and a number of other requirements and procedures. The bill was considered and passed by the Senate on July 25, and a comparable bill (H.R. 3456), sponsored by Zimmer, was considered in the House on September 25. Both H.R. 3456 and S. 1675 were considered and passed by the House on September 26. On October 3 this further precautionary measure aimed at known sexual offenders was signed into law as the Pam Lynchner Sexual Offender Tracking and Identification Act of 1996.[19]

At the Megan's Law signing ceremony, Clinton had been asked about legal challenges by a journalist. In reply he said that he hoped the law, both in its original and enhanced form, would be upheld if it was challenged. He believed that it would be. Before the administration went forward in support, in consultation with Congress, a great deal of legal research had been done. "Congress has done its job," he concluded. "[N]ow it is our job to get out there and defend this law, and we intend to do it if it's challenged. And in the meanwhile, we intend to enforce it."[20]

II

Even before the amendments were enacted to the federal law requiring the release of relevant information to protect the public from sexually violent offenders, there had been challenges to the state version of Megan's Law in her home state of New Jersey. In February 1995 the U.S. District Court, in upholding the registration provisions, held that part of the notification provisions violated the ex post facto clause of the United States Constitution.[21] That decision was appealed, although by the time the case was heard by the U.S. Court of Appeals for the Third Circuit, the Supreme Court of New Jersey had considered the same issues in *Doe v. Poritz*.[22] By a majority of six to one, the court upheld the enforcement of the state's sex offender registration and community notification statutes, and additionally the Attorney General's guidelines on their implementation.

In a lengthy and thoroughly argued opinion, Chief Justice Wilentz, shortly to retire after seventeen years service, held that the state laws did not violate the ex post facto, double jeopardy, cruel and unusual punishment, or bill of attainder clauses of the U.S. Constitution, or analogous provisions in the constitution of the state. Nor did they deprive offenders of the right to equal protection under the law, nor their constitutional right to privacy. Subject to limited modifications allowing for judicial review in the categorization of previously convicted offenders according to the risk of their reoffending, the guidelines promulgated by the Attorney General to implement the laws were valid and immediately effective.

The central issue addressed by the New Jersey Supreme Court, as in challenges heard by federal courts and courts in other states, was whether or not the likely adverse consequences of notifying members of a local community that a convicted sex offender was in their midst amounted to additional punishment. In Wilentz's opinion, the emphasis was put on evidence that in passing the registration and notification laws the intent of the state legislature was clearly protective and not designed to punish. The court had no right to assume, he wrote, that the public would be punitive when the legislature had not. The Attorney General had strongly warned against vigilantism, and that harassment would not be tolerated. The notification procedures had been carefully tailored into three tiers reflecting the degree of risk, the requirements of confidentiality, and the restriction of notification to those likely to encounter the offender. All these factors pointed unerringly toward a remedial intent and a remedial implementation.[23]

Five of the justices joined in the Chief Justice's opinion. The sixth, Stein, J., dissented. While in his opinion it was not yet possible to discern the future effects on those subject to the community and individual notification procedures, he included in the record two accounts of actions recently taken against sex offenders.[24] In the first notification made under Megan's Law in one county, law enforcement officers provided neighbors with the address at which the offender was to reside and distributed photographs of him. Ten days later, a father and son broke into the house looking for "the child molester," attacking a man they wrongly assumed was the released offender. In fact, the unfortunate victim was a truck driver who was staying in the house. The severity of the beating was such that he was hospitalized.

In the second incident, a man was released from prison after serving a sentence for rape. He had informed the authorities that upon his release he intended to live with his mother at her home in New Jersey. Days later he sought and obtained a preliminary injunction in the federal district court, which delayed law enforcement officials from implementing the notification provisions. The news got out, however, enabling the Guardian Angels, a New York-based civilian group, to organize a protest outside the mother's house. It was reported that hundreds of residents and students streamed down the street holding leaflets with the man's photograph handed out by the Guardian Angels. Two young men, local residents, threatened: "We're waiting for him to come down. . . . We're going to beat him up. He can go back upstairs, come down, we'll beat him up again." The leader of the Guardian Angels was quoted as saying that convicted criminals deserved to be treated as outcasts, and that their ostracism would deter others, declaring, "Let the criminal have a taste of being the victim."[25]

Although Stein denied any suggestion that these accounts were typical of the character and nature of the response of the public to the discovery that a sex offender was living amongst them, the cautionary case histories certainly did much to add weight to his conclusions. A fine libertarian analyisis, later cited in the U.S. District Court,[26] then followed:

> The Legislature's value judgment about these laws is entitled to great respect, but that judgment comprises only one part of the constitutional equation. The judiciary's task is to complete the equation by evaluating the legislative determination in the context of settled constitutional principles. Those principles are neither negotiable nor flexible, their importance having been conclusively determined more than two hundred years ago by the founding fathers. In applying those principles, we must bear in mind their origins: "The constitutional prohibitions against the enactment of ex post facto laws and bills of attainder reflect a valid concern about the use of the political process to punish or characterize past conduct of private citizens."[27] . . .

The Constitution's prohibition against ex post facto laws reflects an enduring value that transcends the most pressing concerns of this or any day and age. Today, our concern is with prior sex offenders; in the 1950's the legislative concern focused on Communists; and in the 1860's Congress was determined to punish legislatively those who had supported the Confederacy. Future legislatures will doubtlessly find reasons to deal harshly with other groups that pose an apparent threat to the public safety.

Tested against the historical uses and purposes of punishment, public notice and public ostracism concerning prior sex offenders appear to fall squarely within the parameters of punishment as practiced at the time of adoption of the Constitution. The identification, scorn, and humiliation of sex offenders that public notice will achieve is strikingly reminiscent of the punishments commonly imposed in the colonial period.[28]

The unusually wide choice of avenues for constitutional review meant that many of the state formulations of Megan's Law were open to challenge in the courts. Although the ways differed in which the registration and community notification provisions were implemented, the fundamental questions were the same. Before answering them, the judges had to put out of their minds the notion of striking a balance between the rights of sex offenders and the rights of their victims. That was the language of politics rather than law. What was called for was an analysis of the rights held by every citizen and the constitutional limitations on a government's power to infringe them.

The central question that had to be answered by the courts in reviewing challenges to notification statutes and their enforcement was whether the practices under review amounted to impermissible punishment within the meaning of the ex post facto, bill of attainder, and double jeopardy clauses of the U.S. Constitution.[29] There were other questions too. Was the wording of the statute under review unconstitutionally vague? Did the procedures for determining levels of notification based upon the risk of reoffending conform with the requirements of due process? Did they offend the anti-retroactivity presumption by attaching new legal consequences to completed events? Should the ostracism likely to result from compulsory notification be regarded as an ''unusual punishment'' under the Eighth Amendment?[30] Given the breadth of these questions it is hardly surprising that courts in different parts of the country came up with different answers.

III

A report by the National Institute of Justice published in February 1997 showed that in all of the seven states surveyed there had been constitutional challenges to sex offender notification statutes and their implementation.[31] The most frequent ground for suits was the claim that the ex post facto nature of most state laws, applying the provisions retroactively to offenders who had been sentenced before the statutes came into effect, constituted double jeopardy in that the stigma punished offenders who already had served the punishment imposed by the courts for their crimes. The second most common ground was due process, with the courts in some instances separating, or making subject to judicial review, administrative decisions on the classification of offenders into categories according to potential dangerousness, and taking away from law enforcement agencies the responsibility for implementation. The same reasoning was applied to decisions granting relief from notification. Generally unsuccessful challenges had claimed that notification violated the Eighth Amendment's prohibition against cruel and unusual punishment because of the public stigma alleged to attach to notification.

Modes of implementation can sharpen the focus for legal challenge. In New York it was anticipated that a plan to disclose information in response to inquiries on a special telephone number would eventually reveal the identity of all known sex offenders in the state, believed to total about five thousand,[32] irrespective of the assessed risk of reoffending. After the projected hotline had been made public, but shortly before it was due to become operational in March 1996, it was halted by a temporary restraining order and preliminary injunction granted by the U.S. District Court in Manhattan.[33] In September, the same court in summary judgment held that the public notification provisions of the newly enacted state law constituted punishment, and that they increased punishment after the fact. Hence their retroactive application would violate the ex post facto clause of the Constitution. The registration provisions did not constitute punishment as they did not result in the same excesses or adverse consequences that would follow public notification.[34]

Both the New York and New Jersey decisions were appealed to the U.S. Court of Appeals. The Third Circuit vacated the original judgment of the district court in New Jersey that the notification aspects of Megan's Law violated the ex post facto clause of the Constitution, and affirmed its finding that the registration provisions were constitutional.[35] The outcome of an appeal on a later case from the district court in New Jersey, this time upholding both the notification and registration provisions of the state law,[36] was awaited at the time of writing. The Second Circuit's decision in the New York case was also pending. Given the diversity of opinion, and the fact that in several states, including New York, New Jersey, and Connecticut, the implementation of notification procedures for offenders sentenced before the new laws had come into effect was stayed until the resolution of legal challenges, it seems probable that an opinion of the Supreme Court will be necessary to bring to a conclusion the spate of litigation.

Although no sex offender notification case was on the docket of the Supreme Court in the 1996–97 term, some of the same issues of ex post facto punishment, double jeopardy, and due process were addressed in a convoluted challenge to a related statute enacted by the Kansas legislature. In question was the validity of a new state law authorizing the continued civil confinement of persons convicted of violent sexual offenses after the due date of their release from a criminal sentence if they met certain criteria classifying them as sexually violent predators. The Kansas Supreme Court had stuck down the Sexually Violent Predator Act, which had been passed into law in 1994, on the ground that it violated substantive due process because the appellant, Leroy Hendricks, was being confined without evidence that he had a mental abnormality or personality disorder.[37] The state sought a review of this decision by the U.S. Supreme Court, while Hendricks, the first person to whom the Act had been applied, petitioned the Court to consider the constitutional issues. Both petitions were granted, and oral argument on the consolidated cases of *Kansas v. Hendricks,* and *Hendricks v. Kansas* was heard on December 10, 1996.

Kansas was supported in an amicus brief filed by thirty-eight other states, Puerto Rico, the District of Columbia, and four U.S. territories. Ranged against them in support of Hendricks, was the ACLU and five of its regional associates, the American Psychiatric Association, the National Mental Health Association, and briefs on behalf of the National Association of Criminal Defense Lawyers and several state or county defender associations. As is so often the archetype in criminal and civil proceedings dependent on the mental state of offenders, lawmakers pursue a degree of certainty that doctors are unable to provide.

The division of opinion was reflected by the Supreme Court on June 23, 1997.[38] In a five-to-four decision, the Court upheld the Kansas statute, ruling that states may continue to confine violent sex offenders after the expiry of their sentences of imprisonment, even where their mental condition does not meet the state's normal criteria for civil commitment against the will of the person confined. Writing for the Court Thomas J., joined by Rehnquist, C.J., O'Connor, Scalia, and Kennedy, JJ., held that such civil confinement did not amount to punishment. Three dissenting Justices, Stevens, Souter, and Ginsburg, joined Breyer, J., in concluding that the added confinement imposed upon Hendricks was basically punitive,[39] because he was being restrained rather than treated for his psychiatric and behavioral disorders. Breyer agreed with the majority opinion, however, that the Act's definition of mental abnormality satisfied the substantive requirements of the due process clause. Provided that a state legislature tailored a dangerous sexual offender statute to fit the nonpunitive civil aim of treatment, ensuring that it operated prospectively, so avoiding the constitutional prohibition against the retroactive imposition of new punishments, it would not cross "the Constitution's liberty-protecting line."[40]

The borderline between criminal and civil proceedings was blurred by the requirement for a trial to establish whether a person who had been evaluated initially as a sexually violent predator fulfilled the definition contained in the Kansas law. At the trial, the burden of proof was placed on the state to show beyond a reasonable doubt (the criminal standard of proof) that the evidence supported a finding that the person was a sexually violent predator and thus eligible for civil commitment. In the case of an indigent person, the state was required to provide, at public expense, the assistance of counsel and an examination by health care professionals. The person also had a right to present and cross-examine witnesses, and an opportunity to review documentary evidence presented by the state. If the person was confined, the committing court was obligated to conduct an annual review to determine whether continued detention was warranted. If at any time the court found that the state could no longer satisfy the burden under the initial commitment standard, the person would have to be released from confinement. The thrust of Hendricks's case was that the Act established criminal proceedings. Hence confinement under it necessarily constituted punishment. Thomas, J., rejected this line of argument, saying that the fact Kansas had chosen to afford such procedural protections, did not transform a civil commitment proceeding into a criminal prosecution.[41]

IV

Other than where court-ordered stays were in force, the formulation of the federal Megan's Law had left the door open for a medley of practical ways of notification. State laws typically assigned responsibility to notify to one of four groups: law enforcement agencies; probation or parole departments; local prosecutor offices; or even the offenders themselves. The National Institute of Justice study found that different states, and different jurisdictions within states, conducted notification very differently. Once the implementing agency had been chosen the main elements to be decided upon were how long offenders should remain subject to notification, whether the notification procedure should be mandatory or discretionary, whether it should be proactive or only in response to requests, what offenses should be covered, whether immunity should be provided to implementors, who ought to be notified, whether or not the law should be retroactive, and what items of information should be disseminated.[42]

Almost every respondent to the survey reported that sex offender notification was "very time-consuming and burdensome."[43] Probation officer caseloads often were not reduced to compensate for the additional labor-intensive tasks arising out of the release of sex offenders. Notification backlogs built up, and when offenders moved from one address to another, a frequent occurrence, the whole process had to start again. Neighbors were usually notified by the distribution of flyers door to door, if possible with someone from the agency talking to the occupant. Schools and selected organizations needed to be visited, and the media informed. Practice varied from New Jersey, where a court ruling prohibited notification to the press, to Louisiana, where the offender himself was responsible for notifying the community, and had an obligation to place, and pay for, a notice in the local press.[44]

On the limited empirical information available, it seemed unlikely that notification had any significant effect in protecting the public by reducing recidivism. A study in the state of Washington, the first to enact sex offender registration and notification laws, showed that over a four-and-a-half-year period there was no statistically significant difference in arrest rates for sex offenses between samples of offenders subject to notification, and those who had not been subject to notification before the change in the law. Whereas overall rates of recidivism were similar, it appeared that offenders subject to notification were arrested for new crimes more quickly.[45] Although recidivism may not be greatly affected, notification may nevertheless have a valuable function if the corrosive fear of crime in a local community is reduced, without being replaced by a false sense of security. Perceptions, how people feel, can sometimes count for more than the actuality.

Extremes of community fear, however, can provoke vigilantism or harassment. Nearly all enforcement agencies accepted that notification should be backed up by systematic and sustained efforts to educate communities about the nature of sex offending. If harassment was to be minimized, education strategies needed to be developed and followed up actively with local groups. Dialogues were valuable in informing residents of the crime involved, the ways in which an offender's behavior would be monitored, and how to recognize any signs of relapse. Parents were urged to seek advice on how best to guide and safeguard their children. Such steps as these were seen as essential complements to the warnings against harassment and victimization. In most states local communities were warned that harassment of offenders would be prosecuted, and some states said that the laws might be repealed if they incited vigilantism. That incidents of harassment or discrimination did occur seemed to be the general experience, particularly in housing and employment, but not as frequently or severely as might have been expected from the occasional highly newsworthy case.

The limitations of a federal statute designed to achieve standardization in state practices to meet a situation common to all, in this instance the danger of repeat offenses by previously convicted sex offenders, were illustrated by the differing ways in which state legislators and administrators responded. The apparently clear-cut distinction enunciated at the hearings on Capitol Hill, that the federal law should make notification mandatory rather than permissive, with financial penalties for noncompliance, but that the way in which it was done was for each state to decide for itself, turned out to be less straightforward in implementation. By August 1996 all states had passed legislation requiring the registration of sex offenders, in conformity with the 1994 Wetterling Act. In April of the following year, however, the Council of State Governments was warning member states that public notification systems should be in operation by September 13, 1997, and that failure to meet the deadline could result in a 10 percent reduction in federal law enforcement assistance.[46]

According to a count by the Washington State Institute for Public Policy, as of April 1997 eighteen states had set up active public notification systems, twelve had limited notification, thirteen had public access to registration information, and seven states had no notification or access to records. The latter category included the President's own state of Arkansas. While the eighteen states with active notification systems were seemingly in compliance with Megan's Law, the other twenty-five states with some form of notification, and the seven states with no notification, were in jeopardy of losing some funding through the Edward Byrne Memorial State and Local Law Enforcement Assistance Grant Program. The Department of Justice had drawn up proposed guidelines asking states to submit descriptions of their existing or proposed registration and notification systems. The submissions would then be reviewed to determine the status of state compliance, and suggestions made on how to achieve compliance before a state lost its funding.[47] The timetable was short. States had until June 1997 to comment on the proposed guidelines, and would then need to take action before the September deadline.

V

Gun control, deliberately omitted from the Contract with America and kept at arm's length by the Republican leadership thereafter, returned to the forefront in the House only once during the 104th Congress. That the ban on assault weapons was brought back to the floor at all was the result of an undertaking given to the NRA during the hectic excitement of the first hundred days. According to Elizabeth Drew, a reliable source, a tense meeting had taken place on January 25, 1995, in a conference room at the Speaker's Offices of the House of Representatives between Gingrich, Armey, DeLay, and McCollum with four representatives of the NRA. Gingrich and his colleagues were warned that the NRA membership was getting restive. The congressional leaders should understand, the NRA spokesmen said, that if they didn't take some action soon their membership would "get rid of us and then they'll get rid of you."[48] Gingrich was reported as replying that he had not realized the degree of alienation of the gun people who had been so supportive in the 1994 election. The completion of the Contract was the first priority. Its crime components had been protected from unwanted amendments by being divided into separate bills allowing only of germane amendments. Provided that the NRA desisted from putting pressure on those bills, the assault weapons ban would be taken up later.[49]

The original intention had been to hold votes in both Houses in the spring of 1995. The Oklahoma City bombing caused a postponement, with Dole displaying decreasing enthusiasm about the prospect of scheduling a repeal bill in the Senate. In the House of Representatives, moreover, Republican opinion was divided. The moderates, on whose support the gun control measures enacted in the previous Congress had depended, were apprehensive that it would look as though House Republicans had succumbed to a powerful interest group that had contributed money as well as political influence to the electoral campaigns of some of its members. The polls showed that a clear majority of public opinion was against the notion of scrapping the prohibition on possessing certain assault weapons, and Clinton held all the high cards. Not only would he veto any legislative repeal, but he would be handed an issue that he would relish exploiting with the general public. On the other side was aligned a large and impatient group of ideologically committed Republican freshmen, many of the seventy-four of whom had pledged themselves to support repeal.

And then there was that embarrassing undertaking given to the NRA by the leadership in January 1995.

By March of the following year the moment came when the issue could no longer be delayed. To play it down as far as possible, the vote was scheduled after no more than one hour of debate on the House floor on a Friday morning. Everyone knew that the result would be a symbolic political gesture rather than a decisive step toward a change in the law. Apart from the presidential veto, Republican sentiment in the Senate had cooled still further, and was now distinctly lukewarm. While still majority leader, although soon to resign to contest the presidential election, Dole was asked if he would schedule a Senate vote after the House action. His reply was curt: "I haven't considered it. It's not a priority," he said,[50] adding that he did not think such a bill could pass the Senate.

Brushing aside Democrat objections that a bill with the resounding title of the Gun Crime Enforcement and Second Amendment Restoration Act of 1996 (H.R. 125) had been sent to the floor without being reported by an authorizing committee, or indeed receiving any prior consideration, the debate finally took place on March 22. Despite containing some other provisions, it was the repeal of the prohibitions on certain semiautomatic assault weapons and large-capacity ammunition-feeding devices that dominated the brief, but emotionally charged, proceedings. By a coincidence, the debate was held only days after the news of the massacre of a class of five- and six-year-old children and their teacher at a school in Scotland.[51] It was evident that the scale of the tragedy was fresh in the minds of several of those taking part.

The high point came in a clash between the youthful Patrick Kennedy (Dem. Rhode Island) and a veteran Republican congressman and chairman of the Rules Committee, Gerald Solomon (Rep. New York). The twice-bereaved nephew of the assassinated President and of Senator Robert Kennedy spoke with passionate intensity:

> Families like mine all across this country know all too well what damage weapons can do, and you want to arm our people even more. You want to add more magazines to the assault weapons so they can spray and kill even more people.
>
> Shame on you. What in the world are you thinking when you are opening up the debate on this issue? Mr. Speaker, this is nothing but a sham, to come on this floor and say you are going to have an open and fair debate about assault weapons. My God, all I have to say to you is, play with the devil, die with the devil.
>
> There are families out there, Mr Speaker, and the gentleman will never know what it is like, because they do not have someone in their family killed.[52]

Solomon's angry retort to what he took as a personal attack was not worthy of him, nor of the occasion. Still worse was an off-microphone aside, omitted from the *Congressional Record,* but reported elsewhere, "Let's just step outside."[53] The strength of feeling was not confined to the floor of the

House. After the exchanges with Solomon, another representative complained to the Speaker pro tempore that he had heard and seen applause and clapping in the galleries during Kennedy's speech. Thus prompted, the Chair duly reminded all persons in the gallery that any manifestation of approval or disapproval was a violation of the rules of the House.[54]

When the vote came, the predictable result of a comfortable majority for the bill of 239 voting yea and 173 voting nay, with 19 not voting,[55] displayed to public view the lack of unanimity in the Republican ranks. Not only did Henry Hyde, chairman of the Judiciary Committee, vote against the bill, but so did John Kasich (Rep. Ohio), a Republican with a key role in the 104th Congress by virtue of his chairmanship of the Budget Committee. They were joined by such well-respected moderates as Christopher Shays, Jim Leach, and Douglas Bereuter, the last two demonstrating by their votes that the Middle Western states they represented were not the wholly impregnable strongholds of gun owners'' rights they were sometimes claimed to be.[56] The most senior woman on the Republican side, Marge Roukema (Rep. New Jersey) opposed the repeals, as did Susan Molinari, a rising star, who had voted both for the Brady bill and the ban on assault-style weapons in the previous Congress. Her initiative in ensuring that evidence of the prior commission of sexual assaults should be admissible in subsequent trials has been noted in an earlier chapter. In the summer of 1997, Molinari announced her intention to resign from Congress to take up a career in television.

All taken in all, the episode was an uncomfortable one for the Republican leadership. To insiders who knew the background, the vote to repeal the assault weapons ban, even when contained in a bill of wider application, was explicable. To others, more distant from Capitol Hill, it was a reminder of how doctrinaire ideology and interest group pressure could combine to reinforce a reputation for extremism unlikely to appeal to uncommitted voters in the coming elections. Whether for this reason or not, no more was heard of the assault weapons issue for the remainder of the 104th Congress. For eight of the more vulnerable gun advocates in the House, it was not the end of the story. Having been targeted by HCI as part of its electoral strategy, they went down to defeat in the congressional elections in November.[57] The most notable casualty was Harold Volkmer, a ten-term Democrat who had led the congressional efforts in the 1980s to weaken the Gun Control Act of 1968. Shortly before the 1996 elections he had walked out of the Democratic Convention in protest against Sarah Brady addressing the delegates.

VI

Although resolute in shunning the attempt to lift the assault weapons ban, the Senate was hesitant in its approach toward two less controversial gun-related bills of its own. Both had been taken up as personal causes by individual senators, acting independently of each other, and both bills had the strong support of the administration. The first, sponsored by Senator Kohl, aimed to re-enact in appropriate language the ban on guns in school zones that had been struck down by the Supreme Court in *United States v. Lopez.*[58] The second was an initiative by Senator Frank Lautenberg (Dem. New Jersey) to prohibit anyone who had been convicted of a misdemeanor offense of domestic violence from lawfully possessing a firearm.

Under existing federal law a person convicted in any court, state or federal, of a felony crime punishable by imprisonment for a term exceeding one year was prohibited from possessing or receiving a firearm or ammunition.[59] But it was believed that in many of the numerous domestic incidents of violence each year in which a firearm was present, estimated by the White House at about 88,500 in 1994,[60] the defendant was able to plea bargain the offense down to a misdemeanor, if indeed any criminal charges resulted.

Lautenberg, like Kohl, was a Democrat, but the domestic violence issue was a topical one that had attracted bipartisan support, inside and outside the Congress. The implications for gun control, however, had made it politically controversial. In August 1996, some months after the bill's introduction, and consequent upon energetic lobbying of the White House staff, Clinton adopted the proposal as one of the themes for his campaign speeches designed to appeal to centrists and less-committed voters who might decide the outcome of the presidential election. His recognition of the contribution that could be made by legislative action to curbing the sometimes fatal consequences for women and child victims of domestic violence, if tardy in coming, was crucial thereafter.

The original bill (S. 1632) was introduced in the Senate on March 21, 1996. Despite his best efforts, Lautenberg had been unable to find a Republican co-sponsor. As the bill failed to make progress, he let it be known that when a separate bill sponsored by Senator Kay Bailey Hutchison (Rep. Texas), which aimed to make stalking a federal crime if a person crossed a state line while stalking, was brought to the floor he would be offering his domestic violence bill as an amendment. The Republican leadership then refused to bring the stalking bill to the floor so as to avoid having to face a gun-related amendment. In a letter dated June 18 to Senator Trent Lott (Rep. Mississippi), who shortly before had succeeded Dole as majority leader, Lautenberg reiterated that he was anxious for the stalking bill, which he supported, to be brought to the floor, and confirming his intention to offer his bill as an amendment. The subsequent accusation that he was obstructing the stalking bill was seen by Lautenberg as a Republican spin to divert attention from their own dilemma.

The reason for the Senate leadership's reluctance to allow the bill to be brought to the floor was that, notwithstanding a broad range of bipartisan support, there was a group of conservative Republicans who were strongly opposed because it would extend the range of federal gun control. They wanted the bill to be killed, or postponed indefinitely. They were conscious, however, of the sympathetic reaction of the general public that Clinton was able to exploit so effectively. Yet, when after protracted negotiation, the stalemate was ended and a combined measure incorporating both Hutchison's stalking bill and a slightly modified version of Lautenberg's domestic violence bill reached the floor in July, not one of the critics raised any objection. Whatever the strength of their own convictions, they sensed that to speak out publicly would be bad politics. Following some brief remarks by the two sponsoring senators and the majority and minority leaders, the bill was passed by a late-night voice vote on July 25.[61]

The unanimous consent of the Senate was not the end of the story as the House Republican leadership declined to take up the composite bill, again because of their objections to its gun control language. Back in the Senate, the persistent Lautenberg sought another vehicle to carry his proposal into law. By September, time was running out and the Senate was preoccupied with the final stages of the appropriations process for the fiscal year 1997. Although not governed by any rule of germaneness, the Senate customarily had not allowed substantive new or amended legislation on matters unconnected with the appropriation of public funds to be included in annual appropriations bills. Since winning control in 1994 Republicans had been less restrictive and, once the door was ajar, Democrats were not going to be left outside. Lautenberg was amongst them, offering the domestic violence proposal as an amendment to the Treasury, Postal Service, and General Government Appropriations Bill. The boundaries of relevance were expanded even further when Senator Hutchison succeeded in adding her stalking provisions to the Defense Department Appropriations Bill.

In introducing his amendment during the floor consideration of the Treasury Appropriations Bill on September 12, Lautenberg reminded the senators that if it sounded familiar it was because it was the exact proposal they had passed unanimously in July.[62] He admitted frankly that in view of the House reaction, and the degree of bipartisan support previously shown in the Senate, subsequently shared by both presidential candidates, he had decided to bring the proposal forward again using the only vehicle that held out a realistic hope of enactment. After a debate in which the importance of keeping guns out of the hands of persons with a record of previous violent spousal or child abuse was endorsed in a speech by Senator Wellstone, with supporting statements added later to the record by Senators Murray and Feinstein, the amendment was agreed by ninety-seven votes to two.[63] Outside Congress, the legislation had attracted support from over thirty national organizations, including the National Coalition against Domestic Violence, the National Network to End Domestic Violence, the Children's Defense Fund, the National Urban League, the American Academy of Pediatrics, the YWCA of America, and several church organizations.

The end was now in sight, although there was still one last and potentially treacherous stretch to be traversed on the path through the legislative minefield. Later in September, the Treasury, Postal Service, and General Government

Appropriations Bill was pulled from the Senate floor by the leadership and included in a mammoth omnibus spending bill covering most of the departments of government for fiscal year 1997. Point-by-point negotiations in conference with the House representatives on a number of issues had resulted in alterations being made to some of the provisions in the domestic violence gun ban as approved by the Senate. In an agreement eventually reached early on the morning of Saturday, September 28, Lautenberg had successfully resisted various attempts by opponents of the gun prohibition to weaken it. One was to exclude child abuse, and another to limit the application of the law only to offenders who had been notified of the ban at the time they were charged. Apart from the practical difficulties, such a restriction would have the effect of excluding all previously convicted offenders from the legislation.

Some changes were made in the interests of due process to afford greater protection for the accused. They included a proviso that a person would not be considered to have been convicted of a qualifying offense unless represented by counsel, or had waived the right to such representation, and that the case had been tried by a jury where there was an entitlement to jury trial, or that right had been waived. Another new provision was that a prior conviction would not lead to a firearm disability if it had been expunged or set aside, or was the result of an offense for which the convicted person had been pardoned or had his or her civil rights restored. The definition of the offense that would activate the ban was also revised. As finally enacted, a misdemeanor crime of domestic violence was an offense under federal or state law that had as an element the use or attempted use of physical force, or the threatened use of a deadly weapon.[64] Lautenberg accepted this formulation as an improvement on his earlier version, which did not explicitly include attempts to use force, or threats to use a weapon, if such attempts or threats did not involve actual physical violence. Late in the day as it was, these refinements essentially were the culmination of a deliberative process that had extended over many months.

Very different was another amendment produced without warning during the penultimate negotiations on the Appropriations Bill on September 27–28. The prime mover was Representative Bob Barr, a leading advocate of gun rights with close links to the NRA. Although not a member of the conference committee, Barr was often consulted on firearms-related legislation by the majority leadership in the House. He was again on the Lautenberg measure. The discussions took place in private, and there is no authoritative account of what happened. But the outcome was the addition of a completely new provision, which had not been the subject of any prior consideration either by Congress or the interested parties. Its effect was to remove the existing exemption of persons employed by government entities, notably police officers and military personnel in the performance of their duties.[65]

Suspicious Democrats pointed the finger at Barr, alleging that he had miscalculated in thinking that if the public use exemption was taken out, then the representative police organizations might be mobilized to stop the bill becoming law. If indeed that was the objective, and Barr himself gave no explanation then or later, it misfired. Within days the Lautenberg measure had been signed into law as part of the Omnibus Consolidated Appropriations Act, leaving an unprepared and disunited law enforcement community to sort out their reactions. "How are we . . . to fix this mess which has been brought upon us?" asked an exasperated spokesman for the National Association of Police Organizations.[66]

Under existing law, dating back to the Gun Control Act of 1968, the prohibition of a convicted felon possessing a firearm or ammunition did not apply to government entities, whether federal or state.[67] The incongruous result of Barr's intervention (if it is correct to attribute it to him) was that police and other law enforcement officers would be unable to have the use of a firearm issued to them for the performance of their duties if convicted of one particular type of misdemeanor offense, but would not be subject to the same disability if convicted of a more serious felony offense, or of any misdemeanor offense other than domestic violence. The fact that police regulations generally would not allow for the continued employment of a convicted felon as a police officer, or not in any capacity where the officer would require the use of a firearm, did not alter the confused state into which the law and police practice was thrown by such an ill-considered addendum.

Once the new law had come into effect, the Director of the Bureau of Alcohol, Tobacco and Firearms (ATF) at the Department of the Treasury published an open letter on the Internet informing the public of the change in the gun control legislation. It stated that individuals subject to the disability should "immediately lawfully dispose of their firearms and ammunition." It recommended that firearms should be relinquished to a third party, such as an attorney, the local police agency, or a federally licensed firearms dealer. The continued possession of firearms or ammunition by persons under the disability would be a violation of the law, and might subject the possessor to criminal penalties. In addition, the firearms and ammunition would be subject to seizure and forfeiture.[68] Formal letters were despatched to state and local law enforcement agencies, and to all federal firearms licensees, about the application of the new firearms disability in general, and its effect on law enforcement officers who had been convicted of a qualifying misdemeanor offense in particular. Detailed sets of questions and answers, approved by the Departments of the Treasury and Justice were prepared to assist law enforcement agencies in answering the numerous inquiries they had received concerning the new law. The ATF's own armed agents, and those of the FBI, would be subject to the same provisions, as would military personnel.

The initial response of the police organizations was hampered by a lack of reliable information about how many officers had incurred misdemeanor convictions in the past for domestic violence. Not all of them would be male, since the inclusion of child abuse in the definition of qualifying offenses meant that any female officer who had been convicted of assaulting a child would also be prohibited from having a firearm while on duty in the future. The most credible of the estimates derived from a survey of twenty-five law enforcement agencies. In those localities, which included the nation's fifteen largest cities, the survey found that out of 100,000 officers, 152 could lose their firearms or their jobs.[69] The highest number was in New York City, with the largest police force, although it was the policy of its Police Department not to hire applicants with records of domestic violence.

When they had time to decide upon their policy responses, the police organizations were unable to speak with one voice. The two largest, the National Association of Police Organizations (NAPO) and the Fraternal Order of Police (FOP) both pressed for immediate changes to be made in the law, but sought different solutions. NAPO was adamant in arguing that the governmental exemption should be reinstated.[70] A bill to achieve this objective (H.R. 445) had been introduced in the House of Representatives by a former state trooper and avowed opponent of gun control, Bart Stupak (Dem. Michigan). The FOP did not agree, throwing its weight behind bills introduced in the House by Barr (H.R. 26), and in the Senate by Wellstone (S. 262). Each of these aimed to amend the new law so that the firearms disability would apply only to persons convicted after the date of enactment. The argument put forward by Barr, but not by Wellstone, that the provision was retroactive, and therefore unconstitutional, failed to take account of the structure of the Gun Control Act of 1968. That law punished not the earlier offense, but the subsequent possession of a firearm by a person included in the list of prohibited categories, which had been extended on several occasions.

A third approach, advocated by the National Black Police Association (NBPA), was to maintain the domestic violence gun ban imposing a firearm disability on any person convicted at any time of a misdemeanor crime of domestic violence. The NBPA argued that law enforcement officers should be held to a higher standard, and not a different standard, than other people. At a time when the relationship between the police and the community was "constantly deteriorating," its spokesman said, the NBPA believed that the effort by police unions and the other associations was misguided and would "result in the continued widening gulf between the community and the police."[71]

Yet another alternative was put forward in a letter sent to every member of Congress on February 19, 1997, by sixty-one national and local organizations working to prevent and reduce family violence. Not only should the prohibition on gun ownership for those convicted of domestic violence misdemeanors be maintained, the letter stated, but "the official use exemption for individuals convicted of felony domestic violence offenses should be eliminated." The work done by law enforcement agencies on behalf of battered women was applauded, and they were urged to ensure that their officers were held to the same standards as other citizens in the efforts to reduce gun violence and deaths.[72] The same argument was used by the National Network to End Domestic Violence. A membership organization comprising state domestic violence coalitions representing nearly 2000 shelters and domestic violence programs throughout the United States, the National Network referred to the sensitive matter of some research studies that suggested rates of violence in police officer families were considerably higher than those reported for random families of civilians.[73]

The new law applied not only to state law enforcement officers, but also to federal agencies employing officers with authority to carry firearms. Once the data had been collected there must have been a sense of relief that, with the exception of corrections officers, the statistics showing the number of employees who would be disabled from gun possession because of qualifying convictions was less than might have been expected. None of the 10,870 employees of the FBI surveyed, representing 99.9 percent of the total number employed, were disqualified, and only one officer, a chemist, employed by the ATF. The Federal Bureau of Prisons, with the largest workforce, reported that of the 28,485 employees surveyed (99.9 percent of all employees), eighty were disqualified. The only other agency with a numerically significant return was the Immigration and Naturalization Service, which reported that nineteen out of the 14,470 employees surveyed (99.2 percent) would be disqualified. Agencies reporting that no employees would be subject to the disability included the U.S. Marshal's Service, the Drug Enforcement Administration, the Internal Revenue Service, and the U.S. Secret Service.[74]

Early in March 1997, by now well into the 1st Session of the 105th Congress, the Subcommittee on Crime of the House of Representatives held hearings to try and decide what should be done. In his opening statement from the chair McCollum was circumspect. He said it was unfortunate that the committee had previously had no opportunity to consider several important questions relating to the issue. Now, with the law already in effect, the committee had to ask what were the unique problems associated with applying the ban for crimes of domestic violence only to misdemeanor convictions? Would applying the ban retroactively be unfair, and would it create unreasonable hardship on some people, particularly police officers, who make a living using firearms? What about the ability to identify such past misdemeanor convictions quickly and accurately within the limitations of current criminal conviction records? With a candor unusual in elected politicians, McCollum admitted that he was undecided on what to do about the problem, and was looking forward to hearing the testimony of the witnesses.[75]

As ranking minority member, Schumer followed. People who beat up their spouses, he said, were the last people in the world who should have guns. But the law enforcement community had raised some genuine questions about the application of this law to police officers. Unlike other citizens, their jobs were at stake. While he had not yet taken up a position on either of the bills before the subcommittee, the law enacted the previous year was sound. It was a fact that people convicted of domestic violence were likely to do so again. He believed the controversy had been fomented by the National Rifle Association and others who wanted to see law enforcement put at odds both with the gun control movement and the women's rights movement. That was the real agenda. Barr then launched a caustic attack on the way the new law had been rammed through in the waning hours of the 104th Congress as part of legislation with which it had no connection. Some last minute adjustments had been made to the Senate version to give it a semblance of constitutionality, and to ensure that some provisions "requested by the people of this country" were included. The federal government was now trying to enforce the ban retroactively, despite the fact that it was not the intent of Congress, nor certainly of himself and many other members. No mention was made of the potentially embarrassing matter of how the official use exemption had come to be terminated.

Before the witness panels got under way, Conyers placed a forthright statement in the record. The amendment now proposed by Barr, he said, was an NRA initiative. It would apply only to those people who had been convicted of domestic violence offenses after the ban and allow anyone who had been previously convicted of domestic violence to keep his gun. The NRA had long opposed the prohibitions under the Gun Control Act, and was intent on getting rid of the additional restriction. The NRA's fax alert had stated specifically that the Barr amendment "will hopefully result in the repeal" of the gun ban. If the Lautenberg law had been in effect years ago many women might not have lost their lives. Shouldn't Congress be doing everything possible to prevent such murders in the future? If the Barr measure became law, Conyers forecast that "some man with a record of domestic violence will lawfully purchase a gun and blow his wife away. How can we knowingly allow such a thing to happen?"[76]

The first witnesses who testified before the hearings on March 5, 1997, were representatives of each of the three national police associations, already cited, and the executive director of the National Network to End Domestic Violence. They were followed by a second panel that was concerned with the technicalities of implementation. It comprised representatives of the ATF and FBI, and experts on systems technology and criminal records management.

In reviewing this episode of legislative history, it is hard to avoid the conclusion that such awkward issues, undeniably relevant and important as they were, should have been argued out before, rather than after, the new law had been enacted. The most glaring feature is that the substance of the Lautenberg bill had never been considered at any stage by the House. Although hearings on the issue could have been scheduled by the Crime Subcommittee, the House leadership refused to acknowledge the existence of the bill until the last minute. Fear of the political costs of opposing the bill's aims in public meant that it became law by a side wind, raised on the fringes of the negotiations in private between the majority and minority congressional leaders and the administration, again represented by Leon Panetta, during the final stages of the passage of the Omnibus Appropriations legislation for fiscal year 1997. On the last day of the 104th Congress the compelling objective of the participants was to reach agreement in time to enable all departments and agencies of government to be funded for the imminent fiscal year, without a replay of the destructive confrontation that had disfigured the budget and appropriations process of fiscal year 1996. All else must have seemed a troublesome distraction from the main task.

VII

Another Senate amendment to the Omnibus Consolidated Appropriations Act 1997, included as Section 657 immediately preceding Lautenberg's amendment, which was enacted as Section 658 of the General Provisions title,[77] reaffirmed a previous decision of Congress. In 1990 Senator Kohl had sponsored a provision making it a federal offense for any individual knowingly to possess a firearm at a place the individual knew, or had reasonable cause to believe, was a school zone.[78] The Bush administration's reservations about the propriety of superimposing a federal prohibition on conduct that already was unlawful in several states, intruding into two areas of policy traditionally regulated by the state, namely education and law enforcement, and the President's admonitory warning when he signed the bill into law, were noted in an earlier chapter. Since then, the Supreme Court in the *Lopez* decision had held the Gun-Free School Zones Act to be unconstitutional as exceeding the authority of Congress to regulate commerce under the commerce clause of the Constitution. More precisely, it satisfied neither of two independent conditions. The activity regulated, that is, the possession of a firearm, did not in the aggregate "substantially affect" interstate commerce, nor did the statute contain a jurisdictional element that would ensure, through case-by-case inquiry, that the firearm possession in question affected interstate commerce.[79]

Although the tenor of the Chief Justice's opinion for the majority was to remind Congress that the commerce power was not unlimited, it left the way open for further congressional action, taken either on its own initiative or at the prompting of the administration. The White House was first off the mark with Clinton sending a formal message to Congress within two weeks of the decision in *Lopez*. On May 10, 1995, he transmitted a draft of proposed legislation to amend the 1990 Act in such a way as to provide the necessary nexus with interstate commerce.[80] In the wake of the Court's decision, he said, he had directed Attorney General Reno to present to him an analysis of *Lopez* and to recommend a legislative solution to the problem identified by that decision. Her recommendation was to amend the Act by adding a requirement that the government prove that the firearm had moved in, or that the possession of the firearm otherwise affected, interstate or foreign commerce. The addition of this jurisdictional element would limit the Act's "reach to a discrete set of firearm possessions that additionally have an explicit connection with or effect on interstate commerce" as the Court had stated in *Lopez*, thereby bringing it within the Congress's commerce clause authority.[81]

The Attorney General had advised that the proposal would not require the government to prove that a defendant had knowledge that the firearm had moved in, or the possession of the firearm otherwise affected, interstate or foreign commerce. The defendant must know only that he or she possessed the firearm. It was anticipated that the change would have "little, if any, impact on the ability of prosecutors to charge this offense," as the vast majority of firearms had "moved in . . . commerce" before reaching their eventual possessor.[82]

Although the President's message and the accompanying papers were referred to the House Committee on the Judiciary and ordered to be printed, with Schumer as the ranking Democrat on the Crime Subcommittee acting as the bill's sponsor, the main action took place in the Senate.[83] As he had done five years before, it was Senator Kohl who took the leading role. In the interval, he had continued to keep a watchful eye on youth violence in general and the growing threat of guns in schools in particular. Whereas in 1990 fewer than half of the states had provisions similar to the federal law, by 1995 over forty had adopted a variety of laws to this end. Despite some vigorous examples of enforcement by school boards, police, and prosecutors, the surge in juvenile offending, exacerbated by the rapid expansion of gangs, had resulted in the proportion of students carrying a gun in a thirty-day school period increase from one in twenty in 1990 to one in twelve by 1995.[84] Bringing the point home even more vividly, the National Education Association had estimated that by the time of the Senate hearings on the federal role in controlling guns in schools in July 1995 about 100,000 children nationally were bringing guns to school every day.[85]

Kohl's belief that the problem was national in scope, with a substantial federal interest in safeguarding school environments that had such a vital impact on the quality of education, was shared by the Republican senator, Arlen Specter. As chairman, and formerly ranking member, of the Appropriations Subcommittee on Education, he was one of seven bipartisan co-sponsors of the Senate bill (S. 890) which embodied the legislative solution proposed by the President, but with some additional elements. Diane Feinstein, the author of the assault weapons ban in the 103rd Congress and a stalwart for gun control, was another co-sponsor.

The main difference between the two versions was that the Senate bill incorporated a list of specific findings, the absence of which had contributed to the vulnerability of the 1990 Act when it was exposed to challenge in the courts. Although discussed neither in the Senate hearings held by the Subcommittee on Youth Violence of the Committee on the Judiciary in July, nor in the debates on the floor of the Senate shortly before the end of the session in September of the following year, the findings were not a new element. They repeated, almost word for word, a declaration of nine findings added as an amendment to the U.S. Code by the Violent Crime Control and Law Enforcement Act of 1994[86] while the *Lopez* case was slowly progressing through the appellate courts. It was, however, an instance of locking the stable door after the horse had bolted as Lopez had been tried and convicted under the law as it stood in 1992, two years before the oral hearing of arguments by the Supreme Court in 1994.[87] Consequently the ruling of the Court and the opinions of the Justices were based on their consideration of the 1990 statute without the later addendum.

So much had been said about the absence of any findings as evidence that Congress had perceived a link between gun possession in schools and interstate commerce, that the Kohl bill took no further chances and repeated in the text the findings that lay almost unnoticed in Title 18 of the U.S. Code. As printed in S. 890 they read as follows:

The Congress finds and declares that

(A) crime, particularly crime involving drugs and guns, is a pervasive, nationwide problem;

(B) crime at the local level is exacerbated by the interstate movement of drugs, guns, and criminal gangs;

(C) firearms and ammunition move easily in interstate commerce and have been found in increasing numbers in and around schools, as documented in numerous hearings in both the Judiciary Committee of the House of Representatives and the Judiciary Committee of the Senate;

(D) in fact, even before the sale of a firearm, the gun, its component parts, ammunition, and the raw materials from which they are made have considerably moved in interstate commerce;

(E) while criminals freely move from State to State, ordinary citizens and foreign visitors may fear to travel to or through certain parts of the country due to concern about violent crime and gun violence, and parents may decline to send their children to school for the same reason;

(F) the occurrence of violent crime in school zones has resulted in a decline in the quality of education in our country;

(G) this decline in the quality of education has an adverse impact on interstate commerce and the foreign commerce of the United States;

(H) States, localities, and school systems find it almost impossible to handle gun-related crime by themselves; even States, localities, and school systems that have made strong efforts to prevent, detect, and punish gun-related crime find their efforts unavailing due in part to the failure or inability of other States or localities to take strong measures; and

(I) Congress has power, under the interstate commerce clause and other provisions of the Constitution, to enact measures to ensure the integrity and safety of the Nation's schools by enactment of this subsection.[88]

Then came the crucial new provision, containing the formulation recommended to the President by the Attorney General, but joining it to a description of the existing offense:

It shall be unlawful for any individual knowingly to possess a firearm that has moved in or that otherwise affects interstate or foreign commerce at a place that the individual knows, or has reasonable cause to believe, is a school zone.

The need for painstaking attention to be given to insulating the prohibition from future judicial challenge did not overshadow other considerations during the deliberations of the Senate. During the subcommittee hearings the chairman, Senator Fred Thompson (Rep. Tennessee), one of the most formidable of Republican legislators, had made clear his reservations about whether the problem of youth crime, aggravated by the presence of so many guns in schools, called for a federal solution at all. His stance that Congress should refrain from federalizing an offense that fell within an area of regulation traditionally left to the states and localities was shared by several of the witnesses in their testimony. But others, including a former U.S. Attorney for the Eastern District of Texas, a lifelong Republican and NRA member who had been appointed by President Reagan on the nomination of Senators Tower and Gramm, took a different line.

"If this is not a national issue," said Bob Wortham, "there are no national issues. If this is not a case where the Federal Government needs to come in and add its might, add its power, then there are no issues where the Federal Government needs to become involved."[89] He went on to explain that in Texas the federal and state authorities collaborated in enforcing an active drug-free and gun-free program, in cooperation with school boards, parents, and teachers. Many of the local District Attorneys were sworn in as Special Assistant U.S. Attorneys and prosecuted cases from their counties in the federal courts. As a team, they decided which jurisdiction should be used, state or federal. The severity of the crime was the leading gauge, but the key to the program's effectiveness was that all cases would be prosecuted. After about two years of successful prosecution and outstanding media coverage, the flow of cases had turned into a dribble.[90] The Presiding District Attorney and the Sheriff for Jefferson County submitted letters in support, saying that when the federal Gun-Free School Zones Act had been struck down a tremendous tool had been lost. Both strongly urged the passage of the replacement legislation.[91] While the voices from Texas may not have been representative of state law enforcement officials generally, they were powerful witnesses for Kohl's cause.

For over a year after the hearings no action was taken either in the Senate or the House to progress the school zone gun ban. The executive branch kept the pressure up, and on October 26 the President signed a directive to ensure that any student who brought a gun to school in any part of America would be expelled for at least a year.[92] The extent of the practice of bringing guns to school premises was shown by the reported confiscation of 129 handguns from students at public schools in New York City in the school year 1995–96.[93] But in neither House of Congress was the issue an attractive one for the Republican leadership. Had it not been for the availability of the tactic that Lautenberg had deployed, the probability was that the reimposition of the ban would have failed to pass the 104th Congress.

On the same day, September 12, as the domestic violence amendment was approved by a ninety-seven-to-two majority in the Senate, Kohl offered his bill as an amendment to the Treasury, Postal Service, and General Government Appropriations Act for 1997. In a short speech, with extended remarks printed in the *Congressional Record,* he described the bill as a commonsense, bipartisan, constitutional approach to combating violence in schools. It barred bringing a gun within a thousand feet of a school, with a few exceptions. It modified the previous law to ensure its constitutionality in accordance with the Supreme Court's decision in *Lopez.* He reiterated that the problem was national in scope, and the interstate commerce in guns was exactly what was causing the problem. Car loads of guns were being brought by gangs from Chicago to Madison in his own state of Wisconsin, and from Mississippi to Boston. Although state laws could help to address the national problem, not every state had a law. Nor was every state law adequate. In many states juveniles did not serve any time for violating the laws. In federal cases they did. Under federal law loopholes could be filled, and the most serious violators might be sentenced to up to five years' imprisonment. In conclusion, Kohl said, it did not "make much sense to treat a modest and sensible proposal as a major threat to the Federal-State balance."[94]

Later in the disjointed floor debate on a series of unrelated amendments to the Appropriations bill, Thompson repeated his objections. He believed that forty-eight states had now passed legislation to deal with the problem of guns in schools, and they should be left to address the issue in ways they saw fit. He could not agree to Congress taking over an area which traditionally had been under the auspices of state and local government, taxing people at that level, and then bringing the money to Washington to put in the hands of federal officials to enforce these laws. Popular as the guns in school ban might be, it was wrong to federalize whatever happened to be the rage at the moment, until one system was reached at the federal level. He ended with an eloquent plea:

> That is not the way we have traditionally handled these matters in this country. That is not the way we need to proceed in order to make sure we keep that separation between State and local and Federal Government. So at a time when so many of us are trying to move more and more responsibility back to the States and closer to the people who know how to handle it more effectively, I think it would be indeed ironic for us to be taking this matter, which for 200 years has been the responsibility of State and local government, and federalize it.[95]

Thompson then moved to table the amendment, and called for a vote. The result was twenty-seven voting yea, and seventy-two voting nay. If Senator Hatfield had been present and voting, he indicated that he would have voted nay.[96]

By a decisive margin Kohl's persistence, backed up by the self-evident practicality of his arguments, carried the day. Principled as it had been, it is worthy of comment that Thompson's restatement of the creed that had brought the Republicans to power in the 104th Congress failed to convince about half of the total number of Republican senators. Not for the first or last time, the one-size-fits-all brand of ideology gave way to pragmatism when faced with a specific situation amenable to legislative action. The Kohl amendment survived the pitfalls of the conference without mishap, reaching its final destination in statute law side by side with the Lautenberg amendment on September 30, 1996.

Chapter 9

A New Isolationism

I

The politics of gun control can be looked at in two ways. The first is to see in the cautious approach of the 104th Congress a true reflection of the national mood. Relatively minor legislative changes were made re-enacting the federal ban on guns in school zones and adding persons convicted of a misdemeanor offense of domestic violence to the categories prohibited by federal law from possessing a firearm or ammunition.[1] The vote to repeal the assault weapons ban had been an embarrassing fiasco, contributing to the electoral defeat a few months later of several of its most ardent proponents. No comprehensive proposals to limit the availability of firearms had been put forward by the administration, and had it done so only a few brave spirits believed that such a measure would have had any realistic chance of passing into law.

While up-to-date survey findings showed that majority opinion endorsed stricter controls on the sale of guns and the adoption of safety precautions applicable to other consumer products,[2] the distinctive feature of this body of opinion was its latency. The 1996 National Gun Policy Survey conducted by the National Opinion Research Center (NORC) at the University of Chicago showed the small proportions of those surveyed who participated actively in

204

the public policy debate over firearms. In opposition to gun control policies, 2.8 percent had written letters to a public official, 4.3 percent had joined an organization opposed to gun control, and 5.0 percent had given money to an anti–gun control organization. On the pro–gun control side, 2.6 percent had written to a public official, 4.6 percent had joined an organization, and 6.4 percent had given money. The near equality in the dimensions of the pro- and anti-control groups, with the edge just going to the pro–gun control activists, marked a sharp contrast to the late 1970s.[3] Then the anti–gun control activists had outnumbered the pro-control group by about three to one. But overall the picture was one of a generally passive state of opinion with 92.2 percent of the public showing no indication of active participation. The sparks that had ignited the conflagration precipitating congressional and state action on three strikes and Megan's Law had not been struck.

Over the years the American public has given an impression of becoming progressively desensitized toward the daily loss of life and other serious, although nonfatal, injuries caused by shooting. Only a conspicuously outrageous or large-scale incident, it seems, has the capacity to convert passive support into the activism necessary to get gun control measures passed by the Congress. Since the mid-1990s America has been spared the painful experiences endured by Britain with the killing of sixteen young children and their teacher at a Scottish school by a deranged gunman in 1996, and the even greater loss of life the same year in Australia when thirty-five people were killed and many more wounded in a mass shooting at Port Arthur in the state of Tasmania. Both wanton incidents affronted public opinion nationally and led to a tightening of already strict regulatory systems.

It is not that the United States has been free of multiple killings in which guns have been used. On the contrary, they had become so commonplace that nothing less than the most extreme instances had the power to shock the national consciousness. In the 1960s, the passage of the Gun Control Act of 1968 had come about in the aftermath of the gun murders of President Kennedy, Martin Luther King, and Robert Kennedy. The assassination attempt on Ronald Reagan early in his first term by chance caused the President no more than minor injury, although the permanent disability suffered by his press secretary, James Brady, in the same incident helped to facilitate the passage of the Handgun Violence Prevention Act of 1993 that bore his name.

The step-by-step policy pursued by Clinton, a more committed president on gun control than any since Johnson, was similarly the chosen tactic of Handgun Control, Inc. In building a constituency the experience of victims, and their ability to evoke an emotional popular response, was a central concept. Stardom also played a part. The celebrity status accorded to the Bradys, the courage and fortitude of the invalid husband, and the campaigning skills of the tireless wife, superimposed public faces on a political cause. The invitation to Sarah Brady, a Republican, to address the Democratic National Convention in Chicago in August 1996 when Clinton accepted his party's nomination as candidate for reelection to the presidency, was a recognition of the breadth of appeal of her message. "Every year in this country," she said in her speech, "nearly 40,000 Americans are killed with a firearm":

> More than 100,000 more are wounded. Every two hours another child is killed with a gun. And with each death and each wound, another American dream, another American family is shattered. This must stop. Jim and I decided we must do something about it. Not as Republicans, but as Americans. . . . gun violence is not a Democratic or a Republican problem, it's a problem that affects each and every one of us. It was a Democratic Congress which passed the Brady bill and a Democratic President who signed it, but we could never have passed the Brady bill without the support of a lot of Republicans, including former President Ronald Reagan. And we could never have passed it without the support of law enforcement officials.
>
> But now we need your help. This battle is not about guns. It's about families. It's about children. It's about our future. You can't have stronger families, without safer children. The gun lobby likes to say that Jim and I are trying to take guns away from hunters and sportsmen. The gun lobby is wrong. To the hunters and sportsmen of America we say: Keep your guns . . . just give us the laws that we need to keep guns out of the hands of criminals and out of the hands of our children.[4]

As the 104th Congress gave way to the 105th, the momentum of gradualism was continued. The initiatives: child safety devices fitted to handguns, action against unregulated gun shows, and one-handgun-purchase-per-month laws and other measures intended to counter gunrunning between states, originated from the gun control faction, often with the support of the administration. The obstruction came from the conservative Right, with the formidable backing of the NRA. It was not just organizational strength that had made the NRA so effective an influence on public policy, but its skill at exploiting the sense of righteousness attached to gun ownership. The repetitive "bedrock stand" was that law-abiding citizens are entitled constitutionally to the ownership and legal use of firearms. Comparison with other forms of regulation in the interests of public safety were swept aside with the justification that whereas the Second Amendment to the Constitution guaranteed the right to keep and bear arms, there was no comparable guarantee, for instance, of a right to keep and drive cars. "Hence, governments may constitutionally regulate the sale, ownership, and operation of motor vehicles in ways that they are not free to do with respect to firearms."[5]

A supporting strand of constitutional argument has been deployed to supplement the frequently asserted, but unenforceable and judicially rejected,[6] right to bear arms. This is to challenge the legitimacy and reach of federal authority to regulate firearms on the grounds that such actions are inconsistent with the rights of states as protected by the Tenth Amendment.[7] For the gun lobby, an identification with the popular movement to reduce the size of federal government by shifting more responsibilities to the states, where it was claimed they properly belonged, had many advantages. It reduced the isolation and risk of public rejection brought about by the more extreme gun rights advocates and their fondness for extravagant language uncomfortably reminiscent of the armed private militias. By no means all of the NRA's mass membership shared the fanatical zeal of some of the movement's leaders and propagandists. By them, a calmer and apparently more reasonable posture was appreciated.

Tenth Amendment challenges also held out greater promise in the courts. Accepting the low probability of success in attacking the Brady Act head-on as a violation of the Second Amendment, the NRA encouraged local sheriffs in various rural jurisdictions to file cases based on the Tenth Amendment.[8] The contention was that in mandating background checks to establish if intending gun purchasers fell within one of the prohibited categories contained in the 1968 Act as subsequently amended, the Congress had exceeded its authority under the Constitution by requiring local officials to implement federal policies.

The extra burden placed on local law enforcement officials, in the parlance of the Act described as CLEOs (chief law enforcement officers), resented by some but welcomed by others, was temporary. Because no complete and reliable national records checking system was operational at the time of the Brady Act's passage in 1993, the statute created an interim system for up to five years. During this period the Department of Justice was charged with developing a permanent system that would enable instant checks to be made nationwide. In twenty-seven states with existing or post-Brady laws requiring a check on criminal history records to be made before a license was issued, or where a point-of-sale check was required for each gun purchase, systems were in operation that accomplished by state law the ultimate objective of the federal law: to ensure background checks were made on anyone wanting to buy a gun from a licensed dealer.

It was in the remaining states that the issue arose of who should do the checks, on handgun purchases only during the interim period, and by what authority. A feature of the federal legislation of particular importance to the NRA was that once the permanent checking system was in place, the Brady Act required that federally licensed dealers would need to check records prior to the purchase of any firearm, and not just handguns.[9]

II

The alternative way of evaluating the policy responses to the prevalence of gun violence is to question if the measures taken piecemeal are commensurate with the massive dimensions of the problem. The statistics, seldom presented in their stark simplicity, are a terrible indictment of the unrivalled extent of lethal violence in American society. Table 4 compares the number of homicides in which a firearm was the principal weapon used, together with gun-related suicides and fatal accidents, in the United States, Great Britain, Australia, and Canada. The American totals are not just higher than any of the

Table 4. Firearm-Related Homicides and Deaths: Great Britain, Australia, Canada, and the United States, 1994–1995

	Great Britain	Australia	Canada	United States
Homicides with a firearm	81	67	176	14,733
Rate per 100,000 population	0.14	0.37	0.62	5.60
Non-homicide firearm-related deaths[a]	178	412	960	20,946[b]
Rate per 100,000 population	0.31	2.28	3.36	7.96
National population	56,957,000	18,049,000	28,536,780	263,034,000

Notes: Data for 1995 unless otherwise stated.

[a] Covers fatal accidents with firearms and suicides with firearms. Uncertain causes of firearms deaths are omitted.

[b] Data for 1994: National Institute of Justice, *Research in Brief,* May 1997.

Sources: United Kingdom, Home Office; Centre for Public Policy, University of Melbourne; Centre of Criminology, University of Toronto; Bureau of Justice Statistics, U.S. Department of Justice.

others; they are two orders of magnitude greater. Allowing for the differences in population, social organization, and political institutions, the size of the discrepancy is huge. Australia, like the United States, has a postcolonial history, a dichotomy between state and federal authority, a large immigrant population, and a fiercely protected tradition of individual freedom. Canada shares with the United States a border running all the way across the continent, with much movement over it in both directions. Some of its largest cities are located only short distances from the border. Great Britain is the source of the common law, the English language, and many values that are shared between the two countries. How many Americans, including lawmakers, realize that the annual number of gun homicides per capita recorded in the United States in 1995 was forty times, or about 4,000 percent, more than in Britain?

It is hard to believe that the failings of human nature, the definition of criminal conduct, or the enforcement of the law, can account for a disparity on this scale. The explanation can only lie in the uniquely privileged status accorded to firearms. The latitude allowed to gun owners has resulted in the creation of an arsenal of weapons, legally or illegally held, so massive that no one can be certain of its size with any accuracy. Estimates in the region of 200 million do not seem too high, particularly in view of the most recent indications that about 43 percent of adults live in households which contain guns.[10] Faced with the evidence of virtually every other industrialized democracy, American policies toward gun control call to mind the isolationism of the 1920s and 1930s.

Opinion poll data suggests that it is not so much the general population that is responsible for the prevailing myopia as the political system. The gun control measures enacted with such strife by the 103rd and 104th Congresses, and the state laws that unevenly complement them, are proof enough of the height of the barriers impeding the way to reform. Yet the constitutional privileges claimed on behalf of gun owners have not been endorsed by the courts, which have the duty to interpret and uphold the Constitution. Indeed they have been rejected so often that plaintiffs are now finding it hard to establish standing to bring a suit. For some lawmakers the rights of gun owners undoubtedly are a matter of genuine conviction and principle. For others, however, the Second Amendment can serve as a smokescreen to avoid taking up a position based on the facts and the consequent hassle. During the long drawn-out debates in Congress on the Brady bill the often-heard parrot cry, that the Second Amendment ruled out legislation requiring background checks to be made before the purchase of a handgun, at times owed more to a desire to enhance an elected representative's prospects of re-election than any devotion to the actuality of constitutional principle.[11]

Of all the gun control proposals currently in the arena of public policy the most important is the establishment of a nationwide system of state licensing meeting federal standards, backed up by a register of individual weapons when and if it becomes technically feasible. Re-emerging after more than a quarter of a century in hibernation since Lyndon Johnson's last State of the Union message, a federal initiative has become a realistic possibility because of the increasing tendency by states to require permits or other forms of license as a condition of carrying concealed weapons in public places.

In twelve states a license or permit is required by state law for the purchase of a handgun, and in six of these the requirement extends to long guns as well as handguns. In twenty-six states a record of the sale must be reported to state or local government.[12] While there is no general licensing requirement for the possession of firearms, the need for a permit had been accepted by 1997 in forty-one states as a corollary to the increased risks involved in carrying a concealed firearm. The restrictions vary from state to state, but most require citizens to apply for a license from their local law enforcement agency or the state police.[13] In some states, an applicant must demonstrate a need to carry a concealed weapon. Such reasons include having good reason to fear injury or a need to protect themselves or their property. All states perform some kind of background check on individuals desiring a license, and in most there will be a list of prohibited categories. Ineligible applicants under state laws typically include juveniles, convicted felons, persons subject to bonds pending trial or sentencing for a serious offense, or persons previously ordered to forfeit a firearm.

The proliferation of regulation is estimated by the NRA as exceeding twenty thousand gun control laws. It warns that two challenges face gun owners as a result. They must familiarize themselves with the content of the regulations: "Only by knowing the laws can you avoid innocently breaking one"; and while federal legislation receives much more media attention, state legislatures and city councils make many more decisions regarding "the right to own and carry firearms."[14]

As this brief survey illustrates, there is no novelty in the recourse to permits or licenses as a means of reducing the risk of firearms misuse. In their enthusiasm to extend the claimed right to carry weapons in public, the NRA and its allies tacitly have accepted that the associated risks justify the issue of a license by the state. There should be no argument of principle therefore against state licensing conforming to federal standards.

Because practices vary so widely it is not easy to get an accurate picture of the current situation over the country as a whole. An evaluation of state regulation as of spring 1997 classified nine states and the District of Columbia as having "very strong" restrictions going beyond the minimum Brady requirements. They included the populous northeastern states of Connecticut, New Jersey, New York, and Massachusetts, as well as Illinois, Michigan, and Minnesota. Controls in California were classified as being in the "strong" category, with a ten-day waiting period for all gun purchases, the regulation of secondary sales, and sales records sent to a state agency. In contrast, twenty-seven states, mainly in the South and West, were classified as having "very weak" controls, generally with no restrictions going beyond the Brady Law.[15]

The groundswell of support lying behind the proposals for a federal requirement of registering firearms and licensing gun owners was illustrated by one of the highest proportionate statistics contained in the 1996 NORC report. Eighty-one percent of respondents favored the mandatory registration of handguns and pistols, and 66 percent favored mandatory registration of rifles and shotguns.[16] The trend had been tracked over a long period of years by the NORC with the results published regularly in the *General Social Survey* series. In reply to a constant question: "Would you favor or oppose a law which would require a person to obtain a police permit before he or she could buy a gun?" a steadily growing majority of respondents indicated their support for such a law. In 1987, 70.74 percent of the sample was in favor, and 27.07 percent opposed. By 1994, the proportion in favor had risen to 77.71 percent, while those who were opposed had fallen to 20.34 percent. If the small number of responses shown as "not applicable," "don't know," or "no answer" are eliminated, the 1994 findings can be restated as being 79.25 percent in favor, and 20.75 percent opposed.[17]

The introduction of a national system of licensing in the form of renewable permits issued by states for the ownership and possession of handguns, would be a demonstrable first step toward the acceptance of regulatory standards that are commonplace in other comparable countries throughout Western civilization. To underline the fact that such systems already exist in America, and have proved to be practicable and generally acceptable in their implementation, the Illinois law could be used as a model. Section 2 of the Firearm Owners Identification Card Act provides that, with some exceptions for law enforcement officers while engaged in their official duties and other specified exemptions, "no person may acquire or possess any firearm (or ammunition) within this state without having in his or her possession a Firearm Owner's Identification Card previously issued in his or her name by the Department of State Police under the provisions of this Act."[18]

In New York City, there are currently six different types of handgun license, each with specific restrictions and conditions attached. Licenses are issued to named individuals by the Police Department, and may not be transferred to any other person or location. They are revocable at any time, and an application for renewal must be made every two years. Failure to renew on time is cause for suspension or cancellation. All pistol licensees are required to familiarize themselves with the laws relating to the use of deadly physical force. In June 1997 there were 59,090 active handgun licenses in the city, excluding law enforcement officials, security guards, private investigators, and licensed gun custodians. The total number of licensed weapons carried or possessed amounted to 126, 700.[19]

If combined with restrictions on the quantity of guns purchased, such a federal law would have an immediate practical effect of staunching the present virtually unrestricted movement of deadly weapons from states with weak gun laws into those with strong gun laws. A revealing report commissioned as a prelude to the introduction of legislation in both Houses of Congress in April 1997[20] brought out the full extent of the thriving traffic in guns that are purchased legally, and in large quantities, in states with little or no restriction, and transported via the interstate highways across state lines to the northern and eastern cities where they are sold on the black market.

In 1996 Florida headed the list of states where guns sold were traced to crimes committed in other states, with Texas next. These two states between them accounted for almost 14 percent of guns used in the commission of out-of-state crimes that are traced back to their place of origin.[21] Another basis of calculation, adjusting the number of weapons used in crimes outside the state of origin to the size of the population, put Mississippi at the top of the league table with an export rate of 29.00. This means that for every 100,000 Mississippi residents 29 guns sold in their state were subsequently traced to crimes committed in other states. The routes along which the weapons travel are primarily one way. Interstate 95, known as the Firearm Freeway, is the favored route for illegally transported guns from Florida, Georgia, and South Carolina to New York, New Jersey, and Massachusetts, supplemented by Interstate 55, used by gunrunners from Mississippi to Illinois. It is a sobering fact that more traceable firearms originating from Mississippi were used to commit crimes in the state of Illinois in 1996 (306) than at home in Mississippi (268). In the reverse direction, only 4 guns originating from Illinois were traced to crime in Mississippi. Despite a distance of 1,200 miles, Florida was the largest supplier of out-of-state guns traced to crime in Massachusetts.

III

There can be little reason to doubt that the harmful effects of interstate commerce on this scale would justify regulatory federal legislation without risking a successful jurisdictional challenge. Permit requirements for the purchase of handguns or the carrying of concealed weapons already are in force in a majority of states. They would, as in the case of state drug laws and mandatory sentencing, be strengthened in application by federal legislation designed to achieve a higher and more uniform standard of public safety, so threatened by the epidemic of gun violence. As measured in terms of the frequency of criminal offending, the effect might not be large. But it is reasonable to expect that the fatal consequences of crimes committed in the future would be reduced. The provision of monetary incentives in the form of grants to states for law enforcement purposes is also an acknowledged way of encouraging states to accept objectives set by Congress. Examples discussed in this book are to be found in truth-in-sentencing and violent offender incarceration grants, or the prospect of losing federal funds because of noncompliance, as with Megan's Law. The Supreme Court has stated explicitly that there are a variety of ways, short of outright coercion, by which Congress may urge a state to adopt a legislative program consistent with federal interests. In particular, it has held that Congress may, under its spending power, attach conditions to the receipt of federal funds so long as such requirements meet certain conditions.[22]

The Brady Act had become vulnerable to challenge, not on the primary aim of delaying the sale of a handgun, and later of all firearms, for a period of up to five business days while a check was made to ascertain if the intending purchaser was a prohibited person under federal law, but because of one aspect of the procedure for its implementation. In states where there was no existing system to check on the background of purchasers before a sale was completed by a federally licensed dealer, chief law enforcement officers were required to make "reasonable efforts" to verify that the sale was to a person not within the prohibited categories set out in the Gun Control Act of 1968, as subsequently amended by the Firearm Owners' Protection Act of 1986.[23]

Contrary to popular belief, the Brady law did not mandate a fixed five-day waiting period. Although a "cooling-off" period of some days' delay before a buyer could purchase a gun had been advocated by many of the supporters of the legislation, in the form that the Brady bill was signed into law it did not specify any freestanding waiting period. Five business days was the maximum amount of time allowed for background checks to be made. Depending on the speed of the system, a CLEO might be able to give a dealer the go-ahead almost immediately, or after a few hours, or in some days, or not at all. If within the five-day period a CLEO had neither approved nor denied a sale, the dealer would then be permitted to release the gun to the prospective purchaser.

The enforcement procedure was that once notified of a pending sale by a licensed dealer, a designated CLEO, who might be a local police chief, or county sheriff, or state law enforcement official, would check the application form, submitted with a photo I.D. and written statement, against the available records. Further information might be sought if the details were unclear or incomplete, and reasons given for denial. If the sale was approved, all records of the purchaser's application and the background check had to be destroyed within twenty business days. Although the efficacy of these checks has been questioned,[24] and it is certainly rash to make overblown claims as to the number of gun crimes prevented because of the ease of access to firearms on the secondary market, nevertheless the statistic that between 1994 and 1996 approximately 6,600 firearm sales over the counter each month to potentially dangerous persons were frustrated by Brady Act checks is one that cannot be disregarded. More than 70 percent of the rejected purchasers were convicted or indicted felons.[25]

The U.S. Department of Justice found that most local law enforcement officials were "more than happy to perform this kind of check without being required to do so."[26] But not all were so amenable. In Graham County, Arizona, Richard Mack, described as "a controversial pro-gun, pro-militia figure,"[27] who was the sheriff at the time although subsequently defeated in a re-election bid, assisted by twelve county officers, reviewed between eighty and ninety proposed purchases within the first three months after the Brady Act became law. Only one proposed purchase proved unacceptable. Mack sued the United States in the federal district court challenging the constitutionality of the CLEO provisions, invoking the Tenth and Fifth Amendments. Jay Printz, sheriff and coroner of Ravalli County, Montana, and a longstanding NRA member, had a similar number of assistants to oversee 169 licensed firearms dealers in the county. He averred that he did not have the staff or any mechanism to carry out the duties imposed by the Brady Act. Mack and Printz additionally pointed to laws in their separate states that explicitly prohibited counties from regulating the sale or ownership of firearms.

Sheriff Printz also sued the United States and, in separate actions before different district courts, both he and Mack were successful.[28] The district courts, however, severed the unconstitutional background check provisions from the balance of the Brady Act. The United States appealed both cases to the Ninth Circuit, which reversed the district courts by a vote of two to one.[29] There were comparable suits in some other states, with varying results, before the Supreme Court granted petitions by Printz and Mack to enable oral argument to be heard on their claims of constitutional violation.

The consolidated case of *Printz v. United States* and *Mack v. United States* was argued on December 3, 1996. The underlying question to be resolved by the Supreme Court was whether a decision by Congress to shift the responsibility for enforcing a federal act, and some consequential costs and liabilities, to state or local officers amounted to "commandeering" state or local officers and resources in a way that had been invalidated by the court in *New York v. United States*.[30] The division between the states was clearly demonstrated by the filing of amicus briefs. Whereas eight states filed a joint brief in support of Sheriffs Printz and Mack, thirteen filed an opposing brief in support of the United States. The federal government's cause was fortified by a joint brief filed by eleven U.S. senators.

On the last day of the Court's term, June 27, 1997, the Supreme Court gave its decision. By a majority of five to four, the Justices divided in exactly the same formation as in the *Lopez* case to strike down as unconstitutional the provision for state and local law enforcement officers to conduct background checks on prospective handgun purchasers, and to perform certain related tasks.[31] Justice Scalia, writing for the Court, placed emphasis on the offensive character of a command. ''The Federal Government,'' in his opinion might ''neither issue directives requiring the States to address particular problems, nor command the States' officers, or those of their political subdivisions, to administer or enforce a federal regulatory program. It matters not whether policymaking is involved, and no case-by-case weighing of the burdens or benefits is necessary; such commands are fundamentally incompatible with our constitutional system of dual sovereignty.''[32] The judgment of the Court of Appeals for the Ninth Circuit was reversed, but the Supreme Court did not address the separate issue of the status of the waiting period of up to five business days before a sale could be completed.

The phraseology employed, especially the repetitive use of the word ''command'' shows that even Supreme Court Justices are not immune from the temptation to resort to emotive language to attract support for their viewpoint. Although less militaristic in its overtones[33] than its parent ''commandeer,'' in the language used by the Court in the *New York* and *Hodel* decisions,[34] ''command'' conveys more of an autocratic intent than is obtained by a reading of the statute, the debates on the Brady bill in Congress, or the statements of the President. What was sought from the states was their cooperation in implementing, for an interim period, a public policy that after a lengthy gestation had gained majority consent in the national Congress. Most CLEOs were willing to cooperate in making ''a reasonable effort'' to prevent prohibited or potentially dangerous persons from purchasing handguns. The implications of manpower and cost, in those states where comparable systems of checking records were not already in operation, were hardly an unbearable burden; nor was there any intention to shift political liability for decisions that might be unpopular in some individual cases from federal to local officials. Cooperative federalism was a more fitting description of the policy process than coercion. Less evocative words such as ''require,'' ''direct,'' or ''enjoin,'' were available in the judicial vocabulary, although less suited to Scalia's polemical style.

In the more moderately phrased dissent of Justice Stevens, the provision of the Brady Act that crossed the Court's newly defined constitutional threshold was ''more comparable to a statute requiring local police officers to report the identity of missing children to the Crime Control Center of the Department of Justice than to an offensive federal command to a sovereign state.''[35] He ended his opinion with the conclusion that ''[i]f Congress believes that such a statute will benefit the people of the Nation, and serve the interests of cooperative federalism better than an enlarged federal bureaucracy, we should respect both its policy judgment and its appraisal of its constitutional power.''[36]

Justice O'Connor, in concurring with the opinion of the Court, confined herself to no more than two incisive paragraphs. No doubt with a cautionary eye on the intensely partisan politics of gun control, she made a point of stating definitively that the holding by the Supreme Court "of course, does not spell the end of the objectives of the Brady Act. States and chief law enforcement officers may voluntarily continue to participate in the federal program. Moreover, the directives to the States are merely interim provisions scheduled to terminate on November 30, 1998."[37] She added that Congress was free to amend the interim program so as to provide for its continuance on a contractual basis with the States if it wished to do so, as it had done with a number of other federal programs. Like two other cases, already discussed, which also were decided in the final week of the Court's term, *Lindh v. Murphy,* narrowing habeas corpus relief, and *Kansas v. Hendricks,* on the use of involuntary civil commitment in conjunction with the criminal process, the Court in *Printz* divided by a majority of five to four. The same four Justices, Stevens, Souter, Ginsburg, and Breyer, were in the minority in two of the three cases. In the third, *Lindh v. Murphy,* they were joined by Justice O'Connor to form a majority.

IV

Despite the natural desire of lawmakers and administration officials to protect the fruits of their labor from being struck down by the courts on constitutional grounds, the at times ill-considered style of lawmaking by Congress does call for some means of post-legislative review and relief from unintended or unlawful consequences. As the 1996 and 1997 appropriations processes showed so clearly, the readiness to bypass the formal procedures for substantive lawmaking by the two elected chambers, taking scant notice of the separate stages for authorizing and appropriating public funds, puts too great a premium on last-minute compromises and negotiations. When it comes to implementing the laws passed by Congress, their shortcomings, intended or otherwise, are exposed sooner or later to public view. Again and again, in Anthony Lewis's trenchant comment, "Congress has been saved by the courts from the consequences of a passing folly."[38]

Notwithstanding periodic demands for the impeachment of conscientious judges who have shown their integrity, and faithfulness to the Constitution, by giving an unpopular decision, the active participation of a genuinely independent judiciary is essential to the good health of the American political system. It cannot be taken for granted. In April 1997 leaders of seventy-six national, state, and local Bar Associations wrote to the Speaker of the House of Representatives, Newt Gingrich, urging him to resist any efforts to impeach federal judges because of disagreement with their rulings. Shortly before, Representative Tom DeLay, the majority Whip, had called for Congress to use impeachment as a tool to weed out federal judges whose rulings were "particularly egregious."[39] DeLay's intention "to go after judges" as "part of our conservative efforts against judicial activism" was denounced not only by liberal commentators, but in a stinging public rebuke in the *New Republic.* "It is hard to imagine,'' the editor wrote in a signed article, ''a surer scheme for producing a constitutional crisis than for the party that controls Congress to conduct a campaign of impeachment against judges whose views represent those of the other party.''[40] Judicial activism, it was recognized, flourished on the conservative Right as elsewhere in the political spectrum, not least amongst the Justices of the Supreme Court. In *Printz,* as in other cases turning on the scope of congressional authority, it has been the liberal wing of the Court that has been the defender of judicial restraint, and the conservatives the proponents of judicial activism.

The American political system, if that is an apt description of such a shifting and unpredictable compound of laws and customs, is prone to be swayed by emotion more easily than by reason. If unintentional inequities or violations of rights guaranteed by the Constitution are the result of actions by Congress, then it is for the judiciary to provide remedies. Irritation and resentment are human reactions, on the part of lawmakers like everyone else, but they cool the more quickly if there is an acceptance of a wider public interest lying outside the confines of the Capitol.

That wider interest is the confidence of the public in the discharge by the judges of their duty to interpret and uphold the constitutional rights of individual citizens, regardless of the popularity or unpopularity that their decisions may provoke. There is a fine line dividing legitimate criticism of judicial decisions and the intimidation that can result from vociferous demands for their removal from office. Irresponsible and politically motivated censure that undermines the respect to which judges are entitled, and is aimed at influencing their decisions, is quite simply incompatible with the principle of judicial independence and the maintenance of the rule of law.[41]

In considering congressional action to combat crime over the last two decades, some profound questions arise as to the wisdom and efficacy of the policies adopted. Grounds for criticism are not peculiar to Republican or Democratic administrations, nor to which party controls the Congress. In general, too much reliance is placed on immediate legislative responses to problems with deeply rooted causative factors. The need to accommodate conflicting views hinders the single-minded determination that is so often a prerequisite for the successful pursuit of larger goals. Mistakes occur if public policy fails to achieve its intended effects. Public expectations are raised, then dashed. Faith in the ability of government to lead the nation toward attainable objectives for betterment suffers. Human as well as material resources are wasted. Individual injustice, distortions of process, and indefensible anachronisms in the system of criminal justice are the legacies of misdirected policies.

The underlying reasons why the incidence of violent crime in America is as high as it is lie outside the scope of the study. The focus has been directed toward the policy responses to a social pestilence that has debilitated large parts of American society. That a high proportion of violent offending is concentrated in certain geographical areas and amongst certain groups defined by age and ethnicity has not restricted the spread of a wider sense of danger and fear. The common perception of crime has unleashed exceptionally potent forces of populist opinion, based more often than not on anger, resentment, and a demand for vengeance. The ideals of behavioral reform and improvement inherent in the term "corrections" have given way to the desire to punish and protect the public from victimization. Death penalty statutes are in the ascendant, and the reach of habeas corpus has been restricted. Rates of incarceration nearly doubled between 1985 and 1995, but with little discernible impact on the volume of criminal offending.[42]

Whether or not the punitively inspired changes will add to the safety of individual citizens is in doubt since they depend too heavily on an exaggerated belief in deterrence. Although some crimes, such as organized crime, the more sophisticated importation and trafficking in drugs, and many property crimes, are premeditated and planned in advance, the vast bulk of violent crime is not. Most homicides, assaults, robberies, and sexual offenses are committed on impulse, frequently by assailants who are already known to the victim. The misleading idea that society is divided into two categories, the criminals and the law-abiding people like the rest of us, is woefully disproved day in and day out by the dreary procession through the criminal courts of the "people like us" who have been responsible for so many impulsive sexual assaults, woundings, and killings within families or amongst friends or acquaintances. In such circumstances, the presumed effect of deterrent sentencing is at its weakest.

Even the death penalty seems to lack the deterrent effect that is claimed by its adherents. In Texas, which executed three times as many sentenced offenders as its closest competitors among states since 1976, and four times more than any other state, the murder rate is one of the highest in the country. Since 1990, when the pace of executions began to accelerate, more law enforcement officers have been killed in Texas than in any other state, raising the perverse possibility that police officers may be at greater risk of being killed in states with the highest execution rates.[43]

Understandable as punitive reactions are, and however far-fetched the concept of sending messages by way of legislation to "the criminals" may be, they are infirm foundations for sound policies. Ignorance of the wide variety of circumstances and culpability that characterize criminal offending has to be met with explanation and analysis. There are no short cuts and no ultimate solutions just beyond reach. Violent crime must be distinguished from property crime and the interconnections carefully studied. Just because opinions are strongly and widely held it does not mean that they should be accepted without critical evaluation as the guiding light for legislation. Prevention policies, for example, are neither hard nor soft by any rational definition. Programs should be judged by whether or not they result in fewer crimes than would otherwise have occured.

V

At every point in the structure of law enforcement the pressure of populism makes itself felt. The police, the prosecutors, the judges, juries, and corrections officials are keenly aware of public expectations. State governors and administrators grapple with intractable practical issues such as the avoidance of undue delay in prosecuting defendants, the cost effectiveness of alternative forms of containment if custodial sentences result, the amounts of money available for building, expanding, and operating prisons, and the need to maintain security, order, and adequate standards within them. Federal judges in criminal cases see the inequities that can result from a legislative framework that denies them the ability to punish individual offenders according to the principles of just deserts and proportionality upon which the sentencing guidelines are based. It seems incredible that the flaws in the system of federal guidelines dating from the sentencing reforms of 1984, which had become so unpopular with the judiciary, could be compounded by later statutory enactments. Yet that is what has happened.

In a recent study of mandatory penalties,[44] Michael Tonry brings out the full extent to which they are seen as symbols by the elected representatives who have espoused them. They want to reassure the public generally, he writes, that their fears have been noted and acted on. They do so by making promises that the law can at best imperfectly and incompletely deliver. Instrumental arguments against the effectiveness of mandatory penalties, and normative arguments about injustice fall on deaf ears. Once the votes are cast, elected officials move on to other issues. But the judges, the prosecutors, the defense counsel, and many others have to live with the consequences. They must keep the courts functioning, and that they sometimes devise ways to avoid the application of laws they believe to be uncommonly harsh should come as no surprise. Elected officials, Tonry concludes, should become more responsible about crime control policy, and balance their felt need to make symbolic and rhetorical statements through the passage of legislation with well-established knowledge of how mandatory sentences operate in practice.[45]

There can be no more striking instance of misdirected criminal policy than the course of federal sentencing for cocaine-related offenses. The origins go back to the early years of the evocatively named, but ineffectively waged, War against Drugs. In 1986 Congress enacted an Anti–Drug Abuse Act[46] establishing mandatory minimum penalties for persons convicted of trafficking in a variety of controlled substances. The length of the mandatory sentence was linked to the quantity of the illegal drug distributed, and its potential harmfulness. The Act treated powder cocaine differently from the crack cocaine derived from it by heating cocaine powder mixed with baking soda and water to produce a more immediate and addictive sensation. A person convicted of selling five hundred grams of powder cocaine was made subject to the same five-year mandatory minimum sentence of imprisonment as a person selling five grams of crack cocaine. Similarly, a person convicted of selling five kilograms (5,000 grams) of powder was subject to the same ten-year mandatory minimum sentence as a person selling fifty grams of crack. This discrepancy came to be known as the one hundred-to-one quantity ratio between the two forms of cocaine.[47]

The Anti–Drug Abuse Act of 1988[48] went further by extending the mandatory minimum penalty of five years in prison to simple possession of crack cocaine. It was the only federal mandatory minimum for a first offense of simple possession of a controlled substance. Simple possession without the intent to distribute any quantity of powder cocaine by a first-time offender was a misdemeanor punishable by no more than one year in prison.

Such an inflexible sentencing structure did not accord with the federal sentencing guidelines, the evolution of which is described in chapter 1. In vain the U.S. Sentencing Commission argued that ultimate sentences should be based on more than a measurement of quantity of the drug involved in the offense. The goals of drug-sentencing policy were carefully enumerated. They were that sentences should be commensurate with the dangers associated with a given drug; that five- and ten-year mandatory sentences should be targeted at serious traffickers; that cocaine-sentencing policy should advance the federal government's role in the national drug control effort and rationalize priorities for the use of state and federal resources in targeting drug use and trafficking; and that cocaine sentencing policy and practice should be perceived by the public as fair.

Any consideration of the final goal raised in acute form the issue of whether the one hundred-to-one quantity ratio could be regarded as effective, uniform, and just. While there was no evidence of racial bias behind the promulgation of the sentencing laws, the undeniable outcome was that their impact fell disproportionately on one segment of the population. On the statistics cited by the Commission nearly 90 percent of the offenders convicted in the federal courts of crack cocaine distribution were African-Americans, while the majority of powder cocaine users were white.[50] Thus whatever the original intention, the sentences imposed for trafficking in and simple possession of different forms of the same drug appeared to be, and indeed were, far harsher and more severe in their impact on the racial minorities, Hispanic as well as African-Americans, leading to widespread perceptions of unfairness and inconsistency.

In a powerfully argued analysis of race and the disproportionate sentencing for crack cocaine versus powder cocaine, Randall Kennedy has reminded the most outspoken critics of the differential that at the time of its introduction eleven of the twenty-one black congressmen who were then members of the House of Representatives had voted in favor of the new law.[51] One of them, Charles Rangel, an influential African-American Democrat representative from Harlem, New York, was chairman of the House Select Committee on Narcotics Abuse and Control when the crack-powder differential was enacted. In March 1986 he had been the first person in Congress to draw attention to crack as a new and special danger, noting that what was most frightening about crack was that it had made cocaine widely available and affordable by black youth.[52] Paradoxically, a scrutiny of the legislative history of the measure indicates that rather than having been racially motivated to disadvantage black communities, as some believe, the much higher sentences for crack were intended by Congress to recognize the greater harmfulness of the new drug and to protect those communities, mainly black, which were being devastated by its abuse. The later developments are a classic example of the unintended and unfortunate consequences of insufficiently thought-out legislation.

The perception that crack was more of an integral part of systemic crime than any other drug, particularly the violent street crime associated with open drug dealing, gangs, guns, serious injury, and death, combined with the competitive politics of toughness on crime, meant that legislators in the 103rd Congress had been unable to agree on any amendment to the sentencing law during the passage of the Violent Crime Control and Law Enforcement Act of 1994. The furthest that they were prepared to go was to request a report from the Sentencing Commission on "issues relating to sentences applicable to offenses involving the possession or distribution of all forms of cocaine." The report was to address the differences in penalty levels applying to different forms of cocaine and include any recommendations that the Commission might have to retain or modify the differences.[53] In February 1995 the Commission issued a comprehensive report to Congress in which it recommended unanimously that changes be made, including a reduction in the hundred-to-one quantity ratio between powder and crack cocaine. The Commission was investigating ways to account for the harms caused by cocaine in the sentencing guidelines and would recommend appropriate enhancements and adjustments in the quantity ratio.

By May the Sentencing Commission was ready to send to Congress its proposed changes to the guidelines. The intention was to equate the base sentences for powder and crack offenders by adopting a one-to-one quantity ratio at the existing levels for powder cocaine, with sentencing enhancements for the violence and other harms that were peculiarly linked to crack cocaine. The recommendation was not unanimous, having been agreed by a majority of four to three members of the Commission. The minority dissent contended that the added harms associated with crack cocaine did not warrant a total elimination of the differential. The Commission's recommendation fell on stony ground, both at the White House and on Capitol Hill.

In October, Congress passed, and the President signed, legislation rejecting the proposed guideline changes on cocaine offenses, and also some others on money laundering. In a statement Clinton said that trafficking in crack, and the violence it fostered, had a devastating impact on communities across America, especially inner-city communities. Tough penalties for crack trafficking were required because of the effect on individuals and families, related gang activity, turf battles, and other violence.[54] He accepted that some adjustments were warranted, and noted that the bill he was signing[55] directed the Sentencing Commission to report back after undertaking additional review. Once again, the issue was returned to the Commission for further consideration, this time accompanied by a congressional directive that "the sentence imposed for trafficking in a quantity of crack cocaine should generally exceed the sentence imposed for trafficking in a like quantity of powder cocaine."[56]

By then the scope for further study might seem to have been exhausted since the problem was political rather than technical. Nevertheless, the Commission dutifully addressed itself to the task anew, assessing the concerns raised by Congress, conducting fresh research, consulting with law enforcement and substance abuse experts, and reviewing the vast accumulation of information already in its possession about both powder and crack cocaine, and the changing market for these drugs. The upshot of all this conscientious endeavor was that the Commission reiterated its original core finding that although research and public policy might support somewhat higher penalties for crack than for powder cocaine, a hundred-to-one quantity ratio could not be justified. Attentive to the congressional directive the Commission recommended, this time "firmly and unanimously," that the penalty differential for federal powder and crack cocaine cases should be reduced by adjusting the quantity levels at which the mandatory penalties would be triggered. For powder cocaine it recommended that the current 500-gram trigger for the five-year mandatory sentence be reduced to a level between 125 and 375 grams, and for crack cocaine that the current five-gram trigger be increased to between 25 and 75 grams.

In its *Special Report to the Congress,* the Sentencing Commission urged the adoption of a ratio within the recommended quantity ranges as soon as possible, pointing out that in the interim hundreds of people would continue to be sentenced each month under the existing law. That the laws were not only inequitable, but compared adversely with other approaches in decreasing drug consumption and its related consequences, was shown in a detailed analysis by the Drug Policy Control Center at the RAND Corporation published just a few weeks after the Sentencing Commission had made its recommendation.[57]

The main conclusion of the RAND study was that mandatory minimum sentences were not justifiable on the basis of cost-effectiveness at reducing cocaine consumption, cocaine expenditures, or drug-related crime. Mandatory minimums reduced cocaine consumption less per million dollars spent than the same amount spent on enforcement under the previous sentencing regime. Either type of incarceration approach reduced drug consumption less than putting heavy users through treatment programs, per million dollars spent.[58] The authors acknowledged that long sentences for serious crimes had an intuitive appeal. They responded to deeply held beliefs about punishment for evil actions, and in many cases ensured that by removing a criminal from the streets, further crimes that would have been committed would be prevented. But long sentences are expensive and cocaine control resources are limited. If reducing consumption or violence was the goal, the report concluded, more could be achieved by spending additional money arresting, prosecuting, and sentencing dealers to standard prison terms than by spending it sentencing fewer dealers to longer, mandatory terms.[59]

There is now an overwhelming body of impartially gathered and assessed evidence, economic as well as penological, to support a belated reform in the mandatory sentencing laws for cocaine offenses, and for other drug offenses too. Research findings coincide with practical experience in underlining the need for greater selectivity so that prosecutorial and prison resources can be

concentrated on those offenders engaged in mid-level and more serious trafficking in the most dangerous drugs.

VI

Reform of the mandatory sentencing laws for drug offenses, cocaine especially,
like the nationwide licensing of firearms, currently lies at the outer edge of
what is realistic legislatively. But the limits are not static. They expand or
contract in tune with the constant readings that are made of the state of public
opinion. Of all the lessons to be drawn in analyzing the 1994 crime legislation
and the lesser measures that followed it in the 104th Congress, at the top of
the list is the way in which so many of the provisions that found their way
into law derived from the perceived demands of local, sectional, or national
public opinion rather than the verdict of practical experience, or of any detectable body of coherent principle. The pattern was not confined to crime, or
to those proposals put forward by congressmen or senators. On several important issues, policies originating from or taken up by the administration owed
more to the pollsters and campaign consultants advising the White House than
to the expertise of the Department of Justice.

The future is as unpredictable as were many of the policy developments
in the short period of legislative history covered by this book. The extension
of the death penalty and the restrictions on habeas corpus, the Brady Act, three
strikes, the assault weapons ban, and Megan's Law, were all products of shifts
in public opinion. Some came suddenly, accelerated by outrageous events.
Others built up over a longer period of time. The question now is, What will
be the effect on public attitudes of falling crime rates? If the dominant strain
of punitiveness can be attributed to the sharp increases in the incidence of
crime, particularly violent and lethal crime, that were experienced over two
decades until the early 1990s, will it be moderated by the generally downward
trends reported since 1991, or is it now permanently ingrained in the popular
consciousness?

These are questions to which no answers are yet visible. Early clues may
come seriatim in the response of the President and Congress when faced with
specific situations calling for action. The cocaine-sentencing issue is one such.
Will more room be allowed for toleration of practical considerations based on
the principles of proportionality and fairness than in the past? Public awareness
of the downturn in criminal offending has been ensured by the high-profile
publicity engineered by police chiefs, mayors, state governors, and the President himself, all anxious to claim credit for the effectiveness of policies which
they have espoused. This is not the place for a discussion of the relative causes
of the decline, although it should be noted that the FBI reports of index crimes
in the annual Uniform Crime Reports, commonly referred to as the crime rate,
do not include drug offenses.[60]

What of the role of the media in the coverage of crime, particularly on
television? In 1997 it was estimated that the average American spends 3,400

hours a year "consuming the output of the media." Four-fifths of the total consumption is spent in front of a television set. The overall amount is greater than the hours spent sleeping (2,900 hours) or working (about 2,000 hours). In the average home the television is on for more than seven hours a day.[61] The *Media Monitor* review for 1996 reported that crime news fell by more than half from the 1995 total to a five-year low.[62] Network newscasts[63] began to lose interest in ordinary crimes, focusing more heavily on celebrity crimes and a few high-profile cases. The wrongful-death civil lawsuit against O. J. Simpson generated only 144 stories, about one-sixth of the number reporting his criminal trial and conviction the previous year. In the absence of cameras in the courtroom to supply fresh footage, network attention faded quickly. Even so, the Simpson case generated more stories in 1996 than all murders combined for the second consecutive year.

Although the three main networks have been losing audience share to local stations, cable television, talk radio, and the Internet, they are still the largest national news media, attracting just under half of the total number of viewers. Yet if non-celebrity crime reporting is in decline on network news, it is still firmly ensconced at the head of the list of topics on local television newscasts.

In a survey of one hundred evening newscasts in fifty-six cities across thirty-five states on a single day in September 1995 researchers found that 3.02 percent of airtime was devoted to crime stories, and that crime was the lead story in thirty-seven of the newscasts.[64] A total of 461 separate stories were broadcast, with violent crime as the most common type of crime covered. Although murder is one of the least frequent crimes committed, 63.3 percent of the total time given to crime was spent reporting murders, compared with 10.4 percent to assaults, 5.2 percent to rapes, and 4.9 percent to drug offenses. According to the survey report, presentations tended to focus on "the drama of crime, with stereotypical video of flashing emergency lights, yellow crime scene ribbons, the dead and injured, grieving relatives, and eye witnesses."[65] Rarely did the newscasts explain the context, consequences, patterns, or solutions that surrounded a particular event. Whites were far more likely than blacks to be presented as victims. Only as alleged or identified perpetrators did African-Americans feature in the newscasts to any significant extent, so reinforcing racist stereotypes and negative role models.[66]

VII

It is safe to assume that a very high proportion of all of the killings, woundings, and robberies so repetitively and simplistically depicted in local newscasts will have involved the use of a gun. It is guns that are the unique phenomenon of criminal offending in America. Other countries have experienced high rates of crime and have similarly responded with a greater use of imprisonment. But with the exception of Russia and some other states of the former Soviet Union, no industrialized nation has approached the record U.S. figure of six hundred prison inmates to every one hundred thousand of the population. Rates of incarceration in Western Europe, with some exceptions, have generally been rising over the past decade, but at a much lower rate than the increase of 92 percent recorded in the United States between 1985 and 1995.[67] The statistics in table 5 show that the largest and most populous of the developing nations, China and India, are also far behind America and Russia in their recourse to imprisonment. As with the figures for gun-related homicides, Canada is much closer to Great Britain[68] than it is to its North American neighbor.

The cost to federal and state governments of incarcerating offenders on this scale is huge. In some states, spending on other well-established objectives, for instance the provision of higher education in California, has been cut back to find the money. The risks of riots, escapes, or large-scale disorders cannot be discounted. It is possible that these factors may slow down, or even reverse the upward trend, particularly if sentencing reforms result in fewer less serious drug offenders being imprisoned. The Sentencing Commission 1995 study on cocaine and federal sentencing policy found that 11 percent of imprisoned traffickers were considered to be high-level dealers, 34 percent mid-level dealers, and 55 percent street-level dealers or couriers. These figures relate to drug traffickers sentenced under federal law, typically the more serious cases. A similar analysis of drug offenders sentenced in the state courts, or for possession rather than trafficking, would be likely to show an even smaller proportion of high-level offenders.[69]

Whatever changes lie ahead will need to be contained within the tolerance of public opinion. The NORC surveys already cited, and other findings, have demonstrably established that the general public is ready to accept that no one

Table 5. International Rates of Incarceration, 1995

Nation	Number of Inmates	Rate of Incarceration per 100,000 Population
Austria	6,761	85
Belgium	7,401	75
Canada	33,882	115
China	1,236,534	103
England/Wales	51,265	100
France	53,697	95
Germany	68,396	85
India	216,402	24
Ireland	2,032	55
Italy	47,323	85
Japan	46,622	37
Netherlands	10,143	65
Russia	1,017,372	690
Singapore	8,500	287
United States	1,585,401	600

Source: The Sentencing Project, Washington, D.C., 1997. Reproduced with permission.

should possess a handgun, or possibly any other firearm, without a permit. On investigation, the American love of guns appears to be a male preserve. Most women hate guns; they have seen too often the lethal consequences of accidents involving children, or know victims of domestic gun violence, if they have escaped that fate themselves. In the 1996 congressional elections the electoral impact of women's votes, as part of an incoming tide, was clearly evident in the results.

For the first time, through its Voter Education Fund, Handgun Control, Inc., challenged the NRA's dominance in certain carefully selected races. Twelve contests were targeted, with the assault weapons ban projected as the main issue. In each of them, candidates designated the HCI as the "Dangerous Dozen," and strongly backed by the NRA, had consistent records of voting or positioning themselves against laws like the Brady Handgun Violence Act and the ban on assault weapons. Of the twelve, ten lost. Nine were Republicans, but one, the most prized scalp of all, was the veteran Democrat representative, Harold Volkmer of Missouri. Described as "the NRA's leading House ally,"[70] ten years earlier Volkmer had been a sponsor of the Firearm Owners' Protection Act of 1986 (the McClure-Volkmer amendments), which relaxed some of the restrictions on the interstate trading in firearms that had been in place since 1968. In a statement the following day, Sarah Brady claimed that never before had "NRA-backed candidates suffered so at the polls. It's a new era," she said. "Voters no longer want representatives who have pledged allegiance to the gun lobby. They want Members of Congress who are concerned about public safety."[71]

One of the victors, a registered Republican domiciled in Long Island but running on the Democratic ticket, symbolized the appeal of the public safety platform. Carolyn McCarthy was the widow of a commuter on the Long Island Railroad who had been shot dead by a gunman when returning home from work in New York City. Five others were killed in the incident, and their only child was among the nineteen people injured, being shot in the head. When her representative, Dan Frisa, voted to repeal the assault weapons ban she decided to run for Congress against him. Ten days later, after press speculation that he might be opposed by Mrs. McCarthy, Frisa announced plans to introduce legislation to extend the reach of the assault weapons ban which he had opposed so shortly before. Despite this equivocation, he was defeated in a heavily Republican district with the reputation of having one of the most effective local party organizations in the country.[72]

In the aftermath of the elections, both sides were to claim victory. HCI had shown that it, too, could intervene to prove that votes in Congress could have fatal electoral consequences. To this extent it was adopting its adversary's tactics. The NRA, playing down the defeats of some of its most strongly supported candidates, and the election of such opponents as Senator Paul Wellstone and Representative Dick Durbin,[73] who was running for the Senate, boasted the continued success of its long-standing policy of electing its friends and crushing its foes. While conceding that it might not have won all the races it went in for, indeed losing several of the most conspicuous, the NRA talked of the "ten thousand" races contested at the federal, state, and local levels, claiming an overall success rate of eighty-four percent.[74] As to the congressional elections, it said that nearly half of its supporters who had lost their House seats had been replaced by people of like views on gun legislation, and that in the Senate, where it entered twenty-seven races, it had picked up additional supporters.[75]

VIII

Whereas it would be a premature to write off the NRA as a spent force, the 1996 congressional elections undoubtedly were a watershed. No longer were the gun rights advocates alone in the field; contrary opinion had been turned into votes. Some experienced observers of the Washington scene detected the signs of a paradigm shift of opinion on gun control. Although many congressmen remained hostile to regulation, they became cautious about putting their views on public record. When elected representatives are fearful of expressing opinions that they believe may be unpopular with a majority of their electors, the bounds of the possible are expanded.

Since the introduction of the crime bill in 1993 several steps, large and small, have been taken toward "ending the insanity," in Clinton's phrase, of it being easier to buy or sell a handgun than to obtain a driver's license. Popular opinion, progressively more organized on the part of groups advocating gun control, has enabled legislative and executive actions to be taken that previously were regarded as unattainable. The state of opinion now suggests that it is timely to move on to another, more ambitious objective: to terminate the isolationism of America in its passive acceptance of an annual toll of gun deaths so far out of line with any other comparable nation. Such an objective transcends policies aimed at deterring "the criminals." Deliberate acts of homicide need to be prosecuted vigorously, and when proved punished with all the severity which the law can command. But we should never forget that more than half of the total deaths each year caused by firearms are self-inflicted, or the result of accidents. The issue is one of public safety and life expectancy as much as criminal policy.

Appendix

Violent Crime Control and Law Enforcement Act of 1994

Title XI—Firearms Provisions
Summary

Subtitle A: Assault Weapons

This provision bans the possession, transfer, and manufacture (with some exceptions) of many semiautomatic assault weapons and ammunition-feeding devices that hold more than ten rounds. It amends 18 U.S.C. § 924(c), increasing the mandatory minimum sentence to ten years for the use or possession of such an assault weapon during a crime of violence or drug trafficking crime. The entire set of provisions will be repealed automatically (unless renewed) ten years after the effective date.

Subtitle B: Youth Handgun Safety

This provision renders a federal crime (a) the possession of a handgun or ammunition by a juvenile of less than eighteen years of age, and (b) the transfer of a handgun or ammunition to a juvenile. The penalty imposed for first-time juvenile violators is probation. The subtitle includes a set of wide-ranging exceptions to the prohibition, for example, possession in the course of employment or instruction, or when defending against a burglar. It also permits proceeding against a juvenile violator under the delinquency laws.

Subtitle C: Licensure

Provisions under this subtitle tighten restrictions on the issuance and oversight of federal firearms dealer's licenses. Also included are provisions that require dealers to respond within one day to a request for information concerning the disposition of any firearms, and require a report within two days of any lost or stolen firearms.

Subtitle D: Domestic Violence

Two new offenses are created. One provision makes it a felony to dispose of a firearm to any person knowing that the person is subject to a court order that restrains the person from harassing, stalking, or threatening an intimate partner of such person or such a partner's child, or engaging in conduct that would place the intimate partner in reasonable fear of bodily injury to the partner or his or her child. The court order must, however, have been issued after a hearing at which the prohibited person received actual notice, and must include a finding that the prohibited person represents a credible threat to the safety of the intimate partner or child. The second provision prohibits individuals who are the subjects of restraining orders from possessing firearms.

The subtitle provides that any firearms seized from an individual who is the subject of a restraining order under either of the new provisions must be securely stored and returned to the offender upon the lapse or termination of the restraining order.

Subtitle E: Gun Crime Penalties

The subtitle provides enhanced penalties for gun crimes and makes relatively minor improvements to the firearms statutes.

Notes

Chapter 1. The Politics of Crime

1. A. Hamilton, J. Madison, and J. Jay in P. Ford, ed., *The Federalist* (New York: Henry Holt, 1898), p. 60.

2. Pub. L. 103-322, 108 Stat. 1796.

3. In this context "manipulation" can be taken to mean the conscious adoption of stratagems without regard to their policy implications in order to achieve popularly accepted aims. The author is indebted to Dr. Stanley Katz for this formulation.

4. F. Zimring and G. Hawkins point out that many people have homogeneous images of "the criminal." In *Crime Is Not the Problem: Lethal Violence in America* (New York: Oxford University Press, 1997), p. 12, they suggest that a composite generalized image of criminals incorporating the threatening characteristics of violent crime acts as a factor conditioning public fear.

5. 8 *Media Monitor* (1994), published by the Center for Media and Public Affairs, Washington, D.C. The center is an independent, non-profit research organization that conducts scientific studies of how the media treat social and political issues.

6. See M. Mauer, "The Fragility of Criminal Justice Reform," 21 *Social Justice* 17 (1995).

7. For a commentary on the methodology of victim-reported offenses and police-recorded offenses, see D. P. Farrington and P. A. Langan, "Changes in Crime and Punishment in England and America in the 1980s," 9 *Justice Quarterly* 5, 32–38 (1992).

8. This definition is taken from *A Glossary of Terms Used in the Federal Budget Process,* 3rd ed. (Washington, D.C.: U.S. General Accounting Office, 1981), p. 71. The glossary is recommended in the guidance on *Drafting Federal Law,* prepared by the Office of Legislative Counsel, U.S. House of Representatives.

9. The Hate Crime Statistics Act, passed by the Congress and signed by the Pres-

ident in April 1990 (Pub. L. 101-275, 104 Stat. 140), mandated the collection of data on crimes motivated by religious, ethnic, racial, or sexual-orientation prejudice. Collection commenced on January 1, 1991. The Violent Crime Control and Law Enforcement Act of 1994 amended the Hate Crime Statistics Act to include crimes against the disabled. Federal Bureau of Investigation, U.S. Department of Justice, *Crime in the United States, 1994,* Uniform Crime Reports (Washington D.C.: U.S. Government Printing Office, 1994, p. 3.

10. Ibid., p. 376. The UCR methodology is set out in Appendix I, pp. 376–78.

11. All household members over the age of twelve are interviewed in a nationally representative sample of approximately 49,000 households, amounting to about 101,000 persons. Households stay in the sample for three years and are interviewed at six-monthly intervals. New households rotate into the sample on an ongoing basis.

12. The National Crime Victimization Survey Reports are completed annually by the Bureau of Justice Statistics of the Department of Justice and published under the title *Criminal Victimization in the United States.*

13. Over the five-year period 1990–94 juvenile arrests rose by 21 percent. A general pattern of decreasing levels of violent offending by adults over the age of twenty-five being offset by steadily rising rates of offending by juveniles and younger people was maintained through the mid-1990s. In 1994 the under-twenty-five age group was responsible for 47 percent of the violent crime arrests and 59 percent of property crime arrests. The trend was an alarming one since it was estimated that there would be 23 percent more teenagers in the United States by the year 2005.

14. *Crime in the United States, 1993,* p. 11.

15. *Crime in the United States, 1995,* pp. 274–75.

16. *Crime in the United States, 1993,* p. 14.

17. John J. DiIulio, "Saving the Children: Criminal Justice and Social Policy," in I. Garfinkel, J. Hochschild, and S. McLanahan, eds., *Social Policies for Children* (Washington, D.C.: Brookings Institution, 1996), p. 204. It was calculated, based on data extracted from a report by the Fire and Police Commission in Milwaukee, that in 1991 people living in the city's low-income, predominantly black districts had over thirty times as much chance of being murdered, assaulted, or robbed as those residing in its middle- and upper-income, predominantly white districts (p. 205).

18. *Crime in the United States, 1993,* pp. 18, 29, 32.

19. National Center for Health Statistics, *Health United States, 1993* (Hyattsville, Md: Public Health Service, 1994), tables 42–53, pp. 115–35.

20. The disease categories are deaths from heart diseases (7.3), cerebrovascular diseases (0.5), malignant neoplasms (5.4), neoplasms of respiratory system (0.1), and chronic pulmonary diseases (1.9). Ibid.

21. Los Angeles is the second largest city in the United States, with a population in 1992 estimated at 3.6 million for its crime statistics reporting unit. The city of Sydney in Australia also had a population estimated at 3.6 million. Zimring and Hawkins, *Crime Is Not the Problem,* p. 4.

22. Robbery is defined as the taking of property from the person of another by force or by the threat of force.

23. Zimring and Hawkins, *Crime Is Not the Problem,* p. 5.

24. Ibid.

25. Ibid., p. 6.

26. Ibid., p. 7.

27. Ibid., pp. 10–11.

28. James Q. Wilson, *Commentary,* Sept. 1994, p. 26.

29. *Economist,* Oct. 15, 1994, p. 23.

30. The jurisdiction and organization of the federal and state court systems are clearly described in L. Baum, *American Courts: Process and Policy,* 2nd ed. (Boston, Mass.: Houghton Mifflin, 1990), pp. 21–54.

31. L. M. Friedman, *Crime and Punishment in American History* (New York: Basic Books, 1993), pp. 266–67. Chapter 12 is a finely written historical account of the development of a national system of criminal justice and its limitations.

32. Ibid., pp. 265–67.

33. Art. 1, sec. 8.

34. Pub. L. 88-352, 78 Stat. 243.

35. 85 S. Ct. 348 (1964).

36. 85 S. Ct. 377 (1964).

37. See G. Gunther, *Constitutional Law,* 12th ed., University Casebook Series, (Westbury, N.Y.: Foundation Press, 1991), pp. 147–51.

38. Ibid., p. 93.

39. 115 S. Ct. 1624 (1995).

40. Sec. 5(e)(2) of the Federal Alcohol Administration act of 1935 (First Amendment); provisions of the Ethics Reform Act of 1989 (First Amendment); and sec. 476 of the Federal Deposit Insurance Corporation Improvement Act of 1991 (separation of powers).

41. 5 U.S. (1 Cranch) 137 (1803).

42. It was for this reason that the decision in *Lopez* attracted an unusual volume of scholarly commentary. Of particular interest are L. Lessig, "Translating Federalism: United States v. Lopez," 1995 *Supreme Court Review* 5 (Chicago: University of Chicago Press, 1996), pp. 125–215; and a symposium issue of 94 *Michigan Law Review,* 533–831 (1995), Foreword by L. H. Pollak at 533–53.

43. The Gun-Free School Zones act was enacted as sec. 1702 of the Crime Control Act of 1990 (Pub. L. 101-647, 104 Stat. 4844), and incorporated in § 922 of Title 18, U.S. Code, as subsec. (q)(1)(A).

44. A school zone was defined as in or on the grounds of a public, parochial, or private school, or within a distance of one thousand feet from its grounds.

45. Lopez had been apprehended and charged initially with violating a Texas statute prohibiting gun possession on school premises. A day later, charges were filed against him under the Gun-Free School Zones Act. Upon the filing of the federal charges, the Texas authorities discontinued the state prosecution. See Pollak, Foreword, p. 542.

46. 2 F.3d 1342 (5th Cir. 1993).

47. Rehnquist, C.J., was joined by O'Connor, Scalia, Kennedy, and Thomas, JJ., in the majority, with Stevens, Souter, and Ginsburg, JJ., joining Breyer in filing dissenting opinions.

48. 115 S. Ct. 1630–31, 1634 (1995).

49. Ibid., at 1657.

50. Ibid., at 1658–59.

51. *Washington Post,* Apr. 27, 1995. Professor Tribe is author of *American Constitutional Law,* 2nd ed. (Mineola, N.Y.: Foundation Press, 1988) and has argued a number of cases in the Supreme Court. While the scope of the decision in *Lopez* is not

yet clear, a well-placed source, the minority staff director of the Committee on the Judiciary, U.S. House of Representatives, suggests that it will make Congress more cautious about the use of the commerce clause. See J. Epstein, "Evolving Spheres of Federalism after *U.S. v. Lopez* and Other Cases," 34 *Harvard Journal on Legislation,* 525 (1997).

52. 56 S. Ct. 855 (1936).

53. 115 S. Ct. 1628 (1995).

54. 57 S. Ct. 615 (1937).

55. Ibid., at 624.

56. In the opening chapter of *To Make a Nation,* the political scientist Samuel Beer contrasted the attitudes toward federalism and the use of federal authority by Presidents Johnson and Reagan. The remainder of the book consists of a lively excursion into the history of ideas to support the theory of federalism as a unifying national force and to refute the notion that the Union was no more than a compact between states. The distinction is an important one in practice, since the national theory allows a more generous view to be taken of the powers and responsibilities of the federal government than does the compact view. S. H. Beer, *To Make a Nation: The Rediscovery of American Federalism* (Cambridge, Mass.: Harvard University Press, 1993).

57. Ibid., p. 2.

58. *Public Papers of the Presidents of the United States, 1990,* Book II (Washington, D.C.: U.S. Government Printing Office, 1991), p. 1715.

59. 2 F.3d 1360–1. (5th Cir. 1993).

60. K. A. Bradshaw and D. A. M. Pring, *Parliament and Congress,* rev. and updated ed. (London: Quartet Books, 1981), p. 1. Sir Kenneth Bradshaw was Clerk of the House of Commons from 1983–87, his coauthor being Clerk of Committees from 1976–87.

61. The reasons why American federal statute law differs fundamentally from English statute law are attributed by P. S. Atiyah and R. S. Summers to the many vital respects in which the legislative process in Congress differs from that in Parliament. See *Form and Substance in Anglo-American Law* (Oxford: Clarendon Press, 1987), pp. 306–15.

62. *Washington Post,* Mar. 25, 1995.

63. *New York Times,* Mar. 20, 1995.

64. V. O. Key, *Politics, Parties, and Pressure Groups,* 5th ed. (New York: Thomas Y. Crowell, 1964), p. 661.

65. In *Congress and the Presidency,* 4th ed. (New York: Prentice-Hall, 1986), Nelson Polsby argues that the diversity of power centers in American politics, and the differences in their accessibility to different interest groups, serves to keep the political system open and responsive.

66. Omnibus Crime Control and Safe Streets Act of 1968, Pub. L. 90-351, 82 Stat. 197.

67. Gun Control Act of 1968. Pub. L. 90-618, 82 Stat. 1213.

68. National Commission on Reform of Federal Criminal Laws, *Final Report* (Washington, D.C.: U.S. Government Printing Office, 1971).

69. *Report to the Attorney General on Federal Criminal Code Reform* p. 145. This government document was transmitted to the Attorney General of the United States in January 1989 by the Office of Legal Policy at the Department of Justice. Its author, Ronald L. Gainer, held several senior positions in the Department of Justice between

1963 and 1989, and had been closely involved in criminal law reform and the super-vision of the Department's effort to achieve the enactment of a new federal criminal code. The report was reprinted in full (without its appendices) in 1 *Criminal Forum* 99 (1989). It is a source document of great interest and value. An account from a different perspective has been provided by K. Stith and S. Y. Koh, "The Politics of Sentencing Reform: The Legislative History of the Federal Sentencing Guidelines," 28 *Wake Forest Law Review* 223, at 231–32 (1993).

70. Stith and Koh, "The Politics of Sentencing Reform," 235.

71. Gainer, *Report to the Attorney General on Federal Criminal Code Reform,* p. 171.

72. Ibid., p. 156.

73. Pub. L. 98-473, 98 Stat. 1976.

74. Stith and Koh, "The Politics of Sentencing Reform," 232.

75. Gainer, *Report to the Attorney General on Federal Criminal Code Reform,* pp. 174–75.

76. *Mistretta v. United States,* 109 S. Ct. 647 (1989).

77. For a detailed study of the use of prosecutorial discretion in charging and plea bargaining under the guidelines, see I. H. Nagel and S. J. Schulhofer, "A Tale of Three Cities: An Empirical Study of Charging and Bargaining Practices under the Federal Sentencing Guidelines," 66 *Southern California Law Review* 501 (1992). Dr. Nagel was a member of the U.S. Sentencing Commission at the time of publication, although the article expresses her personal views. In "Plea Bargaining as Disaster," 101 *Yale Law Journal* 1979 (1992), Schulhofer advocates the abolition of plea bargaining.

78. For a critical analysis of why the federal Sentencing Commission and its guidelines have been so much less successful in operation and accepted by so many fewer practitioners than their state counterparts, see M. Tonry, *Sentencing Matters* (New York: Oxford University Press, 1996), p. 84. Failure of management is a factor well documented at pp. 84–89.

79. The symposium papers, together with abstracts and a summary of the pro-ceedings, were published as a special edition, 101 *Yale Law Journal* 1681–2075 (1992). The opening paper by Professor Daniel Freed, an authority on sentencing and editor of the *Federal Sentencing Reporter,* is a thorough and objective analysis of federal sen-tencing in the light of experience in operating the guidelines. The conclusion referred to here is taken from his paper, at p. 1687.

80. *Hearings before a Subcommittee of the Committee on Appropriations, House of Representatives,* 103rd Cong., 2nd Sess., p. 29 (Mar. 9, 1994). Justice Kennedy described these penalties as "very, very harsh and severe sentences."

81. See H. Scott Wallace, "Mandatory Minimums and the Betrayal of Sentencing Reform," 40 *Federal Bar News and Journal* 158 (1993).

82. 101 *Yale Law Journal* 2045 (1992). Marvin Frankel gave the keynote address at the Yale symposium referred to in note 79. His book, *Criminal Sentences: Law without Order* (New York: Hill and Wang, 1973), was a powerful and influential cri-tique of indeterminate sentencing powers.

83. Chapter 2 of the Comprehensive Crime Control Act of 1984, may be cited as the Sentencing Reform Act of 1984 (98 Stat. 1987). Sec. 217 amended the U.S. Code by adding a new chapter 58 on the Sentencing Commission (28 U.S.C. § 991).

84. K. Stith and S. Y. Koh, "The Politics of Sentencing Reform," 223.

85. Ibid., p. 286.

86. Ibid., pp. 261–62.

87. Tonry, *Sentencing Matters,* p. 12.

88. A. J. Reiss Jr. and J. Roth, *Understanding and Preventing Violence,* Report of the National Academy of Sciences Panel on the Understanding and Control of Violence (Washington, D.C.: National Academy Press, 1993), p. 6.

89. Out of a general population in the United States of 248,710,000 in 1990, 1,179,694 persons were incarcerated in federal or state prisons and local jails, an incarceration rate of 474 per 100,000 of the population. L. W. Jankowski, *Correctional Populations in the United States, 1990* (Washington D.C.: Bureau of Justice Statistics, U.S. Department of Justice, 1992), tables 2.1, 2.3, 5.6; and Bureau of the Census, *Statistical Abstract of the United States* 1992 (Washington, D.C.: U.S. Government Printing Office, 1992), table 16. By 1992–93 the total number of inmates had increased to 1,339,695, giving an incarceration rate of 519 per 100,000 of the population. M. Mauer, *Americans behind Bars: The International Use of Incarceration, 1992–1993* (Washington, D.C.: The Sentencing Project, 1994), table 1. By the end of 1994 the number of persons in custody exceeded one and a half million. The total number of prisoners under the jurisdiction of federal or state correctional authorities was 1,053,738 at the year end 1994. Inmates held in local jails, operated by counties and municipalities and administered by local government agencies, are counted on June 30, annually. The number of jail inmates reached the highest level then recorded of 490,442 on June 30, 1994, making an overall total of 1,554,180. About one-third are incarcerated in local jails, and two-thirds in state or federal prisons. Bureau of Justice Statistics, *Bulletin* April and August editions (Washington, D.C.: Office of Justice Programs, U.S. Department of Justice, 1995).

90. Pub. L. 98-473, 98 Stat. 2185. The act formed part of the Comprehensive Crime Control legislation of 1984.

91. Pub. L. 99-570 substituted "a violent felony or a serious drug offense, or both," for "robbery or burglary, or both." The terms were defined in the amending statute. 18 U.S.C. § 924 (e).

92. See "Three Strikes Statutes: Goals, Problems, and precedents," a special edition of 7 *Federal Sentencing Reporter 56* (Sept./Oct. 1994).

93. In *United States v. McClinton,* 815 F.2d 1242, 1245 (1987) the Court of Appeals for the Eighth Circuit noted the absence of a recency requirement in upholding, with some reluctance, a sentence to the mandatory fifteen years activated by three burglary convictions from twenty-five years before a violation of the Armed Career Criminal Act. The total value of the stolen property had been estimated at less than $500 and the defendant was asleep in bed at a motel with a firearm under his pillow at the time of his arrest.

94. 7 *Federal Sentencing Reporter* 69 (1994).

95. Pub. L. 99-570, 100 Stat. 3207.

96. 21 U.S.C. § 841(b)(1).

97. Pub. L. 100-690, 102 Stat. 4181.

98. Ibid., sec. 6371 amending 21 U.S.C. § 844(a). The five-year mandatory minimum was activated also by a second conviction for amounts exceeding three grams, or a third conviction for amounts exceeding one gram. For an account of later attempts by the U.S. Sentencing Commission to eradicate or reduce the discrepancies in sentencing for cocaine offenses, see chapter 9.

99. Ibid., sec. 6481 and sec. 6460 amending 21 U.S.C. § 848(a) and 18 U.S.C. § 924(c).

100. Ibid., sec. 6452, amending 21 U.S.C. § 841 (b)(1)(A).

101. Ibid., sec. 6470, amending 21 U.S.C. § 846.

102. A report on mandatory minimum sentences in February 1994 by the Department of Justice showed that 16,316 federal prisoners, amounting to 21 percent of the total population in federal prisons, could be considered as low-level drug law violators with no record of violence and no previous jail time. Seventeen percent of federal drug prisoners were first-time offenders serving five- to ten-year sentences for carrying quantities exceeding five grams of crack cocaine.

103. *Hearings before a Subcommittee of the Committee on Appropriations, House of Representatives,* p. 29.

104. Quoted in 139 *Congressional Record.* S 15317 (daily ed. Nov. 8, 1993).

105. Pub. L. 101-647, sec. 1703, 104 Stat. 4845.

106. United States Sentencing Commission, *Mandatory Minimum Penalties in the Federal Criminal Justice System,* Aug. 1991.

107. Ibid., p. iii.

108. Ibid., pp. iii–iv.

109. S. R. Gross, "Crime, Politics, and Race," 20 *Harvard Journal of Law and Public Policy* 413 (1997). Sources cited in notes to the article.

110. R. Kennedy, *Race, Crime, and the Law* (New York: Pantheon Books, 1997), p. 157.

111. Ibid., p. 151.

112. Gross, "Crime, Politics, and Race," p. 415.

Chapter 2. Organized Interests and Populist Beliefs

1. "Remarks Announcing the Anticrime Initiative and an Exchange with Reporters," Aug. 11, 1993, *Weekly Compilation of Presidential Documents* 29, no. 32, (Aug. 16, 1993), pp. 1602–4.

2. Ibid., p. 1603.

3. Ibid.

4. For the history of the Brady bill, see R. M. Aborn, "The Battle over the Brady Bill and the Future of Gun Control Advocacy," 22 *Fordham Urban Law Journal* 417 (1995). Richard Aborn, was president of Handgun Control, Inc., at the time of publishing this article.

5. Printed in *Weekly Compilation of Presidential Documents* 29, no. 32, p. 1605.

6. Center to Prevent Handgun Violence, *Proposals for the Clinton Administration to Implement New Gun Control Initiatives Without Passing New Legislation* (1993); cited in Aborn, "The Battle over the Brady Bill," 428–29.

7. Pub. L. 90-618, 82 Stat. 1214; 18 U.S.C. § 922(1).

8. *Weekly Compilation of Presidential Documents* 29, no. 32, p. 1605.

9. Ibid., p. 1606.

10. Aborn, "The Battle over the Brady Bill," 429. A Streetsweeper is a revolving-cylinder shotgun that fires twelve blasts in less than three seconds without reloading. Like the other twelve-gauge shotguns, it failed to meet the sporting purposes test in 18 U.S.C. § 925(d)(3).

11. Previously available as part of the common law in the American colonies, "The Privilege of the Writ of Habeas Corpus" had a place in Article 1 of the United States Constitution, which specified the conditions in which it might be suspended. Not

until a post–Civil War statute in 1867 did federal habeas corpus become available as a remedy to any state prisoner who was held in custody in violation of the Constitution, laws, or treaties of the United States. For a historical survey of the growth and decline of habeas corpus, see G. Hughes, *Occasional Paper VIII,* Center for Research in Crime and Justice, New York University School of Law, 1990.

12. Pub. L. 103-322 authorized the death penalty for the attempted assassination of the President; for large-scale drugs offenses forming part of a continuing criminal enterprise, and for the organizer or leader of such an enterprise who, in order to obstruct the investigation or prosecution of the enterprise, attempts to kill or knowingly directs, advises, authorizes, or assists another person to attempt to kill any public officer, juror, witness, or members of their family or household.

13. *New York Times,* Aug. 14, 1993.

14. In this context "boot camp" means a correctional program of not more than six months' duration involving adherence by inmates to a highly regimented schedule that involves strict discipline, physical training, and work. There is also provision for education, job training, substance abuse counselling or treatment, and after-care. Both the terminology and the regime are borrowed from the Marines.

15. In 1993 forty-one boot camp facilities were operated in twenty-six state correctional systems.

16. 1993 *Congressional Quarterly* 298.

17. The International Parental Kidnapping Act of 1993 (Pub. L. 103-173, 107 Stat. 1998) made it a federal crime for a parent to kidnap a child under the age of sixteen from his or her custodial parents and to remove the child from the United States. The National Child Protection Act of 1993 (Pub. L. 103-209, 107 Stat. 2490) established criminal background checks for child care providers.

18. Janet Reno's nomination as the first woman to serve as Attorney General of the United States was confirmed by a unanimous vote in the Senate on March 11, 1993.

19. For a well-informed account of the passage of the legislation, and the collapse of the hopes of liberal reformers, see M. Mauer, "The Fragility of Criminal Justice Reform," 21 *Social Justice* 14–29 (1995).

20. 1993 *Congressional Quarterly Almanac* 17.

21. Carol Moseley-Braun of Illinois.

22. K. Mfume, *No Free Ride* (New York: Ballantine Books, 1996), p. 320.

23. Mauer, "The Fragility of Criminal Justice Reform," 19.

24. In 1992 African-Americans and Hispanics represented 89.7 percent of all sentences to state prisons for drug possession offenses. M. Mauer and T. Huling, *Young Black Americans and the Criminal Justice System: Five Years Later* (Washington, D.C.: The Sentencing Project, 1995), p. 13.

25. M. Mauer, *Young Black Men and the Criminal Justice System: A Growing National Problem* (Washington, D.C.: The Sentencing Project, 1990); and Mauer and Huling, *Young Black Americans and the Criminal Justice System,* p. 1.

26. Mauer, 21 "The Fragility of Criminal Justice Reform," 19–20.

27. *Washington Post,* Oct. 22, 1993.

28. 139 *Congressional Record* D 1291 (daily ed. Nov. 10, 1993). All references to the *Congressional Record* are to the edition published daily reporting the public proceedings when one or both Houses are in session. The revised and bound edition is not available until some years later.

29. 137 *Congressional Record* H 2879 (daily ed. May 8, 1991).

30. 137 *Congressional Record* S 9086 (daily ed. June 28, 1991).

31. For the history of the Brady bill in the 100th, 101st, and 102nd Congresses, see R. M. Aborn, "The Battle over the Brady Bill," 420–25.

32. Sarah Brady became chairman of the Board of Handgun Control, Inc., in 1989, and also chaired its associated Center to Prevent Handgun Violence.

33. On each vote to close the debate there was a majority of fifty-seven to forty-two, 139 *Congressional Record* S 16332-3 and S 16417 (daily ed. Nov. 19, 1993). Under Senate rules sixty votes are required to end the debate and invoke cloture. It is this rule that facilitates filibusters in the Senate, since more votes are needed to end the filibuster than the simple majority required to pass a bill or an amendment. There is no parallel procedure in the House of Representatives.

34. 139 *Congressional Record* H 10907-8 (daily ed. Nov. 22, 1993).

35. In the version of the Brady Handgun Violence Prevention Act as enacted, a period of up to sixty months (five years) was allowed for the establishment of a national instant criminal background check system without any proviso as to its accuracy. Thirty days after the Attorney General notified licensed gun dealers that the instant check system had been established, they would be required to contact it before completing the sale of any firearm. The provision also applied to licensed importers and manufacturers.

36. 139 *Congressional Record* S 17091 (daily ed. Nov. 24, 1993).

37. "Remarks on Signing the Brady Bill," Nov. 30, 1993, *Weekly Compilation of Presidential Documents* 29, no. 48 (Dec. 6, 1993), p. 2478.

38. The act was named in James Brady's honor as the Brady Handgun Violence Prevention Act of 1993, Pub. L. 103-159, 107 Stat. 1536.

39. 18 U.S.C. § 922(d).

40. Prior to 1993 nothing in federal law prevented an individual from obtaining a firearm simply by filling out a form stating that the potential purchaser was not a felon, had never been dishonorably discharged from a branch of the armed services, nor was under indictment, a fugitive from justice. No verification was required of the information given. Some states had more stringent requirements, and at the time of the passage of the Brady bill, twenty-two states required some form of background check for would-be handgun purchasers. Aborn, "The Battle over the Brady Bill," 417, 418 (1993).

41. Pub. L. 90-351, 82 Stat. 197.

42. Pub. L. 90-618, 82 Stat. 1213.

43. Registration means keeping records of the transfer or ownership of a specific handgun or firearm.

44. Licenses or permits issued to individuals to entitle the holder to purchase, receive, or possess a handgun or firearm.

45. "Remarks upon Signing the Gun Control Act of 1968," Oct. 22, 1968, *Public Papers of the Presidents of the United States, 1968–69* Book II (Washington, D.C.: U.S. Government Printing Office, 1970), p. 1059.

46. Ibid., pp. 1059–60.

47. Ibid., p. 1266.

48. Lyndon Johnson had been a United States senator from Texas, 1948–61, and minority or majority leader in the Senate, 1953–61, before becoming Vice President in 1961.

49. Pub. L. 99-308, 100 Stat. 449 (McClure-Volkmer Amendments).

50. O. S. Davidson, *Under Fire: The NRA and the Battle for Gun Control* (New York: Henry Holt, 1993), p. 80. See also J. Sugarman, *National Rifle Association: Money, Firepower and Fear* (Washington, D.C.: National Press Books, 1992).

51. The data was compiled by Common Cause. See Davidson, *Under Fire,* pp. 79–80.

52. Pub. L. 100-690, 102 Stat. 4181.

53. Pub. L. 100-649, 102 Stat. 3186.

54. *Congress and the Nation,* vol. 8, 1989–92 (Washington, D.C.: Congressional Quarterly, 1993), p. 765. Handgun Control, Inc., was founded in 1974, and its associated Center to Prevent Handgun Violence in 1983.

55. The party breakdown of the voting in the House was Democrats: 179 for and 83 against; Republicans: 60 for and 102 against; Independent: 1 against. In the Senate the voting was Democrats: 48 for and 8 against; Republicans: 19 for and 24 against. 137 *Congressional Record* H 2879 (daily ed. May 6, 1991) and 137 *Congressional Record* S 9086 (daily ed. June 28, 1991).

56. For the historical background of the Second Amendment of the Constitution, and its inclusion in the Bill of Rights, see *To Keep and Bear Arms: The Origins of an Anglo-American Right* by Joyce Lee Malcolm (Cambridge, Mass.: Harvard University Press, 1994).

57. For contrasting views, see Garry Wills, *New York Review of Books,* Aug. 10, 1995, pp. 52–55, and Sept. 21, 1995, pp. 62–73, and W. R. LaPierre, *Guns, Crime, and Freedom* (New York: Harper Perennial, 1995). Wayne LaPierre is executive vice president of the NRA.

58. *New York Times,* July 2, 1996.

59. Ibid.

60. 92 U.S. 588 (1876); S.C., 2 Otto, 542–69.

61. For a study of the historical perspective and judicial interpretation, see W. Freedman, "Terminology and Meaning of the Second Amendment," in *The Privilege to Keep and Bear Arms: The Second Amendment and Its Interpretation* (New York: Quorum Books, 1989), pp. 19–41.

62. 59 S. Ct. 816, 818 (1939). The modern case law is summarized in *The Second Amendment: Myth and Meaning,* a Legal Action Project published by the Center to Prevent Handgun Violence, Washington, D.C. For a scholarly commentary from a contrary viewpoint, see S. Levinson, "The Embarrassing Second Amendment," 99 *Yale Law Journal* 637 (1989).

63. *Lewis v. United States,* 100 S. Ct. 915, 921 (1980).

64. *Maryland v. United States,* 85 S. Ct. 1293 (1965), and *Perpich v. Department of Defense,* 110 S. Ct. 2418 (1990). The statute of 1792 establishing "an Uniform Militia throughout the United States" was described as "obsolete and worthless" by President Theodore Roosevelt in his First Annual Message to Congress in 1901 and was repealed in that year. 14 *Messages and Papers of the Presidents* 6672. The National Defense Act of 1916 reconstituted the militias as the National Guard.

65. *United States v. Nelson,* 859 F.2d 1318 (8th Cir. 1988).

66. 81 F.3d 98 (9th Cir. 1996).

67. Ibid., at 101.

68. Letter, copy on file with author. Burger was already on record as condemning the NRA's interpretation as "one of the greatest pieces of fraud, I repeat the word *fraud,* on the American public by special interest groups, that I have ever seen in my lifetime." Davidson, *Under Fire,* p. 136.

69. M. A. Bellesîles, "The Origins of Gun Culture in the United States, 1760–1865," 83 *Journal of American History* 425–55 (Sept. 1996).

70. Ibid., at 426.

71. Ibid., at 431.

72. Colt's company failed in 1842. He resumed firearms manufacture in 1847, and in 1855 built what was claimed as the world's largest private armory. By the time of his death in 1862, Colt had become one of the wealthiest men of his day.

73. Bellesîlies, "The Origins of Gun Culture in the United States," 452.

74. Ibid., at 453.

75. The Bureau of Alcohol, Tobacco, and Firearms estimated that in 1992 approximately 212 million firearms were available for sale to, or were possessed by, civilians in the United States. The total was made up of approximately 72 million handguns (mainly pistols or revolvers), 76 million rifles, and 64 million shotguns. Most guns available for sale were produced domestically. CRS Issue Brief: *Gun Control*, Library of Congress (Washington, D.C., Feb. 9, 1995), p. 2. The population of the United States in 1992 was 255,458,000. U.S. Bureau of the Census, *Statistical Abstract of the United States: 1994*, 114th ed., Washington, D.C., 1994. Data from a nationally representative telephone survey in 1994 indicated that the proportion of households keeping firearms appeared to be declining. The total number of privately owned firearms was estimated at 192 million. P. J. Cook and J. Ludwig, *Guns in America: National Survey on Private Ownership and Use of Firearms* (Washington, D.C.: National Institute of Justice, U. S. Department of Justice, 1997).

76. The statistic refers to the number of incidents reported of firearm theft, not the number of guns stolen. Crime Data Brief, *Guns and Crime: Handgun Victimization, Firearm Self-Defense, and Firearm Theft* (Washington, D.C.: Bureau of Justice Statistics, Office of Justice Programs, U.S. Department of Justice, 1994).

77. *Crime in the United States 1993*, Uniform Crime Reports published by the Federal Bureau of Investigation, Department of Justice (Washington, D.C.: U.S. Government Printing Office, 1994), p. 18. In 1988, firearms were the weapons used in 10,895 murders; by 1993 the total had risen to 16,189. In 1994 it declined to 15,463 (1994 total corrected in UCR report for 1995). *Crime in the United States 1994*, p. 18.

78. The National Center for Health Statistics of the Public Health Service publishes annual data on firearm deaths based on reports from coroners in each state. Cited in CRS Issue Brief, *Gun Control*, p. 3. Since there is a wide disparity in the information that is entered on death certificates, the statistics cannot be taken as exact.

79. National Center for Injury Prevention and Control, *Firearm Injuries and Fatalities* (1997), p. 2.

80. International research evidence indicating a strong association between rates of gun ownership and gun-related violence was summarized in the British government's evidence to an inquiry by a judge into a mass shooting incident at a school in Scotland resulting in the deaths of sixteen children and one teacher, leaving fourteen others injured, of whom twelve were children. *Lord Cullen's Inquiry into the Circumstances Leading up to and Surrounding the Events at Dunblane Primary School on Wednesday 13 March 1996*, evidence submitted on behalf of the Secretary of State for Scotland and the Home Secretary, Annex G, "Gun Availability and Violent Crime: Research Evidence," pp. 73–83. After opponents to gun control had challenged the research findings, the Home Office Research and Statistics Directorate published a detailed reply. See *Cullen Inquiry: A Reply to Comments on the Research Note in the Government Evidence* (July 1996).

81. "Address before a Joint Session of the Congress on the State of the Union," 140 *Congressional Record* H 33 (daily ed. Jan. 25, 1994).

Chapter 3. Symbolism and Reality

1. All grants carried a matching requirement. The federal share of a grant toward any eligible state proposal for correctional facilities could not exceed 75 percent. Grants for public safety and community policing were subject to a similar matching requirement, although the Attorney General was given power to waive, wholly or in part, the necessity for a nonfederal contribution to the costs of any program, project or activity.

2. *Congressional Quarterly Weekly Report,* Mar. 5, 1994, p. 549.

3. Title XXXI of Pub. L. 103-322 created a Violent Crime Reduction Trust Fund "into which shall be transferred . . . savings realized from the implementation of Section 5 of the Federal Workforce Restructuring Act of 1994 (Pub. L. 103-226)." The amounts to be transferred into the fund over a six-year period commencing with the start of the fiscal year 1995 were specified in sec. 310001(b).

4. Murder, attempted murder, assault with intent to commit murder, assault with intent to commit any felony, assault with a dangerous weapon with intent to do bodily harm. See 18 U.S.C. § 113(a)–(c), 1111, and 1113.

5. F. E. Zimring and G. Hawkins, "Toward a Principled Basis for Federal Criminal Legislation," 543 *Annals of the American Academy of Political and Social Science* 17, 20–21 (Jan. 1996).

6. Ibid., at 21.

7. 139 *Congressional Record* S 15425 (daily ed. Nov. 9, 1993).

8. 1993 *Congressional Quarterly* 296.

9. *Public Papers of the Presidents of the United States,* 1994 (Book II) (Washington D.C.: U.S. Government Printing Office, 1995), pp. 1546–47.

10. Bureau of Justice Statistics, U.S. Department of Justice, *Sourcebook of Criminal Justice Statistics* 1993 (Washington, D.C.: U.S. Government Printing Office, 1994), tables 6.108 and 6.109.

11. 108 S. Ct. 2687 (1988). In two cases the following year, the Supreme Court decided that the imposition of capital punishment on an individual for a crime committed at sixteen or seventeen years of age did not constitute cruel and unusual punishment under the Eighth Amendment. *Stanford v. Kentucky* and *Wilkins v. Missouri,* 109 S. Ct. 2969 (1989). For a note on the constitutional implications of the decision in *Thompson v. Oklahoma,* see 40 *Drake Law Review* 195 (1991).

12. 1993 *Congressional Quarterly Almanac,* p. 295.

13. The vote in the Senate had been ninety-four yeas, four nays, and two absentees. 139 *Congressional Record* S 15070 (daily ed. Nov. 4, 1993).

14. 139 *Congressional Record* S 12446 (daily ed. Sept. 23, 1993).

15. John J. DiIulio, ed., *Courts, Corrections and the Constitution: The Impact of Judicial Intervention on Prisons and Jails* (New York: Oxford University Press, 1990), p. 291.

16. E. S. Storey, "When Intervention Works: Judge Morris E. Lasker and New York City Jails," in DiIulio, ed., *Courts, Corrections and the Constitution,* p. 165.

17. Between 1979 and 1983 the Tombs was gutted and rebuilt as a modern jail incorporating far higher standards than before. Ibid., p. 160.

18. DiIulio, in ibid., p. 7.

19. M. M. Feeley and R. A. Hanson, "The Impact of Judicial Intervention on Prisons and Jails: A Framework for Analysis and a Review of the Literature," in ibid., p. 13.

20. 139 *Congressional Record* S 15747 (daily ed. Nov. 16, 1993).

21. J. J. DiIulio, "Conclusion: What Judges Can Do to Improve Prisons and Jails," *Courts Corrections and the Constitution,* pp. 287–88. For a narrative account of the judicial inspired reforms in Alabama's penal institutions, see L. W. Yackle, *Reform and Regret: The Story of Federal Involvement in the Alabama Prison System* (New York: Oxford University Press, 1989).

22. Feeley and Hanson, "The Impact of Judicial Intervention," p. 25.

23. Ibid., p. 13.

24. The Helms amendment was printed as No. 1159 in 139 *Congressional Record* S 15619 (daily ed. Nov. 10, 1993) and reproduced as sec. 20409 of Pub. L. 103-322, 108 Stat. 1827.

25. 139 *Congressional Record* S 15749 (daily ed. Nov. 16, 1993).

26. Ibid.

27. Ibid., S 15747.

28. Ibid., S 15749.

29. Chief Justice Marshall's judgment is reprinted in G. Gunther, *Constitutional Law* 12th ed. (Westbury, N.Y.: Foundation Press, 1991), pp. 3–10.

30. 139 *Congressional Record* S 15748 (daily ed. Nov. 16, 1993).

31. Ibid. The maxim was cited by Biden at S 15749.

32. 139 *Congressional Record* S 15817 (daily ed. Nov. 17, 1993).

33. See E. R. Alexander, "Confronting the Helms Amendment," in I. P. Robbins, ed., *Prisoners and the Law* (Deerfield, Ill: Clark, Boardman, Callaghan, 1995).

34. The Prison Litigation Reform Act of 1995, enacted as Title VIII of the Departments of Commerce, Justice, and State, the Judiciary, and Related Agencies Appropriation act, 1996. Pub. L. 104-134, 110 Stat. 1321-66.

35. 139 *Congressional Record* S 15391 (daily ed. Nov. 9, 1993). In a later debate, Biden revised the estimate to over 900,000 violent crimes in 1992 which, according to the Department of Justice, had been committed at state and local levels by offenders armed with handguns. 140 *Congressional Record* S 6091 (daily ed. May 19, 1994).

36. 139 *Congressional Record* S 15409 (daily ed. Nov. 9, 1993).

37. The text was printed in 140 *Congressional Record* S 6090 (daily ed. May 19, 1994).

38. A full list of organizations endorsing a ban on assault weapons was printed in 139 *Congressional Record* S 15449 (daily ed. Nov. 9, 1993).

39. Ibid., S 15429.

40. Most of the victims in the shooting at Stockton, California, in January 1989, and all of the dead children, were immigrants from Cambodia or South Vietnam. A vivid description of this incident forms the introduction to O. S. Davidson, *Under Fire: The NRA and the Battle for Gun Control* (New York: Henry Holt, 1993), pp. 3–19. The assault weapon used had been bought openly over the counter shortly before the massacre.

41. Ibid., S 15431.

42. Ibid., S 15456. Dianne Feinstein became 38th mayor of San Francisco in November 1978 after the deaths by shooting at the City Hall of the mayor, George Moscone, and Supervisor Harvey Milk.

43. The vote for tabling the amendment was lost by forty-nine to fifty-one votes. Ibid., S 15461.

44. 139 *Congressional Record* S 15816 (daily ed. Nov. 17, 1993).

45. W. LaPierre, *Guns, Crime, and Freedom* (New York: Harper Perennial, 1995), p. 107.

46. For the *Christian Science Monitor,* 11 Apr. 1994, Franklin Zimring supplied an expert criminological analysis of the likely consequences of the three strikes policy, combining it with the acerbic comment: "Fear of violent crime always presents an opportunity for demagogues." The number of inmates in California's prisons and jails had multiplied fourfold since 1980, a rate of increase well in excess of that in the next three largest states, New York, Texas, and Florida, each of which had high rates of offending.

47. Because of a soaring rate in the California prison population, credit for "good time" authorized the early release of inmates from prison once they had served half of their sentences. No parole board had granted Richard Allen Davis discretionary parole after a hearing. For an account of his progress through the penal system, see J. Toobin, "The Man Who Kept Going Free," *New Yorker,* Mar. 7, 1994, pp. 38–53.

48. *San Francisco Chronicle,* Aug. 6, 1996.

49. Ibid.

50. D. B. Magleby, "Direct Legislation in the American States," in D. E. Butler and A. Ranney, eds., *Referendums around the World: The Growing Use of Direct Democracy* (Basingstoke, U.K.: Macmillan Press, 1994), p. 218.

51. Ibid., p. 234.

52. The estimated resident population of California in 1993 was 31,211,000. U.S. Bureau of the Census, *Statistical Abstract of the United States: 1994* 114th ed. (Washington D.C.: 1994), p. 27.

53. *Washington Post,* Feb. 1, 1989.

54. The result of the vote on November 8, 1988, prohibiting certain handguns was, for: 927,947; against: 663,424.

55. *Sacramento Bee,* Sept. 26, 1994. Contributions recorded as of June 30 in support of three strikes amounted to $880,000, compared with $12,000 raised in contributions by those opposed to Proposition 184.

56. See Los Angeles County District Attorney, Gil Garcetti, as reported in ibid.

57. In the outcome, it was well below this estimate.

58. The definition of "serious crimes" in California law includes virtually all violent crimes that involve injuries to victims or in some cases threats with a deadly weapon. Other offenses may fall within the serious category where there is a potential for injury to victims.

59. See John Van de Kamp, Attorney General of California, 1983–91, quoted in Toobin, "The Man Who Kept Going Free," p. 46.

60. Legislative Counsel's Digest, appended to Act AB 971 to amend section 667 of the California Penal Code, passed by the California legislature and approved by the governor on March 7, 1994.

61. 18 *RAND Research Review,* no. 2 (1994): 5.

62. P. W. Greenwood, C. P. Rydell, A. F. Abrahamse, J. P. Caulkins, J. Chiesa, K. E. Model, and S. P. Klein, *Three Strikes and You're Out: Estimated Benefits and Costs of California's New Mandatory-Sentencing Law* (Santa Monica, Calif.: RAND, 1994).

63. For a technical explanation of the construction and operation of the models, see ibid., pp. 10–16, and appendices C, D, and E, pp. 48–68.

64. Ibid., p. xii, and n.1.

65. Ibid., p. 25.

66. The report of February 28, 1994, by the Legislative Estimates Unit, Offender Information Services Branch of the Department of Corrections, was published in Sept./ Oct. 1994. 7 *Federal Sentencing Reporter* 101–2 (1994).

67. Legislative Analyst's Office, *Status Check,* Jan. 6, 1995, State of California, Sacramento.

68. 7 *Federal Sentencing Reporter* 57 (1994).

69. "Preliminary Report on the Impact of the Three Strikes Law on the Los Angeles County Justice System," Mar. 15, 1995.

70. Judge James Bascue, supervising judge, Criminal Division, Los Angeles Superior Court.

71. "Impact of the Three Strikes Law on the Criminal Justice System in Los Angeles County," Nov. 15, 1995; covering letter from Judge Bascue to Gloria Molina, chair, Board of Supervisors, and chair of the Countywide Criminal Justice Coordination Committee.

72. Ibid., pp. 38–39.

73. Office of the Attorney General, California Department of Justice, *News Release,* Sept. 25, 1995.

74. Justice Policy Institute findings as reported in the *New York Times,* Mar. 7, 1997.

75. California Penal Code, pt. 2, t. 10, chap. 8 § 1385, as amended in 1986 to § 1385(a) and 1385(b). The provision was first enacted in 1872.

76. *The People v. Superior Court of San Diego County* (Romero) (1996), 13 Cal. 4th 497; 917 P. 2d 628.

77. *New York Times,* June 21, 1996.

78. *Los Angeles Times,* July 14, 1996.

79. *New York Times,* June 21, 1996.

80. *Los Angeles Times,* July 14, 1996.

Chapter 4. Partisanship and Compromise

1. *Congressional Quarterly Weekly Report,* Jan. 29, 1994, p. 171.

2. Address before a Joint Session of Congress on the State of the Union, 140 *Congressional Record* H 33 (daily ed. Jan. 25, 1994).

3. Stanley Greenberg, a White House pollster, was reported in August 1994 to have advised Democratic candidates campaigning for the midterm elections in November to concentrate on the passage of three strikes. No other accomplishment, he claimed, came close to it in showing how the administration was giving a central place to crime. *New York Times,* Aug. 5, 1994.

4. A Harvard Law School professor and director of its Center for Criminal Justice, Heymann had been Assistant Attorney General in charge of the Justice Department's Criminal Division during the Carter administration, 1978–81. He had also served as Senior Counsel to Common Cause and as an associate Watergate special prosecutor.

5. *Washington Post,* Feb. 27, 1994.

6. *Los Angeles Times,* Feb. 20, 1994.

7. Ibid. Janet Reno was State Attorney for the 11th Judicial Circuit of Florida, 1978–93.

8. The appointment of Webster L. Hubbell as Associate Attorney General was approved by the Senate on May 28, 1993. A close friend of President Clinton from Arkansas, and a partner in the same law firm as Hillary Rodham Clinton, Hubbell resigned on March 14, 1994, amid allegations that he had overcharged his law firm. He was convicted subsequently and sentenced to twenty-one months' imprisonment for defrauding the firm. Although remaining loyal throughout, he continued to be an embarrassment to the Clintons well into the President's second term.

9. Zoe Baird, vice president and general counsel, Aetna Life and Casualty, and Kimba Wood, judge of the U.S. District Court for the Southern District of New York.

10. Assistant Attorney General in charge of the Civil Division, Department of Justice, 1989–93; Acting Attorney General, 1993.

11. For an informative profile of Ronald Klain and some other younger administration office holders, see R. Shalit, "The Kids Are Alright," *New Republic,* July 18 and 25, 1994, p. 23.

12. Joseph Biden became chairman of the Committee on the Judiciary after the Democrats won a majority in the Senate at the 1986 elections. He was succeeded as chairman by the ranking Republican senator, Orrin Hatch of Utah, after the 1994 elections to the 104th Congress.

13. Shalit, "The Kids Are Alright," p. 25.

14. Ibid., p. 23.

15. J. Rosen, "Crime Bill Follies," *New Republic,* Mar. 21, 1994, p. 24.

16. Shalit, "The Kids Are Alright," p. 25.

17. 108 Stat. 1982.

18. 108 Stat. 1983.

19. 108 Stat. 1984.

20. Even this modest estimate proved too high. In the ten months after the three strikes provision came into force, no more than sixteen federal third-strike cases had been brought in ten districts. Letter of July 27, 1995, to the author from the Criminal Division, U.S. Department of Justice.

21. Rosen, "Crime Bill Follies," p. 23.

22. *An Analysis of Non-Violent Drug Offenders with Minimal Criminal Histories* (Washington, D.C.: U.S. Department of Justice, 1994), executive summary, p. 2.

23. Ibid., p. 3.

24. Ibid., p. 4.

25. Annex to letter from the Attorney General, Janet Reno, to the Hon. Jack Brooks, chairman, Committee on the Judiciary, United States House of Representatives, June 13, 1994, p. 25.

26. The "safety valve" provision was enacted as sec. 80001 of Pub. L. 103-322, 108 Stat. 1985. The section limited the applicability of mandatory minimum penalties in certain defined cases of offenses under the Controlled Substances Act (21 U.S.C. § 841, § 844, § 846) or Controlled Substances Import and Export Act (21 U.S.C. § 961, § 963).

27. Dissenting views of Hon. Jack Brooks, House Report No. 103-489, *U.S. Code Congressional and Administrative News* 103rd Cong. 2nd Sess. (1994), vol. 4: *Legislative History* (St. Paul, Minn.: West Publishing Co., 1995), p. 1836.

28. 140 *Congressional Record* H 3116 (daily ed. May 5, 1994).

29. *New York Times,* May 6, 1994.

30. *New Republic,* July 18 and 25, 1994, p. 31. Joshua Steiner was chief of staff to Lloyd Bentsen at the time.

31. *New York Times,* May 6, 1994.

32. Sponsors included Reps. Patricia Schroeder (Dem. Colorado) and Don Edwards (Dem. California). First elected in 1972, Mrs. Schroeder was the longest-serving woman member of the House of Representatives in the 103rd Congress. Edwards was chairman of the Subcommittee on Civil and Constitutional Rights of the House Committee on the Jucidiary.

33. *McCleskey v. Kemp,* 107 S. Ct. 1756 (1987). McCleskey had petitions considered by the Supreme Court on three separate occasions before his execution in 1991. He had been convicted of the murder of a police officer in the course of an armed robbery in 1978 and sentenced to death.

34. *Washington v. Davis,* 96 S. Ct. 2040 (1976).

35. Ibid., 2041, and White, J., delivering the opinion of the Court at 2047.

36. See H. H. Haines, *Against Capital Punishment: The Anti-Death Penalty Movement in America, 1972–1994* (New York: Oxford University Press, 1996), p. 76. The author analyzes the dynamics of the movement to abolish the death penalty since the ending of a ten-year moratorium on executions between 1967 and 1976 and assesses the prospects for the future.

37. The U.S. district court, after holding an evidentiary hearing, had rejected as flawed the findings of the studies by Professors Baldus, Woodworth, and Pulaski. The studies were published under the titles "Monitoring and Evaluating Contemporary Death Sentencing Systems: Lessons from Georgia," 18 *University of California, Davis, Law Review* 1375 (1985), and "Arbitrariness and Discrimination in the Administration of the Death Penalty: A Challenge to State Supreme Courts," 15 *Stetson Law Review* 133 (1986). The judicial critique of the studies is summarized in 107 S. Ct. 1756 (1987), at 1764–66.The Court of Appeals in the Eleventh Circuit, sitting en banc, assumed the validity of the studies, and addressed itself to the constitutional issues. The Supreme Court followed the same course. The main finding upon which McCleskey relied was that defendants charged with killing white victims in Georgia were 4.3 times more likely to be sentenced to death than defendants charged with killing black victims. There was no statistically significant evidence to support the claim of discrimination on the basis of the race of the defendant.

38. 107 S. Ct. 1756 (1987), 1766, n. 7.

39. Ibid., Powell, J., at 1776. The reasoning was rejected in a dissenting opinion by Brennan, J., at 1783.

40. 140 *Congressional Record* H 2533 (daily ed. Apr. 20, 1994).

41. 140 *Congressional Record* S 5526 (daily ed. May 11, 1994).

42. *Congressional Quarterly Weekly Report,* July 16, 1994, p. 1935.

43. The Heritage Foundation, *Issue Bulletin,* no. 201 (Aug. 1994), summarized the basis for these calculations.

44. 140 *Congressional Record* H 2604–5 (daily ed. Apr. 21, 1994).

45. Ibid., H 2605.

46. Ibid., H 2603.

47. Ibid.

48. Letter from the Attorney General to the Hon. Jack Brooks, June 13, 1994, p. 10.

49. *Congressional Quarterly Weekly Report,* Aug. 13, 1994, p. 2341.

50. 140 *Congressional Record* H 7960 (daily ed. Aug. 11, 1994).

51. Ibid.

52. Panetta had been elected to the 95th–103rd Congresses as a representative of the 17th District of California, 1977–93, and was a former chairman of the House Budget Committee.

53. Rick A. Lazio was first elected to the House of Representatives for the 2nd District of New York in 1992.

54. *Congressional Quarterly Weekly Report,* Aug. 13, 1994, p. 2341.

55. Rep. Charles Wilson (Dem. Texas), quoted in the *Washington Post,* Aug. 12, 1994.

56. *Congressional Quarterly Weekly Report,* Aug. 13, 1994, p. 2342.

57. Ibid.

58. Brooks denounced a "solid phalanx of the Republican Party" for an intent to kill the crime bill. *Washington Post,* Aug. 12, 1994.

59. *Congressional Quarterly Weekly Report,* Aug. 13, 1994, p. 2343.

60. Transcript of a statement by President Clinton, the White House Briefing Room, Aug. 11, 1994.

61. *Washington Post,* Aug. 12, 1994.

62. "Remarks on Crime Legislation on Departure for Minneapolis, Minnesota," Aug. 12, 1994, *Weekly Compilation of Presidential Documents* 30, no. 32, Aug. 15, 1994, p. 1664.

63. *New York Times,* Aug. 13, 1994.

64. In a teleconference thanking the mayors on August 26 the President remarked that Mayor Abramson of Louisville got the prize for making the most telephone calls, having made over two hundred in support of the bill. *Weekly Compilation of Presidential Documents* 30, no. 35, Sept. 5, 1994, p. 1722. The U.S. Conference of Mayors collectively supported the legislation.

65. The National Association of Police Organizations represented more than 160,000 law enforcement officers and 3,000 police unions and associations throughout the nation.

66. "Remarks to the Convention of the National Association of Police Organizations in Minneapolis," Aug. 12, 1994, *Weekly Compilation of Presidential Documents* 30, no. 32, Aug. 15, 1994, p. 1666.

67. *New York Times,* Aug. 13, 1994.

68. "The President's Radio Address," Aug.13, 1994, *Weekly Compilation of Presidential Documents* 30, no. 33, Aug. 22, 1994, p. 1671.

69. Ibid., p. 1672.

70. Rep. Cleo Fields (Dem. Louisiana). *New York Times,* Aug. 18, 1994.

71. As a two-term governor, Castle was precluded under state law from seeking reelection for a third term. In 1988 he had worked closely with Clinton, then governor of Arkansas, in an effort to overhaul the federal welfare system.

72. *Weekly Compilation of Presidential Documents* 30, no. 33, pp. 1685–86.

73. *New York Times,* Aug. 20, 1994.

74. *Congressional Quarterly Weekly Report,* Aug. 20, 1994, p. 2449.

75. Subtitle D of Title IV of the Antiterrorism and Effective Death Penalty Act of 1996 (Pub. L. 104-132) made changes in the procedures for removing and excluding criminal aliens from the United States.

Chapter 5. Ending the Insanity

1. The term "sexually violent predator" was defined in section 170101 of Pub. L. 103-322 as a person who has been convicted of a sexually violent offense and who suffers from a mental abnormality or personality disorder that makes the person likely to engage in predatory sexually violent offenses.

2. Community Protection act of 1990, 1990 Wash. Laws, ch. 3, §§ 101–1406, codified as amended in scattered sections of Wash. Rev. Code. For a note on the Washington State law that permitted police to notify communities about sex offenders residing nearby when the release of information was "necessary for public protection," see 108 *Harvard Law Review* 787 (1995).

3. 139 *Congressional Record* S 15311 (daily ed. Nov. 8, 1993).

4. A majority of states (thirty-eight in 1994) had statutes requiring sex offenders released from prison to register with local law enforcement agencies.

5. Annex to letter from the Attorney General, Janet Reno, to the Hon Jack Brooks, chairman, Committee on the Judiciary, United States House of Representatives, June 13, 1994, p. 13.

6. Linda A. Fairstein was an Assistant District Attorney in New York County and the author of *Sexual Violence: Our War Against Rape* (New York: William Morrow, 1993).

7. *New York Times,* Aug. 21, 1994.

8. *New York Times,* Aug. 17, 1994.

9. *New York Times,* Aug. 25, 1994.

10. Ibid.

11. The chief doorman at the House gallery said the number was two to three times higher than on a normal weekday, and that a similar total of visitors came again the next day when the debate was in progress. *New York Times,* Aug. 22, 1994.

12. Jack Brooks was defeated by the Republican candidate in the 9th District of Texas in the midterm elections on November 8, 1994. Despite many years of steadfast opposition to gun control, the gun lobby intervened against him because of his support for the crime bill. Three decades earlier, as a member of Congress, he had been riding in the motorcade in Dallas when President Kennedy had been shot and killed.

13. 140 *Congressional Record* H 8967–8 (daily ed. Aug. 21, 1994).

14. Ibid., H 9005.

15. A determination that a person was no longer a sexually violent predator would be made by the sentencing court after receiving a report by a state board composed of experts in the field of the behavior and treatment of sexual offenders.

16. 140 *Congressional Record* H 8964 (daily ed. Aug. 21, 1994).

17. *New York Times,* Aug. 25, 1994.

18. 140 *Congressional Record* H. 8991 (daily ed. Aug. 21, 1994). In her statement Rep. Molinari relied on the work of David J. Karp, a senior counsel in the Office of Policy Development at the Department of Justice during the Bush Administration, and a rare advocate for the change. See K. K. Baker, "Once a Rapist? Motivational Evidence and Relevancy in Rape Law," 110 *Harvard Law Review* 563 (1997).

19. The section added three new rules of evidence to the Federal Rules of Evidence. Implementation was delayed for 150 days after the enactment of the Act to enable the Judicial Conference of the United States to transmit to Congress a report containing recommendations for amending the Federal Rules of Evidence as they affected the admission of evidence of a defendant's prior sexual assault or child

molestation crimes in cases involving sexual assault and child molestation. 108 Stat. 2137.

20. *Report of the Judicial Conference of the United States on the Admission of Character Evidence in Certain Sexual Misconduct Cases,* Feb. 1995, p. 2.

21. Ibid., p. 3.

22. Letter to the author from J. K. Rabiej, chief, Rules Committee, Support Office, Administrative Office of the United States Courts, Washington, D.C., July 31, 1995.

23. See *The Federal Rules of Practice and Procedure: A Summary for Bench and Bar,* Administrative Office of the U.S. Courts, Oct. 1993.

24. *Weekly Compilation of Presidential Documents* 30, no. 34, Aug. 29, 1994, p. 1701.

25. 140 *Congressional Record* S 12499 (daily ed. Aug. 25, 1994).

26. 140 *Congressional Record* S 12391–2 (daily ed. Aug. 24, 1994).

27. *Los Angeles Times,* Aug. 26, 1994.

28. 140 *Congressional Record* S 12557 (daily ed. Aug. 25, 1994).

29. The day after the results in the midterm elections, Shelby joined the Republican ranks in the Senate.

30. 140 *Congressional Record.* S. 12600 (daily ed. Aug. 25, 1994).

31. *Washington Post,* Aug. 26, 1994.

32. Ibid.

33. O. S. Davidson, *Under Fire: The NRA and the Battle for Gun Control* (New York: Henry Holt, 1993), p. 23. The account of the origins of the NRA that follows draws on chap. 2, "The Early Years."

34. Ibid., pp. 27–28.

35. Ibid., p. 29.

36. "Remarks at the Annual Members Banquet of the National Rifle Association in Phoenix, Arizona," May 6, 1983, *Public Papers of the Presidents of the United States* 1983, Book I (Washington D.C.: U.S. Government Printing Office, 1984), p. 659.

37. Ibid., p. 660.

38. Davidson, *Under Fire,* p. 39.

39. Lord Cullen, *The Public Inquiry into the Shootings at Dunblane Primary School on 13 March 1996* (Cm. 3386), presented to Parliament by the Secretary of State for Scotland by Command of Her Majesty, Oct. 1996, The Stationery Office, London, p. 3.

40. "Keep your Family Safe from Firearm Injury," brochure published by the American Academy of Pediatrics/Center to Prevent Handgun Violence, 1994.

41. D. Hemenway, S. Solnick, and D. Azrael, "Firearm Training and Storage," *273 Journal of the American Medical Association* 46–50 (1995).

42. K. Tardiff, P. Marzuk, A. Leon, C. Hirsch, M. Stajic, L. Portera, and N. Hartwell, "A Profile of Homicides on the Streets and in the Homes of New York City," 110 *Public Health Reports* (1995), 13–17. Data was collected from the files of the chief medical examiner of New York City, who has responsibility for the certification of unnatural deaths in the five boroughs of the city. All deaths occurring in the calendar years 1990 and 1991 and certified as homicides were eligible for the study.

43. Ibid., p. 13.

44. Ibid., p. 16, and A. Kellermann et al., "Gun Ownership as a Risk Factor for Homicide in the Home," *329 New England Journal of Medicine* 1084–91 (1993).

45. Bureau of Justice Statistics, U.S. Department of Justice, *Sourcebook of Criminal Justice Statistics* 1993 (Washington, D.C.: U.S. Government Printing Office, 1994), p. 203, tables 2.57 and 2.58.

46. U.S. Department of Health and Human Services, *Healthy People 2000: National Health Promotion and Disease Prevention Objectives* (Washington D.C.: U.S. Government Printing Office, 1990), p. 236.

47. Ibid., pp. 236–37.

48. D. McDowall and B. Wiersema, "The Incidence of Defensive Firearm Use by U.S. Crime Victims, 1987 through 1990," 84 *American Journal of Public Health* 1982–84 (1994).

49. Ibid., p. 1984.

50. G. Kleck and M. Gertz, "Armed Resistance to Crime: The Prevalence and Nature of Self-Defense with a Gun," 86 *Journal of Criminal Law and Criminology* 150–87 (1995).

51. Ibid., 180.

52. D. McDowall, C. Loftin, and B. Wiersama, "Easing Concealed Firearms Laws: Effects on Homicide in Three States," 86 *Journal of Criminal Law and Criminology* 194 (1995).

53. W. LaPierre, *Guns, Crime, and Freedom* (New York: Harper Perennial, 1995), pp. 29–39.

54. McDowall et al., "Easing Concealed Firearms Laws," pp. 195–96.

55. Ibid., pp. 201–3.

56. D. D. Polsby, "Firearms Costs, Firearms Benefits and the Limits of Knowledge," 86 *Journal of Criminal Law and Criminology* 207–20 (1995).

57. 346 *The Lancet* 563–64 (1995).

58. Pub. L. 104-208, 110 Stat. 3009–244.

59. *Almanac of Federal PACs: 1994–5* (Arlington, Va.: Amward Publications, 1995), pp. 206–7.

60. *New York Times,* Nov. 10, 1993.

61. Sec. 110102, 108 Stat. 1996–8.

62. Sec. 110103, 108 Stat. 1998–9.

63. Sec. 110201, 108 Stat. 2010–2.

64. Sec. 110401, 108 Stat. 2014–5.

65. Sec. 110511, 108 Stat. 2019.

66. Secs. 110301–7, 108 Stat. 2012–4.

67. Sec. 110302, 108 Stat. 2013.

68. 139 *Congressional Record* S 16931 (daily ed. Nov. 22, 1993).

69. *Winchester Ammunition Press Release,* Nov. 22, 1993, printed in the *Congressional Record* for the same date, S16931 (daily ed.).

70. *Congressional Record* S 16932 (daily ed. Nov. 22, 1993).

71. The epidemiological approach to gun control means an examination of all the elements of human behavior, as well as the mechanical instruments, that form the causative factors of gun violence. Interventions are then designed to address all of the causative factors. The composite strategy adopted by HCI offered the prospect of a greater chance of reducing assaultive behavior than concentration on a single issue. Letter to the author from Richard M. Aborn, President, Handgun Control, Inc., Oct. 16, 1995.

72. S. Verba, K. L. Schlozman, and H. Brady, *Voice and Equality: Civic Volun-*

tarism in American Politics (Cambridge Mass.: Harvard University Press, 1995), pp. 400–405.

73. *Wall Street Journal,* Nov. 2, 1994. Over the previous weeks the U.S. Federal Election Commission records showed that the NRA had put more than $1 million into House and Senate election campaigns, the bulk of it for radio and television advertising.

74. The *New York Times* reported on Nov. 7, 1994, that the NRA had targeted Sasser, spending more than $350,000 in an effort to prevent his reelection to the Senate.

75. The Democrats lost control of the Senate and the House of Representatives, where there had been a Democratic majority for forty years. The Republicans had not controlled both Houses of Congress since 1954.

76. 141 *Congressional Record* H 587 (daily ed. 24 Jan. 1995).

77. Richard Posner is chief judge in the U.S. Court of Appeals for the Seventh Circuit. "The Most Punitive Nation," *Times Literary Supplement,* Sept. 1, 1995, p. 4.

78. In 1993, 98 percent of all felony cases filed occurred in state courts. *1993 Judicial Business of the United States Courts,* Administrative Office of the U.S. Courts; and *Examining the Work of State Courts, 1993,* Conference of State Court Administrators, the State Justice Institute, the Bureau of Justice Statistics, and the National Center for State Courts.

79. Posner, "The Most Punitive Nation," p. 3.

80. *Congressional Quarterly Weekly Report* Aug. 20, 1994, p. 2450.

81. *Weekly Compilation of Presidential Documents* 30, no. 32, 16 Aug. 1993, p. 1603.

82. National Institute of Justice, *Research Report,* "Criminal Justice Research Under the Crime Act—1995 to 1996" (Washington, D.C.: Office of Justice Programs, U.S. Department of Justice, 1997), p. 1.

83. Sec. 110104, Pub. L. 103-322, 108 Stat. 2000.

84. The National Institute of Justice, created by the Omnibus Crime Control Act of 1968, as part of its mandate has the conduct and sponsoring of basic and applied research into the causes and prevention of crime, and the sponsorship of evaluations of major federal initiatives.

85. J. A. Roth and C. S. Koper, *Impact Evaluation of the Public Safety and Recreational Firearms Use Protection Act of 1994,* Final Report (Washington, D.C.: The Urban Institute, 1997).

86. Ibid., p. 2.

87. Ibid., p. 8.

88. Ibid., p. A-1. Mass murder was defined as the killing of four or more victims at one time and place by a lone offender.

89. *Crime in the United States 1994,* p. 18. The 1994 total was corrected to 15,463 the following year, when the annual total of gun murders in 1995 fell to 13,673. *Crime in the United States 1995,* p. 18.

Chapter 6. Processing the Contract

1. N. Gingrich, R. Armey, and the House Republicans, *Contract with America* (New York: Times Books, 1994). Ed. E. Gillespie and R. Schellhas.

2. Ibid., p. 8.

3. Ibid., p. 4.

4. Two of the nonsigners were Cuban Americans representing congressional districts in Florida. They objected to the denial of assistance in the welfare reform proposals for permanent legal residents from Cuba and elsewhere.

5. 1994 *Congressional Quarterly Almanac,* p. 570.

6. E. Drew, *Showdown: The Struggle between the Gingrich Congress and the Clinton White House* (New York: Simon and Schuster, 1996), p. 33.

7. *National Journal,* Feb. 4, 1995, p. 292.

8. Letter to Hon. Henry J. Hyde, chairman, Committee on the Judiciary, House of Representatives, from Sheila F. Anthony, Assistant Attorney General, U.S. Department of Justice, Office of Legislative Affairs, Jan. 26, 1995, pp. 2–3. Emphasis in original. Copy on file with the author.

9. Comment of Tony Blankley, press secretary to Newt Gingrich, quoted by Drew in *Showdown* p. 100.

10. House Republicans, *Restoring the Dream* (New York: Times Books, 1995), p. 17.

11. Ibid., pp. 17–19.

12. *Washington Post,* Mar. 28, 1995.

13. In a fiery speech on the floor of the House, during which he tolerated no interruption, Hyde said "The unstated premise of term limits is that we are progressively corrupted the longer we stay around here. . . . I will not concede to the angry, pessimistic populism that drives this movement, because it is just dead wrong." 141 *Congressional Record* H 3906 (daily ed. Mar. 29, 1995).

14. *Contract with America,* pp. 52–53.

15. The Fourth Amendment to the Constitution, dating from 1791, reads: "The right of the people to be secure in their persons, houses, papers, and effects against unreasonable searches and seizures, shall not be violated, and no Warrants shall issue, but upon probable cause, supported by Oath or affirmation, and particularly describing the place to be searched, and the persons or things to be seized."

16. *Massachusetts v. Sheppard,* 104 S. Ct. 3424 (1984).

17. B. Neuborne, "An Overview of the Bill of Rights," in New York University School of Law, *Fundamentals of American Law* (New York: Oxford University Press, 1996), p. 106.

18. *Mapp v. Ohio,* 81 S. Ct. 1684 (1961). In a dissenting opinion in *United States v. Leon,* 104 S. Ct. 3430 (1984), Brennan, J., said that in case after case he had witnessed the Supreme Court's "gradual but determined strangulation" of the exclusionary rule. In *Ornelas v. United States,* 116 S. Ct. 1657 (1996) Rehnquist, C.J., in delivering the opinion of the Court, said that standards of "reasonable suspicion" and "probable cause," as used to evaluate the constitutionality of investigative stops and searches, were not readily or even usefully reduced to a neat set of legal rules. Rather they were commonsense, nonlegal conceptions that dealt with the factual and practical considerations of everyday life on which reasonable men, not legal technicians, acted.

19. *Statement of Administration Policy,* Executive Office of the President, Office of Management and Budget, Feb. 7, 1995.

20. 141 *Congressional Record* H 1399 (daily ed. Feb. 8, 1995).

21. Ibid., H 1389–90.

22. Ibid., H 1398.

23. Statement of Susan Boleyn, *Hearings before the Subcommittee on Crime of*

the Committee on the Judiciary, House of Representatives, 104th Cong., 1st Sess., Jan. 19 and 20, 1995 (Washington, D.C.: U.S. Government Printing Office, 1996), p. 309.

24. See J. L. Hoffmann and W. J. Stuntz, "Habeas after the Revolution," (1993) *Supreme Court Review* (Chicago: University of Chicago Press, 1994), pp. 66–68.

25. Ibid., p. 118.

26. The authors of the study cited here were Joseph L. Hoffmann, professor of law and Ira C. Batman Faculty Fellow, Indiana University at Bloomington, and William J. Stuntz, professor of law and E. James Kelly Jr. Research Professor, University of Virginia.

27. Congressional Quarterly, Inc., Washington D.C., 1995, pp. 84–87.

28. *Schlup v. Delo,* 115 S. Ct. 851 (1995) and *Kyles v. Whitley,* 115 S. Ct. 1555 (1995).

29. The results of a survey by J. S. Liebman of capital judgments in state courts, which had been reviewed on habeas corpus in the federal courts between 1976 and 1991, showed that 42 percent were found to have been constitutionally flawed on final review. These findings were notified to the Supreme Court in an amicus brief in *Wright v. West,* 112 S. Ct. 2482 (1992), but not published with the case report. A smaller survey, sponsored by the National Center for State Courts estimated that 17 percent of habeas petitions filed by state death row inmates in 1990–92 had been granted by U.S. district courts. *National Law Journal* Oct. 17, 1994, A19. For an authoritative and systematic analysis of the procedural issues in postconviction litigation, see J. S. Liebman, *Federal Habeas Corpus Practice and Procedure,* Vols. 1 and 2 (1988), and 2nd ed. with R. Hertz (1994) (Charlottesville, Va.: Michie Co.).

30. Bureau of Justice Statistics, U.S. Department of Justice, *Sourcebook of Criminal Justice Statistics, 1995* (Washington, D.C.: U.S. Government Printing Office, 1996), p. 604. As of April 30, 1996, there were 3,112 prisoners under sentence of death in federal, U.S. military, and state jurisdictions.

31. Randall T. Shepard, Chief Justice of Indiana, Workshop for Judges of the Seventh Circuit, Kohler, Wisconsin, May 2, 1996.

32. Drew, *Showdown* p. 198.

33. Apr. 21, 1995.

34. Domestic terrorism is defined by the FBI as the unlawful use of force or violence committed by a group of two or more individuals, against persons or property, to intimidate or coerce a government, the civilian population, or any segment thereof, in furtherance of political or social objectives.

35. 1995 *Congressional Quarterly Almanac* 6–6.

36. Letter to Hyde from Anthony, Jan. 26, 1995, p. 4.

37. Cited by R. G. Hood, *The Death Penalty: A World-wide Perspective Revised and Updated* (Oxford: Clarendon Press, 1996), p. 108. Original Source: ABA Section of Individual Rights and Responsibilities, 73 *ABA Journal,* 57–58 (1987).

38. 53 S. Ct. 55 (1932).

39. 83 S. Ct. 792 (1963).

40. *Murray v. Giarratano,* 109 S. Ct. 2765 (1989) per O'Connor, J. at 2772. See also the remarks of Kennedy, J., at 2772–73. A later case relating to the appointment of counsel to act for indigent capital defendants in postconviction proceedings in the federal courts was *McFarland v. Scott,* 114 S. Ct. 2568 (1994).

41. Pub. L. 100-690, 102 Stat. 4181.

42. 21 U.S.C. § 848 (q)(4)(B) amending 28 U.S.C. §§ 2254 and 2255.

43. Stephen B. Bright, "Counsel for the Poor: The Death Sentence Not for the Worst Crime but for the Worst Lawyer," 103 *Yale Law Journal* 1835 (1994).

44. Letter to Hyde from Anthony, p. 5.

45. See N. Lefstein, "Reform of Defense Representation in Capital Cases: The Indiana Experience and Its Implications for the Nation," 29 *Indiana Law Review* 495, 501–3 (1996). Norman Lefstein is dean and professor of law, Indiana University School of Law–Indianapolis.

46. Following the election of Cuomo's Republican opponent as governor, George Pataki, New York became the thirty-eighth state to impose capital punishment. One in five voters cited the death penalty as the most important issue of the election. C. J. Meade, "Reading Death Sentences: The Narrative Construction of Capital Punishment," 71 *New York University Law Review* 732 (1996).

47. State of New York Judiciary Law, § 35.

48. *Hearings before a Subcommittee of the Committee on Appropriations, House of Representatives* 103rd Cong., 2nd Sess., pp. 30–31 (Mar. 9, 1994).

49. Ibid., p. 33.

50. *House Conference Report No. 104–518,* p. 101.

51. *Weekly Compilation of Presidential Documents* 32, no. 17, April 24, 1996, p. 717.

52. 28 U.S.C. § 2261.

53. A "unitary review" procedure means a state procedure that authorizes a person under sentence of death to raise, in the course of direct review of the judgment, such claims as could be raised on collateral attack. 28 U.S.C. § 2265.

54. *Weekly Compilation of Presidential Documents,* p. 720.

55. Ibid., pp. 720–21.

56. 116 S. Ct. 2333 (1996).

57. Ibid., at 2337.

58. Ibid., at 2340.

59. 117 S. Ct. 2059 (1997).

60. Ibid., at 2068.

61. 110 Stat. 1245.

62. 141 *Congressional Record* S 19282 (daily ed. Dec. 22, 1995)

63. Ibid., S 19277.

64. Ibid., S 19278–9.

65. Cited as the Mandatory Victims Restitution Act of 1996, 100 Stat. 1227.

66. *Weekly Compilation of Presidential Documents,* p. 694. The Crime Victims Fund had been created by sec. 1402 of the Victims of Crime Act of 1984, Pub. L. 98-473, 98 Stat. 2170–71. Fines, penalty assessments, proceeds of forfeited bonds, and collateral were deposited in the fund to compensate and assist victims.

67. In reporting the bill to the Senate in 1982 the Committee on the Judiciary commented that "restitution . . . lost its priority status in our courts long ago. . . . As a matter of practice, [restitution] is infrequently used and indifferently enforced." Quoted in Senate Report No. 104-179. (1996) *U.S. Code Congressional and Administrative News,* p. 926.

68. Pub. L. 97-291, 96 Stat. 1248.

69. 96 Stat. 1253.

70. Pub. L. 98-473, 98 Stat. 2170.

71. Pub. L. 101-647, 104 Stat. 4820.

72. 108 Stat. 1904–10.

73. 108 Stat. 1947.

74. 108 Stat. 1815.

75. P. Lane, *Felony Sentences in State Courts 1992* (Washington D.C.: Bureau of Justice Statistics, U.S. Department of Justice, 1994).

76. U.S. Sentencing Commission, *Annual Report 1994,* Table 22.

77. Victims were entitled to mandatory restitution in a total of twenty-six states in 1994. In nine, restitution was mandatory; in eight it was mandatory unless the court found extraordinary and compelling reasons for failing to order restitution; in two it was mandatory, but the court must give reasons, without the requirement that they should be extraordinary or compelling if restitution is not ordered; while seven state statutes described restitution as mandatory, but contained broad language permitting exceptions. Source: National Victim Center, Legislative Database Project, 1994.

78. (1996) *U.S. Code Congressional and Administrative News,* p. 942. This statistic was the basis of the minority views of Senator Simon (Dem. Illinois).

79. Letter to the author from Dr. Marlene Young, executive director, NOVA, Sept. 13, 1996.

80. *California Penal Code,* § 1202.4.

81. The original wording of § 1202.4 was amended in 1984 and 1990, and largely rewritten by legislation in 1994. Further amendments were added in 1995.

82. Letter from Dr M. Young to author.

83. Pub. L. 101-647, 104 Stat. 4822.

84. R. Packard (Rep. California), 41 *Congressional Record* H 1590 (daily ed. Feb. 10, 1995).

85. Gingrich et al., *Contract with America,* p. 54.

86. 141 *Congressional Record* H 1594 (daily ed. Feb. 10, 1995).

87. Ibid.

88. Ibid., H 1597.

89. 141 *Congressional Record* S 2678 (daily ed. Feb. 15, 1995).

90. Ibid.

91. See N. Strossen, "Criticisms of Federal Counter-Terrorism Laws," 20 *Harvard Journal of Law and Public Policy* 531 (1997). Nadine Strossen is professor of law at New York Law School and president of the American Civil Liberties Union.

92. Ibid., p. 540.

93. Ibid., p. 539.

94. *Congressional Quarterly Weekly Report* Apr. 20, 1996, p. 1044.

Chapter 7. Money and Ideology

1. House Republicans, *Restoring the Dream* (New York: Times Books), p. 17.

2. Pub. L. 104-145, 110 Stat. 1345, and Pub. L. 104-236, 110 Stat. 3093.

3. Title VIII of the Omnibus Consolidated Rescissions and Appropriations Act of 1996, Pub. L. 104-134, 110 Stat. 1321, was cited as the Prison Litigation Reform Act of 1995, 110 Stat. 1321–66.

4. After the U.S. Court of Appeals for the First Circuit held that a rape which had occurred in the course of a carjacking did not come within the definition of a

"serious bodily injury" required for an enhanced sentence in accordance with 18 U.S.C. § 2119(2), *U.S. v. Rivera,* 83 F.3d 542 (1st Cir. 1996), Congress passed the Carjacking Correction Act of 1996, signed into law by the President on October 1, 1996 and assigned Pub. L. No. 104-217, 110 Stat. 3020. The amending legislation provided that any conduct that would violate the sections of the U.S. Code regarding aggravated sexual abuse or sexual abuse would constitute serious bodily harm for the purposes of the carjacking offense.

5. D. Teasley, *Violent Crime Reduction Trust Fund: An Overview,* CRS Report, 95-1158 GOV (Washington D.C.: Library of Congress, Congressional Research Service, updated Oct. 3, 1996), p. 3.

6. Letter to Hon. Henry J. Hyde, chairman, Committee on the Judiciary, House of Representatives, from Sheila F. Anthony, Assistant Attorney General, U.S. Department of Justice, Office of Legislative Affairs, Jan. 26, 1995, pp. 10–13.

7. For a commentary on the rise and demise of the LEAA, 1968–82, see J. J. DiIulio, S. K. Smith, and A. J. Saiger, "The Federal Role in Crime Control," in J. Q. Wilson and J. Petersilia, eds., *Crime* (San Francisco: ICS Press, Institute for Contemporary Studies, 1995), pp. 452–55.

8. Letter to Hyde from Anthony, pp. 11–12. Emphasis in original.

9. In the course of a theme hearing on the Justice Department's law enforcement agencies, the Subcommittee on the Departments of Commerce, Justice, and State, the Judiciary, and Related Agencies, of the House Committee on Appropriations, heard oral testimony on March 9, 1995, from the director of the Community Oriented Policing Services program in support of its budget request for fiscal year 1996. Part 7 (Washington D.C.: U.S. Government Printing Office, 1995), pp. 478–80.

10. *COPS Program, Hearing before the Subcommittee on Crime of the Committee on the Judiciary, House of Representatives,* 104th Cong., 1st Sess., Dec. 7, 1995. (Washington, D.C.: U.S. Government Printing Office, 1996), p. 9.

11. 141 *Congressional Record* H 14107–8 (daily ed. Dec. 6, 1995).

12. *COPS Program,* p. 2.

13. Ibid., pp. 2–3.

14. Ibid., p. 4.

15. Ibid.

16. *Weekly Compilation of Presidential Documents* 31, no. 51, Dec. 19, 1995, p. 2206.

17. *COPS Program* p. 5.

18. Requirements for eligibility for Truth in Sentencing Grants were included in sec. 20102 of the Violent Crime Control and Law Enforcement Act of 1994 (Pub. L. 103-322, 108 Stat. 1816). They were that since 1993 a state (a) had increased the percentage of convicted violent offenders sentenced to prison, (b) had increased the average prison time served by convicted violent offenders sentenced to prison, (c) had increased the percentage of sentence served by convicted violent offenders sentenced to prison, and (d) had in effect at the time of application laws requiring that a person convicted of a violent crime should serve not less than 85 percent of the sentence imposed provided that certain conditions relating to repeat offenders were met. 42 U.S.C. § 13702.

19. U.S. Sentencing Commission, *Federal Sentencing Guidelines Manual,* 1991 ed. (St. Paul, Minn.: West Publishing Co., 1990), p. 1.2.

20. M. Mauer, "The Truth About Truth in Sentencing," no. 7 in a series of

Correctional Options published with *Corrections Today* by the American Correctional Association, 1996.

21. The text of the President's letter sent to each individual senator is reproduced in full in chapter 5.

22. Pub. L. 103-322, 108 Stat. 1815.

23. Ibid., sec. 20101(b)(2).

24. Ibid., sec. 20101(b)(4).

25. Ibid., sec. 20102(a)(1) and (2).

26. Ibid., sec. 20104.

27. H.R. 667, following the wording of the Taking Back Our Streets Act of 1995 (H.R. 3), described the Violent Offender Incarceration Grants as General Grants, although the amending legislation as enacted in the Omnibus Consolidated Rescissions and Appropriations act of 1996 (Pub. L. 104-134) reverted to the original terminology.

28. Remarks of Charles Schumer, 141 *Congressional Record* H 1496 (daily ed. Feb. 9, 1995).

29. An undocumented criminal alien was defined in sec. 20301 of Pub. L. 103-322, 108 Stat. 1823, as an alien who had been convicted of a felony and sentenced to a term of imprisonment, and who had entered the United States illegally, or was subject to exclusion or deportation proceedings, or had failed to maintain nonimmigrant status.

30. 141 *Congressional Record* H 1511 (daily ed. Feb. 9, 1995).

31. Ibid., H 1512.

32. Ibid., H 1519.

33. Pub. L. 104-134, 110 Stat. 1321–12 and 13.

34. There were 1,810 Boys and Girls Clubs facilities throughout the United States serving 2,420,000 young people nationally. Clubs were located in 289 public housing sites, and it was estimated that 71 percent of the young people lived in inner city and urban areas. 42 U.S.C. § 13751.

35. State and local drug courts provide specialized treatment and rehabilitation for certain nonviolent offenders. Continuing judicial supervision is integrated with other sanctions and services.

36. Sec. 32401 of Pub. L. 103-322, 108 Stat. 1902.

37. Taking Back Our Streets Act of 1995 (H.R. 3), *Hearings before the Subcommittee on Crime of the Committee on the Judiciary House of Representatives,* 104th Cong., 1st Sess., Jan. 19 and 20, 1995 (Washington, D.C.: U.S. Government Printing Office, 1996), p. 574.

38. Ibid., p. 98.

39. Ibid., p. 275.

40. John J. DiIulio is professor of politics and public affairs at Princeton and director of the Center for Public Management at the Brookings Institution. Joan Petersilia, co-chair of the New Consensus on Crime Policy Group and former director of the Criminal Justice Program at RAND, is professor of criminology, law, and society at the University of California, Irvine. The other members, listed alphabetically, were Professors David Bayley, Alfred Blumstein, Charles Logan, Mark Moore, Dr. Ethan Nadelmann, Professors Anne Piehl, Peter Reuter, Michael Tonry, and James Q. Wilson.

41. *Hearings before the Subcommittee on Crime of the House Committee on the Judiciary,* p. 581.

42. The statistics cited here on youth crime are drawn from a published report to the U.S. Attorney General, "Trends in Juvenile Violence," by Dr. J. A. Fox (March

1996). James Alan Fox is dean of the College of Criminal Justice at Northeastern University, Boston.

43. Ibid., p. 3.

44. P. W. Greenwood, "Juvenile Crime and Juvenile Justice," in Wilson and Petersilia, eds., *Crime,* p. 91.

45. C. L. Sipe, *Mentoring: A Synthesis of P/PV's Research 1988–95* (Philadelphia: Public/Private Ventures, 1996).

46. Ibid., p. 5.

47. Ibid., p. 13.

48. *Policy Framework* (Washington, D.C.: Milton S. Eisenhower Foundation and The Corporation For What Works, 1995), p. 4.

49. The Ford Foundation had been closely involved in the development of the Quantum Opportunities Program since its inception in the late 1980s. The four-year experimental program ran from 1989 to 1993.

50. Mar. 20, 1995.

51. A. Hahn et al., *Evaluation of the Quantum Opportunities Program (QOP)— Did the Program Work?* (Waltham, Mass: Brandeis University, Heller Graduate School, Center for Human Resources, 1994). Six interim research reports were published between 1990 and 1993.

52. *Washington Post,* Feb. 27, 1997.

53. *Policy Framework,* p. 6.

54. University of Maryland, Department of Criminology and Criminal Justice, *Preventing Crime: What Works, What Doesn't, What's Promising,* Office of Justice Programs, Research Report (Washington, D.C.: U.S. Department of Justice, 1997), p. v.

55. Ibid.

56. *New York Times,* Apr. 16, 1977.

57. Fox Butterfield interview with Lawrence Sherman, ibid.

58. *Public Papers of the Presidents of the United States, 1991,* Book I (Washington, D.C.: U.S. Government Printing Office, 1992), p. 362.

59. Ibid., p. 363. In April 1997 George Bush joined in President Clinton's Summit Conference for America's Future, which aimed to promote volunteerism.

60. 140 *Congressional Record* H 7945 (daily ed. Aug. 11, 1994).

61. J. Donnelly, cited in *Washington Post,* Aug. 19, 1994.

62. E. Knight, *Appropriations for FY 1997: Commerce, Justice, and State, the Judiciary, and Related Agencies,* CRS Report 96-618, Washington, D.C.: Congressional Research Service, Library of Congress, 1996, p. 11.

63. Teasley, *Violent Crime Reduction Trust Fund,* p. 11.

64. Knight, *Appropriations for FY 1997,* p. 10.

65. The statistics cited are drawn from Corrections Program Office, *Violent Offender Incarceration and Truth-in-Sentencing Incentive Grants: FY 1996 Implementation Report* (Washington D.C.: Office of Justice Programs, U.S. Department of Justice, 1997).

66. Ibid., p. 3.

67. Pub. L. 104-208, 110 Stat. 3009–14.

68. Pub. L. 104-134, 100 Stat. 1321–15.

69. In 1996 the definition of an undocumented criminal alien was revised to mean an alien who had been convicted of a felony or two or more misdemeanors.

70. For a concise description of the authorization/appropriation process, see W. Kravitz, *Congressional Quarterly's American Congressional Dictionary* (Washington D.C.: Congressional Quarterly Inc., 1993), pp. 16–17.

71. 42 U.S.C. § 13701–§ 13712.

72. Pub. L. 104-134, 110 Stat. 1321–66.

73. E. R. Alexander, "Confronting the Helms Amendment," in I. P. Robbins, ed., *Prisoners and the Law* (Deerfield, Ill.: Clark, Boardman, Callaghan, 1995), pp. 7–73. Elizabeth Alexander is director of the National Prison Project of the American Civil Liberties Union Foundation.

74. Pub. L. 103-322, 108 Stat. 1827, adding 18 U.S.C. § 3626. The section would expire five years after the date of enactment.

75. Alexander, "Confronting the Helns Amendment," pp. 7–74.

76. *Rhodes v. Chapman,* 101 S. Ct 2392 (1981), at 2399. Powell was quoting from the opinion of Warren, C.J. in an earlier case before the Court, *Trop v. Dulles,* 78 S. Ct. 590 (1958) at 598.

77. Examples cited by Alexander, "Confronting the Helms Amendment," pp. 74–75.

78. Congressional Research Service, *Prisons: Policy Options for Congress,* CRS Issue Brief (Washington D.C.: Library of Congress, Jan. 9, 1995), pp. 2–3.

79. Ibid., p. 3.

80. *Hearings before the Subcommittee on Crime of the House Committee on the Judiciary,* p. 247.

81. Ibid., pp. 268–69.

82. *Violent Criminal Incarceration Act of 1995* H.R. Report 104–21, 104th Cong. 1st Sess. (Washington D.C.: U.S. Government Printing Office, 1995), p. 8.

83. Ibid., p. 9.

84. Ibid., p. 15.

85. J. Michael Quinlan, a career corrections official, was director of the Federal Bureau of Prisons, 1987–92.

86. *Prison Reform: Enhancing the Effectiveness of Incarceration, Hearing before the Committee on the Judiciary, U.S. Senate,* 104th Cong. 1st Sess. (S.Hrg. 104-573), July 27, 1995, Serial No. J-104–35 (Washington D.C.: U.S. Government Printing Office, 1996), p. 72.

87. Pub. L. 104-134, 110 Stat. 1321–66.

88. 18 U.S.C. § 3626.

89. Letter to Hon. Henry J. Hyde, chairman, Committee on the Judiciary, House of Representatives, from Sheila F. Anthony, Assistant Attorney General, U.S. Department of Justice, Office of Legislative Affairs, Jan. 26, 1995, p. 18.

90. Pub. L. 96-247, 94 Stat. 349.

91. National Prison Project, 11 *Journal* no. 2 (1996), p. 1.

92. For an account of the earlier intervention by the federal courts in finding prison crowding unconstitutional in New York City and elsewhere, see chapter 3. Consent decrees originating from suits brought by pretrial detainees in New York City jails in the 1970s had generated a judicially administered structure comprising over ninety related court orders and extending to more than thirty discrete areas of prison administration. The decrees had been consolidated for enforcement by Judge Lasker in the district court. With the agreement of the parties, a court-monitoring agency called the Office of Compliance Consultants had been established in 1982.

93. *Plyler v. Moore,* 100F.3d 365 (4th Cir. 1996).

94. *Benjamin v. Jacobson,* 935 F. Supp. 332 (S.D.N.Y. 1996), stayed by 2nd Cir. Aug. 27, 1996.

95. Ibid., at 351.

96. 124 F.3d 162 (2nd Cir. 1997).

97. Guido Calabresi was dean of the Yale Law School, 1985–94. Appointed judge of the U.S. Court of Appeals for the Second Circuit in 1995.

98. Letter to the Hon. Janet Reno, Attorney General of the United States, from Orrin G. Hatch, chairman of the Judiciary Committee, United States Senate, and signed by eighteen senators, July 23, 1996.

99. Pub. L. 104-134, sec. 611(4), 110 Stat. 1321–64.

100. Robert J. Bidinotto, "Must Our Prisons Be Resorts?" *Reader's Digest,* Nov. 1994, pp. 65–71.

101. Ibid., p. 66.

102. Ibid., p. 68.

103. Ibid. While corrections spending increased dramatically at the state level, education budgets did not experience comparable growth. In 1993–94 total education spending was less than in the previous year. *Captive Students: Education and Training in America's Prisons, Policy Information Report* (Princeton: Educational Testing Services, 1996), p. 3. This report also brought out the weakness of literacy skills in a large proportion of the prisoner population.

104. M. Mauer, *Americans behind Bars: U.S. and International Use of Incarceration, 1995* (Washington, D.C.: The Sentencing Project, 1997), p. 17.

105. Religious Freedom Restoration Act of 1993, Pub. L. 103-141, 107 Stat. 1488.

106. One of the sponsors of the 1993 legislation, Senator Hatch, declared during the debate on the Senate floor: "We want religion in the prisons, it is one of the best rehabilitative influences we can have." 139 *Congressional Record* S 14367 (daily ed. Oct. 26, 1993).

107. Pub. L. 104-208, 110 Stat. 3009–66.

108. *New York Times,* Mar. 11, 1997.

Chapter 8. Congress and the Courts

1. The qualifying offenses against victims who were minors, and the meaning of the term "sexually violent offense," were defined in sec. 170101 of Pub. L. 103-322, 108 Stat. 2039.

2. It was not until May 5, 1997, nearly three years after the killing of Megan Kanka in July 1994 that Jesse Timmendequas was brought to trial before the New Jersey Superior Court in Mercer County. Part of the delay was caused by the difficulty of ensuring a fair trial when any juror who knew about Megan's Law would be aware that the person charged with her killing had a prior record of sex offenses. Such information was not usually available to jurors. The following month Timmendequas was found guilty of murder, rape, and other offenses, and sentenced to death. Timmendequas became the fourteenth inmate on New Jersey's death row, although no prisoner had been executed in the state since the enactment of the current death penalty law in 1982.

3. Statement of Hon. Dick Zimmer, *Minor and Miscellaneous Bills (Part 2), Hearing before the Subcommittee on Crime of the Committee on the Judiciary, House of*

Representatives, 104th Cong., 2nd Sess. (Mar. 7, 1996) (Washington, D.C.: U.S. Government Printing Office, 1996), p. 98.

4. See "Prevention Versus Punishment: Toward a Principled Distinction in the Restraint of Released Sex Offenders," 109 *Harvard Law Review* 1711 (1996).

5. *Minor and Miscellaneous Bills (Part 2), Hearing before the House Subcommittee on Crime.*

6. Ibid., pp. 101–2.

7. Pub. L. 103-322, 108 Stat. 2038, at 2042.

8. U.S. Code, *Congressional and Administratative News,* 104th Cong., 2nd Sess., (July 1996), Legislative History of Pub. L. 104-145, p. 984.

9. The full text of the Assistant Attorney General's letter of March 6, 1996, was printed in the House Report on *Minor and Miscellaneous Bills (Part 2)* at pp. 111 et seq.

10. 142 *Congressional Record* H 4452 (daily ed. May 7, 1996).

11. National Child Protection Act of 1993, Pub. L. 103-209, 107 Stat. 2490.

12. 142 *Congressional Record* H 4456 (daily ed. May 7, 1996).

13. Melvin Watt was joined by Maxine Waters (Dem. California) and Robert Scott (Dem. Virginia).

14. 142 *Congressional Record* H 4494 (daily ed. May 7, 1996).

15. 142 *Congressional Record* S 4921 (daily ed. May 9, 1996).

16. Ibid.

17. Pub. L. 104-145, 110 Stat. 1345.

18. *Weekly Compilation of Presidential Documents* 32, no. 20 (May 20, 1996), p. 878.

19. Pub. L. 104-236, 110 Stat. 3093.

20. *Weekly Compilation of Presidential Documents* 32, no. 20 (May 20, 1996), p. 878.

21. *Artway v. Attorney General of New Jersey,* 876 F. Supp. 666 (D.N.J. 1995).

22. 142 N.J. 1 (1995). John Doe is a fictitious name used to refer to the plaintiff individually and others similarly situated. Deborah Poritz was Attorney General of New Jersey, and succeeded Robert Wilentz as Chief Justice of the State Supreme Court in 1996.

23. Ibid., at 74.

24. Ibid., at 125–26.

25. Ibid., at 126.

26. *W.P. v. Poritz,* 931 F. Supp. 1199 (D.N.J. 1996), at 1205–6.

27. *City of Richmond v. J. A. Croson Co.,* 109 S. Ct. 706, at 732 (1989).

28. *Doe v. Poritz,* 142 N.J. 1 (1995), at 147.

29. Sec. 9 of Article 1 of the Constitution of the United States includes the statement: "No Bill of Attainder or ex post facto Law shall be passed." The Fifth Amendment states: [N]or shall any person be subject for the same offence to be twice put in jeopardy of life or limb."

30. The Eighth Amendment reads: "Excessive bail shall not be required, nor excessive fines imposed, nor cruel and unusual punishments inflicted."

31. P. Finn, "Sex Offender Community Notification" (Washington, D.C.: National Institute of Justice, U.S. Department of Justice, 1997), pp. 15–16.

32. *New York Times,* Mar. 8, 1996.

33. *Doe v. Pataki,* 919 F. Supp. 691 (S.D.N.Y. 1996).

34. *Doe v. Pataki,* 940 F. Supp. 603 (S.D.N.Y. 1996) per Chin, J.

35. *Artway v. Attorney General of New Jersey,* 81 F.3d. 1235 (3rd Cir. 1996).

36. *W.P. v. Poritz,* 931 F. Supp. 1199 (D.N.J. 1996).

37. *In re Hendricks,* 912 P. 2d 129 (Kan. 1996).

38. *Kansas v. Hendricks,* 117 S. Ct. 2072 (1997).

39. Ibid., at 2098.

40. Ibid.

41. Ibid., at 2083.

42. Finn, "Sex Offender Community Notification," p. 4.

43. Ibid., p. 10.

44. Ibid., p. 9.

45. Ibid., p.11.

46. Council of State Governments, States Information Center, *Issue Alert,* Apr. 16, 1997.

47. Ibid., p. 2.

48. E. Drew, *Showdown: The Struggle between the Gingrich Congress and the Clinton White House* (New York: Simon and Schuster, 1996), p. 100.

49. Ibid., p. 101.

50. *Congressional Quarterly Weekly Report,* Mar. 23, 1996, p. 803.

51. See *The Public Inquiry into the Shootings at Dunblane Primary School on 13 March 1996* (Cm. 3386).

52. 142 *Congressional Record* H 2675 (daily ed. Mar. 22, 1996).

53. *Congressional Quarterly Weekly Report* Mar. 23,1996, p. 803.

54. 142 *Congressional Record* H 2675 (daily ed. Mar. 22, 1996).

55. Ibid., H 2700–01 (daily ed. Mar. 22, 1996).

56. Jim Leach was chairman of the House Banking Committee and in his tenth term, representing the First District of Iowa. Douglas Bereuter was in his ninth term representing the First District of Nebraska.

57. In ten select cities HCI launched a public education campaign including placing billboards on main streets and highways to inform the citizens of how their representatives had voted on the repeal of the assault weapons ban. Ten out of the "Dangerous Dozen" candidates targeted were defeated in their congressional races. Eight had voted in the House to repeal the ban on assault weapons, and two were NRA-backed candidates for the Senate. HCI *News Release,* Nov. 6, 1996.

58. 115 S. Ct. 1624 (1995).

59. 18 U.S.C. § 922(d).

60. *Congressional Quarterly Weekly Report,* Aug. 31, 1996, p. 2462.

61. 142 *Congressional Record* S 8830 (daily ed. July 25, 1996).

62. 142 *Congressional Record* S 10377 (daily ed. Sept. 12, 1996).

63. Ibid., S10378–80.

64. 18 U.S.C. § 921(a)(33)(A).

65. In the *Atlanta Journal and Constitution* Barr referred to his alternate language, which had been adopted in preference to Lautenberg's language. Oct. 12, 1996.

66. Written testimony of William J. Johnson, general counsel, National Association of Police Organizations, Inc., *Hearing on H. R. 26 and H. R. 445 before the House Subcommittee on Crime,* "Gun ban for individuals convicted of a misdemeanor crime of domestic violence," Mar. 5, 1997, original document, p. 8.

67. 18 U.S.C. § 925(a)(1).

68. Open letter from John W. Magaw, director, Bureau of Alcohol, Tobacco, and Firearms, U.S. Department of the Treasury, Nov. 26, 1996.

69. *USA Today,* Feb. 26, 1997.

70. Written testimony of William J. Johnson, p. 9.

71. Testimony of Ronald E. Hampton, executive director, National Black Police Association, *Hearing before the House Subcommittee on Crime,* original document, p. 1.

72. Letter submitted with the testimony of Donna F. Edwards, executive director, National Network to End Domestic Violence, *Hearing before the House Subcommittee on Crime.* Original document.

73. Donna Edwards testimony, ibid., original document, p. 4.

74. Statistical analysis provided by the Department of Justice. Letter to the author from the Office of the Attorney General, Apr. 16, 1997.

75. Opening statement of Chairman Bill McCollum at the *Hearing before the House Subcommittee on Crime,* Mar. 5, 1997. The report of the Subcommittee had not been published by the year end 1997, but transcripts were available electronically on *Congressional Compass.*

76. Statement of John Conyers Jr., ibid.

77. Pub. L. 104-208, 110 Stat. 3009-369-72.

78. The Gun-Free School Zones Act, Pub. L. 101-647, 104 Stat. 4844.

79. *United States v. Lopez,* 115 S. Ct. 1630–31 (1995).

80. Message from the President of the United States, *Proposed Legislation: The Gun-Free School Zones Amendment Act of 1995,* 104th Cong. 1st Sess., H.R. 104–72, (Washington, D.C.: U.S. Government Printing Office, 1995).

81. Ibid., p. 1.

82. Ibid.

83. The President's message and accompanying report was transmitted on the same day to the Senate and referred to the Committee on the Judiciary. 141 *Congressional Record* S 6459 (daily ed., May 10, 1995).

84. Finding by the Centers for Disease Control and Prevention, cited by Senator Kohl in his opening statement, *Hearing before the Subcommittee on Youth Violence of the Committee on the Judiciary of the United States Senate,* 104th Cong. 1st Sess., on S. 890, July 18, 1995, p. 4. S. Hrg. 104–782 (Washington, D.C.: U.S. Government Printing Office, 1997).

85. Ibid.

86. Sec. 320904 of Pub. L. 103-322, 108 Stat. 2125, amended 18 U.S.C. § 922(q).

87. Pub. L. 103-322 was signed into law on September 13, 1994. The oral argument in *United States v. Lopez* was heard by the Supreme Court on November 8, 1994 and the decision given on April 26, 1995.

88. Text of S. 890 as printed in S. Hrg. 104–782, pp. 103–5.

89. S. Hrg. 104–782, p. 38.

90. Ibid., p. 40.

91. Ibid., pp. 41–42.

92. *Weekly Compilation of Presidential Documents* 31, no. 43, Oct. 30, 1995.

93. *New York Times,* Apr. 2, 1997.

94. 142 *Congressional Record* S 10384 (daily ed. Sept. 12, 1996).

95. Ibid., S 10396.

96. Ibid.

Chapter 9. A New Isolationism

1. When enacted as part of Pub. L. 104-208 the Lautenberg amendment added a ninth category of persons prohibited from purchasing or receiving a firearm or ammunition. The prohibition also applied to persons subject to certain restraining orders relating to domestic violence. The other categories were convicted felons or those under indictment for felonies; fugitives from justice; users of illegal drugs; the mentally incompetent; illegal aliens; persons dishonorably discharged from the military; and persons who have renounced American citizenship. 18 U.S.C. § 922(d)(1)–(9).

2. See T. W. Smith, *1996 National Gun Policy Survey: Research Findings* (Chicago: University of Chicago, National Opinion Research Center Mar. 1997). The survey was carried out in collaboration with the Center for Gun Policy and Research at The Johns Hopkins University, with funding from the Joyce Foundation of Chicago.

3. Ibid., p. 11.

4. Remarks by Sarah Brady, chair of Handgun Control, Inc., Democratic National Convention, press release, Aug. 26, 1996.

5. W. LaPierre, *Guns, Crime, and Freedom* (New York: Harper Perennial, 1995), p. 66.

6. According to Dennis Henigan, director of the Legal Action Project, Center to Prevent Handgun Violence, the NRA has never won a Second Amendment case in any federal court. D. A. Henigan, E. B. Nicholson, and D. Hemenway, *Guns and the Constitution* (Northampton, Mass.: Alethia Press, 1996), p. 3.

7. The Tenth Amendment, the last of the Bill of Rights ratified in 1791, reads: "The powers not delegated to the United States by the Constitution, nor prohibited by it to the States, are reserved to the States respectively, or to the people."

8. Henigan, et al., *Guns and the Constitution,* p. 15.

9. Pub. L. 103-159, 107 Stat. 1539, amending Title 18, § 922 of the U.S. Code.

10. Smith, *1996 National Gun Policy Survey,* p. 9. Over two decades there had been a steady decline in the proportion of adults living in households with guns since a high point of 50.7 percent in 1977. Ibid., p. 13, and table 10.

11. See E. B. Nicholson, "Guns and the Congress," in *Guns and the Constitution,* p. 27.

12. *Compendium of State Laws Governing Firearms, 1997,* compiled by NRA Institute for Legislative Action, Fairfax, Va., 1997. The District of Columbia is included in the listing of states.

13. States Information Center, Council of State Governments, *State Government News,* Feb. 1996, p. 32.

14. NRA Institute for Legislative Action, *Compendium of State Laws Governing Firearms, 1997,* op. cit.

15. Appendix to a report titled "War between the States: How Gunrunners Smuggle Weapons across America," Office of Congressman Charles Schumer, U.S. House of Representatives, 1997.

16. Smith, *1996 National Gun Policy Survey,* table 3, pp. 25–26.

17. General Social Surveys, 1972–1994, *Cumulative Codebook* (Chicago: National Opinion Research Center, University of Chicago, 1994), table 86. GSS analysis by Dr. L. Windeler, Data and Statistics Services, Princeton University Library, 1997.

18. 430 ILCS 65/2 (1996). In its original form the law dated from 1967.

19. Letter to the author from George A. Grasso, Deputy Commissioner, Legal Matters, City of New York Police Department, June 27, 1967.

20. See Schumer, "War between the States."

21. Ibid., table 1: Guns Crossing State Lines, 1996. Source: Bureau of Alcohol, Tobacco, and Firearms. The statistics relate only to guns recorded by law enforcement that are traced back to their place of origin. The actual totals of out of state guns used in crime are likely to be much higher.

22. See *New York v. United States,* 112 S. Ct. 2408 (1992).

23. 18 U.S.C. § 922(d).

24. See J. B. Jacobs and K. A. Potter, "Keeping Guns out of the 'Wrong' Hands: The Brady Bill and the Limits of Regulation," 86 *Journal of Criminal Law and Criminology* 93–120 (1995).

25. These statistics, published by the U.S. Department of Justice in February 1997, were cited by Stevens, J., in his dissenting opinion in *Printz v. United States,* 117 S. Ct. 2387 (1997).

26. Briefing Paper, *Understanding Brady,* Jan. 23, 1997, p. 2.

27. 3 *ABA Preview* 152 (Nov. 18, 1996).

28. *Printz v. United States,* 854 F. Supp. 1503 (D. Montana, 1994), and *Mack v. U.S.,* 856 F. Supp. 1372 (D. Arizona, 1994).

29. 66 F.3d 1025 (9th Cir. 1995).

30. 112 S. Ct. 2408 (1992). For a thorough-going analysis of the principles involved, see E. H. Carminker, "State Sovereignty and Subordinacy: May Congress Commandeer State Officers to Implement Federal Law?" 95 *Columbia Law Review* 1010–89 [1995].

31. *Printz v. United States,* together with *Mack v. United States,* 117 S. Ct. 2365 (1997).

32. 117 S. Ct. 2384 (1997).

33. See Carminker, "State Sovereignty and Subordinacy," at 1005, n. 9.

34. *New York v. United States,* 112 S. Ct. 2408 (1992) and *Hodel v. Virginia Surface Mining and Reclamation Assn., Inc.,* 101 S. Ct. 2352 (1981).

35. *Printz v. United States,* 117 S. Ct. 2401 (1997).

36. Ibid.

37. Ibid., p. 2385.

38. *New York Times,* Apr. 14, 1997.

39. *New York Times,* Apr. 7, 1997.

40. Mar. 31, 1997.

41. See S. B. Bright, "Political Attacks on the Judiciary: Can Justice Be Done amid Efforts to Intimidate and Remove Judges from Office for Unpopular Decisions?" 72 *New York University Law Review* 308 (1997).

42. M. Mauer, *Americans behind Bars: U.S. and International Use of Imprisonment 1995* (Washington, D.C.: The Sentencing Project, 1997), p. 1 and table 3. The 1985 rate of incarceration for the United States was 313 per 100,000 population, rising to 600 in 1995, an increase of 92 percent.

43. Letter from D. C. Leven, executive director, Prisoners' Legal Services of New York, *New York Times,* May 29, 1997. In 1994, nearly half (fourteen) out of a national total of thirty prisoners executed while under the jurisdiction of state and federal correctional institutions were executed in Texas. Bureau of Justice Statistics, U.S. Department of Justice, *Sourcebook of Criminal Statistics, 1995* (Washington, D.C.: U.S. Government Printing Office, 1996), table 6.72, p. 602.

44. *Sentencing Matters* (1996), pp. 134–64.

45. Ibid., p. 161.

46. Pub. L. 99-570.

47. *Special Report to the Congress: Cocaine and Federal Sentencing Policy,* Sentencing Commission, Washington, D.C., Apr. 1997, p. 2.

48. Pub. L. 100-690.

49. *Special Report to the Congress,* pp. 3–8.

50. Ibid., p. 8.

51. *Race, Crime, and the Law* (New York: Pantheon Books, 1997), p. 370.

52. Ibid., p. 371.

53. Pub. L. 103-322, 108 Stat. 2097.

54. *Weekly Compilation of Presidential Documents* 31, no. 94, Oct. 30, 1995, p. 1962.

55. S. 1254, assigned Pub. L. No. 104-38, 109 Stat. 334.

56. *Special Report to the Congress,* p. 2.

57. J. P. Caulkins, C. P. Rydell, W. L. Schwabe, and J. Chiesa, "Mandatory Minimum Drugs Sentences: Throwing Away the Key or the Taxpayers' Money?," (Document MR 827) (Santa Monica, Calif.: RAND, 1997).

58. Ibid., p. 2

59. Ibid., p. 6.

60. M. Mauer, *Americans behind Bars: U.S. and International Use of Incarceration, 1995* (Washington, D. C.: The Sentencing Project, June, 1997), p. 9.

61. Editorial, 2 *Harvard International Journal of Press/Politics* 1–2 (Spring 1997).

62. 11 *Media Monitor 2* (1997).

63. The annual review by the Center for Media and Public Affairs monitors the news stories broadcast on the ABC, CBS, and NBC evening news programs.

64. P. Klite, R. A. Bardwell, and J. Salzman, "Local TV News: Getting Away with Murder," 2 *Harvard International Journal of Press/Politics* 102–12 (1997).

65. Ibid., p. 104.

66. Ibid., p. 106.

67. Mauer, *Americans behind Bars,* table 3, p. 7.

68. The statistics for Great Britain include England, Wales, and Scotland. The Sentencing Project statistics used to compile table 5 show England and Wales with an incarceration rate of 100 per 100,000 in 1995) and Scotland (incarceration rate 110) separately. Both correspond with the Canadian rate of 115 in 1995.

69. Mauer, *Americans behind Bars,* p. 13.

70. Congressional Quarterly, *Politics in America, 1994* (Washington D.C.: C.Q. Press, 1994), p. 892.

71. Handgun Control, Inc./Voter Education Fund, *News Release* Nov. 6, 1996.

72. *New York Times Magazine,* June 22, 1997, p. 22.

73. Both Wellstone and Durbin featured in the list headed "10 Who Gotta Go" published in the *American Rifleman* in November/December 1996, p. 39.

74. E. Drew, *Whatever It Takes* (New York: Viking/Penguin Books, 1997), p. 247.

75. Ibid., p. 248.

Index

267